THE HISTORY OF THE NORTHERN

INTERIOR OF BRITISH COLUMBIA

THE
HISTORY OF THE

NORTHERN INTERIOR OF BRITISH COLUMBIA

BY

A. G. MORICE

1978
Standard Book No. 0919213-97-9

Published by
Interior Stationery (1970) Ltd.
1172 Main Street, Box 2500
Smithers, B.C.
V0J 2N0

Printed by
Friesen Printers
5748-176 Street
Cloverdale, B.C.
V3S 4C8
Head Office: Altona, Manitoba

ADRIEN—GABRIEL MORICE, O.M.I.,
MISSIONARY AND SCIENTIST

Adrien-Gabriel Morice was born on August 27th, 1859, in Saint-Mars-Sur-Colmont, (Mayenne), France. After his studies at the Seminary of Mayence, the Oblate college of Notre-Dame de Sion, near Nancy, he joined the Oblate Order in Nancy in 1877. He went to Autun (1878-1880), was sent as a missionary to British Columbia, and reached Victoria in July 1880. He resided in New Westminster for two years where he completed his ecclesiastical studies and was ordained a priest on July 2nd, 1882, by Bishop Louis d'Herbomez, O.M.I., Vicar Apostolic of British Columbia.

Immediately assigned to Williams Lake mission, he stayed there three years working among the Chilcotin, learning their language and ministering to their spiritual and material needs. In August 1885, he was transferred to a more northerly post and lived at Fort Saint James (Stuart Lake) for the next nineteen years, where he devoted himself to the acquisition of new languages and the origin and customs of his flock. From the beginning of his apostolate in that mission, he bacame acquainted with the dialects spoken in the various Indian villages, for he had always been convinced that religion should be taught in the language of the people. He also thought that the Indians would speak their language for many generations to come and he knew that on leaving the mission schools, the children spoke their mother tongue. He also was of the opinion that English was not as suitable as the native idiom to convey the message of the Gospel to his children of the woods.

This conviction, along with a sincere desire to better understand his dependants, prompted Morice to acquire a thorough knowledge of their history. This led him to gather material and write articles on history, anthropology and ethnography. It was during this period of his life that he published numerous papers on the Dene, and started the preparation of his great works on the Dene race and the Carrier language. He also published his own experience in *Au pays de l'ours noir*.

His missionary life and the visitation of his parishionners demanded extensive travelling, which made him perfectly acquainted with the country in the northern interior of British Columbia, During his travels he jotted notes which resulted in a perfect survey which was accepted by the Provincial Government as the first official map of that part of the country and printed in 1907. The Société geographique de Paris awarded him a silver medal for this work. G. S. Andrews, Surveyor general of British Columbia wrote of this map: "On his parochial and exploratory travels over that enormous area, roughly 300 miles in diameter, he carried with him only a compass, aneroid barometer, chronometer, and a length of cable (for soundings). He used magnetic azimuth for rough triangulation. Over the frozen surfaces of the lakes he made paced traverses on snowshoes, and cutting holes through the ice, he took soundings for depth. By canoe in summer he used his chronometer to proportion out the distance between landmarks along the shore. From mountain tops (with a skilled eye for distance and shape) he sketched what he could see, but not reach on foot. Other inacessible and hidden features were sketched on his manuscript on the advice of faithful native guides and hunters, in whom he found a highly developed topographic sense, and an intimate knowledge of the country."[1] He then adds that subsequent surveys confirmed the accuracy and detail of his map in commendable terms.

However the publication of this map brought many heart-breaks to Morice because of the changes made from his original map, the result of twenty-three years of exploration[2].

Besides this important achievement, Morice published his scholarly book *The History of the Norther Interior of British Columbia, formerly New Caledonia*, which is now the object of a new printing.

While missionary in the North, Morice also published Indian catechisms, hymns and reading-books printed by himself on the very primitive press of the mission. He also devised a special syllabic alphabet which the Indians could readily learn and thus be enabled to read. He even put out from 1891 to 1894 an original newspaper called "The paper which relates"[3] using the same alphabet which he also printed at Fort Saint James for the Carrier Indians.

After leaving his mission field, Morice worked in Kamloops, B.C. (1906-1908), then in Manitoba until 1910, when he became the first editor of the French newspaper *Le Patriote de l'Ouest* at Duck Lake, Saskatchewan (1910-1911), where a fire destroyed his library. He also lectured in anthropology at the University of Saskatchewan where he was awarded an honorary Master of Arts in 1912 and an honorary doctorate in 1933.

While living in Manitoba, he devoted all his time writing on a variety of subjects: ethnology, anthropology, philology and history. The The best known of his writings during this period is his *Histoire de l'Englise catholique dans l'Ouest canadien, du Lac Supérieur au Pacifique (1659-1915)*, of which he gave an abridged English version *History of the Catholic Church in Western Canada: from Lake Superior to the Pacific (1659-1895)*. This is the only comprehensive history of the Catholic Church in Western Canada and no one has as yet attempted to imitate Morice's work. He also published some biographies, a dictionary of the French Canadians and Metis of the Canadian West, and several works of controversy. He contributed articles to many scientific journals such as the *Transactions of the Royal Canadian Institute* (Toronto), *Anthropos* (Vienna), *The Royal Society of Canada, American Anthropologist, Revue de l'Université d'Ottawa, Bulletin de la société neuchâteloise de géographie, Année linguistique* (Paris), and the reports of the *Congres international des Américanistes*.

As a polemist he published, among others, *A Critical History of the Red River Insurrection* and *La race métisse,* the later a correction to Auguste-Henri de Trémaudan's *Histoire de la nation Métisse dans l'Ouest canadien.* He also contributed articles to the *Catholic Encyclopedia* and the *Encyclopedia of Religion and Ethics* and to several minor periodicals and newspapers.

In short, it can be said that Morice was an outstanding brilliant scholar whose writings have a permanent value, although not everyone will share all his points of view or his conclusions. His contribution to science has been acknowledged in all parts of the world and he has received many awards and honors. Among the last is an honorary doctorate from the University of Ottawa.

Energetic, endowed with an extraordinary capacity for intellectual work, Morice laboured until his last day, which occured at Saint Boniface, Manitoba, on April 21st, 1938.

Donatien Fremont wrote in Winnipeg's French newspaper *L Liberté* on the occasion of his passing away: "Western Canada has lost one of its historians, a man of action and a man of study who loved his adopted country with passion, and who leaves to the younger generation the noble example of a laborious and fruitful life." The tribute is entirely deserved.

This new printing of his *History of the Northern Interior of British Columbia* is a worth endeavour which will please all his many friends and admirors, and it is hoped that it will prompt others to prepare editions of several of his works, (some still in manuscript, others now out of print or not easily available), as a monument to the memory of this devoted missionary and remarkable scientist, and for the benefit of scholars in many fields.

Gaston Carriere, O.M.I.,
Ottawa, Canada.

FOOTNOTES

1. *Impressions of Father Morice,* October 23, 1945 (Oblate Historical Archives, Ottawa, Canada).

G. S. Andrews writes again in *Surveys and Mapping in British Columbia Resources Development:* "His catechismic cartographic peregrinations in this huge area covered the years 1883 to 1904, after which he consolidated his sketches and notes into the first detail map of the region, showing with astonishing fidelity the countless lakes, their shapes, with soundings and drainage relationships, prominent mountain features with elevations, trails and settlement." *Transactions of the Seventh British Columbia Natural Resources Conference,* 1954, p.12).

2. A.–G. MORICE, *L'abbé Emile Petitot et les découvertes géographiques du Canada...,* Quebec, Imprimerie L'Action sociale, 1923, p. 56.

On the reaction of Morice, see *The Northern Interior of British Columbia,* in *Transactions of the Royal Canadian Institute,* 1918, pp.25-39.

On the controversy which is still going on, see T. JOST, *Rev. A. G. Morice, discoverer and surveyor, and the problems of the proper geographical names in North Central British Columbia,* in *Revue de l'Université d'Ottawa,* (1967), p.463-476; C.P.V. and Helen B. AKKRIG, *1001 British Columbia Place Names,* 2d ed., Vancouver, Discovery Press, 1970, p.7-8.

I gave a short account of Morice's geographical work in *Essai de toponymie oblate canadienne,* in *Revue de l'Université d'Ottawa,* 28 (1958), p. 365-369.

3. This Indian newspaper was published before the well-known *Kamloops Wawa,* a monthly periodical, printed by Father Jean-Marie LeJeune, O.M.I., at Kamloops, B.C., 1892-1904.

A BIG BRITISH COLUMBIA BOOK

The Historical Work of Rev. A. G. Morice, O. M. I., Is Well Up to Sample — An Idea of the Sort of Book It Is.

British Columbia is regarded as a goldfield, a tourist resort, a baseball district, a fishing-ground, a holdup area or a racetrack, according to the proclivities of the various people who come in contact with it. Apart, however, from the strictly utilitarian dollar-hunter or the strictly sporting game-chaser, there is an increasing public the members of which are sufficiently intelligent to pay some attention to the history of the province and to its intellectual and social development. These will heartily welcome a book so important and so full of information as The History of the Northern Interior of British Columbia, by Rev. A. G. Morice, O. M. I. (Toronto: William Briggs, $2.50). Seldom has it been our lot to review a work so carefully written and so satisfactory in every respect. Its English is scholarly, idiomatic and correct, displaying a use of the language that even Old Countrymen might well imitate; its research is remarkably able and industrious, and its conclusions are sound and judicious. The literature relating to this province may be said to begin with the great book which contains the account of the voyages and travels of the famous Captain Vancouver, and to arrange itself for the most part under three heads, viz., the topographical, the advertising and the historical. Some books, indeed, have aimed at comprehending all three, at any rate in their titles. Thus, in 1862 there was published in London Dr. Rattray's book under the voluminous appellation, Vancouver Island and British Columbia, Where They Are and What They May Become; a Sketch of the History, Climate, Topography, Resources, Capabilities and Advantages, especially as Colonies for Settlement. In addition to the three classes of books mentioned, British Columbia has occasionally figured both in poetry and fiction, enterprising novelists and at times a poet or two having laid their scenes within our boundaries or hung their rhymes upon our mountains or our forests. Father Morice's book is, however, straight history. His long residence in the district of which he speaks has afforded him very rare opportunities for getting at original documents and information. He has had the free run of the old papers of the trading posts. As the faithful missionary pastor for many years over a large stretch of country, the members of his Indian flock have given him the stories of the past that have been handed down from father to son through many generations. As an able philologist he has been quick to recognize the historical values of language and the significance of the names of places and people. To this he has added an industry and persistence in research without which this book, one of the most important contributions to our historical archives, could never have been written. Moreover, he has been solicitous to tell the truth as he found it, without bias and without fear or favor. Nowhere in his work is there to be traced either the flavor of clericalism or the attempt to bolster up preconceived notions. There is no attempt at what is called "fine writing," and there are no "purple patches." We have here a plain unvarnished account of things as they have actually happened in the district lying between the Coast Range and the Rocky Mountains from about the fifty-first to the fifty-seventh degree of north latitude.

Necessarily much of the book is taken up by accounts of the early explorations and the doings of the great fur companies. Broadly speaking, the modern existence of this province began because it contained wild animals whose skins were valuable. Sir Alexander Mackenzie was a fur dealer, and it was in the interests of the fur trade that Simon Fraser explored the great river that bears his name. The Northwest Fur Trading Company and the Hudson's Bay Company would not have come into existence except for this promoting cause. But it is impossible that such operations as were undertaken by these enterprises among the aboriginal inhabitants could go on without much romantic interest mingling with the story of their doings. Prosaic and sordid as were the details of their business, we find in Father Morice's annals, as we look back upon the past, plenty of such material as might yield to the novelist a fertile field for fiction. And that is all the more true because the author has not allowed himself to dress up his statements merely to "please the gallery." He gives us references and corroborations without number; he is exact with regard to distances and dates. But he is not betrayed into twisting the truth for the sake of effect. Therefore while he is not so picturesque as Macaulay, he is more truthful. He is not so eloquent as Parkman, but when we have finished his book we feel that, on the whole, the light he throws upon the past is a little whiter even than that which beams from the pages of that delightful historian. Nowhere is this quality more manifest than in those pages of the work which deal with the various officers of the Hudson's Bay Company who ruled the various trading posts. They live and move before us like real men. We can almost hear them grumble that an Indian "has only brought in eleven beaverskins;" we can almost see the malevolent wink of the eye that goes with their decision to obtain some end they had in view by the distribution among their aboriginal servitors of a supply of potent liquor. We are made acquainted with the tools, appliances and utensils they had at their disposal. For instance, here is an entry from one of the trading post journals: "To-morrow Mr. Douglas, with two fishermen, Bichon and Clermont, and two men to assist them, will proceed to Yokogh to establish the fishery there. This gentleman will not only superintend the fishery, but will also collect the fish which the Indians may have to dispose of immediately, for which purpose he is supplied with leather and other articles of trade." This is one of the first appearances in the narrative of Sir James Douglas, who was to be the first Governor, and his history is gradually traced in just such a realistic and natural way. In doing this, as in other departments of his book, Father Morice occasionally comes across the errors of other historians, notably H. H. Bancroft and Dr. George Bryce, both of whom are brought up before the cold tribunal of fact with somewhat disastrous results to their reputation for accuracy. In like manner we come face to face with Simon Fraser, of whom, by the way, we are given the first portrait ever published; with John Stuart and with Harmon, with Wm. Conolly and Peter S. Ogden. Later in the book we find the account of the first discovery of gold in the country and its effect upon the operations of the fur companies; the introduction of Christian missions, the building of roads, the progress of the fishing industry.

The book is exceedingly well printed and bound, and there are upward of thirty beautifully executed illustrations, besides an original map of the district—probably one of the most correct bits of map-drawing that has been done in the province. It has also two appendices and a good index. In the last of the appendices the author once more reads Dr. Bryce a lesson, this time on prejudice in history-writing. It is such an appendix as might almost bring on an attack of mental appendicitis on the part of its subject.

This review of Father Morices' book was printed in the Vancouver Province on Saturday, July 16, 1904. It referred of course to the first Toronto edition and not to the later London edition, of which this is an enlarged facsimile.

BIBLIOGRAPHY

ADRIAN GABRIEL MORICE, 1859-1938

Au pays de l'ours noir; chez les sauvages de la Colombie britannique; recits d'un missionaire; ouvrage enrichi d'un carte, de 5 photogravures et de 26 gravures par l'auteur. Paris, Delhomme et Briguet, 1897. viii, 305 p. illus., map.

The Carrier language (Dene family); a grammar and dictionary combined. St. Gabriel-Modling near Vienna, Austria, "Anthropos", 1932. 2 v. front. (port) (Linguist-ische bibliothek, t. 9, 10)

The Catholic Church in the Canadian Northwest. Winnipeg, 1936. 83 p. illus., ports.

The Catholic Church is western Canada. Winnipeg, Canadian Pub., 1931. 26 p.

Dictionnaire historique des Canadiens et des Metis francais de l'Ouest. Quebec, Garneau, 1908. xi, 329 p.

Same. Quebec (Laflamme) 1908.

Same. 2m3 3d. augmentee d'un supplement. Quebec, Garneau, 1912. xl 355 p.

Disparus et survivants; etudes ethnographiques sur les indiens de l'Amerique du nord. Winnipeg, 1928. 371 p. front. (port.)

Essai sur l'origine des Denes de l'Amerique du nord. Quebec, l'Evenement, 1915. 245 p. 12 plates, port.

Fifty years in western Canada; being the abridged memoirs of Rev. A. G. Morice, by D. L. S. Toronto, Ryerson, 1930. x, 267 p. front. (port,) 10 plates, 5 ports.

A first collection of minor essays, mostly anthropological. Quesnel, B.C., Stuart's Lake Mission, 1902. 74 p.

The great Dene race, with 23 photogravures and 66 figures in the text. St. Gabriel-Modling near Vienna, Austria, Mechitaristes (1928?) xvi, 256 p. illus., plates, ports., diagrs.

Histoire abrege de l'Ouest Canadien: Grand-Nord. St.
Boniface (1914) 162 p. front. map, illus.

Histoire de l'eglise catholique dans l'Ouest canadien du
Lac Superieur au Pacifique (1659-1905), Winnipeg, West
Canada Pub. Co., 1912 3 v. front., 20 plates, 30 ports.,
fold. map, facsims. (1 fold.)

Same. Nouvelle ed. St. Boniface, 1915

Same. 1921-23 4 v.

History of the Catholic Church in western Canada from Lake
Superior to the Pacific (1659-1895) with maps and illus.
Toronto, Musson, 1910. 2 v. front., 15 plates, 22 ports.,
2 fold. maps, facsims. (part fold.)

The history of the northern interior of British Columbia,
formerly New Caledonia (1660-1880). Toronto, Briggs,
1904. xi, 349 p. front. (fold. map) 9 plates, 19 ports.

Same. 3rd. ed. 1905. xii, 368 p.

Same. London, J. Lane, 1906.

L'Ouest canadien; equisse geographique, ethnographique,
historique et demographique. Neuchatel, Paul Attinger,
1929. 98 p.

Le petit catechisme a l'usage des sauvages porteurs; texte
and traduction avec notes suivi des prieres du matin et du
soir. (Quesnel, B. C.) Mission du Lac Stuart, 1891. 144 p.

Precis de grammaire Nahanaise. (n.p., n.d.) 72 p.

Souvenirs d'un missionnaire en Colombie Britannique. Winnipeg,
1933. 374 p. illus. facsims.

Vie de Mgr. Langevin, oblatde Marie Immaculee Archeveque
de St. Boniface. 3rd. ed. St. Boniface, 1919. 398 p. front.
port., plates
Voyages et aventures de Lebret a La Haye, Lisieux, Lourdes
et Verdun. St. Boniface, 1925. 310 p. plates.

Note: this list of published books of Father Morice, taken
from Smith, is almost certainly incomplete.

FATHER MORICE

Indians dressed only in the skins of wild animals. Red men who were thorough savages and made war on the whites. Miles and miles of desolate country where nomadic tribes wandered. None of the comforts of the most northerly trading post of today.

That was the task which confronted Adrian Gabriel Morice in British Columbia half a century ago, while Father Morice conducted the mission at Lac Lahache on the Cariboo wagon road. That is the scene he looks back on today with happy memories and thoughts of a job well done. For Father Morice is still alive, but his long beard is turning white and he is in his seventieth year. Today he claims that he is the only living missionary who has seen the Indians at their wildest, the red man garbed in blankets and skins, the aboriginee who on rare occasions killed the white man in savage frenzy.

Like the cloistered monks of past centuries, Rev. Father A. G. Morice, O.M.I., new residing in Winnipeg, Manitoba, is one of the original intellectuals of the West. He is or has been anthropologist, missionary, author, musician, lecturer, publisher, newspaper editor, photographer, stenographer, lexicographer, explorer and cartographer—in short, "jack-of-all-trades."

Father Morice has many claims to fame. The greatest marks of success in his own estimation are: He was the first bachelor of arts and the first master of arts of the University of Saskatchewan; he has been admitted without payment into at least a dozen scientific societies; by a unanimous vote he was made the first honorary member of the Royal Canadian Institute; his great four-volume 'History of the Catholic Church in Western Canada was crowned by the French Academy; and he was awarded a silver medal by the Geographic Society of Paris for a map of

British Columbia he made in the early days. This last award came to him as a complete surprise as he had not even sent the society a copy of the map.

But the aged priest will soon have another accomplishment to add to his "jobs well done." He is now finishing what he calls "the greatest work of my life." It is a huge dictionary and grammar of the languages and dialects of the Indian tribes along the Pacific coast. The book is soon to be published and will have about 800 pages and cost nearly $6,000 to print. The combined grammar and dictionary is arranged in a unique style, one that he devised himself for the use of the Indians. Like Thomas Carlyle, who lost his only copy of *The French Revolution* when a servant girl started a fire with the manuscript, this Canadian historian and lexicographer also suffered a terrible loss by fire. Father Morice prepared an Indian-English dictionary some years ago which took thirteen years to complete and his only copy was destroyed in a fire at Duck Lake, Saskatchewan.

Indian dialects, according to Father Morice, are the most difficult in the world to master. In the language of one of the British Columbia tribes the verb "to put" has 100,000 synonyms. He states that he actually tabulated 60,000 of these and that he is sure there are 40,000 more.

It was forty-nine years ago that Father Morice went as a missionary to the Indians of the Interior of British Columbia from his birthplace in Mayenne, France. He was born there just seventy years ago, on August 27, 1859. Victoria, B.C., when Father Morice arrived there, was a little village of a few hundred inhabitants. As there was no transcontinental railroad across Canada in those days the trip to Victoria had to be made by boat from San Francisco.

For a quarter of a century the priest worked among the Indians, carrying Christianity to the wild Chilcotin tribe, teaching them to read and write by means of heiroglyphic language called the Dene Syllabary which he invented himself, and doing countless tasks to improve their manner of living. He even had a printing press out from Montreal on which he printed books and newspapers in the new tongue he devised.

Father Morice came close to losing his life several times when savage tribes threatened him with death if he continued his work. That was in the early days among them when the Indians, particularly the wild Chilcotins, objected to the inroads of the white man. The priest knew their threats were not idle ones as whites had been killed by the redmen a short time before. He persisted in his work, however, and managed to win their friendship.

Ill health forced the missionary to return to civilization twenty-five years ago, but he has not forsaken his flock. At his home, 200 Austin Street, Winnipeg, he still writes for them and of them. Altogether he has had published seventeen volumes and his mammoth dictionary will soon be a fitting climax to his life's work.

WROTE IN ENGLISH

Born at Mayenne, France, August 27, 1859, Father Morice was honored by the French Academy for his four-volume *History of the Catholic Church in Western Canada,* and the Geographic Society of Paris awarded him a silver medal for a map of British Columbia in the early '80's. He was a member of the Vancouver Art, literary and Scientific Association.

He wrote eleven of his works in English, including the history of the Riell insurrection. His memoirs, *Fifty Years in Western Canada,* were published in 1931.

Father Morice was noted for his absent-mindedness and his puckish humor. Once a young priest visited him when he was stationed in the Arctic. It was Father Morice's custom to cook a week's supply of food on Monday, and his stock was running low, so the Hudson's Bay Company factor sent over a quarter of venison so that the visitor would fare well.

COOK BREVIARY

"Can you cook, Father Francois?" asked Father Morice.

"No, I never had to," was the reply.

"Well, I'm not much of a chef, but I'll do the best I can," said Father Morice.

Father Morice's constant companion was a leather-covered, dogeared breviary. After the two sat down and had soup, Father Morice dug down into the venison pot with a fork. Out came the breviary!

KEPT STREAM OPEN

Most of his flock were aboriginals and he treated them like children.

Once a young Indian told the Father that he wanted to go down to Prince George to be married, but he feared that the river would freeze before he was able to return.

Father Morice looked up his weather records and told the Indian that the river would be open for another ten days.

"Give me $10, Peter," he said, "and be sure to come back in ten days."

British Columbia lost one of its notable pioneer figures in the death at St. Boniface, Manitoba, on Thursday of Father Adrien Gabriel Morice, at the age of 79. A priest and historian, one of his thirty books on the Canadian west was *The History of the Interior of British Columbia.*

He left his mark on the land and the people both in this province and in Manitoba. A lake and river in central British Columbia and a village, Moriceton, on the Canadian National's northern line were named after the distinguished padre. The town of Morice in Manitoba is also a tribute to him.

Father Morice spent twenty-five years in British Columbia as a missionary, and at the time of his death he had just completed a check of proofs on his latest book, *The Origins of Catholicism in Winnipeg.*

The priest was the first bachelor of arts and first master of arts graduate of the University of Saskatchewan and the first honorary member of the Royal Institute of Canada.

Among its members the Art Historical and Scientific Society is very fortunate to number Fr. Adrian Gabriel Morice, that distinguished Oblate missionary to the Indians, who, now retired, spends his days in Winnipeg writing about the races with whom he came in contact during the time of his active service. Born in France in 1859, Father Morice looks today ten years less than his age, for the outdoor life which he led for so many years has kept him active in spite of the passing of time.

Ordained a priest in 1882, Father Morice went almost at once to the mission at Stuart Lake, B.C. In the course of his missionary journeys he discovered and named no less than fifteen lakes. Single handed he developed a literature of the Dene's, for he invented a Dene Syllabary, with whose signs he printed several books and even a monthly periodical for his Indians. In 1911, he founded and edited Le Patriote de L'Ouest; the same year he obtained the first degree of Bachelor of Arts from the new University of Saskatchewan, and the following year the first M.A. from the same University, in which he was lecturer in Anthropology. Of late years he has taken an active interest in colonization by French speaking people of the Canadian West.

During all the years he has been in active service as a missionary, and since his retirement from active service he has been engaged in studying ethnology, and has collected two unique libraries, one of ethnological books and one of works on archaeology. He is a member of Canadian, American, English, Swiss and French scientific societies. His essays are in demand in the scientific journals of Europe. His books are numerous and he is still writing. During the last summer he made a pilgrimage to his beloved Dene to once more improve his vocabulary in their language in order to finish a new book on the subject.

FATHER MORICE

Province Apr. 22 '38

British Columbia has had few residents more active or more versatile in their activity than Father Adrien Gabriel Morice, whose death is reported from Winnipeg. The good father came to British Columbia from his native France in the early eighties, while still a very young man, and, after a year or two on the Lower Fraser, became a missionary in the Chilcotin country. For a vast region he duplicated the work of Father Lacombe in Alberta.

His parish was the great central interior, at that time not very well known. Father Morice travelled widely in his great parish, explored the country, prepared maps, taught the Indians everything from catechism to music, studied their language, with its numerous dialects, created a grammar and a syllabary, built up a literature and published books and even a monthly magazine.

He made use of all opportunities, too, to study the history of the north country and to record and compare and check stories and traditions. His History of the Northern Interior of British Columbia places the whole province in his debt.

A man of great energy, great capacity, great learning, Father Morice was a credit to his church, to his race and to his adopted country.

Father Morice, B. BC. Missionary Dead   Sun. Apr. 22, '38

ST. BONIFACE, Man., April 22. Rev. Father Adrien Gabriel Morice, 79, author of about 30 books on the history of Western Canada, died in St. Boniface Hospital yesterday.

The priest, a member of the Oblate order, achieved fame with publication of a dictionary of the Dene, or Carrier, Indian language in the interior of British Columbia.

The Dene language is regarded as the "root" of other Indian tongues.

Father Morice spent 25 years in British Columbia as a missionary.

Father Morice was the first honorary member of the Royal Institute of Canada.

The Geographic Society of Paris awarded him a silver medal for a map of British Columbia in the early 80's.

BUT RIVER FROZE

Three days after the bride and groom left on the return journey, the river froze over. They were forced to cache their canoe and several days later, footsore and weary, they reached the settlement.

"I gave you $10, Father," said Peter, "and you did not keep the river open for me."

"But I told you, Peter, to remain in Prince George only ten days, and you stayed fourteen," replied the missionary. "I waited until the twelfth day. There are 100 trappers here awaiting departure, so I could not hold up their business any longer for the sake of one man."

TRIBUTE TO PRIEST

Father Morice's work has a visual symbol. At the mission, where once the Indians worshipped the totemic gods, there is now a fine church, a tribute to the zeal and devotion of the learned Frenchman.

Funeral services will be Saturday in St. Boniface.

ADRIAN GABRIEL MORICE

Father Morice, missionary priest of the Oblates of Mary Immaculate and author of a number of books, history and anthropology of the Canadian northwest, was born in Mayenne, France, August 27, 1859. He died at St. Boniface, Manitoba, April 21, 1938, in his 79th year.

Father Morice, missionary priest of the Oblates of Mary Immaculate and author of a number of books, history and anthropology of the Canadian northwest, was born at St. Mars-sur-Calmont, France, August 27, 1859. He died at St. Boniface, Manitoba, April 21, 1938, in his 79th year. It is no easy matter to assess the work of this brilliant, hard working but rather controversial man. The History of the Northern Interior of British Columbia, commonly called New Caledonia, was printed in Toronto in 1904, again in 1905, and in London in 1906. Despite the passing of 65 years the work is still a standard British Columbia history and it may well be some years yet before it must join the ranks of books no longer read.

In order to place the work of A. G. Morice in some sort of perspective we can perhaps do no better than to print here the presidential address given by Mr. Walter N. Sage, on January 17, 1958 on the occasion of the annual meeting of the British Columbia Historical Association held on that date at Nanaimo, British Columbia.

This material was provided by Mr. Willard Ireland, Archivist, Provincial, Archives, Victoria, B. C., to which source we give our thanks.

SOME EARLY HISTORIANS OF BRITISH COLUMBIA*

British Columbia in 1958 is celebrating its centenary: "A Century to Celebrate." It is hardly necessary to remind members of the British Columbia Historical Association that we are commemorating the birth of the Crown Colony of British Columbia and not the centenary of the Province. There seems to be some doubt in the public mind on this subject. Let us hope that many of us here will live to see the hundredth anniversary of British Columbia's entry into the Canadian federation, which took place officially on July 20, 1871.

In this centennial year it seemed useful to discuss with you certain of the early historians of British Columbia. I have chosen six—Hubert Howe Bancroft, Alexander Begg, C.C., Rev. A. G. Morice, O.M.I., R. E. Gosnell, E. O. S. Scholefield, and Judge F. W. Howay. H. H. Bancroft was a San Francisco bookseller who collected a huge library of source materials on the history of the Pacific Slope from Central America to Alaska, including British Columbia, employed a large staff, ran a "history factory," and produced *The Works of Hubert Howe Bancroft* in thirty-nine volumes. Alexander Begg, C.C. (Crofter Commissioner), was born in Scotland, lived in Ontario, and came to British Columbia in 1887. In order to avoid confusion with Canadian-born Alexander Begg, author of the *History of the North West* and editor of the *British Columbia Mining Record,* Scottish-born Alexander Begg, who was appointed in 1888 by the Government of British Columbia Emigration Commissioner to investigate the settling of Scottish crofters on Vancouver Island, appended the letters "C.C." to his name. His one important work, *The .History of British Columbia,* published in Toronto in 1894, will be discussed later.

Father Morice was a devoted missionary priest of the Roman Catholic Church, who was distinguished as a historian, an anthropologist, a philologist and linguist, a printer and publisher, and the adapter of Rev. James Evans' syllabic Cree alphabet to the Athapascan or Déné lan-

---

* The presidential address delivered before the annual meeting of the British Columbia Historical Association, held in Nanaimo, B.C., January 17, 1958.

British Columbia Historical Quarterly, Vol. XXI, Nos. 1–4.

guages. An extremely able, versatile priest, he was fond of controversy, and was no admirer of H. H. Bancroft.

R. E. Gosnell and E. O. S. Scholefield, however much they differed from each other in character, training, and attainments, may well be considered together. They had one thing in common: they helped to found and build up the Provincial Library and the Provincial Archives at Victoria. Gosnell was an old-time journalist who had a vision of what the library, and later the archives, might become. Scholefield, who was Gosnell's assistant, and became his successor, was also a man of vision. Above all, he was a collector of books and manuscripts, who, in the stirring days of Sir Richard McBride, secured the funds for the library and archives addition to the Parliament Buildings. It should, however, never be forgotten that Scholefield built upon the foundation laid by Gosnell. Scholefield co-operated with Gosnell in the writing of that large leather-covered volume, produced in edition de luxe, and entitled *British Columbia: Sixty Years of Progress.*

The standard history of British Columbia during the last forty years has been the first two volumes of a four-volume work produced by His Honour Judge F. W. Howay and E. O. S. Scholefield. The full title of these first two volumes is *British Columbia from the Earliest Times to the Present,* that is to 1914. This history will, doubtless, be succeeded by the centennial history of British Columbia, which is now being written by Dr. Margaret A. Ormsby.

Judge Howay is usually recognized as the outstanding historian of British Columbia. Born in Ontario, he was brought west by his mother at an early age. His father had already found employment in the Cariboo. Frederic William Howay's boyhood was spent in New Westminster, a city then filled with memories of the Cariboo and of the Royal Engineers. One of young Howay's friends was a good-looking lad called Richard McBride, better known to us as Sir Richard McBride. Another great friend was a Nova Scotian, Robie Lewis Reid, whom Howay met when they were both trying the examinations held in Victoria for third-class teaching certificates. Reid persuaded Howay to accompany him to Halifax, where they both entered Dalhousie Law School. "Dick" McBride followed them a year later. While attending Dalhousie, Howay began his literary career by writing letters dealing with Nova Scotian affairs to the New Westminster papers. Howay and Reid became law partners in New Westminster and prospered greatly during the early years of this century. In 1907 F. W. Howay became the Judge of the "County Court of Westminster holden in the City of New Westminster." By this time he had begun his serious study of British Columbia and Northwest Coast history and was building up one of the finest private libraries then in existence in this field.

Judge Howay was " learned in the law " and was an extremely accurate and indefatigable worker. He was also a good citizen and interested himself in the New Westminster Public Library. He founded the Fellowship of Arts and was a strong supporter of the Dickens Fellowship. He was a British Columbian, and a " mainlander." He knew Vancouver Island well and was highly regarded in Victoria, but his home was in New Westminster, and as a lawyer he had also practised in the Cariboo. The great contribution of his later life was in the field of the maritime fur trade. Nor should it be forgotten that he was the first President of the British Columbia Historical Association, founded in 1922, and that he held that office until 1926.

Before going more fully into the lives and writings of this group of historians of British Columbia, it would be well to pause for a moment to point out and emphasize the difference between historical source material and historical works. Source materials for historical writing may be drawn not only from archives and libraries, but also from " historical field work," the collection of old-timers' stories, of old letters, newspapers, and pamphlets. Nor can the historian afford to neglect anthropology and its allied sciences. So far we have tended to neglect the history of the native peoples of British Columbia. One important historian, Rev. A. G. Morice, was also a noted anthropologist and a student of linguistics. He was, in fact, an anthropologist before he was a historian. Ever since the early voyages, scientists have been interested in the native peoples, as well as in the flora and fauna of the Northwest Pacific Coast. For well over half a century anthropologists have been working in the British Columbia field, but even the historians have not yet paid sufficient attention to their work.

The historian to-day must be a jack of all trades. He must not only be a frequenter of archives and libraries, he must also be a field worker and collector. He must know enough of the techniques of fur-trading, mining, smelting, lumbering, pulp and paper, fishing, agriculture, hydroelectric power, transportation by land, sea, and air, not to mention atomic energy and guided missiles, to be able to write intelligently on these various and varied subjects. He must be, if not " learned in the law," at least a student of legal, constitutional, and political history. He should be able to read, if not to speak, languages other than his own. Curiosity should be one of his main characteristics. He should always be asking questions, many of which he will never be able to answer. He can never study local history in a vacuum. He must be able to relate it to national, international, and world development.

Above all, the real historian should be humble. He realizes that he knows so little even concerning his chosen field. He should be prepared to admit his ignorance even in his special field and to answer " I don't know." A genuine historian is not a bluffer, nor should he exhibit a "false front" to the world. If possible he should be a man of wide experience and broad sympathies. He must be ready to weigh evidence and criticize. He cannot allow his feelings and emotions to get the better of him. He must stand aside from his work and view it objectively, and yet at the same time be part of his work, just as his work is a large part of him.

In a word, the historian finds and uses source materials, but from them he creates his historical work. It isn't enough to be a good collector, a wide reader, an assiduous searcher in libraries and archives, a scientific weigher of evidence; the historian must also be an artist in the presentation of his materials. He writes best who loses himself in his writing. Then Clio the Muse descends upon him and real creative historical writing begins. It doesn't happen often. Most histories are not masterpieces, but the work of journeymen or craftsmen, who are paid well for what they do but fall short of being great historical writers.

Judged by these severe standards, probably none of the six historians under discussion would reach the topmost rating. That is hardly to be expected. But all of them were important, and at least three of them— H. H. Bancroft, Rev. A. G. Morice, and Judge Howay—made outstanding contributions in the field of British Columbia history.

Hubert Howe Bancroft, 1832–1918, was a Californian of the Californians. In no other State of the Union, and probably in no other place in the world, could a successful bookseller have become the proprietor, manager, and inspiration of a " history factory," which produced volumes on the history and anthropology of the Pacific Slope, but specialized in Old California. He was born on May 5, 1832, at Granville, Ohio, of New England stock and brought up in what he termed in his volume on *Literary Industries* as " an atmosphere of pungent and invigorating puritanism."[1] In 1848 H. H. Bancroft left home to go to Buffalo, N.Y., where he entered the employ of his brother-in-law, George

---

(1) H. H. Bancroft, *Literary Industries,* San Francisco, 1890, p. 63, quoted in John W. Caughey, *Hubert Howe Bancroft,* Berkeley and Los Angeles, University of California Press, 1946, p. 7.

H. Derby, a bookseller. He started at the bottom and hadn't climbed very far up the ladder when, six months later, he was dismissed by the head book-keeper. His brother-in-law provided him with a supply of books on credit and Bancroft went back to Ohio, where he obtained valuable experience as a book-pedlar. By the end of the summer he was able to pay up his debts to his brother-in-law, to buy a suit of clothes and a silver watch. He was invited back to Buffalo to a regular clerkship at the then satisfactory salary of $100 a year.

Azariah Ashley Bancroft, the father of Hubert Howe, in 1850 caught the gold fever and left for California. Two years later George Derby decided to send his young brother-in-law to California with a consignment of $5,000 worth of trading goods. H. H. Bancroft, with his friend George L. Kenny, sailed from New York to Aspinwall, crossed the Isthmus of Panama, and took ship from Panama City to San Francisco. A new day was dawning for Hubert Howe Bancroft.

Professor John Walton Caughey, of the University of California at Los Angeles, has traced in detail in his *Hubert Howe Bancroft, Historian of the West* the adventures of the young Ohioan in the mining camps and boom towns of California. He underwent an extensive and severe training, but in the end he prospered. On a trip east in 1856 he obtained a line of credit and bought $10,000 worth of books and stationery. In December of that year he started in business in San Francisco along with his old friend George L. Kenny. The name of the firm was H. H. Bancroft and Company. Although times were very hard, the Bancroft shop prospered. Kenny was an expert salesman and Bancroft was an excellent office manager.

During the Civil War, California remained on the gold standard at a time when the rest of the country was using depreciated paper currency. Bancroft's business prospered greatly, and the proprietor had sufficient money to visit not only New York, but London and Paris as well. His brother, Albert L. Bancroft, had arrived in San Francisco in 1858. and in 1859 was placed in charge of the blank-book and stationery shop operated by both brothers under the title of A. L. Bancroft and Company. In 1858 H. H. Bancroft married his first wife, née Emily Ketchum, a rather strait-laced young lady, who in the best Victorian tradition undertook to convert her free-thinking husband. Until her death in 1869, Hubert Howe Bancroft was, outwardly at least, very religious. His scepticism reappeared later.

On his various journeys, Bancroft learned much. Even in the Eastern United States he found certain customs and mores which shook his early puritanism. California had remade him, and on his travels to and from New York via Panama he had glimpses of Latin-American civilization. Europe was also a revelation to him. He was much impressed by the European leisured classes, although he despised their disdain for work. He realized that there was something more in life than the accumulation of money. He would use money as a means to an end, and that end was cultural rather than plutocratic. Already he was dreaming dreams.

There is no time even to outline how Bancroft gathered his library, found able assistants, and became a historian. Suffice it to say that if he had not made that vast collection which has been since 1905 the Bancroft Library at the University of California in Berkeley, it would have been quite impossible for later historians and others to have recovered what would undoubtedly have been lost. Even in the case of British Columbia, if Bancroft in the 1880's had not visited Victoria, talked with the pioneers, obtained Sir James Douglas's private papers, and the manuscript histories and narratives of Alexander Caulfield Anderson, John Tod, and many others, we would have lost much valuable material concerning not only the fur trade and the colonial period, 1849–1871, but even the early days of our Province.

Three of H. H. Bancroft's volumes deal with what is now British Columbia: *The North West Coast,* Vols. I and II, and the *History of British Columbia.* Even now at this late date they are essential. No doubt there are errors; for example, Bancroft says that James Douglas married Nellie Connolly. Her name was Amelia. Mrs. Dennis Harris told me over thirty years ago that her father always called her mother Amelia. Bancroft also states that Connolly's first name was not William but James. But these are minor defects. In his review of Caughey's *Hubert Howe Bancroft,* Dr. W. Kaye Lamb quotes with approval a sentence from Bernard De Voto's *The Year of Decision, 1846:* " I have found that you had better not decide that Bancroft was wrong until you have rigorously tested what you think you know."[2]

One charge often levelled at H. H. Bancroft is that he purloined manuscripts, by borrowing them from their authors and refusing to return them. This story was still going the rounds in Victoria thirty to forty years ago. The late James R. Anderson, son of Alexander Caulfield Anderson, told me that Bancroft had stolen his father's manuscript on the *North West Coast.* It is interesting in this connection to note

---

(2) *British Columbia Historical Quarterly,* X (1946), p. 305.

that practically all original narratives in the Bancroft Library at Berkeley are in transcript form. The original manuscript of the *Fort Langley Journal,* 1827–1830, is in the Provincial Archives at Victoria.

Bancroft's historical methods were, to say the least, unconventional, and his works were by no means all his own compositions. He never claimed that they were. His merchandising tactics were also open to criticism. He was, none the less, a great figure in the historiography of the Pacific Slope, and his reputation will, in all probability, increase rather than diminish with the years.

It is, unfortunately, impossible to make a similar statement regarding Alexander Begg, C.C. His one book of importance, *The History of British Columbia,* has always been and still is almost impossible to use. As indicated above, Alexander Begg, C.C., was a Scot. He was born at Watten, Caithness, Scotland, on May 7, 1825, the son of Andrew and Jane Taylor Begg. He was educated privately but later obtained a teaching diploma at Edinburgh Normal School. He taught school for a time at Cluny, Aberdeenshire. Emigrating to Canada in 1846, he taught school in Ontario. His next move was into journalism. In 1854, with H. F. Macmillan, he founded the Bowmanville *Messenger;* later he established the Brighton *Sentinel* and published the Trenton *Advocate.* He sold out his interest in the *Advocate* to his brother Peter, probably in 1855. In 1858 at Brockville, Ont., Alexander Begg married Emily Maria Lake. They had eleven children—six sons and five daughters.

Begg was employed in the Department of Internal Revenue at Ottawa for several years. Apparently he found the comparative safety of the Civil Service preferable to the wear and tear of journalism. In 1869 he accompanied Lieutenant-Governor McDougall on his ill-fated expedition to Red River. Begg had been appointed Collector of Customs for the North-west Territories, but Louis Riel thought otherwise. At Pembina, Begg was turned back, as was McDougall, by Louis Riel's " men of the new nation."

In 1872 Begg, while on a visit to the land of his birth, was appointed Emigration Commissioner in Scotland for the Province of Ontario. His headquarters were in Glasgow, but he lectured all over the country. He persuaded many thousands of crofters to settle in Canada. About two years later the indefatigable Begg was establishing a temperance colony at Parry Sound. He turned once more to journalism and became owner and editor of the *Muskoka Herald* and founded the *Canadian Lumberman.*

The Toronto *Mail* in 1881 sent Alexander Begg as its correspondent in the Canadian North-west. He travelled by Chicago, St. Paul, and Bismarck, N.D. For a time he tried his luck at Dunbow Ranch, Alberta, and imported horses and cattle from Montana. His son Robert A. Begg eventually took over the ranch, and it flourished under his management. Another son, Roderick Norman Begg, in 1887 left Alberta to take a position with the *Daily Colonist* in Victoria, B.C. His father followed in a few months and was appointed in 1888 Emigration Commissioner for British Columbia. It was then that Alexander Begg appended the letters " C.C." to his name.

Alexander Begg, C.C., went to England in 1889 and took up his residence in London, where he remained until 1897, directing the Crofter Settlement scheme. During this period he was elected a Fellow of the Royal Geographical Society and of the Colonial Institute. In 1894 his *History of British Columbia from its Earliest Discovery to the Present Time* was published by William Briggs, Toronto. It is a tedious work, which has no index, and it cannot be classed among the more successful volumes in the British Columbia field.

In 1903 the Beggs left Victoria and settled in New York, where five of their sons and one daughter were engaged in professional work. In March, 1905, at the age of 80, Alexander Begg, C.C., died in New York and was buried in Orillia, where he and his wife had lived for several years beginning with 1877. Mrs. Begg died at the age of 93 in the year 1932. " Old Paste and Scissors," as Begg has been termed by more recent investigators in the British Columbia field, was not a great historian, but in his day he made a useful contribution.[3]

Rev. Adrien Gabriel Morice, O.M.I., 1859–1938, was noteworthy as a missionary, an anthropologist, and a historian. Born at St. Marss-sur-Calmont, France, on August 27, 1859, and educated at Oisseau and the Ecclesiastical College at Mayenne, he was early attracted to the Oblates of Mary Immaculate. He made his final vows in that order in 1879 and was sent to British Columbia in 1880. He had not yet been ordained but, with his companions N. Coccola and J. D. Chiappini, was a scholastic brother of the Oblates of Mary Immaculate. In 1882 he received ordination and was sent to labour among the Chilcotins, whose language he learned to speak. It was one of the Athapascan language

(3) For the above information on Alexander Begg, C.C., *see* Madge Wolfenden, "Alexander Begg versus Alexander Begg," *British Columbia Historical Quarterly,* I (1937), pp. 133–139.

group and introduced Rev. A. G. Morice to the study of what he later termed " The Great Déné Race."

In 1885 he was placed in charge of the Stuart Lake mission at Fort St. James. There he worked out his Déné Syllabery and gave to the Athapascan peoples a written language. What is more, he provided the Carriers of Stuart Lake with a printed language and produced valuable works on his printing-press. Morice became intensely interested in anthropology and linguistics. He talked to the old chiefs and gleaned from them what they knew of the dim period before the white man came. His first book, *Au Pays de l'Ours Noir,* was published in 1897. *The History of the Northern Interior of British Columbia, commonly called New Caledonia* followed in 1904. Bernard McEvoy, of Vancouver, well known to many of us as " Diogenes " of the *Daily Province,* praised Morice's manuscript so highly that the publishing firm of William Briggs, Toronto, accepted it unseen. It was a great success. The *History of the Catholic Church in Western Canada* appeared in 1910, in two volumes. A three-volume French edition was published in Winnipeg in 1912. During his long life (he survived till 1938) Father Morice published many books and articles in the fields of anthropology and history. He wrote well in both French and English, and his writings attracted wide attention in Europe as well as in North America. For a time he was lecturer in anthropology in the newly established University of Saskatchewan, which honoured him by granting him its first B.A. in 1911 and its first M.A. in 1912. These degrees were not honorary, but the reverend father was not required to sit for any examinations.

Rev. A. G. Morice, O.M.I., made a most valuable contribution to the writing of the history and anthropology of British Columbia and the prairies. Of his ability and his versatility, there is no doubt. He was a careful researcher and his work was authoritative. Above all, he was a true son of Holy Mother Church. His devotion to Roman Catholicism led him at times to pass very unfavourable comments on Protestants and other non-Roman Catholics. He disliked H. H. Bancroft, and he was unduly severe in his comments on the Right Rev. W. C. Bompas, successively Anglican Bishop of Athabasca, Mackenzie River, and the Yukon. Although he was always obedient to the rules of his order, he was none the less an individualist, and rumour hath it that his fellow members of the Oblate Order found him somewhat difficult at times.

Father Morice spent nineteen of his best years in British Columbia, nearly all in his beloved New Caledonia. He then crossed the mountains and took up his residence in the Prairie Provinces. He was for years in Winnipeg, and part of his later life was spent at La Fleche, Saskatchewan. He made a great contribution to his church and to Western Canadian culture. Probably the greatest stroke of luck in his life was the finding by Alexander C. Murray, then the Hudson's Bay Company's manager at Fort St. James, of a treasure-trove of old letters and other documents in the attic of the old fort. From these manuscripts Father Morice derived much of his best source material for the *History of the Northern Interior of British Columbia,* which is usually considered his finest piece of historical writing.

R. Edward Gosnell, 1860–1931, was born at Lake Beauport in the Province of Quebec in the year 1860 and was educated in Ontario. For a time he was a school-teacher, then he became a journalist and worked for various Ontario newspapers. Gosnell came to British Columbia in 1888, the year after his marriage to Miss Alice White, and was associated with the Vancouver *News* and *News-Advertiser.* In November, 1893, he was appointed Provincial Librarian, and the next year played a large part in securing the passing by the British Columbia Legislature of "An Act to establish and maintain a Library for the use of the Legislative Assembly and constitute a Bureau of Statistics." He found a library of about 1,200 volumes which was sadly lacking in organization. He had vision and industry and laid the foundations of the present Provincial Library. In 1894 E. O. S. Scholefield became his assistant. Gosnell in 1896 became secretary to the Premier, and held both positions until September, 1898, when Scholefield succeeded him as Provincial Librarian. Mrs. Gosnell died in 1898, a blow from which R. E. Gosnell seems never to have completely recovered. He became restless and changed his posts frequently. He remained secretary to the Premier until 1901, when he was appointed secretary of the Bureau of Provincial Information. Organization was his strong point, and the Bureau prospered. In 1904, however, he lost this position.

Gosnell was always a journalist at heart, and in 1906 he became editor of the Victoria *Colonist.* The next year, 1907, he was a delegate to a conference on education held in London, England. Premier McBride at this time visited England asking "better terms" for British Columbia. He found R. E. Gosnell a useful assistant, and probably a quite convivial travelling companion.

When the Provincial Archives was separated from the Provincial Library in 1908, Gosnell became the first Archivist of British Columbia. He held this position until 1910, when he was succeeded by E. O. S. Scholefield. In 1910 and 1911 he performed special services for the

Attorney-General's and the Treasury Departments. From September, 1915, to December, 1917, he was again secretary to the Premier.

After 1917 we lose sight of R. E. Gosnell for a time. He went back to Ontario and lived for several years in Ottawa. He seems to have been in the employ of the Federal Government for a while, and he also represented the Vancouver *Star* in the Parliamentary Press Gallery. I met him once in 1922, in the Public Archives of Canada, but he was then but a wreck of his former self. He lingered on in Ottawa, but in April, 1931, returned to Vancouver, where he died on August 5th. In many ways his life was a tragedy. He was brilliant, wrote well, and possessed organizing ability. Unfortunately he lacked both stability and sobriety.

None the less, R. E. Gosnell made a great contribution to British Columbia. In 1897 he issued the first *Year Book of British Columbia,* a storehouse of useful information, historical and statistical, concerning our Province. In 1906 he published *A History of British Columbia.* Two of his best works were done by collaboration. R. H. Coats, Dominion Statistician and " Father of Canadian Statistics," took Gosnell's manuscript on Sir James Douglas, prepared for the Makers of Canada series, revised it, drastically cut down its length, and rewrote the volume. It was not really a life of Douglas, but a most useful one-volume history of British Columbia. Dr. R. H. Coats many years ago told me the story of the revision of this volume. My memory may be at fault, but I am almost certain he said that he had never met R. E. Gosnell. Gosnell also joined E. O. S. Scholefield in the production of *British Columbia, Sixty Years of Progress,* which appeared in 1913. It was a weighty tome, beautifully printed, and handsomely bound. Gosnell wrote Part II, the period since federation. On the whole, it was a good piece of writing, probably his best. He was a keen analyst of British Columbia politics and politicians, and he was also well acquainted with the economic development of the Province. R. E. Gosnell may be forgotten to-day, but historical students should study his writings carefully. He knew a great deal about British Columbia and he told it well.

Ethelbert Olaf Stuart Scholefield received much of his early training in library and archives methods from R. Edward Gosnell. He succeeded Gosnell first as Provincial Librarian and later as Provincial Archivist. Was this the result of chance, or of skilful manipulation, or was it by merit? At this late date it is difficult to tell. Probably all these factors entered into Scholefield's advance and Gosnell's decline. By inference we may state that Gosnell was a bit of an enthusiast who dreamed dreams, worked out schemes, did well for a time, and then got tired. Scholefield was a collector and builder. His real monument is the Library and Archives Building and much, if not most, of its contents.

Born at St. Wilfrid's Ryde, Isle of Wight, on May 31, 1875, Scholefield came to British Columbia, along with other members of his family, in 1887. His father, Rev. Stuart Clement Scholefield, was an Anglican parson who was for a time in charge of a church in New Westminster and later was rector of Esquimalt. Ethelbert, in the best English tradition, attended a private school conducted by Rev. W. W. Bolton. He later entered the Victoria High School, where he had a distinguished record. On leaving school he entered the service of the Provincial Library. In 1894 he was assistant to R. E. Gosnell, whom he succeeded as Provincial Librarian in 1898. In 1910 he became Provincial Archivist. These positions he held until his death, after a lengthy illness, on Christmas Day, 1919.

Scholefield was intensely interested in the early voyages of discovery to the Northwest Coast and in the development of Vancouver Island. He was fortunate in his collaborators—R. E. Gosnell and Judge F. W. Howay. The Judge often spoke to me with kindly affection of " little Scholefield," and sometimes commented on his acuteness. He had been a page boy in the Legislature, and he early learned how to get along with men and how to get the best out of politicians. He planned the Archives Memoirs series and edited three of them, which were published in 1918, the year before his death. He died before he was 50, and had he lived out the allotted span he probably would have written much more.

C. B. Bagley, of Seattle, writing in the *Washington Historical Quarterly* shortly after Scholefield's death, after praising him and his work, criticizes him rather severely for his broken promises. He always lived under a terrific nervous strain and was continually making engagements he could not fill. He wrote, as has been well said, " with the printer's devil at the door." His work suffered as a result, but he gave all he had to the Provincial Library and Archives of British Columbia.[4]

And now, at long last, we come to His Honour Judge Frederic William Howay, 1867–1943. How is it possible to recapture the Judge and to contain him within a few manuscript pages? The main events

---

(4) C. B. Bagley, "Death of E. O. S. Scholefield," *Washington Historical Quarterly*, XI (1920), pp. 35–36. I wish to thank Mr. Willard E. Ireland, Provincial Librarian and Archivist, for his kindness in providing me with material on both Gosnell and Scholefield.

of his life have been rapidly sketched above. He was a British Columbian by adoption, but no native-born son could have loved our Province more nor done more to advance the writing of our history. He was easily the greatest historian that British Columbia has as yet produced.

As a boy in New Westminster he became steeped in the early history of the Lower Mainland and of the Cariboo. His father-in-law, William H. Ladner, had come in with the gold-seekers in 1858 and had later taken up land at Ladner's Landing, now Ladner, B.C. The Judge grew up with British Columbia. He witnessed the coming of the railway and vividly recalled " the battle of the terminals." He was a " mainlander," and his sympathies in the struggle between " mainland " and " island " in the 1870's and 1880's were all with the " mainland." It is sad, but amusing, that his resignation of the presidency of the British Columbia Historical Association in 1926 was due to a difference of opinion, which became an open quarrel, between himself and a learned Justice of the Supreme Court, residing in Victoria, on the date of the birthday of British Columbia. Judge Howay was adamant in upholding the date, November 19, 1858, and the place, Fort Langley, B.C.

The Judge was a tireless worker and he was also fiercely accurate. He checked and rechecked his references, and although he made mistakes—we all do—he tried to keep them to a minimum. He exhibited his legal training in his handling of materials. On the whole he wrote well, but he spoke better than he wrote. There are few brilliant passages in his writings, but he has checked his facts, and the burden of proof is now, as it was during his lifetime, on anyone who challenges his statements. But under all this legal and historical armour there beat a kind and generous heart. He did not " suffer fools gladly," but to any serious historical student he would open his stores of learning and his wonderful library. Time meant nothing to him on such an occasion. I owe the Judge a debt which I can never repay. He checked over the manuscript of my thesis on " Sir James Douglas and British Columbia," not only chapter by chapter and page by page, but line by line. It was excellent training, from which I profited greatly.

Law and history, however, were only part of the Judge's repertoire. He was widely read in English literature, especially in Dickens. He was himself not only a Dickensian, but to a great extent a character which had walked right out of Pickwick Papers. He was a bit of an actor and delighted in dressing up and taking part in the Twelfth Night revels of the Fellowship of Arts. He wrote for many years the addresses to be spoken by the May Queen and the May Queen-elect at New Westminster. He was once awarded a good citizenship medal, and an elementary school in New Westminster was named after him.

To list all the historical and other honours Judge Howay was awarded would be tedious. He had an international reputation. A Fellow of the Royal Historical Society of London, he was also a Fellow of the Royal Society of Canada, of which august body he was president in 1942. He received the Tyrrell gold medal in history from the Royal Society of Canada. He was for many years the representative of the four western provinces on the Historic Sites and Monuments Board of Canada. There are now four members carrying on the work which once he attempted alone.

After Judge Howay's death in 1943, Dr. W. Kaye Lamb prepared a bibliography of his writings which was published in the *British Columbia Historical Quarterly,* Vol. VIII, No. 1, January, 1944. There are in it 286 items, stretching from 1902 to two posthumous publications in 1944. Later Dr. Lamb added a few more items. There is no time to discuss this lengthy list, but it proves beyond argument that Judge Howay worked and wrote hard.

There was, of course, another side to the story. There always is. Judge Howay, as was Father Morice, was often involved in historical arguments, and I have known him to become quite heated. Usually he had the backing of the older and more reputable Canadian historians, but occasionally he and they went just a bit beyond what was needful in trying to smash an opponent. Dr. J. B. Tyrrell and Judge Howay tried on one occasion to demolish Dr. A. S. Morton, but Morton put up a good argument and, as usual, was unconvinced.

These six early historians of British Columbia all made their contributions. Without them there would be irreparable gaps, not only in source materials, for they were all collectors with the possible exception of Alexander Begg, C.C., but also in the comprehension of what actually occurred in the early days of the white man on the Northwest Coast and on the Pacific Slope. It would be hard to find six men more unlike, but their work somehow now seems to intertwine and to form a firm foundation upon which we and subsequent generations of historical investigators in British Columbia can build.

WALTER N. SAGE.

VANCOUVER, B.C.

THE HISTORY OF THE NORTHERN

INTERIOR OF BRITISH COLUMBIA

Rev A. G. Morice, O.M.J.

THE HISTORY

OF THE

NORTHERN INTERIOR

OF

BRITISH COLUMBIA

(FORMERLY NEW CALEDONIA)

[1660 TO 1880]

BY

THE REV. A. G. MORICE, O.M.I.,

Honorary Member of the Philological Society of Paris, of the Natural History
Society of British Columbia, and of the Art, Historical and Scientific
Association of Vancouver ; Corresponding Member of the Can-
adian Institute, of the Historical and Scientific Society
of Manitoba, of the Geographical Society of Neuf-
chatel (Switzerland), and Member of the
Ethnological Committee Brit.
Ass. Adv. of Science.

WITH MAP AND ILLUSTRATIONS

JOHN LANE, THE BODLEY HEAD,
VIGO STREET, LONDON W., 1906.

PREFACE.

THE present volume is an enlargement of a paper the writer had prepared on Aboriginal History, embodying facts which, on account of the light they throw on the manners and customs of the natives in pre-European times, he thought it well to preserve for posterity. As he went on in his studies, he soon discovered that only a part of the history of British Columbia had so far been written ; that which is most interesting and, from a certain point of view, most important, has to this day never been presented to the public. Who knows, for instance, that long before Victoria and New Westminster had been called into existence, the province had been settled in a way, and had possessed a regular capital—at Stuart Lake—whence a representative of our own race ruled over reds and whites? Not one in a thousand Canadians or even British Columbians. The record of these times and ways of life which are irrevocably past has never been written, not to say published, and the only author who has ever touched on some of the events with which we will soon entertain the reader, Hubert Howe Bancroft, is so irretrievably inaccurate in his remarks that his treatment of the same might be considered well-nigh worthless. Nay, two months have scarcely elapsed since there was issued in this city, under the auspices of that same Hudson's Bay Company to which we shall have so frequently to refer, a little pamphlet, in which we read that " although McKenzie came west . . . in 1793, it was not until thirty years later (or in 1823) that the first post was established in British Columbia." What of the six most important forts which flourished long before that date in the northern interior of the province, and whose aggregate formed one of the most valuable districts under the management of the fur-traders ? Yet, if any set of individuals ought to be familiar with the early history of British Columbia, it must surely be the members of that trading corporation, whose immediate predecessors discovered and kept under sway more than half of its territory. *Ab uno disce omnes.*

This apparently unaccountable ignorance shall be our excuse for offering the present volume to the kind appreciation of Canadian and other readers. The originality of the material of which it is mainly composed and the novelty of the scenes it records have, in our humble opinion, rendered it imperative that we should enter into details and tarry on minor facts which, under other circumstances, might well have been passed over with a brief mention. We have aimed at giving a faithful picture of the times, persons and places of which we have written. The reader will judge of the degree of success which our efforts have met with.

It is hardly necessary to mention that none of the letters and other manuscript documents we quote from was written with a view to meet the critical eyes of modern readers. Therefore it is but fair to remark that, out of consideration and regard for the proprieties of grammar and orthography, we have occasionally taken slight liberties—though as seldom as possible—with the recorded utterances of the Hudson's Bay Company and other writers, while religiously conserving their sense or meaning.

Had it not been for the courtesy of Mr. A. C. Murray, the gentleman in charge of Fort St. James, on Stuart Lake, this little work could never have been made what it is. For the generous access he gave us to all the old papers, letters, journals, account books, and memoranda in his keeping, we beg to return our sincerest thanks. The same is also due to such gentlemen as the Hon. Senator R. W. Scott, Secretary of State for Canada, who kindly put at our disposal a photograph of the first British Columbian, Simon Fraser, whose portrait has hitherto never appeared in print; to Messrs. R. E. Gosnell and E. Scholefield, of Victoria, for the loan, by the former, of a volume of unpublished letters by the pioneer traders and the blocks of some illustrations, and for the readiness with which the latter laid open for our benefit the well-guarded riches of the Legislative Library at the provincial capital. Finally, the services of Archbishop Orth, of Victoria, call likewise for public acknowledgment, as do also those of Messrs. A. P. McInnes, of Alexandria; G. Hamilton, an old Hudson's Bay Company officer; James Bain, D.C.L., the obliging Librarian of Toronto, and last, though not least, Bernard McEvoy, the well-known poet and journalist, who so kindly lent us his valued aid in seeing the work through the press.

VANCOUVER, B.C., July, 1905.

CONTENTS.

INTRODUCTION.

PAGE

The Country and Its Aborigines.—Boundaries—Flora—Lakes and streams—Fish and game—Various native tribes—Manners and customs of the same—Their probable origin—Original seat of the Babines - - - - - - - - - - - I

CHAPTER I.

Earliest Historical Times.—Na'kwœl and his iron axe—Lost and found —Quick with his bow—His son killed by his wives—Prompt retribution—A great patriarch—Chinlac and its sad fate—Spitted through the ribs—A raid on the Chilcotins—Battling with spear and armor—Why Khalhpan could not dance - - - - 9

CHAPTER II.

Still Pre-European Times.—A new chieftain—A dishonorable adventure—Stuart River massacre—K'wah tries to avenge it—A successful attack—Between "two fires"—Hostile reception of the victors— K'wah becomes a gambler—Blood pays for an insult—Firearms first heard of—The Beavers oppress the Sekanais—The latter retaliate - 20

CHAPTER III.

Discovery by Alexander Mackenzie.—The fur-trade in the east—Alexander Mackenzie—He crosses the Rockies—Liquor in great demand —He ascends the Parsnip River—First intercourse with the Carriers —Dread on both sides—An exciting episode—Panic and discouragement—A blind man opens the eyes of the adventurers—All's well that ends well - - - - - - - - - - - 33

CHAPTER IV.

First Foundations.—Mackenzie turns litterateur—Simon Fraser—First view of Stuart Lake—Fraser prepares his great expedition—Difficulties from nature and from men—A well named river—The Fraser—Ready, ye warriors !—Surprise and consternation—First trading—Lake Stuart—Its aborigines—Errors of Bancroft and others - - - - - - - - - - - 50

CONTENTS

CHAPTER V.

PAGE

Founding and Exploring.—Erecting a new fort —The pioneers starve—
And then complain of their abundance—Fraser Lake—A large bill
—Reinforcements—Fort George founded—Disagreeing authors all
in the wrong—Fraser's trip to the sea-coast—"Awful and forbidding appearance" of the river—Native ladders for a trail along an
abyss—The river not the Columbia—Bancroft unfair to Fraser   67

CHAPTER VI.

Stuart and Harmon at Stuart Lake.—Stuart succeeds Simon Fraser—
Harmon comes to Stuart Lake—The first drunken orgy—'Kwah is
chastised—Cremation of a Carrier—Harmon and McDougall go to
Babine—Received with a display of war clubs and axes—The very
first mail within British Columbia—Stuart's shortcomings—Massacres and murders—Conflict between the rival companies—Amalgamation of the latter - - - - - - - - -   84

CHAPTER VII

The Hudson's Bay Company in New Caledonia.—The Company's
Charter—Its organization—The servants and their grades—The
clerks and the apprentices—A privileged class—Original status—A
new Deed Poll—An American proud of his title—Lord paramount
—Hudson's Bay Company forts—The Company's influence detrimental to the moral welfare of the Indians—Fire-water and
vendettas - - - - - - - - - - -   102

CHAPTER VIII.

William Connolly Succeeds Stuart.—Governor Simpson—Forts Alex-
ander and Chilcotin are founded—Bancroft mistaken—Warlike
Indians—Fort Babine erected—Bancroft wrong again—Poor Mary !
—Douglas comes upon the scene—He acts as Connolly's fisherman—
Did he found Fort Connolly?—Difficult times—Furs, furs—A buffoon
causes a war - - - - - - - - - - -   120

CHAPTER IX.

An Episode and its Consequences.—A fanciful account of the occurrence
—The heroical rôle attributed to the wrong party—The real facts—
"The man he killed was eaten by the dogs ; by the dogs he must
be eaten"—The aggressor on the defensive—Dr. Bryce's mistakes
—Bancroft's dramatized version of the affair—The Governor at
Stuart Lake—How the Company had the last word—But Douglas
had to leave - - - - - - - - - - -   139

CONTENTS

CHAPTER X.

Connolly and Dease at Stuart Lake.—Greed for furs—Fisher has recourse to tricks to get them—Lively correspondence—The original Tête Jaune Cache—Fifteen dogs on the tables—An alert in the woods—Dease arrives at Stuart Lake—Why Connolly was relieved of his post—Opposition traders on the Skeena—A clerk on strike—John McLean at Stuart Lake—First burial among the Carriers   153

CHAPTER XI.

Peter S. Ogden takes Charge of the Country.—Ogden's antecedents—His characteristics—The trickster tricked—Resources of the different posts—Salmon—The engagés—Hard on evil-doers—A boorish officer and a clerk in a tight place—A philippic—Caught in his own net - - - - - - - - - - - 171

CHAPTER XII.

The Country and its Resources.—A new route established—Salmon and staple food—How that fish is caught—Articles of trade—Odd items—Canoes and guns - - - - - - - - - 186

CHAPTER XIII.

Peter S. Ogden Governs.—An undesirable post—Anderson's census—Its inaccuracies—'Kwah falls sick—And dies—Ogden asserts his authority—The wails of a culprit—A quick-tempered officer—Uprisings among the natives—A deserter causes trouble—Campbell's expedition - - - - - - - - - - 193

CHAPTER XIV.

Among the Babines.—A new fort wanted—Domestic troubles of the officer in charge—McBean is removed—His instructions to his successor—Morwick pays his imprudence with his life—The avenging expedition—Treachery wins—Cameron despondent—A double murder and its consequences—Even D. McLean is apprehensive - - 208

CHAPTER XV.

First Catholic Missions.—Canadian priests on the Columbia—Ogden asks for contributions towards their maintenance—Father Demers goes to Stuart Lake—His description of the voyage—Missionary work—Degraded Indians—Among the Shushwaps—Father Nobili—The devil apes the Almighty—False prophets - - - - 224

ix.

CONTENTS

CHAPTER XVI.

PAGE

Manson's Tribulations.—Manson succeeds Ogden—How McIntosh died—Desertions more and more numerous—The officers leave one after the other—An unfaithful man—The manager is disgusted—The terrible Waccan—His manifold services—A deserter caught—Anderson's new route is tried—And found wanting   -   -   -   241

CHAPTER XVII.

Alexis Bélanger and His Avenger.—An unnatural joy—Alexis is cast away—One of his tricks—More disdemeanors—A provocation—Shot while steering—D. McLean and his principles—" Where is Tlel "—Approval of a crime—Forced to scalp—Was that right ?   -   260

CHAPTER XVIII.

" Club Law " in New Caledonia.—The personnel of the district—Manson dissatisfied—Pack-trains under difficulties—A curt officer—Paul Fraser is killed —Manson reproved—Trouble with the chief—Annihilation threatened—Half-hearted reconciliation—The " Prince of darkness "—Douglas on the Crimean War—First symptoms of the gold craze   -   -   -   -   -   -   -   -   -   -   275

CHAPTER XIX.

Golden Cariboo.—First discoveries—Hill Bar—New mail facilities—The Horsefly discovered—The Cariboo mines—Fabulous yields—An overland party reaches the gold fields—Shipwreck and consequent hardships—Gruesome scenes of cannibalism   -   -   -   -   -   291

CHAPTER XX.

Improvements and Trials.—New seekers after gold—The Cariboo waggon road—A newspaper in the wilds—Improved conditions at Stuart Lake—The smallpox—Traders and miners—Down on free traders—The bottle is called into requisition   -   -   -   -   30

CHAPTER XXI.

From Chilcotin to Omineca.—The Waddington Trail—The Chilcotins—Fourteen whites massacred—The Bentinck Arm massacre—The causes of the rising—Punitive expeditions—D. McLean is shot—Some of the murderers are captured—Their fate—The Western Union Telegraph Co.—Mining in Omineca—A steamboat at Stuart Lake   -   -   -   -   -   -   -   -   -   -   -   313

CONTENTS

CHAPTER XXII.

PAGE

Some of the Later Pioneers.—Lively scenes near Fort St. James—Judge P. O'Reilly—Themis at fault—G. Hamilton succeeds P. Ogden— P. Dunlevy and his trading ventures—A mystified official—James Reid—Strenuous life finally crowned with success - - - 324

CHAPTER XXIII.

Laudetur Jesus Christus!—First Anglican missions—Various Catholic expeditions—Father McGuckin—Bishop D'Herbomez visits the district—At Stuart Lake and Babine—Father Lejacq—A rebellious medicine-man comes to grief—Danger from alien races—A mission is established near Fort St. James—The first resident missionaries and their flock - - - - - - - - - - 333

Appendices - - - - - - - - - - - 345

Index - - - - - - - - - - 357

xi.

ILLUSTRATIONS

                                                                                    PAGE

Rev. A. G. Morice, O.M.I.   -   -   -   -   -   -   *Frontispiece*

Map of New Caledonia   -   -   -   -   -   -   -   -   -   1

Shaman or "Medicine Man"   -   -   -   -   -   -   -   -   10

Taya, son of 'Kwah   -   -   -   -   -   -   -   -   -   16

"Grosse-Tête," Julian, Thomas and Athanase, descendants of 'Kwah -   22

Iron Dagger   -   -   -   -   -   -   -   -   -   -   25

Sir Alexander Mackenzie   -   -   -   -   -   -   -   -   34

Daniel W. Harmon   -   -   -   -   -   -   -   -   -   34

Sir George Simpson   -   -   -   -   -   -   -   -   -   34

Sir James Douglas   -   -   -   -   -   -   -   -   -   34

A Carrier Fisherman   -   -   -   -   -   -   -   -   -   40

Simon Fraser   -   -   -   -   -   -   -   -   -   -   54

Kœzi, daughter of 'Kwah   -   -   -   -   -   -   -   -   88

Fort St. James To-day   -   -   -   -   -   -   -   -   104

Old Fort St. James   -   -   -   -   -   -   -   -   -   114

Doubly "Carriers"   -   -   -   -   -   -   -   -   -   160

Peter Skene Ogden   -   -   -   -   -   -   -   -   -   172

Packing Through the Mountains   -   -   -   -   -   -   -   184

Salmon Trap   -   -   -   -   -   -   -   -   -   -   188

Indian Crooked Knife   -   -   -   -   -   -   -   -   191

Iron Skin Scraper   -   -   -   -   -   -   -   -   -   191

'Kwah's Grave   -   -   -   -   -   -   -   -   -   -   198

Rocher Deboulé and the Skeena River   -   -   -   -   -   208

Carrier and Carried   -   -   -   -   -   -   -   -   -   224

John Tod   -   -   -   -   -   -   -   -   -   -   236

A. C. Anderson   -   -   -   -   -   -   -   -   -   236

Bishop Demers   -   -   -   -   -   -   -   -   -   236

Hon. John Work   -   -   -   -   -   -   -   -   -   236

James A. Grahame   -   -   -   -   -   -   -   -   -   236

Fort McLeod   -   -   -   -   -   -   -   -   -   -   242

"Jem" Boucher   -   -   -   -   -   -   -   -   -   284

The Cariboo Waggon Road   -   -   -   -   -   -   -   305

Hon. Senator James Reid   -   -   -   -   -   -   -   332

Rev. J. M. McGuckin, O.M.I.   -   -   -   -   -   -   336

Stuart Lake Mission   -   -   -   -   -   -   -   -   342

History of the Northern Interior of British Columbia.

INTRODUCTION.

The Country and Its Aborigines.

NEW CALEDONIA, the country to which we wish to introduce the kind reader, was the nucleus out of which the present province of British Columbia was evolved. Authors disagree as to its boundaries. Thus, while Alexander Begg, to whom we owe a " History of the North-West," assigns to that district rather too modest dimensions when he states[1] that it extended only from 52° to 55° latitude north—thereby excluding part of the Chilcotin region—his namesake, Alexander Begg, the author of the latest " History of British Columbia," sins the other way by stretching its southern limits as far as Colville, in the present State of Washington.[2] Although it included at one time Kamloops and the adjoining territory, it might suffice for the ethnographer to call it simply the region peopled by the Western Déné Indians ; but as this statement would not probably add much to the knowledge of most readers, we will describe it as that immense tract of land lying between the Coast Range and the Rocky Mountains, from 51°30′ to 57° of latitude north.

This region is mostly mountainous, especially in the

---

1. " History of the North-West," p. 158.
2. " History of British Columbia," p. 12.

north, where lines of snow-capped peaks intersect the whole country between the two main ranges. Endless forests, mostly of coniferous trees, and deep lakes, whose length generally exceeds considerably their breadth, cover such spaces as are not taken up by mountains. The only level or meadow lands of any extent within that district lie on either side of the Chilcotin River, where excellent bunch grass affords lasting pasturage to large herds of cattle and horses.[1]

The Douglas fir preponderates in the southern half of the country, but cannot stand the cold prevalent north of 54°40′, while the three different species of spruce which cover the northern part of the district hardly appear within its more temperate zone. The black pine is fairly common all over the country, and it is always indicative of a dry, sandy, and usually level ground, just as the poplar and the aspen betoken a moist and rather rich soil. Apart from the animals to which they give shelter, these woods afford but very meagre resources adapted to the wants of man. These are reduced to some varieties of berries, prominent among which is the service berry, the fruit of the *Amelanchier alnifolia*, which the aborigines compress into flat cakes and keep in their larder for use in any emergency.

Lakes and rivers are practically numberless. The most important among the former are : Lake Stuart, with its tributaries Lakes Rey, Soullier, Tremblé and Tatla; Lakes Babine and Augier ; Lakes Morice, Dawson, and Emerald,

---

1. H. H. Bancroft, in his "History of British Columbia," asserts that "the lake country from Chilcotin to Fort Fraser and beyond is generally open " (p. 37), a statement which is far too comprehensive. The lakes of that country, and those immediately to the north of it, R. Greenhow gravely declares to be "frozen over more than two-thirds of the year." ("History of Oregon and California," p. 29), which assertion will seem strange to people who, like the present writer, have annually navigated their waters from the middle of May to the middle of December, practically ever since the year 1885.

which are the headwaters of the Nechaco; Lakes Loring and McAulay, whence issues the Bulkley River; Lakes French and Fraser, Peters and Vowell, whose waters flow into the Nechaco; Lakes Cambie, St. Mary's, McLeod, Bell, Turner, Nation, Quesnel and Chilco. The map will show the respective position of each.

The chief streams, apart from the Fraser, are the Nechaco, which, some sixty-five miles from its mouth, receives the Stuart, which drains the lake of the same name, together with Lakes Tatla and Tremblé, through the Middle and the Thaché Rivers; the Blackwater, a stream of minor importance, called West River by Sir Alex. Mackenzie, who ascended its valley on his way to the Pacific; the Quesnel, which heads in the lake of the same name, and the Chilcotin (more properly Tsilhkhoh), which takes its source in the lake called Chilco by the whites, and waters the finest part of the country. Bear Lake and Babine Lake, with their outlets, as well as the Bulkley, belong to the basin of the Skeena, which may be said to form the north-western boundary of the district; while the Parsnip and the Finlay, with their tributaries the Pack, Nation, Omineca, etc., flow into the Arctic Ocean, after having forced their way through the Rockies under the name of Peace River.

Most of these lakes and rivers contain excellent fish, two (sometimes three or more) kinds of trout, whitefish, land-locked salmon, ling and a multitude of carpoides and other inferior fish. A few sturgeon are occasionally caught in Lake Stuart and outlet, but that fish is unknown in the other basins. These sheets of water become also annually the rendezvous of myriads of ducks, geese, and other aquatic fowls, some of which, as the grebe, abound to such an extent that, for a fortnight or so, they are daily taken by the hundred in a single locality.

3

As to the fauna, its representatives are fairly numerous.
The natives class them into venison and fur animals.
Among the former are the moose and the cariboo, whose
habitat is mostly on the mountains of the north, while the
deer, plentiful in the south, does not seem to cross the
limits of the Douglas fir. The various fur-bearing animals
are the grizzly and the black bears,[1] the beaver, foxes of
different color, though they are the offspring of the same
parents; the marten and fisher, the otter, the mink, and
other game of minor value.

These, from time immemorial, have been trapped or
chased by the American representatives of the human
species who call themselves *Déné* (men), and are divided
into four main tribes. From north to south these are:
the Sekanais, on the west slope of the Rocky Mountains
and throughout the adjoining territory, almost as far as the
53rd degree of latitude; the Babines, who inhabit the
shores of the lake called after them and the Bulkley
valley, though many of them hunt also in the vicinity of
Lakes French and Cambie; the Carriers, who have villages
all the way from Stuart Lake and tributaries to Alexandria, on the Fraser; and, finally, the Chilcotins, who now
mainly occupy the valley of the river to which they have
given their name.

These tribes, though all belonging to the same ethnic
group of aborigines, differ not a little as regards language,
manners, and customs, and even physical appearance.
Thus the Sekanais, for instance, are slender and bony,
with fairly delicate features, very small eyes, and thin lips.
The Carriers are stouter and more heavily built, with
coarser traits, thicker lips, and quite large eyes. The
Babines and Chilcotins are shorter than the Carriers, with

1. The brown bears in the district belong to the same species as the
black ones.

broader shoulders and, the former at least, with even thicker lips and flattish faces. A fifth tribe, that of the Nahanais, roams through the territory immediately to the north of the Babines and the Sekanais, though on great occasions they usually repair to their villages at Thalhthan and in the vicinity of the Rockies. Several of their women are almost fair complexioned.

These four or five tribes form what we call the Western Dénés. They have all very black and straight hair, dark eyes, small hands and feet, and a complexion of a swarthy brown, though they are, as a rule, fairer than their heterogeneous neighbors, the Shushwaps.[1]

None of them originally had any village chiefs in our sense of the word. Indeed, the Sekanais, who are quite nomadic and without houses or villages, were formerly destitute of any kind of chiefs, but kept wandering in quest of game under the nominal leadership of the older heads of related families. As to the Babines, the Carriers, and the Chilcotins, they possessed what they called *tœneza*, hereditary "noblemen," who owned the hunting grounds and were the honorary heads of various clans or gentes. Succession to rank or property invariably followed the female line among the Babines and the Carriers, while among the Chilcotins and the Sekanais heredity was, as amongst us, always on the side of the father.

These tribes concurred in their religious ideas. They believed in a future world, and had some confused notions of a Supreme Being who governed the universe through the instrumentality of spirits, whose object was to protect or injure the individual. In the first case, they were what

1. For a fanciful classification of those tribes and a pessimistic account of their characteristics, and of all things British Columbian in general, we would commend D. G. F. Macdonald's "British Columbia and Vancouver's Island," p. 126, *et seq.*

is now called totems or tutelary genii, and the second were the immediate cause of disease, wherewith they were sometimes confounded. The latter had, however, to yield to the incantations of a certain class of men known among us as shamans,[1] who, supposedly endowed with supernatural powers, were regarded almost as the masters of life and death.

In case of death the bodies were buried among the Chilcotins and the Shushwaps, burned among the Carriers, the Babines and the Western Nahanais, but left uncared for among the Sekanais and some Nahanais, who simply dropped thereon the brush shelter used as a temporary residence in the course of their incessant wanderings. Only in the cases of prominent or much beloved members of a band were the remains placed on a rough scaffolding out of the reach of wild beasts, or encased within the hollow or hollowed trunk of an upright tree.

Among the Carriers, the widow of a deceased warrior used to pick up from among the ashes of the funeral pyre the few charred bones which would escape the ravages of fire and *carry* them on her back in a leathern satchel—hence the name of the tribe—until the co-clansmen of the deceased had amassed a sufficient quantity of eatables and dressed skins to be publicly distributed among people of different clans, in the course of an ostentatious ceremony called "potlatch," a ceremony which prevailed among all but the Sekanais and the Eastern Nahanais tribes.

To the customs in vogue among their congeners, the Babines added that of letting their women wear, from the time of their puberty, a labret or plug of bone or hardwood, perhaps half an inch and more in diameter, between the teeth and the lower lip, which was thus distended out of all reasonable proportions. This caused the French Cana-

1. Or medicine-men.

dians in the employ of the early fur-traders to call the whole tribe Babines, or "Lippy People."

Hunting and fishing have always been practically the only means of subsistence of the Western Dénés, and their prospects in life are generally of the most precarious character, inasmuch as hunger and dire famine are not unknown to them, especially when the run of salmon, which is the daily bread of all but the Sekanais, has been a failure.

These aborigines are, for the most part, possessed of strongly religious instincts. The Sekanais are the most honest and moral; the Carriers the proudest and most progressive; the Chilcotins are violent and none too scrupulous, while for loquacity and conservativeness the Babines have few superiors.[1]

With regard to their origin, the short space at our command in this little sketch evidently debars us from entering into anything like an adequate discussion of that intricate question. All we are prepared to state, after a careful survey of their languages, manners and customs, is that: 1st, They are undoubtedly of a mixed origin; 2nd, they have come from the north-north-west; 3rd, they had, in their early history, commerce, perhaps through intermarriage, with peoples of Jewish persuasion or origin.

As it is, none but the Babines have any reminiscence of a home different from that they now occupy. If we are to credit the Ackwilgates (or Western Babines) and their neighbors, the Kitksons, a Tsimpsian tribe which has the same tradition, the original seat of the whole Babine tribe would have been on a flat along the left bank of the Bulkley, a short distance above the mouth of the Bear River.

1. For the most complete account of those Indians to be found in the earlier works we would refer to W. C. Hazlitt's "British Columbia and Vancouver Island." His information, however, is all second hand, and, at times, hardly reliable. As to his description of the geographical features of the country, it is as inaccurate as could be expected from a man writing in 1858, entirely from hearsay.

Kitksons and Babines then lived in close proximity and intermarried freely, when a squirrel[1] having, one day, crossed the river on top of the weir erected for the capture of salmon, the natives, frightened at the sight of such an ominous occurrence, and dreading the sad fate it portended, immediately scattered in all directions. The Kitksons went down to the Skeena, and the Babines took refuge in the shelter of the woods, whence they subsequently emerged to settle, some on the lake now called after them, others near the fall in the Bulkley, at the place known to-day as Moricetown.

There they lived and thrived on the large supply of salmon which the impediment in the stream kept at their doors, until the year 1820, or thereabouts, when a large piece of the rocky cliff overhanging the same river at the place now called Ackwilgate, some thirty miles below, having fallen across the stream, this barred it so completely that it formed a cataract of sufficient height to prevent the fish from getting up to the Moricetown fall. Threatened with starvation, the Western Babines went in a body, armed *cap-à-pie*, and forcibly took the new terminus from its owners of Tsimpsian parentage.

In course of time, the rock, which was to give a name to the new place—Fallen Rock—wore away to such an extent that salmon could return to their former haunts up the river ; but the Babines or Ackwilgates have since retained possession of both fisheries.

So much for the Babines and their traditions. We now come to the real history of their congeners, and the authentic account of their doings immediately before, and ninety years after, the advent of that superior race which was to revolutionize their ideas, manners and customs, and whose not always too edifying deeds we shall also have to record.

1. The Kitksons say a double-headed squirrel.

CHAPTER I.

Earliest Historical Times.

1660-1765.

NA'KWŒL is the first really historical aborigine mentioned by the Carrier Indians of Stuart Lake. His name has come down to the present generation as that of one who was the personification of old age, and after a careful computation based on the various data forming our original chapter and many others not furnished here, the date of his birth cannot be set later than the year 1660. He grew up to attain, in course of time, the honored position of *tœneza*, or hereditary nobleman, of the Stuart Lake sept, and he is likewise famous as having been the first Déné who could boast the acquisition of an iron axe or adze.

This came to him about 1730, probably by way of Tsechah, an Indian village close to what is now Hazelton, on the Skeena. Whatever may have been the origin of the wonderful implement,[1] it is said that, on acquiring it, Na'kwœl convoked his fellow-tribesmen to a great banquet or ceremonial feast, where all the guests could admire it hanging above them from one of the rafters of the large lodge where they were assembled.

That implement was, of course, considered exceedingly

1. From Chapters III., IV. and V. will be seen how comparatively common were iron wares in New Caledonia at the time of its discovery by Mackenzie and Fraser ; and the fact that the latter found, near the 49th parallel, some of them which seemed of Russian manufacture, goes to show the ease with which such goods travelled in pre-European times. (See Appendix B.)

valuable, and its possession was the means of considerably enhancing the notable's prestige among the entire Carrier tribe.

At that time it was customary for those Indians to migrate, at the approach of every winter, to a place where firewood was plentiful enough to supply the needs of the different families grouped around their chiefs or *tœnezas*, and to erect, for use during the cold season, large huts of slender logs with spruce-bark roofs and doorways covered with brush. One day, when some of Na'kwœl's family were cutting boughs for the entrance to his lodge, the line which fastened his adze to its handle getting loosened, the blade suddenly dashed off and fell among the branches already cut. After searching among these, it became apparent that the instrument must have dropped down in the snow, where it could not be found until the services of the medicine-man had been resorted to.[1]

Physically, Na'kwœl was short and very corpulent, a feature quite rare among the western Dénés. As to his psychological disposition, a little episode is to this day related, which goes to illustrate the man and his times.

As he was, one winter day, on the ice of Lake Greenwood, busy cutting up some cariboo, which friendly neighbors had killed for him, footsteps on the frozen snow told him of the approach of a native from Natleh, Fraser Lake. Immediately seizing his bow and arrows,

---

1. The native chronicler goes on to relate how that shaman, who enjoyed a wonderful reputation even among his peers, had a personal totem or familiar genius, in the shape of a skunk-skin, which he wore hanging from his neck. This, during his trances, he used to press in his hands, when it emitted a piercing scream. On the occasion of Na'kwœl's loss, in the midst of dancing, singing and beating of drums, the shaman squeezed his skunk-skin, upon which it cried as if the animal had been alive, and, detaching itself from the neck of the medicine man, it made for the heap of boughs, wherein it plunged and remained for a while. When it came back, it bore in its mouth the lost adze blade !

A SHAMAN OR "MEDICINE MAN."

Na'kwœl aimed his weapon at the stranger, exclaiming at the same time :

"We have decreed against intercourse with people from Natleh. What does this fellow come here for?"

Undisturbed by the threats, which he feigned not to notice, the stranger leisurely limped on and finally joined Na'kwœl's assistants, by whom he was hospitably entertained. Then, bending his own bow, with the arrow aimed at Na'kwœl, this accidental guest exclaimed :

"Now, old Na'kwœl, your pretensions are altogether too preposterous, and you speak like a man without sense. Look at this, my arrow! Were I so minded, I could sink it right now between your ribs."

Na'kwœl had two sons, A'ke'tœs and Chichanit, both of whom wielded great influence among their co-tribesmen. Yet the former, who is the first known to-day of a line of hereditary chiefs, the fourth of whom died of old age some fifteen years ago, met with a tragic and, at the same time, rather inglorious end, being done to death by his own wives. The elder of these was called Chalh'tas, and seems to have been a genuine virago ; while the other, known as Atéte, was of a milder disposition.

Now, A'ke'tœs was constantly tormented by the demon of jealousy. He loved, on that account, to isolate himself and force his partners to share his cheerless seclusion, a step which occasioned many a family dispute, at the end of which his groundless suspicions asserted themselves with renewed vigor. On the other hand, he was believed to be endowed with malefic powers, a gift the possession of which is sure to prove fatal among the natives.

One day, as the family stayed on Long Island, at the outlet of Lake Stuart, while the whole tribe was stationed at Tsauche, about five miles to the south-west, on the shores of the same lake, A'ke'tœs had a violent altercation with Chalh'tas, which resulted in the latter accusing him of the death of her two children, but lately deceased. Upon this blows ensued, when the woman, falling on him, called upon Atéte to help her kill him, under pain of being herself done to death if she refused. Then they shamefully mutilated his remains, which they conveyed to the mouth of a stream emptying on the opposite side of the lake, and buried them in the sand.

Then, hiding his quiver among the rocks of the Stuart River, near the water's edge, they hastily fled to Fraser Lake, where they declared that, after one of their usual disputes, A'ke'tœs had tried to put them to death, when they had made off with his canoe, whereupon he had pursued them in the water and gone beyond his depth. On the ground of that story, canoes searched for days every nook of the river, where only the missing man's quiver was found, until later on his mangled remains were accidentally[1] unearthed, whereupon the anger of old Na'kwœl and of his son Chichanit knew no bounds.

Several years elapsed, when Atéte, who had been but an unwilling accomplice in the murder, tired of her exile, and resolved upon returning to her native land and telling the whole truth. But as she neared Stuart Lake her return was revealed to Chichanit, who sallied out and killed her with his bow-point—a sort of spear affixed to one end of his bow, a weapon quite common among the ancient Carriers. Then, repenting of his act, committed just when the woman endeavored to explain that she was innocent, he decided to spare her surviving co-partner on condition that she would come back and allow him to take her to

1. As the imagination of the natives must mix the marvellous or extraordinary with the common and ordinary, the Indians do not fail to say that a rainbow, one end of which plunged where the body had been buried, was instrumental in causing its discovery.

wife in memory of his late brother. Messengers were sent who brought her back, and thenceforth she attended upon Chichanit, as was usual with widows preparatory to their being re-married to their late husband's nearest kin.

Meanwhile, Na'kwœl was constantly smarting under the pain caused by the untimely death of his eldest son. Though he was now well advanced in years, he used to visit Chichanit's lodge and reproach Chalh'tas with her crime, in which case blows would generally follow words, to all of which she had to submit with as much equanimity as her own haughty nature would allow.

One day, when she was unravelling with a small stone knife the strips of willow bark, the filaments of which were intended as the material of a fish net, her father-in-law became so violent that, unable to stand his abuse any longer, she grabbed him by the hair, and, throwing him to the ground, stabbed him in the neck with her diminutive implement. Fortunately for her intended victim, her knife broke in the old man's collar-bone before it could inflict serious injury, whereupon Na'kwœl called for help in terms which are still recited for the sake of their quaintness, and his son, running to his assistance, killed the woman with his bow-point.

Na'kwœl was now aging considerably. After many years passed in the company of his only remaining son, he grew to be so old that, according to tradition and the accounts of eye-witnesses, his hair, after having been snow white, had become of a yellowish hue. He fell into such a state of decrepitude that his knees and elbows were covered with scaly excrescences, resembling a sort of parasitic moss. His hearing failed him, and his eyelids drooped until he became the very picture of old age. Basking in the sun on a rock emerging from the shallow water, which is still shown near the outlet of Lake Stuart, he would at times send forth loud cries, as of rage at seeing himself so powerless against the ravages of time ; then, bathing in the tepid waters, he would exclaim, on coming out :

"*Ha ! tcilhyaz nasœstlœn a !*" (Ah ! here I am, a young man again !)

Some time before his demise, he is reported to have assured people that it was not without some design from above that he had been permitted to live so long, and that when he should die, Na'kal, the mountain which rises from the eastern shore of the lake, would dance in his honor. The natives date from his death the fall of part of a spur thereof, which the infiltration of water detached from the main body of the mountain.

The exact date of Na'kwœl's death can, of course, only be guessed ; but from all accounts it cannot be far from 1765, as the old chief was certainly more than a centenarian when he passed away. Indeed, considering the longevity of the Indians, especially those of the old stock, he probably lived to see his hundred and tenth birthday.[1]

About twenty years before his death a most melancholy event, which was to cause a permanent change in the ethnographical map of the country, had happened at the confluence of the Stuart and Nechaco Rivers. There stood at that time a flourishing village called Chinlac, the population of which was allied by blood and dialect to the Lower Carriers of what is now called Stony Creek. The principal chief was a certain Khadintel, a man who enjoyed the consideration of his subjects, and who must have been well up in years, since he had two wives with a large number of children.

---

1. Taya, the late head chief of the Stuart Lake band, a son of 'Kwah, who saw Na'kwœl and lived for some time with him, had hardly a grey hair at eighty. An elder brother, whom the writer has known, was quite hale a few days before he died, aged about a hundred years.

For some time previous to 1745, the report had been current amongst his people and their friends of other localities that the Chilcotins intended to avenge on him the death of one of their notables, and, agreeable to anticipations, a very large band of those Southern Dénés did come in due time, and in one morning practically annihilated the whole population then present at Chinlac. A few only owed their life to their temporary absence or to a speedy flight.

At the time of the catastrophe the head chief, Khadintel, was on a tour of inspection of his snares, some distance down the Nechaco. He had reached the rapid next to the confluence of the two rivers, paddling up in a large canoe with two other men, when he suddenly caught sight of a large number of canoes coming down stream.

"The Chilcotins!" he exclaimed. "Run up the bank and flee for your lives. I am the one they want, and I alone ought to die."

His companions were no sooner out of sight than a volley of arrows was whizzing around him, which he so dexterously dodged that, partly because his life appeared charmed to his aggressors, and partly because they thought it prudent to keep for any possible emergency the few remaining arrows in their possession after the great expenditure of them they had made in the morning, Khalhpan, the captain of the war party, ordered a suspension of hostilities. Then, addressing his bold adversary, he said:

"Khadintel, you have the reputation of being a man. If you are such, dance for me."

Whereupon the Chinlac chief commenced the dance of a *tœneza* on the beach of the river, just to show that his heart was above fear and emotion. When he had finished he warned his departing enemy that, in the course of a few years, he would return his visit.

The spectacle which met Khadintel's eyes on his return
to his village was indeed heart-rending. On the ground,
lying bathed in pools of blood, were the bodies of his own
two wives and of nearly all his countrymen, while hanging
on transversal poles resting on stout forked sticks planted
in the ground, were the bodies of the children ripped open
and spitted through the out-turned ribs in exactly the same
way as salmon drying in the sun. Two such poles were
loaded from end to end with that gruesome burden.

Aided by his two companions, Khadintel religiously
burnt all the bodies, and placed the bones which had
partially escaped destruction in leather satchels adorned
with long fringes which, in the course of time, he entrusted
to the care of the surviving relatives of Khalhpan's
victims. Then he prepared the vengeance due to such an
unprovoked crime and, early in the spring of the third year
after the massacre, he found himself at the head of a large
band of braves he had gathered from among the few survivors of the Chinlac population and the allied villages of
Thachek, Nulkreh (Stony Creek) and Natleh (Fraser Lake).

Having reached the Chilcotin valley, at a place which,
from the topographical details now furnished by the old
men, must be identified with the plain where the modern
village of Anarhem stands, the avenging party beheld
from the top of the third terrace, or last of the superposed
plateaus, in the thickets of which they discreetly passed
the night, a long row of lodges, indicating a very large
population.

Khalhpan, the Chilcotin chieftain, had a younger brother
known as 'Kun'qus, a man most powerfully built and of a
very amiable disposition. Expecting reprisals for his
brother's misdeed, that influential Chilcotin had built a
palisade round his house, wherein he lived with a wife
taken from among his own tribe and a second partner, a

TAYA.

(A son and second successor of 'Kwah.)

Carrier woman, with her little brother, whom the members of Khalhpan's expedition had brought him from Chinlac.

He had just gone to prepare laths for the erection of a salmon trap, when, early in the morning, he was surprised to hear, all of a sudden, the uproarious clamors of the avenging party who, from different points of vantage, were storming his village. Running home in all haste, he gave the alarm to the sleeping population, and as he rushed into his house he passed his Carrier wife and her brother escaping in the direction of their attacking countrymen. He lost some time in trying to pursue them armed with a war-club which, to defeat his purpose, the woman had previously fastened to the wall of the lodge.

By that time, several Chilcotins had already fallen before the rage of the Carriers, when 'Kun'qus, aided by his first wife, hastily donned his double armor, consisting of a device made of dried rods of hardened amelanchier wood, over which he spread the *pesta*, a sleeveless, tunic-like cuirass of moose-skin covered with a coat of glued sand and gravel. Thus attired, he went out and started shooting wildly until his supply of arrows was exhausted, keeping between his legs, till he fell pierced by an arrow, a little son of his, whom he loved above all his other children.

The Carriers, who now recognized him, seeing him practically powerless, assailed him from all parts. But with a large stone dagger, whose blade he had mounted at the end of a stick, he kept them all at bay, so that they could hardly hurt him, inasmuch as their missiles were of no avail against his double armor. In this predicament they remembered the boast of a confederate, a little man of insignificant parentage named Yœntœlh, who had previously offered to catch the big Chilcotin for them. Bidden to make good his boast, Yœntœlh rushed at 'Kun'qus, leading him to use his lance, which he skilfully dodged at the very instant that he seemed doomed to destruction, and grasping its shaft before 'Kun'qus could strike again, gave his countrymen the long-sought-for opportunity. Seizing the warrior from every available quarter, they snatched from him all the native finery in which he was attired, a beautiful ceremonial wig adorned with dentalium shells, a costly breastplate, and a necklace mostly of the same material. Then, under a heavy stroke from a war-club launched on the forepart of his head, 'Kun'qus fell down never to rise again. Then, falling on his helpless body with all kinds of weapons, they made of it an unrecognizable mass of flesh.

The Carriers had now gratified their lust for vengeance. Indeed, the destruction of Chinlac was more than avenged. There the Chilcotins had set up two poles loaded with children's bodies, while the Carriers did not return to their country before they had put up as a trophy three such poles with similarly innocent victims.

Meanwhile, Khalhpan, the primary cause of the whole trouble, had been vainly sought for by the avenging northerners. He was absent, and did not come back until a short time after their departure. His feelings can be imagined when he came in sight of his village, now transformed into a solitude, peopled only by dogs howling around the mangled remains of their masters. Taking with him a few of the fugitives he found gloomily prowling about the field of carnage, he set out in pursuit of the retreating Carriers.

These had just forded a river at a point where a sand-bank in the middle cut it in two, and they were in the act of putting on their foot-gear again, when Khalhpan was sighted on the opposite side of the stream. Khadintel immediately advanced to meet him.

" People say that you are a man, and you would fain pass yourself off as a terrible warrior," he said, in the best

Chilcotin he could command. " If you be such, come on, Khalhpan ; come on, and retreat not."

Whereupon the Chilcotin chief advanced as far as the sand-bank ; but at the sight of his powerlessness against such a host of enemies, he began to cry and to turn back.

"Now, Khalhpan," insisted his triumphant foe, "when, all alone against your people, I was cornered on the river bank and you wanted to kill me, I danced at your bidding. If you are a man, dance now for me, as I did for you."

But his adversary merely returned as far as the sand islet, when the sight of the multitude facing him, and the remembrance of all his relatives gone and of his beloved daughter, now dragged into slavery, were too much for him. He requested his adversary to spare her life, and broke into violent sobbing, which seeing, Khadintel, in tones full of scorn, cried across the river :

" Khalhpan, it is upon men that we came down to avenge a great wrong. I see that you are a woman, therefore I allow you to live. Go in peace, and weep to your heart's content."

The affront to the Carrier tribe was thus washed out in blood, but the destruction wrought by the Chilcotin marauders remained irreparable. In the course of time, the few persons who had escaped the massacre of 1745 settled among their friends of Thachek and Lheitli (Fort George). As to their own village, a bare spot on the right bank of the Stuart River, and the several trails leading out of it, are all that now remain of what was formerly the home of a thriving community.[1]

1. After the destruction of his native village Khadintel remarried, and by his last wife he had a daughter named Samalh'ti, who died in 1842 at the age of about ninety. She was then older than another woman who died recently among the Dénés leaving after her four generations of descendants. Samalh'ti is our authority for the date of the Chinlac massacre.

CHAPTER II.

Still Pre-European Times.

1765–1791.

ALLIED to Na'kwœl's family was a certain Tsale-kulhyé, the first now remembered of a line of hereditary chiefs, whose regular seat was Pinche, on Lake Stuart. He was born about 1735, and he was probably a little younger than the first A'ke'tœs, whose sister or cousin he must have married, since his eldest son ultimately succeeded to the latter's name and rank. This circumstance accounts also for his own incorporation into the Stuart Lake tribe.

Tsalekulhyé seems to have been of a rather troublesome disposition, and he must have been something of a profligate, as the first incident in connection with which his name is mentioned does certainly not redound to his credit. A member of the Sekanais tribe was wont to make periodical visits to the Stuart Lake band of Indians, whom he had befriended. One evening a commotion arose in the camp, and, while trying to ascertain the cause of it, the stranger beheld his own sister bleeding to death from an arrow wound received at the hand of Tsalekulhyé. What the reason of such a rash act was is not known, but can easily be surmised. Infuriated at the sight of his dying relative, the Sekanais shot Tsalekulhyé, and made for the woods. Happily for the latter the wound inflicted was not serious, and he soon recovered.

In his second encounter with an adversary, fate was not so favorable to him. About the year 1780, an influential member of the Naskhu'tin sub-tribe happened to die near the confluence of the Blackwater River with the Fraser, where those aborigines had but recently a village. As the loss of the Indian was much felt, his relatives consulted the shaman, who declared that Tsalekulhyé was responsible for his death. Bent on vengeance, his friends, in great numbers, started armed *cap-à-pie* for what is now called the Stuart River.

The natives were not at that time so sedentary as they are to-day. As we have already seen, they shifted their winter quarters as the need of fuel required, though, as spring opened, the ancestors of the population now stationed near the southern end of Lake Stuart moved generally to the mouth of Beaver Creek, some five miles to the south-west of the outlet of that lake. There they subsisted mainly on small fish, carp and trout, with an occasional duck or goose, until the middle of August, when they transferred their penates exactly to the outlet of the lake, where they set their weirs and traps. Finally, late in September, they migrated again up the lake, and dispersed themselves along the shores and on the several islands, where the women caught whitefish and trout in the preserves allotted them by hereditary right, while the men trapped the various fur-bearing animals.

Early in the spring of 1780, or thereabouts, those Indians were camped in three large detachments on the upper course of the Stuart River. Their southermost party occupied a site still pointed out, slightly above Hay Island, when a canoe came up with the alarming news, gathered from friendly Indians, that a large force of Naskhu'tins was on its way up to avenge its dead. Tsalekulhyé was then visiting his swan snares, and had repeatedly been told that he was the man especially wanted by the southerners He therefore hastened to rejoin his friends in the lower encampment.

Doubtful of their ability to resist the aggressors, the members of that party decided to move up and join the other two allied bands. But a heavy snow-storm came on, which caused a slight postponement of their departure. This delay sealed their fate. All of a sudden, a great outcry was raised on the top of the bank, and, before the Stuart Lake people could take in the situation, arrows were whizzing about, spears flying in all directions, and war-clubs stunning right and left, amidst the most hideous yells and vociferations of the attacking party. Two *tœnezas,* or headmen, were among the assailed. Both of them were slain and mutilated, as well as other less conspicuous members of the band, while most of the women the Naskhu'tins could lay hands on were taken prisoners and enslaved. As to Tsalekulhyé, the involuntary cause of the disaster, he took to the water, and was on the point of escaping, when he was recognized, killed and horribly mutilated.

Such had been the swiftness of the enemy's movements, and the consequent confusion of the assailed, that the former had but two persons wounded during the whole affray.

Among Tsalekulhyé's relatives present on the spot were four brothers, the youngest but one of whom, a lad of possibly fifteen summers, named Nathadilhthœlh, succeeded in swimming across the river, loaded, at first, with a sister and a brother only a few years old, whom, to save himself and sister, he had to let go and condemn to a watery grave. He is the same whom we will see called *Mal-de-gorge* in the old Hudson's Bay Company journals. Both his elder brothers were killed before his own eyes, and, while he bade his sister run as fast as her legs would carry her along the

"GROSSE-TÊTE," JULIAN, THOMAS AND ATHANASE.

(Son, grandson, great-grandson and great-great-grandson of 'Kwah.)

border of ice clinging to the shore and announce the sad news of their misfortunes to the next band of Indians, he himself stood in the vicinity of the doomed camp waiting for the end of the massacre, out of reach of hostile eyes and arrows.

Next morning three large canoes came down, and those who owed their lives to flight and the blinding snow-storm, together with the courageous Nathadilhthœlh, made bold to return to the scene of the disaster, where, amidst noisy mourning, the dead bodies of the fallen, with the exception of that of Tsalekulhyé, which could not be found, were placed on a pile of dry wood and burned.

Now, Tsalekulhyé had two sons, 'Kwah, a young man about twenty-five years old, who had just been married, and was destined to become a very prominent figure in the annals of Stuart Lake, and Œhulhtzœn, a few years younger, who was as yet single. Both brothers were on a hunting tour at the time of the massacre of their co-tribes-men.

Great was their surprise and indignation when they were told on their return of what had happened in their absence. 'Kwah was then but a young man, without title or claim to consideration other than that which he owed to his father's rank, to which, according to the Carriers' hereditary law, he could not even aspire. Yet it was universally conceded that to him and his relative, Nathadilhthœlh, must fall the task of avenging the victims of the Blackwater Indians. Many were even for immediate action ; but more moderate counsels prevailed, as the old men knew well that the Naskhu'tins, expecting reprisals, would be on their guard. They resolved, therefore, to wait until one or two years had elapsed without hostilities, wishing to lead the southern Indians to suppose that their crime would remain unpunished.

23

In the meantime 'Kwah went across the Rocky Mountains to get a supply of tanned skins to make moccasins for his prospective followers. On his return, he assembled quite a little army of braves from the Stuart Lake and Stony Creek villages, and went on to execute what he considered a filial duty.

But he had gone no farther than Tsinkœt or Head Lake, seven miles to the south of Stony Creek, when dissensions or fears arose among his people, as it was openly hinted that some of the Stony Creek Indians related to the Naskhu'tins intended to become traitors by giving warning of his approach. In the face of that lack of accord among his braves, 'Kwah turned back with regret, proclaiming before all his irrevocable abandonment of all hostile designs on the southern Indians.

This was, however, but a subterfuge on his part; for he had no sooner reached his native place again than, taking with him but seven tried men, among whom was Nathadilhthœlh, he embarked for the confluence of the Nechaco with the Fraser, where Fort George now stands, thus changing completely his route and rendering impossible treachery at the hands of Indians friendly to the Naskhu-'tins. On reaching the Fraser, the little party abandoned their canoe and continued their journey on foot, following all the time the left bank of that river.

Summer was then well on, since when they arrived opposite the first camp of the Naskhu'tins, which was composed of but a few persons, they spied them busy catching salmon. Retreating somewhat for the sake of greater secrecy, they built a large spruce bark canoe and profited by a dense fog to gum it, as otherwise the smoke of the fire required to melt the gum would have given the alarm—an Indian will smell smoke for miles. The little band of Naskhu'tins had just feasted on a fat bear, and were sleeping soundly when they were rudely awakened by the outcries of 'Kwah's followers. In a large house, with a doorway at each gable-end, lived with his brother and family a *tœneza* known under the name of Tsohtaih. While his brother precipitately rushed out of the lodge, only to find death at the hands of one of his aggressors, who pierced him with his spear, Tsohtaih made his exit with his son by the opposite door and took to the water. He might have made good his escape had it not been for 'Kwah himself, who noticed the two fugitives and, seizing a canoe, set out in pursuit of them.

The contest was altogether too unequal, and before Tsohtaih could swim away any considerable distance, 'Kwah was dealing him out repeated thrusts of an iron dagger (which is still in the possession of one of his sons at Stuart Lake), until he had been reduced to the state of an almost shapeless mass of flesh and blood. His son, a young man of perhaps twenty years of age, shared his fate, while on land a child of but a few months was seized and thrown into the river by one of the northerners in memory of his own brother who had been similarly treated by the Naskhu'tins. After this exploit, 'Kwah's "warriors," whose limited numbers did not allow him to undertake greater deeds, as he knew that the alarm was sure to be given by the women-folk who had escaped or been allowed to go in peace, hastily decamped and set out to return by land to their native country.

KWAH'S
DAGGER

Now it happened that the main body of the Naskhu'tins was stationed some distance farther down the Fraser, while still a little lower was the camp of T'sœlkwet, a most irascible Indian, allied by family ties to some of the victims of the Stuart River massacre. In the main group of Indians stood the lodge of a man who was now married to one of the women previously brought down from Tsale-kulhyé's ill-fated winter quarters. That man had become much attached to his wife, who had with her one of her little daughters sharing her enforced exile. As the Indian was in the act of fetching from his trap the salmon caught in the course of the night, he was horrified to find among his fish the disfigured body of Tsohtaih, which had floated down until stopped by the fishing weir.

Guessing what had happened, and, on second thought, fearing for the safety of his wife, he tried to neutralize the effect of his first cry of surprise by declaring to all questioners that there was nothing the matter. Then he hurriedly retired to his shack, and, seizing his war-club and dagger, he made his wife sit at his feet while he told the curious of his discovery.

Enraged at the sight of the mangled remains of their headman, the Naskhu'tins immediately strove to vent their anger on the foreign woman and her daughter; but, with all the ardor which love and despair could inspire, her husband successfully warded off all attacks on her, so that, unable to accomplish their purpose—inasmuch as they could not use arrows for fear of killing their countryman—they resolved to turn their attention to the authors of Tsohtaih's death, who were now beating a hasty retreat.

The Naskhu'tins had hardly left when T'sœlkwet, who had heard of the whole affair, assembled his own relatives and set out on the tracks of the pursuers with the avowed object of lending a helping hand to the Stuart Lake Indians in case of a conflict. Vainly did the outraged Naskhu'tins endeavor to deter him from his undertaking. The irate old man would listen to no entreaties and he equally scorned all threats. Finding themselves unequal to the task of successfully meeting two wide-awake enemies, attacking from opposite quarters—as the natives generally show little bravery except in ambuscades or against a sleeping adversary—they had to give up the pursuit.

Meanwhile 'Kwah's fellow-villagers in the north had transported themselves a short distance above the mouth of the Thaché River on Lake Stuart, when he returned with his little party of followers, all smeared over the face with charcoal, as became native "warriors." Upon seeing them back the Indians there assembled seized their bows and arrows, shooting at random in the direction of the oncomers, brandishing towards them their spears, daggers and war-clubs, and gratifying them with quite a noisy demonstration.

But this was only feigned hostility and the accomplishment of a sort of traditional rite customary on such occasions. 'Kwah and his men were in their estimation *me*, that is, legally impure, for having shed human blood, and the unfriendly reception was intended as a protest and a preservative against any bodily ill which might otherwise have befallen them as a consequence of their latest deeds.

One of the headmen finally put an end to the tumult, and invited the whole assemblage to a repast composed mainly of an immense number of *kesæl*, or land-locked salmon, a small fish one of which each guest took, and, in the case of some personal ailment, applied to the diseased limb or part of the body, the *kesæl* being considered, under the circumstances, as possessed of particularly great curative properties.

In the eyes of his fellows, young 'Kwah was now a man ; but a man, among the primitive Carriers and not a few of their descendants, is not supposed to be above the gambling passion. One of his friends was a youth whose father bore the significant name of *Utzi-lla-e'ka*, which may be freely translated Arrow-Heart or Keen-edged-Heart. His natural crankiness and disposition for harboring a wrong were proverbial. Yet he must have been an influential member of the band, since he rejoiced in the possession of an iron axe, an implement which was still exceedingly precious among the natives of the Stuart Lake valley.

Taking this with him as an aid in camp-making, Arrow-Heart's son left one day on pleasure bent for Thachek, in company with the hero of the late Blackwater expedition. Arrived at that place, which was then a populous village,[1] 'Kwah and his companion soon took to gambling. Time and again luck was against them, until they lost article after article of their wearing apparel. Reduced to a state of almost perfect nakedness, and yet hoping against hope, Arrow-Heart's son ventured to stake half the value of his father's axe, which likewise went over to his opponent. Disheartened, and thinking his companion would be more lucky, he turned over the remaining half of the implement to 'Kwah, only to see it immediately lost.

Dejected, and in the thinnest attire, the truant couple returned to their people, who were then camped on Stuart River, some fifty miles below the lake from whence it flows. Maddened at the loss of his axe, Arrow-Heart broke into reproaches against 'Kwah, whom he accused of being the final cause of its going over to the Thachek people. To placate the old man, who had a bad reputation and was credited with an unwelcome familiarity with the black art of sorcery, 'Kwah, after protesting that the fault was not his, presented him with a marmot robe and a beautiful necklace of dentalium shells, which, however, the irate parent of a gambler spitefully declined to accept.

1. As is shown by the large number of stone arrow-heads and other ancient weapons still found in the soil on the original site of that village.

Time went on without softening his hostile sentiments. 'Kwah would offer him the first-fruits of his hunts, only to see them thrown away with disdain. One day, when he was embarking in a small canoe in order to follow his wife, who had just left with the family impedimenta in a craft of her own, Arrow-Heart appeared on the bank, and in a shrill voice addressed him thus :

"You good-for-nothing orphan, who live on the bones of the village, why did you take my axe away from me?"

Wounded to the quick by those epithets, than which none can be more opprobrious in the eyes of a Déné,[1] 'Kwah seized his bow and arrows and shot his insulter through the heart. This was the signal for his quondam partner in gambling to spring out of his lodge in hot pursuit of the now retreating homicide, who made for the south as swiftly as the sluggish stream and his own exertions would allow. Finding his progress too slow by water, he landed and darted away, keeping close to the river, where he soon overtook his wife, who was paddling leisurely in her own canoe. Together they crossed to the eastern side, and both started for the hunting-grounds of friendly Sekanais, among whom they stayed a full year or more.

At length, deeming the anger and resentment of Arrow-Heart's people sufficiently cooled down, he returned to Stuart River with a plentiful provision of dressed skins, which he publicly distributed as an atonement for his deed.

By that time, however, the Sekanais themselves were in no very happy position, owing to a circumstance which none of them could have foreseen. Aborigines of the eastern slopes of the Rocky Mountains,[2] they had been

1. In the eyes of the Dénés there is no condition so lowly as that of an orphan or a widow.

2. As proved by their own language and by the following statement of Harmon, one of the first white men who ever came in contact with them (a

gradually driven into the recesses of that lofty range, where they had acquired their name,[1] and finally to the west thereof, by a section of their own tribe now constituted into a distinct branch of the great Déné family, the Beaver 'Indians, who for many years had been at enmity with their parent stock. Of late years an element had forced itself into the conflict which was telling terribly against the Sekanais proper. " Detonating bows " due to strangers in the east, who came nobody knew whence, were playing havoc among the less favored mountaineers, who, on several occasions, were slaughtered like sheep in the most treacherous manner. Parties of Beavers armed with guns would play with the fright inspired by their weapons, and, discharging them in the midst of the unsophisticated Sekanais, would kill them to the last.

Thus it came to pass that no mountain fastnesses could afford them shelter or anything like real security. Moreover, as fright is contagious, the terrible deeds of the Beavers went to the ears of the far-away Carriers, who to this day have remained persuaded of their innate lust for carnage. So much so, indeed, that hardly a summer now passes without some parties of the Western Dénés running home with the intelligence that bodies of Beaver Indians are lurking in the woods, evidently bent on slaughter.

To some of our readers an explanation of this reversal of fortunes is hardly necessary. It was but the natural

statement which we had never noticed until some time after the foregoing had been written) : " They [the Sekanais] are a small part of a tribe who, but a few years since, came from the east side of the Rocky Mountains" (" An Account of the Indians Living West of the Rocky Mountains," p. 265, New York reprint). Why their numbers were so insignificant the reader will soon see. Another proof of that author's wonderful sagacity is his remark to the effect that " the people who are now called Si-can-nies, I suspect, at no distant period, belonged to the tribe called Beaver Indians." (*Ibid, ibid.*)

1. The true name of that tribe is *Tsĕʼkĕhne*, "People-on-the-Rocks," *i.e.*, the Rocky Mountains.

result of the approach of the Canadian traders representing the North-West Company. Fire-arms and fire-water, the one a relative blessing and the other an unmitigated curse, which are but too often yoked together, were now within measurable distance of the Rocky Mountains, leaving behind them a trail of blood and indescribable debauchery. The white man, in his march from the east, was almost in sight, bringing in the folds of his mantle, along with undoubted boons for the natives, the plague of drink and consequent disorders, which was to thin their ranks to such an alarming extent.

For a score of years or so the bulk of the Carrier tribe was to remain free from the contamination of the new invasion; but, as we have seen, the Sekanais, who were to meet sooner the pale-faced strangers, were being, in the meantime, decimated by their death-dealing engines.

The last bloody encounter, wherein, as usual, the victims were all on one side, took place near a hill between the Rockies and the Carrier's territory, whose name is still mentioned by the natives. A party of Beavers came on, requesting the Sekanais to tell their children not to mind the report of their arms, which they were going to discharge for the fun of it, when suddenly all the adult Sekanais fell bathed in their blood.

This was the last butchery at the hands of the insolent easterners, and it was not destined to go unavenged even before the introduction of fire-arms among the Sekanais. The latter began to feel shy of their congeners, who were constantly crossing the Rockies, apparently to parade their wonderful arms, and would not so easily listen to their protestations of friendship and peace. We are told that a band of Beavers, having broken into a camp of Sekanais while professing the most amicable intentions, one of the latter, who enjoyed the respect of his tribesmen,

31

immediately made for the woods and travelled for some distance on the snow, cutting or bending as he went the bush tops, with the object of drawing to his movements the attention of bands of congenerous huntsmen possibly roaming in the vicinity. He then returned to his original camp, where the easterners were still to be seen, enjoying the hospitality of his own people.

Several parties of nomadic Sekanais noticed the silent signals left on the frozen snow and through the bush, and, unable to read them to their own satisfaction, followed the freshest tracks of the Indian to solve the enigma. These led them to the Sekanais camp, where the Beavers were now in an insignificant minority.

This gradual grouping of natives who could not bear them any possible goodwill seems to have given the alarm to the strangers, who thenceforth never went about without being armed to the teeth. One day, when one of them was conversing with the inmates of a Sekanais tepee, squatting on the ground with one of his feet hard on the handle of an iron dagger, the Indian who had so cleverly brought in such a concourse of his fellow-tribesmen professed admiration for the beautiful weapon and asked to be allowed to examine it. But the Beaver would not even momentarily part with it, so that the Sekanais had to forcibly wrench it from under his foot, and, plunging it into the stranger's breast, thereby gave the signal for the massacre which ensued. The Beavers were taken by surprise and, unable to seek and drop under the hammer of their guns the few grains of powder which at that time did duty as a percussion cap, they were overcome and annihilated by their hosts.

CHAPTER III.

Discovery by Alexander Mackenzie.

1792–1793.

FOR more than a century the Hudson's Bay Company, a commercial corporation with which the reader will in due time become better acquainted, had been claiming the monopoly of the fur trade over the vast basin of Hudson Bay and its tributaries, while their claim over the western territories adjoining what was then Canada had come to be disputed by several merchants of Montreal, on the plea that the said territories originally belonged to French Canada and that the English company's pretension to trade thereon was condemned by the very letter of its own charter. This, they argued, expressly specified that the lands handed over to the new corporation were those which were not actually " possessed by the subjects of any other Christian Prince or State" at the time of its formation. As individual efforts could not have much effect on the powerful company, the chief fur-dealers of Montreal, among whom Joseph Frobisher and Simon McTavish were the most prominent personalities, united their interests in 1783, and constituted themselves the North-West Fur-Trading Company.

But the new concern had hardly been brought into existence when, at the instigation of a troublesome character, an American named Peter Pond, a few fur-dealers, among whom was a young man known as Alexander

Mackenzie, of whom we shall presently have much to say, formed themselves into a rival corporation.

As a consequence, the fur trade for a time presented the ludicrous spectacle of small localities enjoying the competition of three different posts, kept by men bitterly hostile to one another. This bitterness having resulted in the violent death of a certain John Ross, a *bourgeois* or partner representing the interests of the minor North-West company at Lake Athabaska, the two Canadian concerns coalesced in 1787, and Alexander Mackenzie was entrusted with the post so suddenly vacated by John Ross.

Alexander Mackenzie was a Scotch Highlander, born at Stornoway, who had come to Montreal about 1779, when he entered the service of Gregory, Macleod & Co. Of a restless and somewhat impetuous disposition, he was by nature inclined to be biased, and, if crossed in his plans, he would become rather self-assertive and stubborn. But his very defects were simply excesses of good qualities, and they admirably fitted him for the tasks he was so gloriously to achieve.

Possessed of a fairly good education, the young man does not seem to have taken kindly to the drudgery incident to the daily life of a fur-trader. Adventure and the search after glory were much more congenial to his tastes. These he successfully followed in his first expedition down the noble stream which now bears his name. That journey was effected during the summer of 1789, and it served only to whet his appetite for excitement and fame. It was also a welcome preparation for the more difficult task which remained in store for him.

There had been some contention as to the probable distance from Lake Athabaska to the Pacific Ocean, which the expeditions of adventurers belonging to various

SIR ALEXANDER MACKENZIE.
(See p. 34.)

SIR GEORGE SIMPSON.
(See p. 120.)

DANIEL W. HARMON.
(See p. 85.)

SIR JAMES DOUGLAS.
(See p. 128.)

nationalities had made fairly known. There, according to native reports, "white men were to be seen who wore armor," whereby were meant either the Spaniards or English, or even the aborigines of the coast, who, as will appear further on, were often taken for whites by the natives of the interior, and amongst whom the use of armor was quite common. An expert had finally decided that the distance to the *grande mer de l'ouest*, as the Pacific was called by the French Canadians of the time, must be very great. But this only urged Mackenzie to reach it by land.

During his expedition to the Arctic Ocean he had more than once deplored his want of astronomical knowledge and the lack of the proper instruments. To obtain this desideratum, he crossed over to London in 1791, there acquired the necessary information, and returned in the spring of 1792, when he sent ahead of his expedition two men to prepare timber for houses and palisades wherein to winter, so as to be able to make an early start in 1793.

Mackenzie was the discoverer of New Caledonia and, therefore, of the interior of British Columbia. Nay, as the skippers who visited the North Pacific coast never ventured inland, he might with reason be put down as the discoverer of the whole country. On that account, the smallest details entered in his Journal, the aspect of the country, and the nature of its fauna, such as they appeared to him, but more especially his account of his first encounters with the natives are, in our eyes, invested with an importance which could hardly be exaggerated. Having left Fort Chippewayan on the 10th of October, 1792, he arrived ten days later at the last post established on the Peace River, "amidst the rejoicing and firing of the people, who were animated with the prospect of again indulging themselves in the luxury of rum, of which they had been deprived since the beginning of May, as it is a practice throughout the North-West neither to sell nor give any rum to the natives during the summer,"[1] which implies that the contrary was the case in the course of other seasons.

The very first pages of Mackenzie's Journal are valuable as giving us an insight into the policy followed by the North-West Company with regard to their subordinates. We therefore continue our quotation :

"As they [the Indians, who must have been Beavers] very soon expressed their desire of the expected regale, I called them together, to the number of forty-two hunters or men capable of bearing arms, to offer some advice . . . and I strengthened my admonition with a nine gallon cask of reduced rum and a quantity of tobacco."[2]

Leaving the new establishment, he crossed the Rocky Mountains up to the junction of the Parsnip and the Finlay, and, a short distance west thereof, he met, on the former, the men he had sent to prepare his winter quarters. With them he found an Indian chief, together with about seventy of his men, who, from their conduct and familiarity with fire-arms, seem to have been Beavers encroaching on Sekanais territory.

His tent had no sooner been pitched than he summoned them together, reproached them with their past mis-behaviour, after which he gave each of them "about four inches of Brazil tobacco," and "presented them with a quantity of rum," adding the somewhat naïve recommend-ation that they should use it with discretion ! In spite of the bitter cold, he had to wait until the 23rd of December before the house that was being erected for him was in-

1. "Journal of a Voyage Through the North-West Continent of America," London, 1801, pp. 125, 126.

2. *Ibid.*, p. 126.

habitable. He then set his men to build five more houses for themselves, and thenceforth his life was that of a fur-dealer, occasionally visited by the trappers, and subsisting on the game of the country, which, happily, was quite abundant.

On the 1st of January, 1793, he was, as usual, awakened by volleys from his men's muskets, and, in return for their good wishes, he treated them "with plenty of spirits." [1] Five days afterwards he mentions the firing of the Indian guns as a mark of sorrow at the death of a member of the tribe, a circumstance which goes to prove that fire-arms were already common in that part of the world. Intoxicants do not seem to have been much scarcer, since he adds in a foot-note, that when those Indians "are drinking, they frequently present their guns to each other, when any of the parties have not other means of procuring rum."

In April the supply of liquor was exhausted among the natives, who sent an embassy to him to "demand rum to drink." [2] Having at first refused to comply with their request, their threats forced him to yield to their importunities.

At the opening of the spring he received a valued reinforcement in the person of Alexander Mackay, who was destined to meet with a violent death on the ship *Tonquin*, which was captured by the Coast Indians. Finally, on the 9th of May, 1793, Mackenzie left for his perilous expedition in a birch-bark canoe 25 feet long, 4¾ feet beam, and 26 inches hold. Therein he found place for 3,000 pounds of baggage and provisions, together with a crew of nine French Canadians, whose names are worthy to be transmitted to posterity. Besides Mackay and his

1. "Journal of a Voyage Through the North-West Continent of America," London, 1801, p. 137.
2. *Ibid.*, p. 150.

chief, there were Joseph Landry, Charles Ducette, Baptiste Bisson, François Courtois, Jacques Beauchamp, and François Beaulieu. These were accompanied by two Indians, who were to act as hunters and interpreters.

Ascending the Parsnip River, the explorer met with several elk and herds of buffalo, two noble animals which have since disappeared forever from those quarters.[1] Then beaver succeeds to the larger game, and Mackenzie declares that in no part of the world did he see so much beaver work.

On the 9th of June he meets with the first party of undoubted Sekanais, a body of natives who had heard of white men, but had never seen any. They immediately took to flight, and on his sending his men to parley with them, the latter were received with the brandishing of spears, the

---

1. The buffalo was never indigenous to the Carrier country, and the Stuart Lake Indians call it by a Cree word; but they knew of the elk, which went as *yezih*, a Carrier term. The Sekanais have a native name of their own for the buffalo, which circumstance confirms Mackenzie's account as to its originally being found west of the Rockies. He also mentions having seen several enclosures to drive in and capture the larger game, contrivances of which the present writer had given a description long before he had seen Mackenzie's Journal.

Mr. Malcolm McLeod is no doubt mistaken when, in the course of his note xlvii to McDonald's "Peace River," he claims that Sir Alexander Mackenzie confounds the moose with the elk. These are two very distinct animals, the first of which (*toeni*, in Carrier) is still to be found within the territory of our Indians, while as to the latter (*yezih*, in Carrier), the oldest aborigines claim to have seen or heard of specimens of it long ago on the west side of the Rocky Mountains. That this kind of deer did really exist at one time within reach of their arrows is shown by the fact that when they first saw a horse they called it a domestic elk (*yezih-lhi*, elk-dog), a name it has retained to this day. Mackenzie was also evidently of that opinion, since on p. 205 of his Journal he distinctly mentions the "moose, elk and reindeer." Harmon is no less explicit in his "Concise Account of the Principal Animals which are Found in the North-Western Part of North America." After mentioning the buffalo and the deer, he comes to the elk, which, he says, "is about the size of a horse," after which he describes separately the moose and the cariboo.

display of bows and arrows, and loud vociferations. Having
succeeded in dispelling their fears, the explorer soon
noticed iron work in their possession. On inquiry he
found that they got it from people who lived up a large
river (the Carriers), who in turn procured it from others
who dwelt in houses (the Coast Indians), to whom it was
furnished by men like Mackenzie himself, who travelled in
canoes large as islands on the "stinking lake," the sea.
They professed to know of no stream that emptied therein,
but mentioned a large river whose "inhabitants built
houses, lived on islands, and were a numerous and warlike
people."[1] This is the first implied reference we find in the
whole field of literature to the Fraser and the Carrier
Indians.

Having persuaded one of the Sekanais to accompany
them in the capacity of guide, Mackenzie and party
reached (June 12th) a lake two miles long, which was no
other than the source of the Parsnip. After a portage of
only 817 paces, they came to another lake, whence they
entered a small stream which was to try sorely their
patience, and which, for that reason, they called the "Bad
River." This might be described as a generally shallow
creek with a rocky bottom, where rapids, whirlpools,
eddies, and treacherous rocks succeeded each other with
hardly any interruption. The party's canoe fared badly
along this wild river, getting broken with several holes in
the bottom, when the crew had to jump into the water, and
the whole cargo was wrecked, though afterwards recovered
with the exception of the bullets, which were irretrievably
lost.

As a climax, the guide, on whom they had counted to
introduce them to the terrible Carriers, deserted on the
15th, and they were left alone to contemplate the "Great

1. Mackenzie's Journal, p. 204.

River," which they reached in the course of the same day, and which Mackenzie took to be the Columbia, though he occasionally calls it *Tacoutche-Desse*, after his Eastern Déné interpreter.[1] This, as everybody knows, was nothing else than the large stream which nowadays goes by the name of Fraser River.

On the 19th of June his men saw, without being able to entertain them, a small party of Carriers, who fled at their approach, and by threatening signs with their arms (which, besides the usual bows and arrows, consisted of spears and large knives), deterred them from attempting anything like friendly intercourse.

On the morrow he passed a house which seemed to him so novel that he describes it minutely, along with " a large machine . . . of a cylindrical form," which was none other than a salmon basket. After meeting several other lodges built on the same model, mostly on islands, he cached in the ground ninety pounds of pemmican, and, on June 21st, somewhere between what is now Quesnel and Alexandria, he came upon the first party of Carriers with whom he could hold intercourse. His account of his experience with them is so graphic that, in spite of its length and owing to the importance of the occurrence to the historian and the ethnographer, we will reproduce it almost in its entirety. It is but fair to fully notice the risks the great explorer ran, and the wonderful tact with which he came out of them without injury to himself or his people.

" We perceived a small new canoe that had been drawn up to the edge of the woods, and soon after another appeared with one man in it, which came out of a small

1. The Carrier name is *Lhtha-Khoh*, which is no doubt responsible for the word Tacoutche (*tche* means mouth) the desinence of which (*Khoh*) is the Carrier equivalent of the Eastern Déné *desse*, river.

A CARRIER FISHERMAN.

With one of Mackenzie's " machines " in the background.

river. He no sooner saw us than he gave the whoop to alarm his friends, who immediately appeared on the bank, armed with bows and arrows and spears. They were thinly habited, and displayed the most outrageous antics. Though they were certainly in a state of great apprehension, they manifested by their gestures that they were resolved to attack us if we should venture to land. I therefore ordered the men to stop the way of the canoe, and even to check her drifting with the current, as it would have been extreme folly to have approached these savages before their fury had in some degree subsided. My interpreters, who understood their language, informed me that they threatened us with instant death if we drew nigh the shore, and then followed their menace by discharging a volley of arrows, some of which fell short of the canoe and others passed over it, so that they fortunately did us no injury. As we had been carried by the current below the spot where the Indians were, I ordered my people to paddle to the opposite side of the river, without the least appearance of confusion, so that they brought me abreast of them. My interpreters, while we were within hearing, had done everything in their power to pacify them, but in vain. We also observed that they had sent off a canoe with two men down the river, as we concluded, to communicate their alarm and procure assistance. . . ."

This circumstance induced him to leave no step untried in order to establish friendly intercourse with them before the arrival of the expected reinforcements. So he goes on to say :

" I left the canoe and walked by myself along the beach, in order to induce some of the natives to come to me, which I imagined they might be disposed to do when they saw me alone without any apparent possibility of receiving assistance from my people. . . . At the same time, in order to possess the utmost security of which my situation was susceptible, I directed one of the Indians to slip into the woods with my gun and his own, and to conceal himself from their discovery ; he also had orders to keep as near me as possible without being seen, and if any of the natives should venture across and attempt to shoot me from the water, it was his instructions to lay him low ; at the same time he was particularly enjoined not to fire till I had discharged one or both of the pistols that I carried in my belt. . . .

"In the meantime, my other interpreter assured them that we entertained the most friendly disposition, which I confirmed by such signals as I conceived would be comprehended by them. I had not, indeed, been long at my station and my Indian in ambush behind me, when two of the natives came off in a canoe, but stopped when they had got within a hundred yards of me. I made signs for them to land, and as an inducement displayed looking-glasses, beads, and other alluring trinkets. At length, but with every mark of extreme apprehension, they approached the shore, stern foremost, but would not venture to land. I now made them a present of some beads, with which they were going to push off, when I renewed my entreaties, and after some time prevailed on them to come ashore and sit down by me. My hunter now thought it right to join me, and created some alarm in my new acquaintance. It was, however, soon removed, and I had the satisfaction to find that he and these people perfectly understood each other.[1] . . . I expressed my wish to conduct them to

1. Mackenzie's interpreter must have been previously acquainted with the Carrier dialect, or the explorer is mistaken as to the ease with which his Indian conversed with the strangers, as a Sekanais and, *à fortiori*, a Beaver who knows but his own idiom can hardly understand a Carrier. The probability is that each party used all he knew of the other's vocabulary, added to the words which, with slight variations, are common to both tribes.

our canoe, but they declined my offer ; and when they saw some of my people coming towards us they requested me to let them return, and I was so satisfied with the progress I had made in my intercourse with them that I did not hesitate a moment in complying with their desire.

"During their short stay they observed us and every-thing about us with a mixture of admiration and astonishment. We could plainly distinguish that their friends received them with great joy on their return, and that the articles which they carried back with them were examined with a general and eager curiosity ; they also appeared to hold a consultation, which lasted about a quarter of an hour, and the result of which was an invitation to come over to them, which was cheerfully accepted. Nevertheless on our landing, they betrayed evident signs of confusion, which arose probably from the quickness of our movements. . . . The two men, however, who had come with us appeared, very naturally, to possess the greatest share of courage on the occasion and were ready to receive us on our landing ; but our demeanor soon dispelled all their apprehensions."

Having secured their confidence by gifts of trinkets and the like, he was informed that the river on which they had embarked was long, with a very strong current and several rapids which no man could safely shoot. Mackenzie's new friends described their immediate neighbors, the Shush-waps, as "a very malignant race, who lived in large sub-terranean recesses," and they did their best to dissuade him from continuing farther, if he valued his life at all. According to their reports, the Shushwaps then possessed iron arms and utensils, which they procured from neighbors in the west, who obtained them from people like Mackenzie.

But he was not to be easily dissuaded. Taking along

1. "Journal," pp. 242-5.

two of his new acquaintances to secure him a favorable reception from the Indians he would meet on his way down, he was just leaving for the south, when a canoe was sighted which was manned by three men, one of whom cautioned him to wait until next day, as the messengers he had noticed detaching themselves from the main group had gone down to alarm the people, who would certainly oppose his passage.

On the morrow he left early with his two Carrier guides, only to fall in with another body of hostile Indians. The guide went to them, and, " after a very vociferous discourse," one of them was persuaded to approach them, a man who presented a " very ferocious aspect," after which his example was followed by his companions, to the number of seven men and ten women.

A little farther down he had a repetition of his recent encounter, and he states that so wild and ferocious was the appearance of the Indians that he entertained fears for the safety of the guides sent to conciliate them. At the main village—which was afterwards to be called Alexandria, in memory of his eventful trip—he found, among the Carriers, a Beaver Indian and four Shushwaps, and he was not a little astonished to be addressed in Cree by a Sekanais woman who had been taken prisoner by a band of " Knisteneaux."

There, a map of the southern course of the river was drawn for his benefit, to show him the madness of his enterprise, while he was told that, after only seven days' march due west, he could obtain his object by following a route to the " stinking lake," where the Indians themselves used to procure brass, copper and trinkets. From that quarter they also got iron bars eighteen inches long, which they fashioned into axes and arrow and spear points.

As he had not more than thirty days' provisions left, he

held a consultation with his men, the result of which was that they would return up the river to the stream (Black-water), whose valley they would follow by land to reach the coast.

On their way up they divided into two parties. To lighten their craft, Mackay followed the shore on foot with the two eastern Indians and one Carrier, who had promised to guide them to the sea. On getting to the rendezvous they had agreed upon, Mackenzie and his crew were greeted by a story from Mackay and the easterners, which we had better allow the explorer to relate in his own words.

"They—Mackay and companions—informed us that they had taken refuge in that place with the determination to sell their lives, which they considered in the most imminent danger, as dear as possible. In a very short time after they had left us, they met a party of Indians whom we had known at this place, and were probably those whom we had seen to land from their canoe. They appeared to be in a state of extreme rage, and their bows bent with their arrows across them. The guide stopped to ask them some questions, which my people did not understand, and then set off with the utmost speed. Mr. Mackay, however, did not leave him till they were both exhausted from running. When the young man came up, he then said that some treacherous design was meditated against them . . . but refused to name the enemy. The guide then conducted them through very bad ways, as fast as they could run ; and, when he was desired to slacken his pace, he answered that they might follow him in any manner they pleased, but that he was impatient to get to his family, in order to prepare shoes and other necessaries for his journey. They did not, however, think it prudent to quit him, and he would not stop till ten at night.

"On passing a track that was but lately made, they began to be ferociously alarmed, and on inquiring of the guide where they were, he pretended not to understand them. They then all lay down, exhausted with fatigue, and without any kind of covering ; they were cold, wet and hungry, but dared not light a fire from the apprehension of an enemy. This comfortless spot they left at dawn of day and, on their arrival at the lodges, found them deserted, the property of the Indians being scattered about as if abandoned forever.

" The guide then made two or three trips into the woods, calling aloud and bellowing like a madman. At length he set off in the same direction as they came, and had not since appeared. To heighten their misery, as they did not find us at the place appointed, they concluded that we were all destroyed, and had already formed their plans to take to the woods and cross in as direct line as they could to the waters of the Peace River, a scheme which could only be suggested by despair."[1]

At this recital, a general panic seized those around Mackenzie, and, unloading everything except six packages, which he left to the care of four men, the leader was prevailed upon to return to the camp of the previous night, which was more propitious for defence. There he saw to it that the party's arms were in good order, filled each man's flask with powder, and distributed one hundred bullets, while some of the men were employed in melting down shot to make more.

While they were busy with these warlike preparations, an Indian landed where they stood, who, on perceiving them, bolted away with the threat that he would hasten and join his friends, who would come and kill the intruders.

They passed an uneasy night and kept strict watch

1. "Journal," pp. 263-4.

over their surroundings. Early next day they returned to Mackay, who complained that his men were discontented and wanted to go home. Indeed, while Mackenzie was taking observations at noon they went so far as to load, on their own accord, his canoe to return east. Feigning not to notice dissatisfaction, he let them go by water while he followed over land.

Here a little incident still added to their apprehensions. His men had already got to an Indian house, there to pass the night, when, by inadvertence, he let go an arrow, which, to his alarm, struck the lodge they had just entered. That was too much for their strained nerves. They thought themselves attacked by the mysterious Carriers, and the explanation their chief gave them of the accident served only to increase their fears. The arrow was without any head, and yet it had penetrated more than an inch a hard, dry log.[1] Why remain in the power of a people possessed of such means of destruction? moralized his crew.

About midnight a rustling noise was heard in the woods which created a general panic, while their dog remained in a state of nervous restlessness until two, when the sentinel informed Mackenzie that he saw something like a human form creeping along on all-fours. This ultimately proved to be a blind old man, who was welcome as a means of clearing up the mystery which had attended the Indians' actions for the last few days. He explained that, shortly after they had passed on their way to the sea coast, natives had arrived from up the river who had declared them to be perfidious enemies; and their unexpected return so soon after they had proclaimed that they were

1. "I have been assured, by one of the most respectable Factors, that he has seen an Indian pierce an inch plank with an unbarbed arrow, shot from his bow, the mere wooden point passing through and protruding on the other side" ("Journal of the [Protestant] Bishop of Montreal," p. 97).

47

going to follow the river to its mouth had confirmed those rumors and created a panic of which he had been one of the victims, since, unable to follow them, he had been left to his fate.

At these words Mackenzie must have remembered with dismay the pleasure he had taken in firing off his gun to show the extent of his power, and the unspeakable fright they had manifested on hearing its report. This circumstance had now turned against him, and he and his men were in the ludicrous position of people haunted by the apprehension of those whom fear had driven away from them.

The next day, which was the 28th of June, was employed in making a new canoe, and on the 29th they were agreeably surprised at beholding their Carrier guide, with a companion, making for their camp. He declared tha the had spent his time in search of his missing family, who had fled like the others.

On Tuesday, 2nd July, 1793, the whole party reached the mouth of the Blackwater, where Mackenzie harangued his men, declaring his firm and irrevocable resolution to go west, even though he might be left alone. Then he made another cache, left his canoe on a scaffolding, and handing each of his white companions a pack of some ninety pounds, with a gun and ammunition—the Indians grumbling with only half that weight—he directed his steps in their company towards the village of the Naskhu'tins, which was then eleven miles distant from the mouth of the Blackwater River, on a lake called Pœncho.

There he found, as usual, several articles of European manufacture, among which he mentions a lance resembling a sergeant's halberd, which had lately come from the sea coast. Taking care to send two couriers in advance to predispose people in his favor, he proceeded west, and in the course of a few days he met a woman from the coast all bedecked in ornaments of various kinds.

After crossing two mountains the whole party came upon an arm of the sea, now Bentinck Inlet, among troublesome Indians, where the indefatigable explorer wrote on a rock, " Alexander Mackenzie, from Canada, by land, the twenty-second of July, one thousand seven hundred and ninety-three."

In another month, August 24th, the intrepid voyagers were safely back at Fort Chippewayan.[1]

1. While some authors are evidently unfair to S. Fraser, who was the first British Columbian of note, others, like the writer of a sketch of the Hudson's Bay Company, in a booklet on the " History of the SS. *Beaver*," are hardly just to the memory of Alexander Mackenzie when they state that " Simon Fraser . . . appears to have been the first white man to cross the Canadian Rockies in charge of an expedition " (p. 6). That same author is scarcely more accurate when he writes, immediately after the above astonishing statement, that Fraser discovered, in 1806-07, the river that bears his name. (See Chapter V.) On the other hand, Dr. A. Rattray unduly antedates Mackenzie's discoveries in the west when he says that " the Rocky Mountains formed an impassable barrier until Sir Alexander Mackenzie crossed them in 1790 " ; and that author is furthermore inaccurate in stating that the Scotch explorer traced " the Peace River and the head-waters of the Fraser River to their source " (" Vancouver Island and British Columbia," p. 7), which he did in neither case. Nay, most authors seem more or less at sea when it is a question of early British Columbia chronology. One would hardly believe that a writer with such a reputation for historical accuracy and critical acumen as R. Greenhow enjoys, in spite of the too evident anti-British complexion of his writings, could have stated in his " History of Oregon and California " (p. 264), that the Fraser was never traced to its mouth before 1812, instead of 1808, as we will see in the course of this work. The same author, referring (*ibid.*, p. 290) to the foundation of the *third* N. W. Co. fort west of the mountains, writes (accentuating the appositeness of his remark by the use of italics) : " This was the *first* settlement or post of any kind made by British subjects west of the Rocky Mountains ! " (See footnotes to pp. 54 and 65 of the present work.)

CHAPTER IV.

First Foundations.

1794-1806.

NOT unaware of the importance of his discoveries, Alexander Mackenzie resolved to publish his Journal, and, after preparing it for the printer, he visited Scotland, only to return to Canada in 1795 without having accomplished his object. Thenceforth he was to stay in Montreal, there to act in the capacity of a partner of the North-West Company. Just then his services were badly wanted, for in that very year several partners having seceded from the Canadian concern, owing to the autocratic ways of its chief, Simon McTavish, they set up a rival corporation, which soon became known as the X Y Company. With the love of independence which characterized Mackenzie, he was only too inclined to join the seceders. Yet he was persuaded to stay another three years with the North-Westers.

In 1799, however, he finally severed his connection with them, crossed over to England, published in 1801 his "Voyages," and was knighted by George III.

Sir Alexander's services to geography and ethnography were very valuable, and well deserved the recognition they received. His journey to the Pacific, especially, was an exceedingly dangerous venture, and the fact that he emerged without bloodshed from his many difficulties speaks volumes for his tact and prudence. His observations on the manners and customs of the people he encountered betray an able and evenly balanced mind. We could almost wish that the chronicler had been more particular about place names and topographical matters in general, as it is with the extremest difficulty that a person, however well acquainted with the territory he explored, can follow him. Moreover, while he notes the passing of several unimportant streams flowing into the Parsnip River and elsewhere, we look in vain in his journal for any mention of such large rivers as the Pack, or McLeod, whose waters differ so much from those of the Parsnip, into which it empties itself, and even the Nechaco, which is as important as the Peace west of the Rockies.[1]

From a purely literary standpoint, his Journal, though revised by his cousin, Roderick Mackenzie, stands open to criticism. Again, its author does not seem to have been blessed with anything like a keen ear, nor any aptitude for native languages. On pages 257-8 of his volume he gives us brief vocabularies of the " Nagailer or Chin Indians," and of the "Atnah or Carrier Indians," which are philologically worthless. Moreover, his so-called Carrier vocabulary is made up of Shushwap words, while its " Nagailer " counterpart is intended to reproduce words which, in the mouth of his informants, were evidently Carrier.

In the course of that same year (1801), the explorer returned to Canada, and, freed from the bonds which had so far kept him with the McTavish concern, threw himself body and soul into the X Y Company, of which he became the directing spirit.

1. In his own Journal, Fraser occasionally notes some of these omissions, and in one instance he supposes that Sir Alexander must have been asleep when he passed a large stream he never mentions. Whereupon H. H. Bancroft becomes very wroth, forgetting that Mackenzie is himself candid enough to confess that it happened to him more than once to doze in his canoe ("Journal," p. 183).

It does not fall within our province to describe here the heated contentions, the bitter rivalries, the fights and the brigandage which ensued between the opposing factions. Suffice it to say that McTavish's death, in 1805, removed the main cause of the whole trouble, and the following year the divided parties were reunited into one. What we are concerned with is the territory traversed by the indomitable Scotchman and its fate after it became known to the traders.

The bitter struggle between the rival factions in the east forced them to concentrate, instead of extending, their energies, and the newly-discovered fields west of the Rocky Mountains had to wait for the restoration of peace before anything could be done for them. Four years after Mackenzie's voyage, in the course of 1797, a certain James Finlay did, indeed, ascend that part of the Peace River which now bears his name, after which he followed that explorer's route along the Parsnip almost to its source; but that was merely travelling, and it is safe to say that no tangible benefit thereby accrued to the fur trade or the Indians.

As for the older Hudson's Bay Company, it was far too conservative and too much devoid of initiative to have dreamed of establishing itself in a distant country just revealed to the world through the exertions of one of its natural enemies. Nay, it was only reaching the middle of the continent when Alexander Mackenzie was visiting the Pacific Coast.[1]

1. The unaccountable ignorance of the early history of British Columbia to which we have referred in our Preface manifests itself in many ways. Will it be believed that the author of the sketch of New Caledonia in the " Diction- ary of Well-known British Columbians," an important work published at Vancouver four years ago, honestly supposes that the Hudson's Bay Company had no precursors in the fur-trade within the limits of the Province? He does not seem to have ever heard of the North-West Company!

As that gentleman was leaving, in 1792, on his memorable journey, a youth of sixteen[1] was entering the service of the North-West Company, who was to be the man of whom his employers would avail themselves to reap the first-fruits of Mackenzie's voyage. Sir Alexander had discovered the land ; Simon Fraser was to establish the first trading-posts therein.

Born at Bermington, on the Hudson, of a Scottish United Empire Loyalist, a Captain Fraser, who died in prison after he had been captured by the Americans at Burgoyne's surrender, he was taken by his widowed mother to Upper Canada, in the vicinity of Cornwall, where he passed his infancy. In 1792 he joined as clerk the ranks of the North-West Company, and ten years afterwards he obtained the honorable position of a *bourgeois* or partner, a fact which is certainly the best proof of his ability, and should silence the attacks of such writers as H. H. Bancroft, who never tires of belittling him. To be made a partner of a powerful commercial company at twenty-six is certainly no sign of a soft brain, of lack of education, or of administrative incapacity.

After a first appointment to Grand Portage, he was sent to Lake Athabaska, and in 1805, new men and more abundant resources having been added to the North-West Company by the absorption of its active rival, the X Y Company, it was decided, at a conference held at Fort William, the headquarters of the entire concern, to extend the Company's activities west of the Rocky Mountains. Fraser was chosen as the man best fitted for the purpose.

In the spring of that same year (1805), one of his subordinates, James McDougall, who was to make his mark as a popular fur-trader in the wilds of the extreme west, had already visited the sheet of water which empties itself into

1. Others wrongly say nineteen.

53

the Parsnip River and which was soon to be called McLeod Lake. Pushing still farther west, he had even reached a lake some fifteen miles east of the present Fort St. James, which, his guide having told him was within Carrier territory, has remained to this day known as Carrier Lake or Lac Porteur.

In compliance with his orders, Fraser proceeded in the autumn of the same year to a place on the Peace, immediately east of the Rockies, where he established a post under the name of Rocky Mountain Portage. There he left fourteen men (two clerks and twelve servants), and went up with six others as far as a tributary of the Parsnip, the Pack River, which Mackenzie had overlooked, and which would have immensely lightened the difficulties of his progress during the first half of his voyage. This stream he entered and ascended until he came in view of a narrow lake, seventeen miles long, which he named McLeod, in honor of a friend in the service, Archibald Norman McLeod.

There, on a peninsula formed by a tributary (Long Lake River) and its outlet, by latitude 55° 0′ 2″ north, he founded the first permanent post ever erected within what we now call British Columbia.[1] This was to accommodate the trade with the Sekanais Indians, and for a short time it even 'served as a supply house for the forts later established among the Carriers. It has existed to this day without a year of interruption.

Leaving three men at the new post, he returned, in November, to winter at the Rocky Mountain House with his three remaining companions and the fourteen men he had left there.

The three French Canadians now stationed at Fort

1. Or, at all events, west of the Rocky Mountains. In a " History of B.C., adapted for the use of Schools," O. H. Cogswell wrongly states (p. 34) that Fort McLeod was established in 1806. Even Nicolay supposes that Fraser did not cross the Rockies before that date (" The Oregon Territory," p. 98).

SIMON FRASER.

(From a photo by James Hawes, Cornwall, C. W., kindly furnished by Hon. R. W. Scott.)

McLeod were pioneers among the many fur-traders who were to toil and die on the west side of the Rockies. They might be considered the very first resident British Columbians. Their first immediate superior was La Malice, who was, however, soon to be replaced by James McDougall. The trio may not have enjoyed their enforced solitude on the shore of Lake McLeod. They certainly do not seem to have pulled well together, and before many months had elapsed, La Malice, who was a worthless kind of a fellow, had left on the pretence that his men would not do their duty.

Things were going more smoothly at the parent house, immediately to the east of the mountains, where good humor, if nothing of a less peaceful character, was maintained by means of copious libations of rum.

On the 28th of January, 1806, McDougall was sent on a second expedition to McLeod Lake. Taking with him a limited store of tobacco, beads and ammunition, he set out, accompanied by two Canadians and an Indian, and that time he even went so far as the site of the present Fort St. James, near the outlet of Lake Stuart, which he was the first white man to behold. Where the imposing structures and dependencies of that establishment now stand was then to be seen a thick forest of spruce. One of these trees he blazed and adorned with an inscription whereby he claimed the spot in the name of the Company he represented. One of the few Indians he saw, a man apparently of little worth, called Tœyen or Shaman, whom he wished to invest with some sort of authority, he presented with a piece of red cloth, thereby securing his good offices in a possible hour of need. This done, he returned east.

On the 9th of February, two Canadians, Farcier and Varin, were sent to La Malice with an assortment of axes, knives, and other articles most in demand at McLeod Lake.

Meantime, Fraser was laying plans for his projected expedition to the westward, and in April, 1806, he had five bales of goods made up and carried to the western end of the portage, there to remain ready for the early spring.

Moreover, fully realizing the importance and difficulty of that undertaking, he was feeling his ground in advance and studying the geography of the country he intended to endow with its first trading establishments. His text-book was no other than the Indians, not always quite reliable or properly understood, who occasionally called at his place. Thus, under date of 23rd April, 1806, he records in his Journal the arrival of natives from the Finlay River, near the source of which he is told that there is "a large lake called Bear Lake, where the salmon come up, and from which there is a river that falls into another . . . that glides in a northwest direction. . . . It is in that quarter they get their iron works and ornaments; but they represent the navigation beyond that lake as impracticable, and say there are no other Indians excepting a few of their relations that ever saw white men thereabout, and to get iron works they must go far beyond it, which they perform in long journeys on foot."

"We cannot understand what river this is," adds the chronicler, who thereby confesses his ignorance as to the lake itself. Bancroft is not so self-diffident. In a foot-note he peremptorily solves the problem. "It is Babine Lake here referred to," he says.[1]

We are sorry to contradict so voluminous a writer, but the lake above mentioned is simply Bear Lake, sometimes called Connolly by a few strangers, and the river that exercises the mind of Fraser is the Skeena. Bear Lake is within Sekanais territory, and is frequently visited to this day by the Finlay River Indians. The source of their

1. "History of the North-West," Vol. II., p. 96.

supply of implements of European manufacture was merely the tribes of Tsimpsian parentage stationed along the Skeena, who obtained them from their congeners on the coast. The Sekanais of that early period probably did not even know of Babine Lake, and the only inaccuracy in their report is that relative to the proximity of Bear Lake to the Finlay, which, as the present writer has personally ascertained, is one hundred and eighty miles instead of " half the length of the Rocky Mountain Portage."

This item of information seems to have preyed on Fraser's mind, and two days later he adds, after further inquiry from new arrivals, the unwelcome circumstance that, though that river seems to have nothing in common with the Columbia (he means the Fraser), it is through it that they get most of their goods, among which he mentions guns and ammunition. One of the reasons which prompted his superiors to send him west was to forestall the Americans, of whom they seem to have vaguely heard in the east. It must, therefore, not have been without a pang that he had to chronicle the fact that, according to his informants, "white people came there in the course of the summer ; but, as they came on discovery, they had little goods. I have seen a pistol," continues Fraser, " brass-mounted, with powder and ball, which they say they had from them."

This was dismal intelligence indeed for a fur-trader who was just on the point of setting out to establish new posts where he thought he had not been preceded. Had he been better acquainted with the ways of the Déné nation, he would have known that its members call whites anybody who conforms to the whites. Those who traded occasionally at Bear Lake were only Tsimpsians from the coast. Nay, the Skeena valley, precisely on account of the monopoly claimed by the Tsimpsian adventurers, is one of the territories of any importance within British Columbia which has remained the longest free of any real white man.

Before his departure for his important journey, which, after information furnished by James McDougall, he foresaw would be long and tedious, Fraser received, on the 27th of April, Archibald McGillivray, who came from the east to take charge of the Rocky Mountain Fort during his absence. Prudence suggested as early a start as possible in May, in order to avoid the June freshets; but one of his men, the truant La Malice, did not arrive until the 17th of that month, and a woman he brought with him, and for whom he is said to have paid £300 sterling, caused still further delay. Fraser would have none of her in his expedition, and La Malice refused to go without her. Finally, his employer, short of men as he was, had to yield.

At length, after he had sent to Fort Chippewayan two canoes loaded with furs, together with an account of his operations up to date, Fraser left on the 20th of May, 1806. After a portage of fifteen miles, two canoes were loaded, when it was discovered that a third was necessary, which was entrusted to La Malice. Fraser had with him an able lieutenant in the person of John Stuart, a young clerk, who was to be more or less identified in after years with the fur-trade west of the mountains. Among his crew was also a young half-breed, Jean Baptiste Boucher, who, under the nickname of "Waccan," we will likewise have to mention more than once in the following pages.

On the 28th of May they came upon two natives, who, though they had never seen a white man, were possessed of guns, which they had obtained from relatives among the Beaver Indians. At noon of the same day, they entered the Parsnip, whose banks they were sorry to find

58

overflowed, so that their progress was necessarily very slow,[1] the passage over rocks, through driftwood and rapids occasioned by the high water, rendering their leaky canoes unwieldy and far from safe.

Nation River was passed on the 2nd of June, and three days afterwards they encamped two miles up the Pack or McLeod River. There all the goods which were not destined to outfit Fort McLeod were cached, when they proceeded to the post where McDougall, now in charge, was anxiously awaiting them. New canoes were now made and two Sekanais engaged to introduce them to the land of the Carriers.

Ignorance of the geography of the country was to lead Fraser to repeat the mistake already made by Alexander Mackenzie, and cause him to seek the Fraser by way of the Parsnip and Bad Rivers, instead of through Crooked River and what we now call Giscome Portage. We do not see Bancroft's object in insisting that both Fraser and Mackenzie *could not* have gone by way of that portage, since, by their own account, there cannot be the shadow of a doubt that they *did not*, the former going so far as to state explicitly that, when he reached the head-waters of the Parsnip, he was told by a Sekanais that, were he at McLeod Lake, he could show him a shorter and better route than that he was on.

At first Fraser was only following Mackenzie's itinerary of 1793, and experiencing the same difficulties, increased, however, by the unusual state of the water, resulting from the lateness of the season, the first explorer having been

---

1. H. H. Bancroft, who is constantly bickering at Fraser's shortcomings, real or imaginary, contrasts his slowness with Mackenzie's quicker movements. Had that author lived a few years in the north of British Columbia, he would certainly not show himself so partial and fault-finding, as he would then know the immense difference a week or two of warm weather will make in the state of our rivers.

fully a month in advance of Fraser, who started from the eastern side of the Rockies, and had, moreover, to deliver freight at Fort McLeod. Then, again, La Malice became sick to the point of showing symptoms of delirium, and all the other men complained of some ailment, a circumstance of which Bancroft takes occasion to have another fling at poor Fraser, who, he seriously asserts, should have had better men in his fort!

Arrived at the terrible Bad River, which was now swollen by the freshets, La Malice was sufficiently recovered to make trouble and thwart his employer by threatening to remain behind, a step which Fraser was too kind-hearted to allow.

At ten o'clock on the 10th of June they were in sight of the Fraser, and the next day they encamped at the confluence of the Nechaco. Up that beautiful river the brigade encountered other enemies in the shape of grizzly bears, two of which they chased. "One man was caught and badly torn, the dogs coming up just in time to save his life. The wife of one of the hunters escaped a horrible death by throwing herself flat on her face, the enraged brute, in consequence, passing her by in pursuit of her flying husband." [1]

The first Carriers sighted by the expedition must have been the survivors of the Chinlac massacre recorded in our first chapter, as they were met at the confluence of the Stuart and Nechaco Rivers,[2] to the number of thirty men, arrayed in robes of beaver, lynx, and marmot skins.

The 26th of July, 1806, was a rather windy day on what

1. Bancroft, "History of the North-West," pp. 108-9.

2. To the best of our knowledge all the authors, without a single exception, confound the two rivers, though in reality they are very distinct streams. The Stuart River drains Lake Stuart, in the north, while the Nechaco, which is a most important river, issues from Lakes Emerald, Dawson and Morice, in the west.

the Indians then called Lake Na'kal, the surface of which was being ploughed into deep furrows. The soap-berries were ripening, and most of 'Kwah's people were camped at the mouth of Beaver Creek, to the south-west of the present Fort St. James, when what appeared to them two immense canoes were descried struggling against the wind, around a point which separated them from the outlet of the lake.

Immediately great alarm arises in the crowd of natives. As such large canoes have never plied on Carrier waters, there is hardly a doubt that they must contain Tœyen's friends, the wonderful strangers from "the country beyond the horizon" he had been told to expect back. Meanwhile, the strange crafts are heading for Beaver Creek, and lo! a song the like of which has never been heard in this part of the world strikes the native ear. What can that mean? Might not this be a war party, after all?

"No," declares Tœyen, who, donning his red piece of cloth as an apron, seizes a tiny spruce bark canoe lying on the beach and fearlessly paddles away. On, on he goes, tossed about by the great waves, until he meets the strangers, who, recognizing him by his badge, bid him come on board. His fellow-tribesmen, now seeing in the distance his own little canoe floating tenantless, take fright.

"They have already killed him," they exclaim. "Ready, ye warriors ; away with the women!"

At this cry, which flies from mouth to mouth, the men seize their bows and arrows, and the women and children seek shelter in the woods. But the curious crafts, which, on coming nearer, prove to be large birch-bark canoes, are now within hearing distance, and Tœyen cries out to the men on shore to be of good cheer and have no fear, as the strangers are animated by the most friendly dispositions.

The fugitives are hastily recalled, and Simon Fraser, with John Stuart and his other companions, put ashore in the presence of a crowd of wondering Carriers.

Lake Stuart was discovered, and a new province was added to the geographical conquests of the North-West Company. To accomplish this it had taken Fraser's party only seven days less than Mackenzie had required to reach the seacoast from his winter quarters.[1]

On landing, Fraser's men, to impress the natives with a proper idea of their wonderful resources, fired a volley with their guns, whereupon the whole crowd of Carriers fell prostrate to the ground. To allay their fears and make friends, tobacco was offered them, which, on being tasted, was found too bitter, and thrown away. Then, to show its use, the crew lighted their pipes, and, at the sight of the smoke issuing from their mouths, the people began to whisper that they must come from the land of the ghosts, since they were still full of the fire wherewith they had been cremated. Pieces of soap were given to the women, who, taking them to be cakes of fat, set upon crunching them, thereby causing foam and bubbles in the mouth, which puzzled both actors and bystanders.

All these phenomena, however, were soon explained away, leaving no suspicion in the native mind, but a most pronounced admiration for the foreigners and their wares. That this last impression was not quite reciprocal is gathered from one of Fraser's letters, wherein he describes his new acquaintances.

"They are," he writes, "a large, indolent, thievish set of vagabonds, of a mild disposition. They are amazing fond of goods, which circumstance might lead to imagine that

1. It should be borne in mind that, besides starting from the east instead of the west side of the Rockies, Fraser had to ascend two important rivers which Mackenzie did not even see.

they would work well to get what they seem to be so fond of; but then, they are independent of us, as they get their necessaries from their neighbors, who trade with the natives of the seacoast."[1]

Trading and bartering were started on the spot. The natives, who received illusory substitutes for their fur coats and robes, were instructed thenceforth to exert themselves and procure as many as possible of the skins enumerated to them.

The first introduction over, the young founder set his men to work at clearing the ground for a new fort at the exact spot McDougall had marked out, just one mile to the north-west of the outlet of the large sheet of water which, called at first Sturgeon Lake, was finally christened Stuart Lake, as a compliment to Fraser's chief companion.

The latitude of the new place was 54° 26′ 52″, by longitude about 124° 30′. It stood on a bay with shallow waters, not on a peninsula, as Bancroft says.[2] To the beauty of its surroundings even fault-finding John McLean was to bear testimony when, forty-three years later, he wrote the following description, which is about accurate, though by no means adequate:

"Fort St. James, the depot of New Caledonia district, stands near the outlet of Stuart Lake, and commands a splendid view of the surrounding country. The lake is about fifty miles in length, and from three to four miles in breadth, stretching away to the north and north-east for about twenty miles. The view from the fort embraces nearly the whole of this section of it, which is studded with beautiful islands. The western shore is low, and indented by a number of small bays formed by wooded

1. Quoted by Bancroft, "History of the North-West," Vol. II., p. 109.
2. *Ibid, ibid.*

points projecting into the lake, the background rising abruptly into a ridge of hills of varied height and magnitude. On the east the view is limited to a range of two or three miles by the intervention of a high promontory, from which the eye glances to the snowy summits of the Rocky Mountains in the distant background. I do not know that I have seen anything to compare with this charming prospect in any other part of the country; its beauties struck me even at this season of the year, when, nature having partly assumed her hybernal dress, everything appeared to so much greater disadvantage."[1]

McLean hardly does justice to the beautiful mountains which rise on either side of Lake Stuart, one of which towers 2,600 feet above the surface of the water, while on the opposite shore another, though less prominent, is still higher. These reminded Fraser of the absent fatherland so often vaunted by his mother, and led him to call the whole country New Caledonia.[2] Then, again, the lake is

1. "Notes of a Twenty-five Years' Service in the Hudson's Bay Territory," London, 1849, Vol. I., p. 241-42. . . Lake Stuart lies 2,250 feet above sea level, instead of barely 1,800, as C. Horetzky would have it ("Canada on the Pacific," p. 79), and his error is so much the less comprehensible as that author was a land surveyor, who had several aneroids with his party.

2. Barret-Lennard wrongly says that Capt. Cook was responsible for that name ("Travels in British Columbia," p. 19).

While we may overlook the many geographical errors committed in describing Fraser's progress by the few authors (Bancroft, Masson, Bryce) who have referred to it, we must be allowed to question the propriety of Mr. Masson's express statement to the effect that Fraser established a fort he named New Caledonia about fifty miles from the mouth of the Stuart River. Dr. Bryce reiterates that assertion, though in vaguer terms, on page 142 of his own book, "The Remarkable History of the Hudson's Bay Company." Now, there has never been a vestige of such an establishment, and none of the oldest aborigines has ever heard of it. Fraser's limited personnel did not warrant three foundations without receiving reinforcements. Stuart, the very man who is credited with having been placed in charge of that mythical post, was in reality sent to see and report on the region of Lake Fraser. Fraser

wider than our author thinks. By actual measurement it is in places over six miles broad.

Thus was the second fort established west of the mountains.[1]

It was intended as a rendezvous for the natives of the whole lake, the exact number of whom could hardly be realized in the haste of the first visit. Both McDougall and Fraser, seeing only one fraction of the entire population, do not seem to have been much impressed by its importance; but it is safe to say that they scarcely met one-quarter of the Indians claiming the lake or its immediate vicinity as their habitat. Yet the former states that he saw some fifty natives hovering about the lower end of the lake. If we take these to be hunters and heads of families, as McDougall no doubt meant it, and if we give

himself writes to his partners in August, 1806: "We have established the post [not the posts] beyond the mountains, and will establish another in the most conventional (*sic*) place we can find before the fall," meaning Fort Fraser. It is probable, however, that both Masson and Bryce refer only to that place which was to be known later as Fort St. James. In that case, both of them are wrong, the former as to distances (Fort St. James being fully ninety miles from the mouth of Stuart River), and the latter as to the site of the place (said fort being not on Stuart River, but on Stuart Lake). On the other hand, Masson can hardly be accurate in writing that Fraser "passed the summer" at the lake called after him, since he had not yet so much as seen it on the 3rd of September.

1. To show how history is written in some quarters, here is a sentence from Macfie's "Vancouver Island and British Columbia," p. 203: "In 1806, the *first* fur-trading post ever established in British Columbia was erected *a short distance* from the great bend of Fraser River by the officer of the *Hudson's Bay Company* after whom that stream was named." The italics are ours, and represent as many egregious blunders.

Even Alex. Begg, who is generally accurate in his "History of the North-West," evidently labors under the impression that no trading post was erected "across the Rocky Mountains until about the year 1810" (Vol. I., p. 117), a statement which, owing to its obliging qualificative, is elastic enough to disarm the critic. The fact that, in the exceedingly valuable Chronological Table appended to the third volume of his work (also p. 141, Vol. I. of he

four children to each—a very fair average for the Carriers —the numbers of that band must have been something like three hundred souls.

But, fourteen miles farther north, at the mouth of the Pinche River, on the same body of water, there was, and still remains, a village of Carriers who were somewhat less numerous, though more sedentary. Again, a very large settlement stood at the mouth of the Thaché River, the principal affluent of the lake, just opposite the site of the present village, and another powerful clan, that of the Beavers (which should not be confounded with the tribe of the Beaver Indians east of the Rockies), had their homes on the same stream, at a place called Grand Rapid, perhaps eighteen miles above. Finally, on a minor tributary, flowing into the northern end of the lake now called the Portage, were a few bands of Carriers, mostly fishermen, living on the fine whitefish abounding in that quarter. All told, one thousand souls is a conservative estimate for the Stuart Lake population at that early period.

same), he duly records with the proper dates the foundation of Forts McLeod and Stuart, seems to imply that his ideas concerning the geographical position of these posts were somewhat vague, inasmuch as a few lines further he repeats his original assertion in the entry: " 1810. The North-West Company pushed across the Rocky Mountains." At that date it already possessed four stations within that territory.

The above is almost the sum total of the references to New Caledonia matters to be found throughout the three large volumes which form that would-be " History of the North-West." For that reason not a few will, no doubt, be tempted to compare it to the tragedy of Hamlet with Hamlet left out. It is in reality a history of Central Canada, always well-meaning and generally accurate, the work of a man whose possible preferences of race or creed seldom interfere with what he conceives to be his duty as an historian, an accomplishment which is shared by very few of those who have treated of the topics covered by his work.

CHAPTER V.

Founding and Exploring.

1806-09.

BY this time Fraser must have had enough of La Malice, than whom few people seem to have been more aptly named. So, to get rid of him and, at the same time, further the interests of his own corporation, he sent him, as the work on the new fort was getting well under way, with letters, first to McDougall at Fort McLeod, and then further east to the partners he had left at the Rocky Mountain House, whence he directed him to take to Fort Chippewayan canoes loaded with the equipments of the new posts up to McLeod Lake.

On the other hand, August was now drawing to a close, and as salmon was extraordinarily slow in making its appearance, the limited supplies he had brought from the east were soon exhausted. Berries, with a few small fish and an occasional fowl, became the only means of subsistence left the fort-builders. At the same time, McDougall, who, from the better equipment of his own establishment, was supposed to be in a position to help them, was begging the starving Fraser for some ammunition and a hunter to keep him alive.

Therefore, to disperse his forces and thereby render their lives less precarious, as well as with a view of keeping his promise to establish another fort before the fall the young commander sent John Stuart with two men over land to the south, where, about forty miles from his

67

present quarters,[1] he had been told was another lake with a numerous native population. Stuart's mission was to spy out the land and report to his chief at Chinlac, the meeting-point of the Stuart and Nechaco Rivers.

John Stuart left on the 28th of August, and Fraser, with the remaining men, now in really straitened circumstances, were putting the last touches to what, in the course of time, was to become the " formidable establishment of Fort St. James."

To take away as many mouths as possible, with a hope of feeding them more easily with the fruits of the chase or other adventitious resources of travel, and, at the same time, to keep his own appointment with his clerk, the young *bourgeois* started with three men on the 3rd of September, leaving a certain Blais temporarily in charge of the new post. But when chief and subordinate met again at Chinlac, so encouraging was Stuart's report on the place he had just visited, that Fraser resolved to repair thither in person, and, in company with his friend, who had to turn back, he poled up the Nechaco to the short tributary issuing from the lake, which, to return the compliment his superior had paid him, Stuart had already called Fraser Lake.

There the combined party erected a fort on a large bay near its outlet.[2] Salmon then came up with a vengeance. Meal after meal, and day after day, it formed the *pièce de résistance* on all the tables, so that people who had pined

1. Bancroft (" History of British Columbia," p. 571) calls it 25 miles, and adds : " Sixty miles south-easterly was Fort George, 80 miles north-easterly was Fort McLeod, and 100 miles north-westerly was Fort Babine." Now, by the original trail, Fraser Lake was over 45 miles from Stuart Lake ; Fort George is at least 150 miles, and old Fort Babine was 140 miles distant.

2. Not "a Hudson's Bay station," nor " at the head of the river " Fraser, nor " probably the first fur-trading establishment ever opened in British Columbia," as Rattray has it.

for its arrival were now reduced to the necessity of complaining of its frequency in their menu.

Fraser Lake is a quiet little sheet of water about thirteen miles long by scarcely three at its greatest breadth. Then, as now, both ends were the sites of a native village, and in the course of time Fort Fraser was to become the resort of numerous Indians. Close by what is now called Stony Creek there was the important settlement of Thachek, to which we have already referred more than once, and another village six miles off, on what is now Gordon Lake. Hehn Lake, the source of the Mud River, had another flourishing settlement ; while on St. Mary's Lake, in the south, were two or three lesser villages. Finally, on French Lake, in the west, and one of its tributaries, Peters Lake, were colonies of Carriers, whose settlements were but a portion of those which dotted the forest to the source of the Blackwater and the seats of the Chilcotins in the south. So many localities which were to become dependent on the new fort for their supplies could not but have rendered it extremely valuable to its founders.

To while away the weary hours of building inspection, Fraser set about exploring the surrounding country. In the course of his peregrinations he found, at Fond du Lac, or the western village, "some spoons and a metal pot," which attested previous intercourse with the Coast Indians. In this connection a little incident, quite insignificant in itself, happened, which shows that he knew how to win the sympathy of the natives by conforming to their whims even in small matters. A chief had died and been cremated, and a memorial post was being erected, which contained, as usual, the few charred bones picked up from the funeral pyre. Thereon Fraser, after a most solemn ceremony, engraved his name, to the immense satisfaction of the warriors assembled.

The building operations over, he left a man in charge with a few servants, and returned with the others to his new home at Stuart Lake, where he passed the winter.

In the fall of 1806 he sent Stuart for the goods La Malice was to have brought by the canoes from Athabaska, only to ascertain that no canoes had come and, therefore, no goods or provisions were available. That was sad news indeed, yet the traders made themselves as comfortable as possible, and, if we are to credit Bancroft, Fraser and McDougall even took to themselves temporary wives from among the natives in their respective vicinities.

Thus closed the second year of the incipient settlements within New Caledonia. Fraser was at Stuart Lake, McDougall at McLeod Lake, and Blais at Fraser Lake. As to Stuart, he spent his first winter west of the Rockies with his immediate superior.

The main question was now that of outfitting and supplies. Fraser's own experience had shown him the extreme difficulty of the water route. It was his original intention " to get the goods taken across land "[1] to the new posts. But the failure of La Malice to bring to its destination the much wanted outfit seems to have momentarily dissuaded him from following the leanings of his own judgment in the matter. So we see him, in the early spring of 1807, dispatching a canoe filled with such pelts as he had collected to ask for a new equipment and some more men. His request was favorably received, and in the autumn of that year two canoes, loaded with merchandise, were sent him under the leadership of Messrs. Jules Maurice Quesnel and Hugh Faries.

Those gentlemen were also the bearers of important instructions from headquarters. It was rumored that the

1. MS. Letters, No. 8.

Americans, under Captains Lewis and Clarke, had reached from the south the mouth of the Columbia River, and were rapidly annexing the country in virtue of the right of discovery. On the other hand, it was but too evident that the Parsnip and Bad River route was hardly practicable to supply the new forts with their annual outfits. Much too long and difficult, it was dangerous to the crews, and especially to the goods, which could not reasonably be expected to reach their destination safely. The overland route, if shorter, was much too expensive, and the native packers hardly reliable as yet. Therefore, to forestall, if possible, the Americans in their adventures around the mouth of the Columbia, and eventually find a cheap route for the yearly brigade of the Canadian trading concern, Fraser was asked to undertake, at his earliest convenience, the careful and complete exploration by water of the large stream which everybody took to be the Columbia.[1]

A pretty difficult task, sure enough ; one which would probably not have been set before anybody had its full extent been realized. But Fraser was a man of courage, as even his detractors are bound to admit ; he was not the one to shirk a duty.

With the new personnel brought him by the canoes from the east, the young superintendent of the new domain was enabled, in the fall of 1807, to erect a new post, and thereby establish the fourth link in the chain of forts wherewith he intended to bind the country to the interests of his employers. This time, the junction of the Nechaco with the " Great River " he was to explore was the chosen site. The native population thus accommodated was not

1. As did also Alex. Begg as late as eleven years ago, when he wrote that Fort George was established in 1807 " on the main stream of the Columbia " (" History of the North-West," Vol. I., p. 240), and entered the following event in his Chronological Table : " 1808. Simon Fraser and John Stuart explored the Columbia."

to be so numerous as that doing business with the other posts established by Fraser ; but its territory was one exceedingly rich in furs, and then the new place might prove to be nothing but a stepping-stone towards the foundation of another fort still farther south. Hugh Faries was the first man in charge of the new post, which received the name of Fort George, in honor of the then reigning monarch.

Considerable discrepancy occurs among the several authors as to the date when Fraser set out on the expedition upon which his fame was to rest. Masson and Bryce say that the start was effected on the 22nd of May, 1808. The former is very obscure concerning the identity of the place whence he left, which he says was " the mouth of the little river he names Fraser, probably the one which bears to-day the name of Nechaco" (a fine *little* river, indeed !). This would mean Fort George. Dr. Bryce is more explicit. " On May 22nd a start was made," he writes, " from the forks,"[1] which is but another name for Fort George. But in his " History of British Columbia," Begg says that Fraser left Fort George on the 26th of May.

Now, we venture to assert that none of these historians is correct, either as to the date or as to the locality. Though Fraser's Journal, such as published by Mr. Masson, dates his departure on May 22nd, and though it is evident from the context that he commenced his diary at Fort George, his next date is " Sunday, 29th," after which all the other dates follow consecutively, and without any hint at a mistake in writing 29th instead of 23rd. On the other hand, it is perfectly certain that between Fraser's 22nd and 29th day of May only a short day's distance was covered, and there was no stop over anywhere. Finally,

1. "The Remarkable History of the Hudson's Bay Company," Toronto, William Briggs, 1900, p. 143.

local tradition is positive that he started from Stuart
Lake, his headquarters, not from Fort George, a new place,
hardly fit as yet for habitation, which lies at a distance of
three days' journey by water to the south-east. It is, therefore, but natural to infer that he left Stuart Lake on the
22nd of May, remained one day at Fort George, and finally
departed for the unknown on Saturday, May 28th.

If the mention of the 22nd as the first date in his journal
is not a typographical error due to Mr. Masson's printers,
it may be easily explained away by the supposition that,
leaving Stuart Lake on the 22nd, he entered that date,
intending to commence immediately his diary ; but on
remembering that the route between Stuart Lake and
Fort George was now fairly well known, he had decided
to make his first entry coincide with his departure from
the latter place.

His lieutenants in this expedition were J. Stuart and J.
M. Quesnel. He had, moreover, with him nineteen
voyageurs, among whom was again the "Waccan" of his
first journey, together with two Indians, the whole party
in four canoes.

Starting on his "terrific voyage," as Dr. Bryce aptly calls
it, he had, fifteen miles from Fort George, a foretaste of
the difficulties that lay in store for him, when he nearly
wrecked one of his canoes "against a precipice which
forms the right bank of the river." This was his first
acquaintance with the Fort George canyon, and there he
was more lucky than the present writer, who once lost a
man at that identical spot. Next day he was shooting
the Cottonwood River canyon with his canoes, whose
cargoes had previously been portaged over to the lower end
of the rapid, where he cached three bales of dried salmon.
That day he did not go farther than the mouth of the river
which, on his return, he was to call Quesnel, after his
second lieutenant.

On Monday, the 30th, horse tracks told him of the approach of a new nation, that " very malignant race " upon which Mackenzie had turned his back. At Soda Creek the excited Atnahs despatched couriers on horseback to announce his approach to their friends in the south, and in order to make his intentions perfectly clear, he is prevailed upon to wait there a full day.[1] He employs part of his enforced leisure in explaining the nature of the wonderful engines of destruction he carries with him, the like of which he tells the natives they will soon be in a position to procure from his people if they allow him to pass. Thereupon he fires several shots, whose reports astonish them so much that " they drop off their legs."[2]

After meeting large crowds of aborigines, who showed themselves rather friendly, and who, he says, were inveterate smokers, his progress was barred, on the 1st of June, by a new and even greater difficulty than those so far experienced. For two miles there was a strong rapid with " high and steep banks, which contracted the channel in many places to forty or fifty yards." No wonder, then, if " this immense body of water, passing through this narrow space in a turbulent manner, forming numerous gulfs and cascades, and making a tremendous noise, had an

---

1. He mentions in this connection a *Tahowtin* woman married to a Shushwap, whereupon his annotator remarks, by way of identification : *"Nate-ote-tain*, Harmon. They lived on the Nateotin River. Cox . . . calls them *Talkotins.*" It is a hard task to keep serious in the face of these explanations. By *Nate-ote-tain* Harmon means *Nato-o'tin*, people of Nato or Babine, Babines ; and the sub-tribe Fraser refers to are the *Lhtha·o'ten* (a contraction of *Lhtha-khoh-'ten*, people of the Lhthakhoh or Fraser River), whereby are designated the southernmost Carriers. Cox's '*Talkotins* is a rendering of the same word by a person who has no ear for the native languages. A distance of at least four hundred miles separates the *Lhtha-o'ten* from the nearest *Nato·o'tin.*

2. Journal (in Masson's " Bourgeois du Nord-Ouest "), p. 160.

awful and forbidding appearance."[1]   Finding the banks too steep to allow of a portage, he launched, by way of an experiment, one of his canoes lightly loaded and manned by his five best men, only to see it drawn into an eddy, to be "whirled about for a considerable time, seemingly in suspense whether to sink or swim, the men having no power over her."   Led from that dangerous vortex into the main current, the little craft was now flying from one danger to another, until the last cascade but one, where, in spite of every effort, the whirlpools forced her against a rock, upon which the men were fortunate enough to alight, thus barely escaping with their lives.

"During this distressing scene, we were on the shore looking on and anxiously concerned ; seeing our poor fellows once more safe afforded us as much satisfaction as to themselves, and we hastened to their assistance ; but their situation rendered our approach perilous and difficult. The bank was extremely high and steep, and we had to plunge our daggers at intervals into the ground to check our speed, as otherwise we were exposed to slide into the river.   We cut steps in the declivity, fastened a line to the front of the canoe, with which some of the men ascended in order to haul it up, while the others supported it upon their arms.   In this manner our situation was most precarious ; our lives hung, as it were, upon a thread, as the failure of the line or a false step of one of the men might have hurled the whole of us into eternity.   However, we fortunately cleared the bank before dark."[2]

Fraser now finds further progress by water impossible. Here are some of the inducements held out to him by land :

"As for the road by land, we could scarcely make our way with even only our guns.   I have been for a long

1. *Ibid.*, p. 163.
2. Fraser's Journal, p. 164.

period among the Rocky Mountains, but have never seen anything like this country. We had to pass where no human being should venture ; yet in those places there is a regular footpath impressed, or rather indented, upon the very rocks by frequent travelling. Besides this, steps which are formed like a ladder by poles hanging to one another, crossed at certain distances with twigs, the whole suspended from the top, furnish a safe and convenient passage to the natives down these precipices ; but we, who had not the advantage of their education and experience, were often in imminent danger when obliged to follow their example."

The natives now seriously advised him to abandon the water route altogether, whereupon the "courageous and conscientious man" asserts himself when he cannot help writing : "Going to the sea by an indirect way was not the object of the undertaking. I therefore would not deviate."[1]

On that same day he furnishes us with the earliest written mention of the Chilcotins when he writes : "There is a tribe of Carriers [he means Dénés] among them, who inhabit the banks of a large river which flows to the right ; they call themselves Chilk-odins."

On June 2nd he finds the river has risen eight feet in twenty-four hours—something quite usual for that torrent-like stream—and tries to find horses for Mr. Stuart, who has had enough of the river, and he wastes a good part of the day in anxious suspense, as none of the Indians seem really willing to part with their animals. His patience is, however, rewarded on the morrow, when he gets four horses, one of which on that same day tumbles, with his load, over a precipice and is lost.

One of his men employed in portaging the baggage almost met with a similar fate one day later. Having missed the narrow path, he "got into a most intricate and

1. Fraser's Journal, p. 165.

perilous situation. With a large package on his back, he got so engaged among the rocks that he could neither move forward nor backward, nor yet unload himself without imminent danger. Seeing this poor fellow in such an awkward and dangerous predicament, I crawled," writes Fraser, "not without great risk, to his assistance, and saved his life by causing his load to drop from his back over the precipice into the river."[1]

Continuing by water, he has hardly anything left to mention but precipices of immense height, tremendous whirlpools, treacherous breakers, and dashing cascades, until he is obliged to confess that his is, indeed, a hopeless undertaking. Yet he will not give it up. For four long days more the painful task goes on ; sometimes shooting rapids where he is cautioned to leave his canoes altogether, and then portaging goods and craft over high hills, precipices and ravines, with such terrible walking over the sharp stones that "a pair of shoes [moccasins] does not last the day, and the men have their feet full of thorns."

On the 9th of June " the channel contracts to about forty yards, and is enclosed by two precipices of immense height, which, bending over each other, make it narrower above than below. The water, which rolls down this extraordinary passage in tumultuous waves and with great velocity, had a frightful appearance. However, it being absolutely impossible to carry the canoes by land, all hands, without hesitation, embarked, as it were *à corps perdu*, upon the mercy of this awful tide. . . . Thus skimming along as fast as lightning, the crews, cool and determined, followed each other in awful silence, and when we arrived at the end we stood gazing at each other in silent congratulation at our narrow escape from total destruction."[2]

1. Fraser's Journal, p. 168.

2. *Ibid.*, pp. 170-71.

In the face of such a perilous undertaking, a modern writer cannot refrain from exclaiming : " How difficult it is to distinguish small from great actions ! Here was a man making fame for all time, and the idea of the greatness of his work had not dawned upon him."[1]

Neither has it as yet dawned upon another who writes of Fraser's achievement : " By this *easy* and *pleasant* service, he secured for the perpetuation of his name the second largest river in this region." The italics are ours, but as to the statement itself, it can proceed from but one man, Hubert Howe Bancroft ![2]

The natives here drew for the explorer a map of the river, which they declared absolutely impracticable, dissuading him at the same time from trying to follow it by land, as there was no beach, no shore, but steep, high mountains and precipices, which they would have to ascend and descend by means of rope ladders. Nothing daunted by these warnings, Fraser continued with his canoe, only to find the rapids getting worse and worse, "being a continual series of cascades intercepted with rocks and bounded by precipices."

On the 10th of June, finding further progress physically impossible, he had to confess himself conquered by nature, which confronted him with difficulties increased a hundredfold by the high stage of the water. Therefore, on Sunday, June 11th, leaving his canoes by the stream, he buried in the ground such articles as could not be carried along, and

1. " History of the Hudson's Bay Company," by G. Bryce, p. 145.

2. " History of the North-West Coast," Vol. II., p. 119. The same author ungenerously adverts to the fact that Mackenzie had seen part of the Upper Fraser before that stream was explored and identified as quite distinct from the Columbia, and indirectly contests the right of Fraser to name it. The Mackenzie River is but the lower course of a long stream which is called Finlay near its source, and then Peace, Athabaska, and Slave. Would anybody pretend that no white man had seen and navigated any of these parts of the same river before 1789? Should we then conclude that the Mackenzie is misnamed ?

started on foot with his men, loaded with eighty-pound packs, hoping for better luck in keeping at a distance from the surging waters.

It is not within the scope of this work to follow him through the many hardships he had still to undergo at the hands of nature and of men, especially as he is now within sight of the Thompson River, and consequently on the limits of New Caledonia. Yet, for the sake of any possible antiquarian who may happen to read these lines, we cannot omit to mention his reference to the Askettihs,[1] a nation "dressed in their coats of mail," which at first received him with a volley of arrows. Their village, he writes, "is a fortification of one hundred feet by twenty-four, surrounded by palisades eighteen feet high, slanting inward, and lined with a shorter row, which supports a shade, covered with bark, constituting the dwellings."

As he gets nearer and nearer the tide-water he meets with increasingly numerous European wares, among which he mentions "a copper tea kettle and a gun of a large size, which are probably of Russian manufacture,"[2] and, farther down, a sword of tremendous proportions made of sheet iron. From Yale he takes to the water again, having in one place to snatch a canoe by force from an Indian, who refuses all sorts of payments, and who finally accompanies him, trembling and sobbing at the thought of the terrible natives they will meet at the mouth of the river.

This Simon Fraser finally reaches, and our hero does not return before he has set his eyes on the Gulf of Georgia,[3] and ascertained that the river he has explored

1. Presumably the Lillooet Indians.

2. Journal, p. 178.

3. By which circumstance will be seen how much truth there is in the following autograph note by Malcolm McLeod to the Journal of Sir George Simpson's famous journey across the American continent, in the copy of the

empties itself into the Ocean, about four degrees of latitude north of the mouth of the Columbia.

His object was accomplished, and the world was soon to learn that the Fraser was a totally different river from the Columbia.

And now, having reached the goal of his ambition, he could well retrace his steps. Yet at the hour of triumph he narrowly escaped paying with his life the penalty of his daring. Followed by a flotilla of canoes manned by hostile Indians, as he returned to the village, where sheer necessity had compelled him to take a canoe by force, he found 'the inhabitants of that locality so excited that he feared the worst. His people wanted to take to flight

same now in the possession of the present writer : " Simon Fraser, after whom (wrongly, I think) the river has been named, never navigated it within over 250 miles of its mouth, nor did any of the Nor'-West Co.; but, fearing the attempt, hauled up his canoes at the mouth of a small stream on the left, which consequently was named by him Canoe River."

The above is a fair sample of the attempts made by Hudson's Bay Company men and others of Bancroft's turn of mind to depreciate Simon Fraser's achievement. That the latter had to yield for a moment to the tremendous difficulties opposed to his progress by water everybody knows, and we are also free to admit that Sir Geo. Simpson did navigate, in 1828, the very stretches of river which Fraser had avoided twenty years earlier. But he who feels inclined to imagine that this circumstance detracts from the latter's glory thereby only betrays his own ignorance. Fraser's voyage took place in the month of June, and he did not reach the sea before the beginning of July, that is, just at the time when the river called after him is a boiling torrent, dangerous to navigate even outside of its regular cañons, whilst Simpson's descent of the same was not effected before some time in the autumn (9th and 10th of October), when the river is for all purposes of navigation an altogether different stream. The reader will easily believe this when he is told that the present writer once lost a man by drowning while trying to shoot in plain daylight a rapid which he afterwards passed by night without the least difficulty. The victim of the accident was about the best canoeman to be found in the country, but then he should not have been so foolhardy as to attempt in June what can easily be accomplished in October.

As to the fact that S. Fraser did reach the salt water there cannot be the shadow of a doubt. Bancroft quotes A. C. Anderson as saying : "In 1808

and return through the fastnesses of unknown mountains, where those who might escape the darts of their pursuers were sure to find death by starvation. Yet such was the ascendancy he had acquired over them that he actually made them swear before God to stay together and abide by his counsels.

The return journey was painful, though without remarkable incidents, and by the 6th of August he was back at Fort George. Strange to say, while the descent of the river had required forty days, the ascent of the same was made within only thirty-three days.

After that "*easy* and *pleasant* service," Simon Fraser proceeded east to report on his achievements, and on May 16th of the following year (1809) he was for one day the guest at Fort Dunvegan, on the Peace River, of the very man who was, shortly after, to continue in the west the work he had so brilliantly commenced—we mean Daniel Williams Harmon.

As a reward for his services Fraser was promoted, in 1811, to the charge of the whole Red River department,

Fraser and Stuart started with bark canoes to descend the Fraser, and with great difficulty and perseverance reached a point near to where New West-minster has since been located" ("History of the North-West Coast," Vol. II., p. 119). On the faith of that assertion by an Hudson's Bay Company man whom we had every reason to believe well informed, we stated in the previous editions of this work that Fraser had "to turn back at the place where New Westminster now stands." But an examination of his Journal leaves no room for doubt as to his having actually reached the Pacific. Under date July 2nd he writes : " Proceeding on for two miles we arrived at a place where the river divided in several channels." (In Masson's " Les Bourgeois du Nord-Ouest," Vol. I., p. 199). By this the explorer evidently means the different arms of the Fraser which combine to form the delta just below what is now New Westminster, inasmuch as he almost immediately after states explicitly : " At last we came in sight of a gulf or bay of the sea." As if to make us doubly sure about this point Fraser goes on to say : " On the right shore we noticed a village called by the natives Misquiam." Now this same village is still in existence under the name of Masquiam, and the shore of its site is bathed by the salt water.

which then extended as far west as the Liard River. Due recognition of his merit was also offered him in the shape of a knighthood, which, however, the insufficiency of his means did not allow him to accept. In 1816 he was present at the unfortunate affair of the Seven Oaks, when Governor Semple, of the Hudson's Bay Company, lost his life in the conflict with the North-West Company people; and when, shortly afterwards, Lord Selkirk took Fort William in retaliation, Simon Fraser was one of the partners arrested and sent to Montreal.

After the excitement of those stirring times he must have returned to the West, for, under date March 13th, 1820, Sir John Franklin, the ill-fated explorer of the north, mentions one " Mr. Frazer " as being then stationed among the Chipewyans, who was probably none other than the founder of New Caledonia.[1]

Having retired from the service about the time of the coalition of the two companies (1821), he married the daughter of Captain Allan McDonnell, of Matilda, Ontario, and he died at St. Andrews, in the township of Cornwall, on the 19th of April, 1862, aged eighty-six.

Simon Fraser was a Catholic—a circumstance which goes some way to explain Bancroft's unwarranted antipathy—and, though not a model of perfection, he was " ambitious, energetic, with considerable conscience, and in the main holding to honest convictions." These very encomiums have escaped Bancroft himself, who naturally hastens to qualify them to the extent of practically withdrawing them.[2]

Some have taken pleasure in alluding to Fraser's pretended illiteracy. He was no scholar, not any more than

1. " Journey to the Shores of the Polar Sea," Vol. II., p. 6.

" History of the North-West Coast," Vol. II., p. 89.

Sir A. Mackenzie, or even John Stuart, who is credited with having had a liberal education. The unpublished letters of the trio lay no claim to elegance or even grammatical correctness. But in the case of Fraser, the reason of his literary shortcomings almost redounds to his glory, since it is no other than the straits his family was reduced to by the death of its chief, Captain Fraser, in the American prisons, where the service of his king had led him.

Simon Fraser, though an altogether self-made man, became the founder of New Caledonia, the explorer of the main fluvial artery of British Columbia, and one of the first residents of that province. Less brilliant services would entitle him to the respect of every Canadian.

CHAPTER VI.

Stuart and Harmon at Stuart Lake.

1809-21.

THOUGH Simon Fraser had passed three full years within New Caledonia, establishing forts and directing their personnel, he was still supposed to be the head of the Rocky Mountain House. To keep him any longer in the wilderness of the extreme west would have been paramount to a non-recognition of his achievements. Therefore, on his promotion, his first clerk, John Stuart, was named his successor in the command of the new district. At the same time, in August, 1809, another clerk, A. R. McLeod, with a number of working-men, were sent to his aid.

The new commander hardly relished the title which bound him to a country where he knew by experience that life was so difficult. Instead of stationing himself at the fort on Stuart Lake, which was the most central of all the new establishments, he preferred to spend most of his time at Fort McLeod, which was then more within reach of those commodities which seem indispensable to civilized life. Thence he would leave with the returns of his district, which he would personally take to Rainy Lake or Fort Chippewayan, and return with the equipments destined to his own posts.

Then, as much later on, the staple food of all the servants was dried salmon, and a shortness in the annual

84

run of that fish would mean vastly impoverished circumstances for the men and increased anxiety for the mind of the chief officer. Now, it happened that the salmon season of 1810 was a failure, and when Stuart crossed over to headquarters, at Fort Chippewayan, he must have availed himself of that circumstance to inveigh against the difficulties of his charge. The result was a letter signed by three partners, requesting D. W. Harmon, then at Fort Dunvegan, to go and superintend the affairs of New Caledonia, unless he preferred to accompany Mr. Stuart as second in command.

Harmon was then thirty-two years of age, having been born in 1778, in the State of Vermont, whence, on the 28th of April, 1800, he had set out for Montreal and joined the ranks of the Nor'westers. He passed four years at Swan River, where he took to wife, after the fashion of the traders of that time, a French Canadian half-breed girl of fourteen, who, after she had presented him with fourteen children, is said to have remained a handsome woman, "as straight as an arrow." Soon thereafter he was sent to Peace River, where Stuart found him stationed.

In pursuance of his double-edged orders, Harmon, who was a most conscientious man, elected to go and help Stuart rather than supersede him in his charge.[1]   There-

1. Stuart's connection with the management of New Caledonia affairs was apparently so slight, and his title so nominal, that we have long hesitated whether Harmon was not the *de jure* as well as *de facto* ruler of the same. Two considerations strongly militate against this supposition. First, as late as October 29th, 1814, Harmon writes himself (Journal, p. 206, New York reprint): "I have received a letter from Mr. John Stuart, who has arrived at McLeod Lake, desiring me to go and superintend the affairs of Fraser's Lake, and to send Mr. La Roque, with several of the people who are there, to this place [Stuart Lake]," whereupon he immediately declares, as if he believed himself under the obligation to obey, that he " shall depart " on the morrow, a clear proof that he regarded Stuart as his superior. In the second place, by his own implicit admission, Harmon was as yet but a clerk in the North-West

fore, on the 7th of October, 1810, he left Dunvegan with his young family, together with Stuart, who was to remain nominally the superintendent of the district, and three days later he was at Fort St. John, where his men were at once set to the task of preparing provisions to make up, at least partially, for the deficiency of salmon in New Caledonia.

By the 1st of November the whole party had reached Fort McLeod, where Harmon first saw the Sekanais, whose destitute condition appealed to his kind heart. There Stuart chose to stay for the winter, with James McDougall as clerk, and, on the 3rd of November, Harmon, accompanied by thirteen servants, left for Stuart Lake, where he arrived in the afternoon of the seventh.

Harmon has left us a most valuable journal of the doings and happenings during his stay in New Caledonia, which proves him to have been as truthful a man as he was keen an observer. From it we glean that the new place impressed him favorably, though of the natives themselves he seems to have acquired but a poor idea. He is, we believe, the first author to dub the Carriers " Tacullies," a term he translates " people who go on the water." [1] Unfortunately the natives .know of no such name in their language, though for some time they have been calling themselves, and all American aborigines, Takhelhne, a word the meaning of which cannot be ascertained and which is undoubtedly of extraneous origin.

Harmon had hardly made himself at home in his new post when he was called upon to witness a scene which

Company's service as late as 1818, while five years before that time Stuart was a partner in the same (Cox's " Columbia," p. 109). In common with those who had long held that rank in the Canadian Company, he was made a Chief Factor when the latter disappeared to make way for the Hudson's Bay Company.

1. A rather fanciful translation, we must say. *Thakhelhne* would almost have that meaning.

told him of the difference between the East and the West. This was the cremation of a woman, whose corpse was burnt amidst " a terrible savage noise, howling, and crying [on the part of her near relatives] and a kind of singing [by people of a different clan]."

On the 1st of January, 1811, he was at Fraser Lake, where he had sent men to rebuild the fort previously burnt through the negligence of a native girl they were bringing up. That day furnishes him with occasion for an entry which, to us, is of a melancholy interest, in view of the demoralizing influence of the evil whose introduction among the natives it chronicles. We copy from his Journal :

" This being the first day of another year, our people have passed it, according to the custom of the Canadians, in drinking and fighting. Some of the principal Indians of this place desired us to allow them to remain at the fort that they might see our people drink. As soon as they began to be a little intoxicated and to quarrel among themselves, the natives began to be apprehensive that something unpleasant might befall them also. They therefore hid themselves under beds and elsewhere, saying that they thought the white people had run mad, for they appeared not to know what they were about. . . . It was the first time that they had ever seen a person intoxicated."[1]

On June 16th of the same year he furnishes us with the first mention of the Babine Indians, one of whom had come to the fort with his son and a number of Carriers in six wooden canoes, a circumstance rather remarkable for that early period. Questioned as to their country, they told him of the Skeena River, which " a number of white people ascend in barges every autumn to trade with the Indians who reside along its shores." These traders Har-

1. Harmon's Journal, pp. 196-97.

mon imagines to be Americans. They were simply Indians from the seacoast.

And now, as usual, famine stares him in the face. On August 2nd, five dried salmon were all that remained in store for his whole establishment. He had therefore to send up to Pinche all his personnel—men, women and children— to gather berries as a means of prolonging their lives until the arrival of the salmon would relieve their distress. On the 23rd of September of the same year he relates an incident which might have had the most serious consequences for the safety of his growing establishment, an incident which links the past or pre-European times with the new period, when the whites had become the makers of history.

Our readers have not forgotten 'Kwah, the warrior, the gambler and the slayer of his insulter. He was now a man enjoying the greatest consideration amongst his fellow-Carriers, and his name had become great in adjoining villages. He had succeeded a dead warrior as A'ke'tœs, thereby attaining the rank of a "nobleman," and he was in most prosperous circumstances. Indeed, he was soon to rejoice in the possession of four wives, whom he would station, each with her offspring, at the four corners of his lodge. Yet it took two or three years for the newcomers to notice him and realize his true position in the tribe. Tœyen, as we have seen, was the first appointed chief in our sense of the word. Then McDougall's mistake being seen, he was deposed, to be replaced by another man, who, in turn, had to yield his rank to 'Kwah.

The latter was still comparatively fresh in the enjoyment of his high estate when Harmon came from the east, and it would seem as if the arrogance proper to *parvenus* had then been hovering about the mind of the new chief. To show his power and influence over the whites, he tried to force the new clerk to advance credit to a worthless

KŒZI.

(One of 'Kwah's daughters.)

fellow, a pretension which the trader resented considerably.
Words followed words, when 'Kwah asked the obdurate
Harmon :

" Have you ever been to war? "

" No," replied his interlocutor, who added that he had no
wish to take the life of a fellow-creature.

" Well, I have been to war, and I have killed a number
of my enemies," said the savage, who then asked for a
piece of cloth for his own use.

Complying with his request, Harmon saw kind after
kind of stuff sullenly refused until, unable to restrain himself any longer, he seized a square yard-stick, wherewith he
administered him a severe wound on the head. 'Kwah then
called out to his companions to take away Harmon, who
was then mercilessly pelting him, only to see his orders
disregarded by the Indians out of fear of the whites, who
were supposed to be hidden within the building.

Some time afterwards the Chief made a feast, to which
he invited Harmon. This gentleman feared some treachery; yet, unwilling to betray his true sentiments in the
face of the Indians, he accepted the invitation. Arming
himself with two pistols, in addition to the sword he constantly carried as a North-West Company officer,[1] he went
to 'Kwah's lodge with his interpreter, who was also similarly
armed. There he met "nearly an hundred Indians
assembled." In the course of the feast, the Chief made a
speech, to the effect that had he been similarly treated by
anybody else than the white man, he would have either lost
his own life or taken that of the person attacking him.
But now, he said, he considered himself as Harmon's *wife*,
who had used him in exactly the same way that he himself

---

1. These gentlemen also wore a red coat with large brass buttons, knee-
breeches and a three-cornered hat with panache. Cf. "Traditions Indiennes
du Canada Nord-Ouest," by E. Petitot, Alençon, 1887, p. 329.

used his own wives when they misbehaved. He ended by thanking him for what he had done him, since it had given him sense.[1]

Whereupon Harmon moralizes : " It will be seen by this account that the white people have a great ascendency over the Indians, for I believe that this chief is not destitute of bravery."[2]

Quite so, we will add ; but his own usually righteous course and lack of haughtiness in dealing with the natives was a good deal responsible for the fortunate turn of affairs. Harmon might also bless his star that, instead of a cranky, vindictive individual, such as abound in all the tribes, he had met a sensible man, who was not above confessing a wrong. Otherwise the issue of the conflict would certainly not have been to his advantage.

On New Year's Day, 1812, Harmon initiates us to the great times he had with his people and the Indians. On the previous year the latter had simply assisted as puzzled and somewhat terrified spectators at the baneful effects of "fire-water" on Canadians ; but even pious Harmon could be progressive. His friend McDougall had come to pass the holidays at Stuart Lake. After dinner several of the Carrier and Sekanais headmen were invited to do away with the remnants on the tables and "drink a flagon or two of spirits." Fateful flagon, which once tasted was to swell into gallons and kegs, how many hundreds—if not thousands—of thy victims have been prematurely laid into the grave !

---

1. After which Harmon records a naïve remark of the dusky Chief, which shows that he was not without realizing that the incident might have unpleasant consequences : " Quâs then told the Indians," writes the chronicler, " that if he ever heard of any of them laughing at him for the beating which he had received, he would make them repent of their mirth." "Journal," p. 177 (New York reprint, 1903).

2. *Ibid., ibid.*

On the 13th of the same month he assisted at the incineration of a man who had been married to two women. His account of the event is precious, and corroborates in every way what the present author has written on the same subject after modern informants.

"The corpse was placed on a pile of dry wood," he writes, "with the face upwards, which was painted and bare. The body was covered with a robe made of beaver-skins, and shoes were on the feet. . . . His gun and powder horn, together with every trinket which he had possessed, were laid by his side."[1]

After the fire had been lighted, his wives, one of whom stood at the head and the other at the feet of the corpse, kept patting it,[2] while burning, with both hands alternately, a ceremony which was interrupted by turns of fainting arising from the intensity of the heat. "If they did not soon recover from these turns and commence the operation of striking the corpse," continues the chronicler, "the men would seize them by the little remaining hair [3] on their heads and push them into the flames in order to compel them to do it. This violence was especially used toward one of the wives of the deceased, who had frequently run away from him while he was living."

Will the reader believe that over twenty years elapsed before the whites among the naturally progressive Carriers had the courage to interfere and become responsible for the first burial of an Indian? Some there are, no doubt, who, in view of the inhuman cruelties perpetrated on the widows at the cremation of corpses, would think that an earlier intervention would have been but the accomplishment of civilization's duty towards an inferior race.

1. Harmon's Journal, p. 216 (original edition).
2. Harmon, not knowing the reason of that act, says "striking."
3. The rest had been burnt in the course of the "ceremony."

Mr. McDougall was still at Stuart Lake. As that gentleman seemed to have a special knack of procuring peaceful introductions to the savage races—a specialty probably based on his knowledge of the Sekanais dialect—Harmon profited by his presence to go and visit that tribe of Babines of which he had already seen two representatives.

Starting on the 30th of January, 1812, accompanied by twelve servants as a bodyguard and two Carriers as middle-men and interpreters, the two friends, after seven days' travel over frozen lakes, met Indians who had never seen a white man. On reaching their first village, the inhabitants manifested great surprise and alarm at the sight of the pale-faced strangers. Harmon writes in this connection :

" As their village stands on a rise of ground, near to a large lake, they saw us coming when we were at a consid-erable distance from them ; and the men, women, and chil-dren came to meet us, all of whom were armed, some with bows and arrows, and others with axes and clubs. They offered no offence ; but, by many savage gestures, they manifested a determination to defend themselves in case they were attacked. . . .

"The day following we proceeded on our route, and during our progress we saw four more of their villages. . . . They showed us guns, cloth, axes, blankets, iron pots, etc., which they obtained from their neighbors, the Atenâs, who purchase them directly of the white people."[1]

Then the chronicler records the fact that the population of the villages they visited formed an aggregate of about 2,000 souls. How melancholy, after this statement, to think that those numbers, since the advent of the whites, should have dwindled to scarcely 250 !

To the spring of 1812 must be referred the very first long-distance transmission of a letter within the territory of

1. Harmon's Journal, pp. 218-19 (original edition).

British Columbia and beyond it. On the 6th of April six couriers arrived from Fraser Lake, bringing a letter addressed to the manager of the North-West Company at Stuart Lake by David Thompson, the explorer of the river that bears his name. The letter was dated Ilk-kay-ope Falls, Columbia River, August 28th, 1811. It had taken exactly eight months and eight days to reach its destination, and had been carried by Indians of all the various intervening tribes, a wonderful example of honesty and of respect for written paper.

In the meantime the superintendent of the whole district, John Stuart, though residing mostly at McLeod's Lake, was paying occasional visits to Stuart Lake and even to Fraser Lake. He seems to have been one of those well-meaning men who, unconscious of their own idiosyncrasies, make life a burden to others. We have no doubt that much of the blame which has been laid at the doors of his former superior, Simon Fraser, might with justice be addressed to him. Fraser has been accused of being naturally quarrelsome, and yet Stuart managed to pass three years and make two long and trying expeditions in his company; while, after the explorer had been separated from him, Stuart appears as a man who has lost his bearings, trying life with the one only to wish for another. Some years after the time of which we write he had just been appointed to a good post, on the east side of the mountains, when he was already speaking of leaving on the ensuing spring, which fickleness prompts a correspondent to write: "Such a short stay was hardly worth his removal from the Bas de la Rivière. Upon the whole, he is a good man; but a person would require to be possessed of the patience of Job and the wisdom of Solomon to agree with him on all subjects."[1]

1. John M. McLeod, of Fort Simpson, to John McLeod, sen. MS. letter.

Poor McDougall could not boast such exalted accomplishments. As, barring the long absences caused by voyages to the east and lesser trips to the west, they had already lived two years together, a change was deemed in order. So Stuart came west to pass the winter with his trusted friend, Harmon, who had now, on the bank of Lake Stuart, a flourishing establishment employing twenty-one laboring men, one interpreter, and five women, besides children. The North-West Company was certainly not niggardly in its treatment of its officers and clerks.

But Stuart's company seems to have been portentous of evil, inasmuch as both himself and Harmon with their interpreter were almost massacred by the Indians of Fraser Lake, whither they had gone to buy furs and salmon. Whatever may be said of the cause of the affray, about which Harmon is not clear, " eighty or ninety of the village armed themselves, some with guns and the others with axes and clubs, for the purpose of attacking" the visitors. By mild measures, however, they succeeded in appeasing their anger.

In the latter part of that winter Harmon took a trip to his old home, Fort Dunvegan, returning to New Caledonia in time to see Stuart depart, in April, for the far south in quest of a water communication to replace the overland route through Fort McLeod, which was so slow, so expensive and admitted the introduction of so limited supplies.[1]

1. It was in the course of that journey that John Stuart was, with Messrs. John George McTavish and Jos. La Rocque, instrumental in buying out Astor's Pacific Fur Company in the name of his own North-West Company (16th October, 1813), a transaction which, originally caused by the British American war of 1812, was to lead to the foundation, shortly afterwards, of that important Fort Vancouver, on the lower Columbia, to which we will have so frequently to refer in the course of the present work. Not any too greatly enamoured with his northern solitude, J. Stuart found means and ways to prolong his stay in the south by leading in November, 1813, a trading expedition to the interior of the Columbia district, and, when back

During his absence the management of the affairs of the whole district fell, as a matter of course, on Harmon's shoulders.

Had the poor man been at the same time entrusted with the task of repressing crime and dealing out justice within the limits of New Caledonia, his hands would have been more than full. In the space of a single week he has to record two shocking murders, occurring one among the Sekanais and the other nearer home, among the Carriers who traded at his own fort. In spite of its sickening details, we think a reproduction of that part of his Journal which bears on the double tragedy will help us to form a correct idea of the manners and morals prevailing among the Indians of New Caledonia in pre-Christian times :

" *Saturday*, June 12th, 1813.—A Sicauny has just arrived, who states that a little this side of McLeod's Lake, where he was encamped with his family, an Indian of the same

again among the snows of New Caledonia, his thoughts reverted to the friends he had left under more favored climes. In a letter dated 25th April, 1815, he gives expression to ideas concerning the latter country and its aborigines, some of which will bear reproduction here :

"The salmon failed with us last season," he writes. "This generally occurs every second year, and completely so every fourth year, at which period the natives starve in every direction. They are of a lazy, indolent disposition, and as a livelihood is rather easily procured, seldom give themselves much trouble in hunting the beaver or any animal of the fur kind. We have no buffalo or deer, except the *caribou* (reindeer) ; and not many even of those ; so that, properly speaking, we may say that water alone supplies the people of New Caledonia with food.

"The natives are numerous, and live stationary in villages of the same description as those on the lower part of the Columbia. In their looks and manner they bear a great affinity to the Chinooks. The meaning of their national name is ' Carriers ' ; but the people of each village have a separate denomination. . . . The Carriers are naturally of an open and hospitable disposition, but very violent, and subject to sudden gusts of passion, in which much blood is often shed. However, those quarrels are soon made up and as soon forgotten " ("Adventures on the Columbia River," by Ross Cox, p. 193, one-vol. edition).

tribe rushed out of the woods and fired upon them and killed his wife. Her corpse was immediately burned on the spot. . . . All the savages who have had a near relation killed are never quiet until they have revenged the death either by killing the murderer or some person nearly related to him. This spirit of revenge has occasioned the death of the old woman above mentioned, and she undoubtedly deserved to die ; for, the last summer, she persuaded her husband to go and kill the cousin of her murderer, and that merely because her own son had been drowned.

"*Sunday*, 20th.—Yesterday an Indian of this village killed another who was on a visit from the other end of this lake, just as he was entering his canoe to return. The former approached the latter and gave him five stabs with a lance, and ripped open his bowels in such a shocking manner that his entrails immediately fell upon the ground and he, of course, immediately expired. The murderer made his escape, and the chief of the village wrapped the corpse in a moose-skin and sent it to his relations. Notwithstanding this conciliatory act, the people of this place are apprehensive that the relatives of the person murdered will make war upon them, and they will therefore set out to-morrow to go to a considerable distance down this river, where they will pass a greater part of the summer until harmony is restored between the two villages.

"This murderer has a wife who is known to be a worthless woman, with whom he supposed the person murdered had had improper intercourse, and it was to avenge this that the act was committed. All the Carriers are extremely jealous of their wives, while to their unmarried daughters they cheerfully allow every liberty."[1]

Meanwhile Stuart was on the eve of returning from his fruitless search after the much-wanted new route. He

1. Harmon's Journal, pp. 230-31 (original edition).

directed Harmon to Fraser Lake to make room for himself as he intended to pass most of 1815 at Stuart Lake. Harmon was thereby relegated to the minor post of Fraser Lake, whence he occasionally sallied out, going once as far as Blackwater in quest of pelts.

He had hardly been edified by the Indians of Stuart Lake. But unchristianized savages of the same race are pretty much the same everywhere. He perceived this when, on the 18th of June, 1815, his new place received a visit from a band of eight Babines, who, on their arrival, began to gamble, as was usual at that time. The strangers being constantly winners, bad feeling was engendered, which developed into open disputes. The restoration of the property won only prevented a serious conflict; but a coolness between the two factions was visible, which culminated in one of the Babines being shot just as he embarked in his canoe. Which seeing, his fellow tribes-men hastened their departure, but not without vowing vengeance on the murderer of their friend.

In the spring of 1816 Harmon, having heard of the serious illness of two of his brothers, began to feel home-sick, and would fain have severed his connection with the North-West Company had he not been strongly advised to the contrary by George McDougall, a younger brother of James, the pioneer trader of Fort McLeod. Perhaps to dissipate by travelling those yearnings after the home circle, he left shortly after (May 8th) for Fort Chippewayan on Lake Athabaska, returning on the 1st of September of the same year. The ensuing winter he took a jaunt of twenty-three days on the Fraser River, where he barely escaped being massacred with his companions.

An Iroquois with his wife and two children were less lucky, since about the same time they were killed, while asleep, by two Carriers of Stuart Lake on whose beaver

G   97

preserves they were encroaching heedless of protest or remonstrance. The reader will, no doubt, be surprised to hear of Iroquois in the far west. They came in the rear of the Canadian traders, generally as hired servants, but sometimes also as freemen, trappers, and hunters. In the vicinity of Jasper House, on the eastern slope of the Rocky Mountains, they even formed quite a little settlement of their own.

In the spring of 1819, after a residence of eight years and a half in New Caledonia, Harmon was off to Montreal, whence he came back to the North-West in the course of the following year. During that trip, which he probably intended to be final, he was accompanied by the mother of his children, whom he then formally married, a step none of his confrères in the service ever had the courage to take in connection with the unions they had formed with native women.

Mr. Malcolm McLeod, in his notes on McDonald's Journal of Sir George Simpson's voyage through northern America, calls Harmon a Chief Factor,[1] and states expressly that he finds his name in the list of Chief Factors and Chief Traders in the original Deed Poll issued at the time of the coalition of the North-West and Hudson's Bay Companies. This must be an oversight on the part of Mr. McLeod. Harmon, who so far had been serving in the capacity of clerk,[2] was then appointed a Chief Trader only, and his name as such appears on the Deed Poll of 1821, being the eighth in seniority. As he is believed to have retired almost immediately from the service, we fail to see how he could have been promoted to a Chief Factorship.

Daniel Williams Harmon was, as we have seen, a most conscientious man, and, especially since September, 1813,

1. P. 104.

2. At all events he was not yet a partner in 1818.

he invariably acted as a God-fearing gentleman, going even to the length of composing prayers for his daily use, prescribing for himself days of fasting, and crowning his attempts at self-improvement by doing justice to the woman he had made his life consort. He was an affectionate father and, generally, a very sociable man, who greatly appreciated the company of his equals.[1]

While he was absorbed in the task of developing and consolidating, under Stuart's presidency, the various establishments founded by Fraser in the west, a band of French Canadian half-breeds, led by a Cuthbert Grant, and acting in the interest of the same North-West Company which Harmon was faithfully serving, were capturing Fort Douglas, on the Red River, after having killed Robert Semple, the Governor of the Hudson's Bay Company, and twenty of his men who had dared to come in the open and meet the invaders. This bloody affair, which took place on the 19th of June, 1816, had evidently been prompted by the North-West Company. Many of its active members had the strongest objections to the settlement of the Red River valley, which for some years had been going on under the patronage of Lord Selkirk. That gentleman had purchased for the purpose a large tract of land from the Hudson's Bay Company, and his interests were, on that account, supposed to be identical with those of the Nor'westers' deadly enemies.

As a consequence of the high-handed measures taken in these troubled times, the seizure of forts, pelts and other property by both contesting parties, the noble Earl had to bear the brunt of long and costly legal battles in the Canadian courts. For the part he had taken in the capture of Fort William he met with adverse verdicts, and when he laid the responsibility of the Seven Oaks skirmish at the

1. As a linguist, at least as regards the Déné dialects, he was a failure.

doors of a few prominent North-West Company partners, the courts also refused to be convinced by his arguments.[1]

These results could not but add new force to the fire of bitterness and discontent which was secretly burning within the bosoms of the two opposing companies and, on one side at least, keep up the thirst for vengeance. But the death of Lord Selkirk, which occurred in April, 1820, came as a God-sent sedative to heal the wounds opened on the Manitoban plains by the muskets of the French half-breeds. As it became evident that neither faction would yield to the other so long as they enjoyed a separate existence, it was agreed that a coalition of the conflicting interests was the only means of effecting a lasting peace. Therefore, on the 26th of March, 1821, the two corporations coalesced under the name of the Hudson's Bay Company.

1. At this late date the action of the Canadian courts is open to criticism, and we are afraid Dr. Bryce is not far from right in his strictures on their judgments. ("History of the Hudson's Bay Company," p. 256.) But that writer is evidently carried away by his feelings when he speaks of Semple's fall as of a murder. A homicide, to become murder, must be premeditated and induced by wilful malice. Where is Bryce's evidence to show that Grant's band had come with the object of taking away Semple's life? They considered themselves a war party bent on taking Fort Douglas, and thus retaliating for the capture of Fort Gibraltar. Had not the Governor sallied out with his men, followed by a piece of cannon, his life would most probably have been spared. Moreover, we must not forget that Grant always contended that the first shot in the affray had been fired by the Hudson's Bay Company people at Semple's order. At all events, he precipitated the conflict by foolishly attempting to grasp the gun of the half-breed messenger sent to parley with him. That Dr. Bryce does not refer to the Indian who is said to have given the *coup de grace* to the wounded Governor, is shown by the fact that he connects the " murder " of Semple with " six of the North-West partners." Lastly, he repeatedly styles the whole unfortunate affair " the skirmish of Seven Oaks." Useless to remark that skirmishing is not murdering. It may be noted, in passing, that Harmon's account of the affair lays all the blame on the Hudson's Bay Company people; but that gentleman had probably been misinformed by parties too friendly to the North-West Company.

According to the Deed Poll then promulgated, the yearly profits of the new concern were to go sixty per cent. to the proprietors who furnished the capital, and forty per cent. to the " wintering partners," as the trading officers were then called. These were now divided into two distinct classes, based mostly on seniority in the service, that of the Chief Factors and that of the Chief Traders. The forty per cent. interest in the Company's profits was subdivided into eighty-five shares, of which a Chief Factor was to receive two and a Chief Trader one. Twenty-five of the former class and twenty-eight of the latter were appointed, in equal numbers, from among the officers of the two companies residing in the country, the remaining seven shares being allotted to various deserving persons from amongst the employees of both concerns.

Thus ended, after thirty-eight years of bitter struggles and brilliant achievements, a trading corporation which had been noted chiefly for its dash, its daring, and an indomitable spirit of initiative and combativeness which was seldom tempered by any scruples.

CHAPTER VII.

The Hudson's Bay Company in New Caledonia.

THE corporation which came thus to reap where others had sown, and was to have such a paramount influence on the destinies of the natives of New Caledonia, was then one hundred and sixty-one years old, having been incorporated in 1670. On May 2nd of that year King Charles II. of England granted his cousin, Prince Rupert, the Duke of Albemarle, the Earl of Craven and fifteen other noblemen or merchants of London, a charter endowing their corporation with the vastest powers over the land tributary to Hudson Bay, with a view to trade with the natives thereof, administer justice, and exercise all the rights of a sovereign over the said country.

It is worthy of remark that the actual originators of the exploration which led to the formation of the Company were two Frenchmen, Radisson and Groseillers, while its bitterest enemy and most formidable competitor in years to come was to be a corporation which was supposed to represent the French element in Canada.

We have not to dwell here on the long contest between the North-West Company and the Hudson's Bay Company, nor is it necessary to recite the rivalry, bitter struggles, and final hostilities which culminated in the bloody affair of Seven Oaks. Indeed, we will not even attempt an appreciation of the latter corporation's action on the country over which it had such a lasting and jealously enforced monopoly. Our task is humbler and more restricted in scope. What we are concerned with is its bearing on the aborigines of New Caledonia, and the doings of its representatives west of the Rocky Mountains. Before we proceed with our account of successive events within that territory, a few words on its constitution and the workings of the same from 1821 to this day, as well as the character of the influence it exercised over the Western Dénés, will certainly not be out of place.

When, for the sake of peace and in the interest of all the parties concerned, the North-West Company united with the Hudson's Bay Company, there originated a new organization, in which was retained only what seemed best in each corporation. The result was an association which for efficiency would seem to have no possible rivals, except the modern religious Orders of the Roman Catholic Church, with whose government and organic conformation it has many points of similarity. The vast extent of territory now under the undisputed control of the Hudson's Bay Company was divided, for the sake of trading purposes, into three principal departments, the Northern, the Southern, and the Western, which, in their turn, were subdivided into districts with a leading fort or capital, where the chief officer resided.

New Caledonia formed the most important district of the Western Department, the other parts of which, with the exception of the Pacific or Coast division, almost seemed to exist only to supply goods to the posts of the northern interior. The main depot of the Company west of the Rockies was Fort Vancouver, on the lower Columbia River. Such forwarding and distributing quarters were presided over by Chief Factors, or superior officers, some of whom were also in charge of the most

important trading posts. This brings us to the consideration of the Company's personnel and its organization.

This was most elaborate, and the lines between the
different classes in the service were at all times strictly
drawn. Generally speaking, it was composed of three
categories : there were the officers or commissioned gentlemen, the clerks and the servants.

Among the latter promotion was naturally out of order,
each man pursuing the vocation his abilities or training
fitted him for. Yet, even in that lower class, there were
degrees which were implicitly recognized, the highest
of which was that of interpreter. Then came, in the
order named, mechanics, guides, steersmen, bowmen or
bouts, fishermen, middlemen (or common boatmen), and
apprentices.

Each one's wages varied according to the value of his
services and the number of years he had been in the Company's employ. The best paid among the *engagés* or
servants were the interpreters. Fifteen years after the
union of the two corporations, their salary averaged £22
per year. One who had seen thirty-four years of service
received as much as £35, while two others had to be content with £15. Irrespective of seniority in the ranks, the
wages of the *bouts*—men who helped the steersmen from
the opposite end of the boat—were £24, and those of the
common boatmen £19.

The servants lodged in quarters distinct from those of
the officers and clerks, and every Saturday afternoon
received their rations for the ensuing week. Their fare, as
will appear in the course of this work, was of the poorest ;
but it is safe to remark that, except when boating or packing, their exertions were on a par with their menu, and
they were hardly expected to yield the amount of work
required of regular laborers in civilized parts of the world.

FORT ST. JAMES TO-DAY.

Employees, while getting goods at specially low prices, were strictly forbidden to trade with the natives, and an infraction of this rule was visited with a fine, generally of two pounds sterling.

Intermediate between the servants and the clerks were the so-called postmasters. These, as a rule, were taken from the ranks of the servants, and were men whose education, too defective to allow them to aspire higher, was yet of such a character as to permit of their keeping accounts and being in charge, at least *ad interim*, of minor posts. As late as 1850 their wages varied between thirty and sixty pounds sterling.

As to the second class, it was composed of the clerks and the apprentices. The latter were young men with a fairly good education, who entered the service with an engagement generally for five years. At the expiration of the first year they were entitled to £20, and the salary was augmented by £5 every subsequent year, except the two last, when the increase was £10 per annum, unless they had not given satisfaction. This gave them £50 for the last year of their apprenticeship, when they could pretend to the title of clerk. These figures are those prevalent in 1850. Twenty years earlier they were less by £5 in every case.

Though they may then have continued to keep the accounts of a post and do such clerical work as circumstances demanded, their new position fitted them for the Indian trade and the charge of a regular fort.[1] In 1836 the salary of the clerks in New Caledonia varied between £50 and £100 a year.

1. A circumstance which goes to show that one did not need to be a Chief Trader to preside over a post, as a C. W. McCain seems to think when he writes that "a Chief Trader . . . was the one in charge of a Fort." ("History of the SS. *Beaver*," p. 9.)

The clerks, even when in a subordinate position in an important establishment, sat at the officers' mess and, as a rule, had rooms in the same house. They were called gentlemen, and in letters were addressed as " Mr."

After the amalgamation of the North-West and Hudson's Bay Companies, a certain Charles McKenzie, who had by a native woman a son with a good education, received at the Red River Seminary, complains that the successor to the two concerns would not recognize the right of such children to promotion. "The Honorable Company are unwilling to take natives even as apprenticed clerks," he writes somewhat bitterly, "and the favored few they do take can never aspire to a higher status, be their education and capacity what they may."[1]

Whatever may be the truth of this statement as regards the management of the Company in the east, it certainly cannot apply to New Caledonia. In 1836 there were in that country two half-breed clerks in charge of forts, one of whom received a higher salary than a fellow clerk hailing from Scotland. Nay more, the following pages will show us the son of a native woman presiding over the whole district.

We now come to the privileged class of the commissioned gentlemen. These formed a veritable oligarchy, and, together with the title of Esquire, to which the clerks had no right, their names, when written by a third party, were coupled with the grade they had reached in the hierarchical scale. None of them received any salary, their remuneration consisting of shares in the Company's profits, so that their very title was a powerful incentive to exertion towards furthering the Company's interests. Upon their promotion they were sent a commission accompanied by a covenant, which they had to execute in

1. Quoted in Dr. Bryce's " History of the Hudson's Bay Company," p. 175.

the presence of a superior officer. The burden of this was a promise of fidelity to the Company.

And here we might as well enter into a few details unknown to the public concerning the intimate history of this privileged class, the inner workings of the system which established it, and the profits or remuneration that yearly accrued to its members.

In the old Company—by contradistinction to the recast of the same in 1872—there were, as we have seen, only two grades of commissioned officers : the Chief Factors and the Chief Traders. We remember that the former received two shares of the Company's yearly profits, while the latter could claim only one. But when we are told that, from the time of the coalition to 1872, the average value of a share was £360, we realize that even a Chief Trader met with an adequate remuneration. Of course, this varied from time to time, and there were a few outfits which yielded insignificant returns, or which even resulted in an actual loss to the Company. Thus, on the trade of the first year after the disappearance of the North-West Company, there was a loss of upwards of forty thousand pounds sterling, which cost the wintering partners £196 7s. 1d. per share. The following year (outfit 1822), the returns were on their way up to the normal amount, being then £203 8s. 9d. Again, in 1869, the year before the transfer of the country to Canada, there was a loss of thirty thousand pounds, caused entirely by the first Riel insurrection.

Originally, certain Chief Factors and Chief Traders were allowed to retire from the service before June 1st, 1822, and for seven years thereafter received the benefit of their commissions. After five years' service as commissioned officers, three Chief Factors and two Chief Traders could withdraw annually, with the full benefit of their respective commissions for one year and of half the amount of their shares for the remaining six years. Vacancies to a commission were filled by the Chief Factors voting for three different names, and the Governor and Committee in London usually chose the men recommended by the lesser Governor residing in the country.

In course of time a Board of Managers was formed, which had in hand the affairs of the whole Western Department and whose seat was at Fort Vancouver. It was composed of Chief Factors whose long and faithful services entitled them to the rest afforded by that position, which was more or less of a sinecure.

In 1834 a new Deed Poll was issued in place of that of 1821, which was abrogated. One of its clauses was to the effect that, in the event of a loss on a year's trade, the wintering partners would not be called upon to make the same good. The number of Chief Factors was also reduced and the number of Chief Traders raised. The new Deed Poll did not, like the old one, make provision for a specified number of each ; so that, until its abrogation in 1871, there were seldom more than fourteen or fifteen Chief Factors on active service, while Chief Traders varied according to the number of shares held by officers who had retired.

On June 1st, 1872, the Hudson's Bay Company was reorganized on a new basis and a third Deed Poll then came into force. By that arrangement the number of grades was increased, and to meet this change the old 40 per cent. gain coming to the commissioned officers was subdivided into 100 shares instead of 85 as before. Since that time the Company is nominally composed of the following grades : Inspecting Chief Factors, who originally received three of the new shares, but now get only their travelling expenses over and above what they have a right to in virtue of their commission ; then come the Chief

Factors with 2½ shares, the Factors with 2, the Chief Traders with 1½, and Junior Chief Traders with 1 share.

Great dissatisfaction was expressed at the time of its adoption at the new arrangement, which the wintering partners contended sacrificed their rights and made light of their interests. Since its promulgation the average value of a share has fallen from £360 to £211. Of late years it has been the policy of the Company to discontinue the granting of commissions and give fixed salaries to the gentlemen in its employ.

The titles of the original Company were greatly coveted, and, at this distance, we can well afford a discreet smile at the unveiled satisfaction of an American who, forgetting the democratic principles professed by all good representatives of his nationality, wrote to a brother officer, seemingly with the blush of a flattered maiden, on his promotion to one of them :

" I return you many thanks for your kind congratulations on my promotion to a Tradership. I have every reason to believe that such is the case, having a letter from Sir George Simpson informing me that my interest as Chief Trader was to date from 1st June, 1853, and sending me his sincere congratulations on the event. Mr. Douglas was, no doubt, aware of it when we were at Langley. As Sir George's letter is dated Lachine, 28th February, and passed the Cowlitz postoffice on the 11th of May, 1853, and Chief Factor Ogden addressed me as Chief Trader McLean in a letter of the 11th of June, surely there can be scarcely a doubt on the subject, and I must confess that it is more than I expected. It is to your kindness that, in a great measure, I owe my having been promoted, and, believe me, I will ever remember it."[1]

These officers, especially the Chief Factor in charge of

1. D. McLean to D. Manson, February 6th, 1854.

an important post, enjoyed the greatest consideration and were treated with every mark of respect. As to the latter, J. W. McKay, himself an old Hudson's Bay Company man, has written of his greatness an account which is too graphic not to be reproduced here.

"This exalted functionary," he writes, "was lord paramount ; his word was law ; he was necessarily surrounded by a halo of dignity, and his person was sacred, so to speak. He was dressed every day in a suit of black or dark blue, white shirt, collars to his ears, frock coat, velvet stock and straps to the bottom of his trousers. When he went out of doors he wore a black beaver hat worth forty shillings. When travelling in a canoe or boat, he was lifted in and out of the craft by the crew ; he still wore his beaver hat, but it was protected by an oiled silk cover, and over his black frock he wore a long cloak made of Royal Stuart tartan lined with scarlet or dark blue bath coating. The cloak had a soft Genoa velvet collar, which was fastened across by mosaic gold clasps and chains. It had also voluminous capes.

"He carried with him an ornamental bag, technically called a 'fire-bag,' which contained his tobacco, steel and flint, touchwood, tinderbox, and brimstone matches. In camp his tent was pitched apart from the shelter given his crew. He had a separate fire, and the first work of the boat's crew after landing was to pitch his tent, clear his camp, and collect firewood sufficient for the night before they were allowed to attend to their own wants. Salutes were fired on his departure from the fort and on his return.

"All this ceremony was considered necessary ; it had a good effect on the Indians ; it added to his dignity in the eyes of his subordinates, but sometimes spoiled the Chief Factor. Proud indeed was the Indian fortunate enough to be presented with the Chief Factor's cast-off hat, however battered it might become. He donned it on all important occasions, and in very fine weather it might constitute his entire costume.[1]

As to trading with the Indians, this was attended to by one or more of the clerks, aided by an interpreter, generally a half-breed. As is well known, the unit of value was equal to that of a prime beaver-skin of any weight, though of the full grown animal; smaller beaver, martens and the like being quoted as so many parts of a made beaver. Until about 1862, when flour, bacon, sugar, and tea were for the first time introduced as articles of trade in New Caledonia, the fort stores contained merely a few indispensable implements, such as kettles, axes and knives, together with a limited supply of guns and ammunition, wearing apparel, and blankets. A gratuity of ammunition was given to each out-going hunter.

Much has been said about the large profits realized by the Hudson's Bay Company in the course of the last century. There can be no doubt that, after the disappearance of its powerful rival, the North-West Company, its returns were of the most satisfactory character, though probably no credence should be placed in the stories of guns being originally bartered for piles of beaver-skins reaching to the end of the guns standing alongside of them. In New Caledonia its expenses were enormous; yet the traders managed to make this district pay handsomely. Discreet as the authorities are about such matters, more than once their official letters betray their satisfaction at the turn of affairs in that country.

In the course of 1845, business in the fur line does not seem to have been so bright as usual; but the governor, Sir George Simpson, consoles himself with the thought

1. Year Book of British Columbia, p. 24 (first edition).

that "the district may shortly recover its conspicuous standing with regard to profits."[1]

Sure enough, the sagacious governor was a good prophet, for three years later Thomas Lewes writes from Colville: "You will observe from the account current that New Caledonia has made rather handsome returns this outfit, and an apparent gain of £6,914 12s. 11d."[2]

As to the credit and debts given to the Indians, it has been said that the Company had recourse to that expedient to keep them in subjection.[3] This charge cannot be substantiated as regards New Caledonia. To the sorrow of those who had to see them paid, large debts were indeed allowed the Indians; but the latter were mostly responsible therefor, being at times exorbitant and almost threatening in their demands. In fact, the credit advanced them is rather a token of the kind-heartedness and liberality of the traders, who, until a relatively recent date, had no competition to fear.

With regard to the re-engagement of servants dissatisfied with the service, so much could not be said in favor of the Company, and the writer has the best of reasons for stating that means not too honorable were sometimes resorted to in order to make them renew their engagement. Service, in many cases, was becoming so irksome after a few years, especially with men placed under autocratic officers, that the correspondence of the higher authorities is replete with requests to such as were at the head of the different forts to use their best endeavors to prevent the *engagés* from leaving the Company's employ.

In fact, in the course of time, desertions and retirements became so numerous that the Company hit upon a plan

1. MS. letter to D. Manson, June 16th, 1845.

2. MS. letter to D. Manson, April 23rd, 1848.

3. See J. E. Fitzgerald's "Hudson's Bay Co. and Vancouver's Island," p. 138.

which yielded the best of results, inasmuch as it urged the natives round the forts to work and exertion. An unsigned letter, probably from Sir James Douglas, dated 12th of April, 1854, has the following:

"In your letter of the 2nd of October allusion is made to the employment of Indians to make up for the deficiency of white servants, a very proper measure, and you must provide goods for the payment of such service."[1]

The Hudson's Bay Company's forts in New Caledonia consisted of quadrilateral enclosures, of an area varying according to the importance of the place, built of stout upright logs, flanked by two bastions at the farthest angles. These were square, tower-like buildings, furnished each with a small cannon and a stand of large muskets. The palisade, which was from fifteen to eighteen feet high, admitted of no chinks between its component parts, and was provided with a large, heavy gate in front of the fort, and a smaller one on the opposite side. The front gate had a wicket for every-day use, and the whole was made of the most solid material. Inside of the palisade, and contiguous thereto, ran a gallery about four feet below the top of the same, which facilitated communication between the two bastions.

Within the enclosure were the quarters of the servants, generally a very long building with many partitions, the store (which at Stuart Lake was originally in the gentlemen's house), salmon shed and meat house, residence of the officer in charge, and of his clerks, etc.

What was the effect of the Hudson's Bay Company on the native population of New Caledonia? The writer sincerely wishes he had not to answer that question; but the close association of the two races during the last eighty years renders imperative the consideration of the result of

1. MS. letter to D. Manson.

FORT ST. JAMES

As it stood in James Douglas's time.

such commingling. Both written and oral information is not wanting to force on us the conclusion that the influence of the superior race was decidedly detrimental to the best interests of the Western Dénés.

Instead of lifting the lower race up to the standard of Christianized Europeans, the latter, in too many cases, stooped to the level of the savages they had come to as the representatives of a wonderful civilization. Gambling, Indian fashion dancing, face-painting, potlatching or heathen feasting, rendering murder for murder, the lax observance of the Lord's Day, disregard of the sanctity of the marriage tie—nay, in two cases at least, even polygamy— were not only countenanced, but actually practised by the Company's officers and servants.[1] The cremation of the dead fell with time into desuetude; but that custom was replaced by others of an equally obnoxious nature, which the whites taught the aborigines: such as scalping, which was quite unknown among the Western Dénés, and that which has sounded the death-knell of morality, peace, and order among the natives who have been cursed with its introduction—we mean the drinking of intoxicants.

Of course, we are well aware of the gravity of our charges; but, were it necessary, nothing could be more easy than to prove them, even by the Company's own official documents, laconic as they usually are when it is a question of happenings which might throw discredit on the concern. These are naturally reticent concerning the wild orgies among the fort employees, and the large kettlefuls of liquor which the officers—even to the Chief Factors—caused to be distributed among the native guests

1. The two cases of polygamy were those of officers, each of whom was at the head of a fort. One of them, a pure white man, who could hardly speak of the natives without dubbing them rascals and scoundrels, co-habited simultaneously with two of their women, and afterwards attained the rank of a Chief Trader.

of the pagan feasts, at which they themselves did not scruple to assist as participants; but they contain enough to tell us of the motives to which they yielded in propagating that evil among the aborigines.

We purposely say propagating that evil. As to its introduction into New Caledonia, the responsibility for that fateful step undoubtedly belongs to the North-West Company, members of which had supplied liquor to the Western Dénés even before they crossed the Rocky Mountains to establish themselves in the west. They were so much the more guilty, as they could not adduce the stimulating influence of trade competition to excuse their conduct. Once introduced, it was difficult for the new company, whose personnel remained practically unchanged in New Caledonia, to stop the evil. Indeed, several of its officers hardly deemed it an evil at all.

As early as 1831, William Todd, of McLeod Lake, writes to headquarters, at Stuart Lake: "Mr. Connolly—the officer in charge of the district—previous to his departure from here, made them [the Sekanais Indians] very liberal promises of spirits and tobacco should their hunt, on his arrival in the fall, be found to equal his expectations." [1]

A year had not elapsed, when Thomas Dears, then in charge of Fort Connolly, writes also: "Those Indians I saw were somewhat disappointed in not receiving a gratuity of spirits. I am of opinion that if a small quantity was allowed them, each according to his merits, it would be a stimulant [No doubt it would.—ED.] to exertion, and, at any rate, it would entice them to visit the fort oftener." [2]

Ten years later, the officer momentarily presiding over the whole district decides, in his official capacity, "Regarding rum to be given to the Indians, I would recommend

1. To P. W. Dease, August 28th, 1831.
2. February 5th, 1832.

that the usual allowance be given to those who pay their debts."[1]

This was evidently written in answer to a consultation regarding the advisability of continuing the custom of furnishing intoxicants to the natives, and said consultation must have been the result of some occurrence which caused the local manager to question the wisdom of following in the footsteps of his predecessors. What this occurrence may have been can easily be guessed by any one who knows the effect "fire-water," even taken in small quantities, has on inferior races.[2]

The directing minds of the Company, though not realizing the extent of the evil, made laudable efforts to check its ravages. In 1831, among the resolutions of their Annual Council, held at Norway House, we find one prohibiting the sale of liquor to the Indians, and regulating that "not more than two gallons of spirituous liquors and four gallons of wine be sold at the depots to any individual in the Company's service, of what rank soever he may be."[3]

1. Paul Fraser to H. Maxwell, of Babine, March 29th, 1832 (*sic* for 1842).

2. This being so, we fail to see how one can reconcile with the real state of affairs the following statement in an official letter written on the 1st of February, 1837, by Governor G. Simpson to J. H. Pelly, then at the head of the Hudson's Bay Company in London : "Drunkenness is now . . . quite unknown . . . in the country known by the name of New Caledonia . . . , the introduction and use of spirituous and other intoxicating liquors having been strictly prohibited" (Appendix to "Report from Select Committee on the Hudson's Bay Company," p. 420). At the time when the above was penned liquor was being supplied by the pailful to the Indians of the very capital of New Caledonia on the occasion of their "potlaches," and we will see, p. 197 of this work, the superintendent of the Company's affairs in the far North-West declare, in the course of that very year 1837, that the natives of that place "have fully sufficient [rum] already."

3. Resolution 95.

And, as the evil seemed to be growing, eight years later the same body orders that "the brewing of beer and distilling of spirits be interdicted at all establishments and posts belonging to the Hudson's Bay Company."[1]

Yet, so late as 1848, D. Manson, the gentleman then in charge of the district, speaks of a keg of rum which was regularly kept for the use of the Sekanais Indians, and we have the best of evidence for stating that, long after that date, intoxicants figured prominently in the Company's transactions with the natives.[2]

King Charles's charter had given the officers of the Company "power to judge all persons belonging to the said Governor and Company, or that shall live under them, in all causes, whether civil or criminal, according to the laws of this kingdom, and to execute justice accordingly." Now, during its many years of supreme control over the native populations, in the midst of which it had established its posts, many unlawful acts were perpetrated and even crimes committed. But there is not one instance on record of a person having been tried for an offence and punished accordingly. When the victim of a foul deed belonged to the Company's personnel, prompt action was, indeed, invariably taken ; but even then there was not the semblance of a trial. He who had killed was killed, sometimes the innocent sharing the fate of the guilty, exactly as was practised by the Indians themselves, a circumstance the latter knew how to utilize to silence the Company's employees who, for the sake of their trade, tried to put a stop to the series of reprisals which followed. Regular arrests and trials would, no doubt, have been sometimes difficult and well nigh impossible ; but it is safe to say that, in several cases, cool, impartial justice might have

1. Resolution 78, June 7th, 1845.
2. To Sir Geo. Simpson, February 20th, 1848.

easily enough taken the place of that which everybody regarded as revenge and retaliation, prompted less by the exigencies of society than by the impulse of feelings and the thirst for blood.

As to the observance of Sunday, we will simply remark that the Hudson's Bay Company in New Caledonia seems to have considered the Lord's Day as the proper time for travelling, which in the north, especially in winter, means packing, felling trees, cutting firewood, sometimes in large quantities, etc. Until a comparatively late date, Sunday trading and outfitting were also weekly occurrences in that district.

The redeeming features of the Company's people in the north were their undoubted honesty in dealing with the natives, the superior quality of their goods, their humane conduct towards the poor and needy, and the assistance they gave the first missionaries and their immediate successors in the way of free passages in their boats and a most generous hospitality at their forts.

CHAPTER VIII.

Last Years of Stuart's Stay in New Caledonia.
William Connolly Succeeds Him.

1821–1828.

THE person who was to harmonize the discordant elements within the new corporation, and reconcile the Nor'westers to the loss of their autonomy, was a young man, a mere clerk of the Hudson's Bay Company. This was George (afterwards Sir George) Simpson. A son of the eldest brother of Thomas Simpson's mother, he had been born in Ross-shire, Scotland, and had engaged for eleven years in commercial pursuits, when, in 1819, he cast his lot with the Hudson's Bay Company, which was then battling furiously with its enterprising rival. Early the following year he sailed from England to Montreal, whence he made for Lake Athabaska, where he wintered.

Of a pleasing appearance and gentlemanly address, with blue eyes and finely chiselled features, he was rather below the average in stature ; but his suavity of manners and a quiet dignity of deportment, which never left him, stamped him as a man who was bound to make his mark in the world. That habitual affability was only ruffled when, in the course of his travels, he was hampered by companions whose easy-going ways jarred on his nerves and did not allow him to live up to his reputation of being one of the very swiftest travellers on record. He would then urge them on with an impetuosity which is said to have once cost him a ducking which was not on his programme. " A stalwart French voyageur, who was a favorite with the Governor [Sir George], was once, in crossing the Lake of the Woods, so irritated by the Governor's unreasonable urging that he seized his tormentor, who was small in stature, by the shoulders and dipped him into the lake, giving vent to his feelings in an emphatic French oath." [1]

As to his administrative abilities, there can be no question. The fact that for fully thirty-nine years—that is, until the date of his death, which occurred in 1860—he remained the trusted Governor of the Hudson's Bay Company in America suffices by itself to prove it.

We have not to enter here into the details, or even give the outlines, of his administration. Norway House, on Lake Winnipeg, became the American headquarters of the Company. There, in conjunction with a few tried Chief Factors, forming a sort of legislative assembly and executive council combined, he used to direct the affairs of his vast corporation, listen to complaints or requests, judge litigious cases, review annually the interests of the many posts under his jurisdiction, and close the whole proceedings by a series of resolutions embodying the changes in the personnel of the " gentlemen "—that is, the officers and clerks—for the ensuing year. [2] Copies of said resolutions were then distributed among the various heads of districts.

In the beginning a great reduction in the number of posts was, of course, in order, several having been established simply out of a necessity based on competition, in the days of the two rival corporations. These con-

1. " The Remarkable History of the Hudson's Bay Company," by G. Bryce, p. 270.

2. As to the servants, they were, with regard to changes from one place to another, under the special jurisdiction of the manager of their district.

flicting interests having never penetrated into New Caledonia, a reduction in the number of forts there was not necessary. On the contrary, with the increase in the personnel resulting from the abandonment of many establishments in the east, expansion and multiplication of posts became the order of the day.

We have seen the pioneer traders for a number of years painfully transporting their supplies overland from the east through Fort McLeod. This necessitated long voyages, in the course of which the goods had to cross the continent and be packed by men along difficult portages, chief among which were the Rocky Mountain Portage and that between McLeod Lake and Stuart Lake, a distance of at least eighty miles. To obviate these difficulties John Stuart had gone in search of a water communication between the Fraser and the Columbia, failing to find which he suggested the advisability of getting the New Caledonia outfits from the Columbia, but *via* Okanagan and the newly founded establishment at Kamloops. As the lower Fraser was unavailable for the purpose, it had to be avoided, and horses were to pack the goods between the Columbia and the terminus of navigation on the former stream. This arrangement necessitated the establishment of a dépôt, or warehouse, to receive the goods and store them for safe keeping pending the arrival of the canoes from Stuart Lake. Hence the erection, in 1821, of a new fort on the Fraser, just at the place where Sir Alexander Mackenzie turned back, in memory of whom the new post was called Alexandria.

In the course of time this became an important establishment, which was not only a depot for the northern posts, but a sort of embryo granary which supplied them with the limited quantity of wheat that could be raised in its immediate vicinity.[1]   Moreover (and this was perhaps the argument that had the most weight in the eyes of the Company), it accommodated a large number of Indians who, unhappily, adding to their innate immorality the vices of the whites, especially the abuse of intoxicants), were soon to decrease rapidly.   To-day their once populous village and adjacent settlements are practically a desert ; but even ten years after the erection of the fort the native population in that quarter must still have been numerous, since on the list of Indians to whom credit had been advanced by the gentleman in charge, on February 12th, 1831, the writer has found the names of one hundred and sixty-nine hunters. This would give a minimum of six hundred souls.   The amount of their debts varied between one-half and twenty-one " skins," or twenty-one times the value of a " made beaver."

The preceding year (1830) that post had received, among other pelts, 1,832 beaver-skins, to which must be added 22 beaver robes, 8 large dressed beavers, 1 small dressed beaver, and 50 bear-skins.

Somewhat later an outpost of Alexandria was established on a tributary of the Chilcotin River, which, after many trials and varying fortunes, had to be abandoned, owing to its isolation and consequent expensiveness, but especially on account of the troublesome disposition of the natives who frequented it.

The author of that most valuable work, the Year Book of British Columbia,[2] follows Bancroft, who states expressly that Fort Chilcotin was established " about the same time " as Alexandria.[3]   To anyone familiar with the geography of the country and the innate restiveness of the Chilcotin

1. The first Fort Alexandria stood on the left side of the Fraser.

2. R. E. Gosnell, Victoria, B.C., 1897, p. 73.

3. " History of the North-West," Vol. II., p. 461.

Indians, such a statement calls for confirmation. That Bancroft is mistaken as to the date of the foundation of that fort (which cannot be 1821, as the Year Book has it on the faith of that author's somewhat vague assertion) is made evident by the following statement from William Connolly's journal, which is undated, except for the very explicit mention of the years 1825-26. It is in the handwriting of that gentleman, who had never been in New Caledonia before the end of 1824, and written probably in 1826:

"The intelligence Mr. McDougall (George) conveys in regard to Alexandria is not very agreeable. The Indians in that quarter, having had some serious misunderstandings a few years ago with the Chilcotins, the latter, in revenge, lately murdered three of the former when they were hunting in the vicinity of the Chilcotin River, and the others, in retaliation, perpetrated a like deed upon two young men of the Chilcotin tribe who were amongst them. Since this occurred all intercourse between the two tribes has been broken off, and both being apprehensive of being attacked, the Chilcotins retreated beyond our reach for the present, which prevented Mr. McDougall from making them the promised visit, and the others have, since that unfortunate affair, done nothing.

"This event, I am afraid, will be an obstacle to the establishment of a post on the Chilcotin River for the present."[1]

In course of time Fort Alexandria became the seat of a Chief Trader, who had under him a clerk in charge of Fort Chilcotin. Both, however, were under the jurisdiction of the Chief Factor at Stuart Lake.

While the Hudson's Bay Company was thus implanting itself in the south of the district, it was extending its influence in the north by means of a new fort it was

1. From a fly-sheet torn off an old journal book.

establishing on the northern shore of Babine Lake, among the numerous Indians whom Harmon and Jas. McDougall visited in 1812. Trading excursions had yearly brought to the doors of those aborigines the wares of the Canadians, in competition with those they indirectly received from the Pacific coast. With the ever-increasing number of servants to support, it was felt that a permanent post in that quarter would be of the greatest benefit to the whole district, were it only as a means of procuring the salmon on which the inmates of the different posts subsisted. The run of that fish failing along the basin of the Fraser, recourse might be had to that of Lake Babine, which is one of the tributaries of the Skeena.

A new post was therefore erected, in 1822, on the northern bank of Lake Babine, in latitude 55° 4'. For over twenty years it bore among the Hudson's Bay Company's people a name which, in the old papers of the time, is variously spelt Kilmaurs, Killmars, and Kilmers. Nowadays that place is known as Old Fort Babine.

Here we must again take exception to one of Bancroft's assertions. This author states, in his " History of British Columbia "[1] that " the post of Babine was built by Chief Trader Brown in 1826-27." But in the minutes of the Council held in 1825 at the temporary Norway House, Chief Trader William Brown is explicitly mentioned as being in charge of that fort, with Charles Ross as clerk. At the time mentioned by Bancroft, Fort Kilmars was already in a flourishing condition, with P. C. Pambrun at its head. The Stuart Lake journal even records the fact that, four men having been sent to bring the returns of that place, these proved to be so abundant that four additional men had to be despatched to help those originally sent.[2]

1. P. 58.
2. Journal, April 4th, 1827.

The year 1824 was the last which John Stuart passed as the manager of the New Caledonia District. In the autumn of that year he was succeeded by William Connolly,[1] an Irishman, with a half-breed family, who crossed the Rocky Mountains with supplies and twenty-four men, whom he had brought from Norway House.

On returning from that country, for which he does not seem to have had too great a liking, John Stuart went over to the east side of the mountains, and two years afterwards, (December 10th, 1826), we find him stationed at Lesser Slave Lake. On the 5th of January, 1827, his thoughts revert to the country of his first trials, and he writes from Edmonton: " Most of the Crees attached to Fort Assiniboine had in summer crossed the mountains in war excursions and, I believe, killed some of the most valuable Indians of Western Caledonia ; but this is a conjecture."[2]

Five years afterwards he was promoted to the command of the Mackenzie District ; but six months later he was already tired of his new position and was speaking of retiring therefrom.[3] Yet he did not act at once on his original intention, and stayed some time longer at the Forks of the Mackenzie River, a step he had to regret, as we learn from an unpublished letter he wrote to his friend John McLeod. That communication is dated March 2nd, 1834, and reads partly as follows :

1. Bancroft, in his " History of British Columbia," wrongly calls him James. In his " History of the North-West," he speaks sometimes of a James, sometimes of a William, Connolly, and a careful study of his text reveals the fact that the two are really one and the same individual. On the other hand, the anonymous author of the article " Douglas" in the " Biographical Dictionary of Well-known British Columbians," calls the same gentleman John Connolly.

2. MS. letter to J. McLeod.

3. March 16th, 1833.

" I had a fair prospect of passing one of the most comfortable and pleasant [seasons] I experienced in the Indian country, when a circumstance I could neither foresee nor suspect [occurred]. Poor unfortunate Mary, of whom, in common with me, you always had a high opinion, fell over head and ears in love, and commenced an intrigue that nearly terminated my life. Of this, although aware she had ceased to treat me as her husband, I had not the smallest suspicion until 7th February, when the poor infatuated victim of delusion retired publicly into the bed-chamber of that vile Abenekis, the abominable Anreon, under a written promise that he would both protect her and turn me out of the house. But the result turned out different from [that] which either of them expected. Shortly after I entered the room, and before he could make use of his pistols, I suddenly seized the bravado by both arms and ordered Mary to her own room, and the next day I sent her to Fort Liard, where she will remain with Mr. McPherson until open water."

He then solaces his wounded feelings by stating that " the thief and villain who seduced his ' wife ' is now leaving the district." After which he adds : " Poor Mary, I both pity and forgive her. . . . I cannot again trust her. . . . Had she continued her former attention . . . until I reached Norway House, she most certainly would have become my wife."

Inasmuch as he asserts that his love for her was gone forever, and that he cannot now marry her, one may be pardoned for not seeing his reasons for taking her away from the man she loved, who was as much her husband as himself, and who was probably willing to make her his wife. He ends by saying :

" I have now only to say that, along with the returns, I will take my departure for England, from where it is probable I will steer for the south of France, and in that fine climate endeavor to spin out a frame for a few years that is nearly exhausted by excess of labor and care, ingratitude and disappointment."

Such were his plans at the time he wrote ; but again his natural inconstancy, or perhaps circumstances over which he had no control, caused him to alter them ; for on leaving the service he settled at Forres, in Scotland, where he died in 1846.[1]

William Connolly, whom we have already seen coming to succeed him in the management of the Company's affairs west of the Rocky Mountains, had originally served in the North-West Company, and he is often honorably mentioned in the Journal of Sir John Franklin (Vols. I. and II.). In the winter of 1819-20 he was the resident partner representing his corporation at Cumberland House[2], and upon the amalgamation of the two rival companies he was made a Chief Trader, while now (1824) his undoubted business abilities were recognized by his being entrusted with the charge of a much larger field.

The year that he assumed command over New Caledonia there came to that country a young man who was in after years to become the principal maker of history within British Columbia. This was James Douglas, a scion of the noble house of the same name. Born in 1803, on the 11th of August, in Demerara, British Guiana,[3] of a Catholic mother, he was educated at Lanark, Scotland, and at seventeen he entered the service of the North-West Company at Fort William. With the petulance which occasionally asserted itself within him, he resented the

1. J. Stuart, who had been made a Chief Factor in 1821, was the maternal uncle of Lord Strathcona and Mount Royal.

2. "Journey to the Shores of the Polar Sea," Vol. I., p. 95.

3. Not in Jamaica, as most authors have it.

coalition of the two companies and the practical absorption of his own by the English concern, and he was on the point of returning to Scotland when he was persuaded to remain in the service by John McLoughlin, a high officer in the new corporation, who had taken a liking for the youth.

John Stuart had just been relieved of the task for which he seemed to have so little taste, and his successor was directing his steps towards his new charge, when young Douglas was despatched to that distant country, the bugbear of apprentices in the service. In 1825 we find him at McLeod Lake, in company with John Tod, who had accompanied Stuart on his last voyage to the western lands in 1823, and as he was giving satisfaction, we see the Annual Council of the Company recommending that he be " engaged for a term of three years from the expiration of his contract, at £60 a year."

Owing to the late foundations, New Caledonia had about attained the high-water mark of its prosperity, and it may serve our purpose to glance at the personnel then stationed at the different posts. In 1825, at Stuart Lake, W. Connolly, who was appointed a Chief Factor that very year, had command over the whole district, and was assisted by three clerks, James McDougall, P. C. Pambrun,[1] and J. M. Yale. The last named gentleman had momentarily left

1. This Pambrun (Pierre Chrysologue) had already a history of his own. Born at Vaudreuil, in the Province of Quebec, he had served as lieutenant in the regiment of the Canadian Voltigeurs, who had distinguished themselves in the war against the United States. Entering the Hudson's Bay Company soon after, he was the officer sent with five boats to bring from Fort Qu'Appelle 600 sacks of pemmican wherewith to victual the Red River colonists, who were threatened with starvation through the machinations of the North-West Company; but he was overtaken on his way down the Assiniboine by the employees of that concern, who seized his stores and made him a prisoner (12th May, 1816) about a month before the Seven Oaks skirmish, a

his station, Fort George, pending an investigation into an occurrence of which we will soon have more to say. John McDonnell was in charge of Fraser Lake without an assistant clerk, while at McLeod Lake John Tod had with him Jas. Douglas ; at Alexandria Geo. McDougall was aided by William B. McBean, and at Babine Chief Trader Brown had Charles Ross for a companion.

Among the country produce of that early date we find the following mentioned in the old account books of the district : Birch bark, gum (or pitch, which sold at 1d. per pound), sturgeon oil, pemmican, Indian rice, buffalo robes (quoted at 5s. each, while samples of an inferior quality retailed at 2s. 6d.), snowshoes, dressed buffalo, reindeer and moose-skins, parchment (mostly for windows), buffalo tongues, which could be had at 6d. apiece, etc.

But to return to our new arrival, Clerk J. Douglas. His stay at Fort McLeod was not long, and he was soon called to Stuart Lake to help in the many branches of service incident to such an important post. In view of the exalted functions he was to exercise in after life, it is refreshing to read, after a lapse of eighty years, a few of the entries in the Journal of the Stuart Lake Fort wherein he is mentioned. Such passages, at the same time, give us an idea of the truly strenuous life the early traders had to lead in the isolated and undeveloped west.

circumstance to which he probably owed his life, as on the day of that bloody affair he happened to be detained at Portage la Prairie by those who were responsible for its occurrence.

He subsequently crossed over to New Caledonia, and, after a short stay at headquarters, he was entrusted with the direction of Fort Kilmars, where we have already seen him. A few years thereafter he migrated to the south, and on the 18th of November, 1838, he was in charge of the important Fort Walla-Walla, on the left bank of the Columbia, where he received with the cordiality of a Catholic gentleman the two first priests sent to Oregon, the Revds. F. N. Blanchet and M. Demers ("Historical Sketches of the Catholic Church in Oregon," p. 47).

One of their first cares, indeed the care that had precedence over all others, was to find the means of subsistence for themselves and their numerous retinue of servants. To procure fish they had started a fishery at " Montée," or the mouth of Beaver Creek, the place across the lake where they had met the first Indians in 1806 ; but the returns of that establishment were usually so indifferent and at all times so uncertain that the authorities at headquarters deemed it expedient to found a second fishing station at *Petit Lac* (or Small Lake), the head-waters of the river that falls into the lake at the Portage, where fish were said to be abundant. The new clerk, James Douglas, was entrusted with the care of that fishery, as can be seen by the following extracts from his immediate superior's Journal :

" *Saturday*, 10th November, 1827.—Received from the [old] fishery fifty-nine whitefish, the produce of two nights. Clermont brought over the greater part of the nets. . . . To-morrow Mr. Douglas, with two fishermen, Bichon[1] and Clermont, and two men to assist them, will proceed to Yokogh [or *Petit Lac*] to establish the fishery there. This gentleman will not only superintend the fishery, but will also collect the fish which the Indians may have to dispose of immediately, for which purpose he is, provided with leather [dressed skins] and other articles of trade.

"*Sunday*, 11th.—Mr. Douglas, with five men, set out for the fishery of Yokogh. They are well provided with nets, having eight of small thread, three of willow, and four of Holland twine. . . . Most of the dogs are also sent to the fishery.

" *Wednesday*, 14th.—Vadeboncœur came from the fishery and informed me that these two days back they had not taken a sufficiency for their consumption. I ordered them

---

1. This name is hardly decipherable in the MS.

to come across to-morrow to prepare to go and join Mr. Douglas at the other fishery."

After this we see the future knight and Governor of British Columbia continually hauling with dog sledges the fish he had taken at his establishment or procured from the neighboring Indians.[1]   Indeed, on the very eve of his departure from the district, he is still busy with fish and furs, as is shown by this other passage from the same Journal:

"January 1st., 1830.— . . . Mr. Douglas also returned from his trip.   In the way of furs he was more successful than had been expected, having collected, principally among

---

1. " Magnus esse vis ? a minimo incipe " (Wilt thou be great? learn first to be little) is an old maxim which most historians cannot apparently imagine as applicable to Sir James Douglas.   To them he was such a great man that they seem to think he never was little, in so far, at least, as social standing is concerned.   As soon as they introduce him upon the scene of the western province, they clothe him with a halo of consideration which is quite dispropor-tionate to his age and surroundings.   They show him to us as a man in authority (forgetting that he was a mere youth at the time) gravely studying people and situations, founding forts and practically doing at Stuart Lake what he was destined to do at Victoria.   " From the time Douglas arrived on the Pacific coast, in 1824," writes his biographer in the " Dictionary of Well-known British Columbians," he was practically at the head of the Company's business, and while McLaughlin was nominally his superior [what about Connolly ?] Douglas was not only the mind which conceived, but the hand which carried into effect all the enterprises of the Company. . . . On his arrival in New Caledonia he set himself without delay to study the conditions of the country, its geography and hydrography, and the languages and charac-teristics of the various tribes of natives with whom he would have business dealings.   He spent four [it should be six] years in the interior of New Cale-donia . . . and during this period he founded several forts and had a number of encounters with the savages, in which his prudence, address and courage made him feared and respected by the natives "—so much feared (?) that, for the sake of personal safety, he had finally to leave the country and his own father-in-law.   Others represent him as a Chief Factor in charge of Fort St. James at a time when he was merely the head fisherman of the establishment.   There should be nothing derogatory to his undoubted great-ness in the assertion that he learned to obey before he could command.

the Kuzche Indians, about 110 pounds' weight of excellent furs, chiefly beaver and marten. But the fish trade has entirely disappointed us, only about 1,600 having been procured, part of which the dogs have brought to the Fort by Mr. Douglas' men."

James Douglas is very generally credited with having established Fort Connolly, on Bear Lake. Begg and others go even so far as to say that he founded *several* such posts within New Caledonia,[1] an assertion which is erroneous on the face of it. That fort is conceded to have been erected in 1826. On the other hand, Bancroft states[2] that Douglas made, in August, 1827, a journey down the stream he called Connolly River, a circumstance which would seem to imply that he wintered at the new place. Indeed, some authors give the date of the foundation of Fort Connolly as 1826-27. Without absolutely disputing the accuracy of these statements, we will remark that, in view of the incontrovertible facts in the possession of the writer, those assertions give rise to some difficulties.

We have to deplore the loss of that part of the Stuart Lake Journal which would have prevented all controversy on the subject. As it is, the few sheets before us relating to that epoch which time has spared are our excuse for the doubts we venture to express as to the accuracy of the various authors regarding that point. In a manuscript document signed by William Connolly, and dated Walla-Walla, July 18th, 1826, Mr. Douglas is directed to "proceed to Okanagan with [the horses] intended for New Caledonia"; and, under date March 27th, 1827, the Stuart Lake Journal says that "Mr. Douglas arrived in the afternoon from Alexandria, which place he left on the 19th." In the face of these two unpublished statements

1. "History of British Columbia," p. 135.
2. "History of the North-West," Vol. II., p. 488.

we fail to see how Douglas could have established Fort Connolly in 1826, especially as Bear Lake, in the midst of which it stood,[1] is a place difficult of access, which cannot well be reached from the south before July, and is situated at the very opposite extremity of the district from that where Alexandria stands, with a distance of over four hundred miles intervening.

Yet it is certain that the fort had been erected before 1827, as we see Connolly sending thither supplies and merchandise by dog trains as early as March 20th of that year. But then Charles Ross, not James Douglas, is mentioned as being in charge, as the following entry will show :

" *Tuesday*, March 25th, 1827.— . . . About midday two men cast up from Connolly's Lake with intelligence from Mr. Ross that he had got a considerable increase to the furs he had when he wrote Mr. Connolly last, and that he would be in want of several essential articles for his summer trade, which, though the season is advanced and much necessary work remains yet to be done, Mr. Connolly is determined to supply him with. It is certainly much to be regretted that Mr. Ross did not forward the news sooner ; for, not expecting such a demand and such an addition to the returns, Mr. Connolly had made no provision for it, and notwithstanding there are fifteen disposable men about this place, five only can be depended upon for any voyage ; two of that number are wanted to prepare wood for the canoes and raise bark, so that three only remain. As for the other ten, they are such drones that if any of them were sent, they would not be back for embarkation ; and then there is still the Babine furs to be brought here, a trip to McLeod's Lake, and Mr. McDonnell's voyage to the Upper Forks to be made."

1. The original Fort Connolly stood on an island.

We are drifting from Fort Connolly, and yet always concerned with the drudgery of life in New Caledonia. That post, therefore, was established in 1826 for the benefit of the northern Sekanais Indians who roam in the vicinity of the very Bear Lake whose identity had so much exercised Fraser's mind as he was on the point of starting on his first voyage of discovery.

The journal of the central fort has become to us so much the more precious as its earliest part has come down to us in the shape of unconnected fragments. This will be our excuse for reproducing the following passages, than which no words of ours could better illustrate the difficulties under which men and masters then labored in that isolated country.

Chief 'Kwah, our old acquaintance of the second chapter, who was not unknown to Harmon, as we have seen, is mentioned on almost every other page as "old Qua," together with the quantity and quality of the furs he brings in. One day he is shown us as making his appearance at the fort "with a most shabby hunt, consisting of only eleven beavers." What a good hunt that would be to-day, especially considering that the old man's expeditions were short and frequent! It was not considered so at that time, and "in consequence [he was] treated with the greatest indifference." Lo! the poor Indian, whose worth and claim to the dignity of manhood are measured by the number of animal skins he hands the white trader, who will perhaps make thereon a profit of 500 per cent.!

From the natives we pass to the servants of the "gentlemen." They do not fare much better. Witness this little incident :

"*Monday*, 31st March, 1827.— . . . René and Dubois arrived about midday with the furs brought by the latter as far as *Rivière au Maskeg*, where he was found by René in a state of extreme debility, originating in sickness and heightened by privations, having, since the 25th inst., had no other nourishment than that derived from a single dried salmon."

The old document now takes us back to Fort Connolly and initiates us into some of the cares weighing upon the administration of the district.

"*Friday*, 2nd November, 1827.—A further supply of ammunition, etc., was also packed for Connolly's Lake, to which post four or five men are to be sent for the winter, a step which the existing scarcity of provisions rendered indispensable, as it is only by proportioning the burden of each post to its means of subsistence that we will be enabled to escape the unsparing ravages of want."

Fraser Lake now comes in for a share of the chronicler's attention.

"*Monday*, 12th November, 1827.— . . . The best summer trade I have seen at Fraser's Lake ; but unfortunately a melancholy circumstance took place a few days ago just nigh the fort. The Grand Sauvage being encamped at a small lake with his family, three of the Simpson River Indians[1] came upon him at night and, in revenge of the murder of one of their relations, killed his wife and wounded his daughter and a child. The woman being a near relation of Yascho and the Sycuss[2] Indians, couriers had been sent with the intelligence, and Yascho was at the village when Williams passed, but Mr. McDonnell had not seen him. He was apprehensive he would be unable to prevail upon them to remain quiet, and should they determine on going immediately to revenge the death of their relation, it will inevitably ruin the fall hunts and the

1. The Skeena was originally called Simpson River by the Hudson's Bay Company's people.

2. Or Stony Creek.

returns will suffer, as that band are the principal beaver hunters of Fraser's Lake."

Who said that a Hudson's Bay Company man's intellectual vision was limited to a pack of furs?

The above occurrence—which, insignificant as it may appear, finds its place in a work like the present, whose aim is to reflect in its pages the particular manners of the times referred to—recalls to mind a massacre of innocent persons which then saddened another part of the district. A band of Sekanais had come to enjoy the hospitality of their Carrier friends at Pinche, on Lake Stuart. It happened that an Indian of that place, noted among his kindred for his innate disposition to buffoonery, blackened his face, as was customary with native " doctors," to impose on the credulity of the strangers, at whom he stared wildly as they were returning to their eastern mountains.

The party was headed by a chief who, owing to an accident caused by his own gun, was called *Pouce-coupé*, or Thumb-cut-off, by whites and reds alike. Unfortunately, as they were on their way back to their hunting grounds, one of the Sekanais died after a very short illness. Persuaded that his death was the work of the Pinche " medicine-man," the whole party retraced their steps, bent on revenge.

Arrived at the south end of Lake Rey, which is parallel to Lake Stuart, the Sekanais stealthily came upon a party of Carrier women, with a man, camped on an island. Falling on them unawares, they killed the women and wounded the man, who, feigning death, managed to escape on the ice ; then, running for dear life on the rugged surface of the ice, without any foot-gear or hardly any clothing, he was pursued by the whizzing of bullets and arrows, which he so dexterously avoided that thenceforth he was considered as possessed of no inconsiderable supernatural powers.   137

Whatever may be said of J. Douglas's connection with the establishment of Fort Connolly, one thing is certain. Early in 1828, or thereabouts, he married, Scotch fashion, the daughter of his superior at Stuart Lake, Nellie Connolly, a maiden of perhaps fifteen summers, who was to be known in after life as Lady Douglas. The youth's good fortune must have excited the secret envy of his less favored fellows. At twenty-five, with a comely wife and the brightest prospects based on his new connection, what more could he desire? And yet, as we shall see presently, that very year was to be the turning-point in his life, a year fraught with peril and pregnant with the most momentous consequences.

We must preface our explanations with a remark. Hardly five years had elapsed since J. M. Yale, then in charge of Fort George, having absented himself (1823) to pay a visit to Stuart Lake, had been stupefied to find, on his return home, the mangled bodies of his two workmen in one of the outhouses, alongside of one of their own axes, wherewith they had been done to death by two Fraser Lake Indians. For his apparent neglect, Yale [1] was visited with suspension from his charge and ordered to headquarters at Stuart Lake pending the verdict of the Council of the Company. There we momentarily saw him, in 1825, acting as third clerk to Mr. Connolly.

His conduct having been fully investigated and himself absolved from any blame, he was reinstated in his functions at Fort George. The next chapter will tell us the sequel to this affair.

1. After whom Fort Yale was to be called in after years.

CHAPTER IX.

An Episode and its Consequences.

1828–1830.

FOR almost forty years Sir James Douglas is the central figure in the history of British Columbia. He was a man of many attainments and of undoubted ability, a true leader, whose memory will ever live as that of the first successful Governor of that province. His bust, which adorns the façade of the magnificent Parliament buildings at Victoria, as well as the obelisk erected in his honor in front of the imposing pile, tell of the appreciative gratitude of the people of the Pacific Coast.

Yet there is certainly no presumption in assuming that not one in a thousand Canadians is aware of the fact that to the Indian Chief of Stuart Lake, a man whom the Hudson's Bay Company Journal of that period delights in belittling, James Douglas owed his life and, indirectly, his subsequent promotion to all the honors in the gift of the Company, as well as his nomination to the post of representative of Queen Victoria on the Pacific Coast. A word from "old Qua," that lowly native to whom he used to show the cold shoulder when his hunt had not been up to expectations, would have cut short his incipient career and sent his ghost to the present abode of his ancestors.

Dr. Bryce, in his " Remarkable History of the Hudson's Bay Company," relates the incident, partly after McLean, and manages to crowd so many inaccuracies into his record of the same and his references to New Caledonia in general, that we think it not irrelevant to enter into some details concerning that most fateful episode in Sir James's early life. We will begin by Dr. Bryce's version of the event:

" Douglas had as his headquarters Fort St. James, near the outlet of Stuart Lake, *i.e.*, just west of the summit of the Rocky Mountains," he writes on page 398. " He determined to enforce law and do away with the disorder which prevailed in the district. An Indian, who some time before had murdered one of the servants of the Hudson's Bay Company, had been allowed to go at large. Judgment being long deferred, the murderer thought himself likely to be unmolested, and visited Stuart Lake. Douglas, learning of his presence, with a weak garrison seized the criminal and visited vengeance on him. The Indians were incensed, but knowing that they had to deal with a doughty Douglas, employed stratagem in their reprisals. The old Chief came very humbly to the fort and, knocking at the gate, was given admittance. He talked the affair over with Douglas, and the matter seemed in a fair way to be settled when another knock was heard at the gate. The Chief stated that it was his brother who sought to be admitted. The gate was opened, when in rushed the whole of the Nisqually tribe. McLean vividly describes the scene which ensued:

" ' The men of the fort were overpowered ere they had time to stand on their defence. Douglas, however, seized a wall-piece that was mounted in the hall, and was about to discharge it on the crowd that was pouring in upon him, when the Chief seized him by the hands and held him fast. For an instant his life was in the utmost peril, surrounded by thirty or forty Indians, their knives drawn, and brandishing them over his head with frantic gestures, and calling out to the Chief, "Shall we strike? Shall we strike?"

" 'The Chief hesitated, and at this critical moment the interpreter's wife (daughter of an old trader, James Mc-Dougall) stepped forward, and by her presence of mind saved him and the establishment.

" 'Observing one of the inferior chiefs, who had always professed the greatest friendship for the whites, standing in the crowd, she addressed herself to him, exclaiming, "What, you a friend of the whites, and not say a word in their behalf at such a time like this! Speak! You know the murderer deserved to die. According to your own laws the deed was just. It was blood for blood. The white men are not dogs; they love their own kindred as well as you. Why should they not avenge their murder?"

" 'The moment the heroine's voice was heard the tumult subsided; her boldness struck the savages with awe. The chief she addressed, acting on her suggestion, interfered, and being seconded by the old Chief, who had no serious intention of injuring the whites, and was satisfied with showing them that they were fairly in his power, Douglas and his men were set at liberty; and an amicable conference having taken place, the Indians departed, much elated with the issue of their enterprise.' "

Now this is very pathetic and even smacks slightly of the drama; but the bare, cold facts are somewhat different, if we are to believe eye-witnesses—one of whom is still living near the writer—and the many Indians, children or contemporaries of eye-witnesses, who all agree in the following details.

For some reason, the nature of which cannot now be ascertained, two young men had killed two of the Company's servants, as we have seen at the end of the preceding chapter. One of them had already paid the penalty of his crime by being secretly slain by the Company's people, who had burned his remains in such a way as to suggest an accident as the cause of his death.[1] Several years elapsed when, in the summer of 1828, his survivor, Tzœlhnolle, hazarded a visit to the Stuart Lake Indians. These, however, he found to be absent to a man, and of the women-folk left in the camp only one is mentioned, who had but lately been delivered of a child. Mr. Connolly was likewise away, having gone down to Alexandria to take up the outfit for the following year, so that Mr. Douglas was left temporarily in charge of the place.

On being told of the presence of Tzœlhnolle, that gentleman immediately took with him a few of the fort men, armed with hoes and other garden implements, and made for the untenanted lodges of the Indians.

Apprised of his coming by the sick woman, Tzœlhnolle, who could easily have escaped by flight, stupidly chose to hide himself under a pile of skins and other household impedimenta, where he was found and brought to Douglas, who, seizing him by the hair, asked for his name. The now terrified young man answered that he was called Nœl.

"You lie!" exclaimed Douglas, who fired at him with his blunderbuss; but owing to the efforts of the youth to free himself from his grasp the ball went wide of the mark, whereupon, with hoes and the remnants of a camp-fire near by, his assistants stunned the Indian and reduced his lifeless body to the condition of a shapeless jelly. Then, by order of Douglas, they passed a stout rope around his neck and proceeded to drag him in the direction of the

1. Bancroft says that he had been killed by the Blackfeet ! How awkward of him to have gone hundreds of miles expressly to be killed by Indians of whom none of the Carriers even so much as knew the name!

fort. " The man he killed was eaten by the dogs ; by the dogs he must be eaten," declared the inexorable clerk.

Several days, perhaps some weeks, afterwards, 'Kwah returned with his followers. Tzœlhnolle's father also came from Fraser Lake. The Chief was indignant at the treatment meted out to the young man, who was a distant relative of his, and urged, no doubt, by the entreaties of his desolate father, he resolved to give a good lesson to the young clerk.

Followed by a large number of his people, he boldly went into the Indian hall, which at that time was also the trading-room, within the dwelling-house of Connolly and his clerks, and was greeted by Douglas, who, expecting trouble, had previously taken the precaution of having one of the little cannons mounted in the bastions brought into the hall. At the sight of the excited crowd he seized the wall-piece, but was immediately taken hold of by 'Kwah and others, who began to reproach him with his cruelty to his victim and demand compensation therefor.

Naturally, quite a commotion arose as a consequence. The fort employees came from all parts to their master's rescue, but soon realized their own powerlessness against such numbers of natives. One of them, however, had the presence of mind to go for the other cannon,[1] which was rudely snatched from him by the crowd, which Nancy Boucher, the interpreter's wife, managed to keep outside.

Meanwhile Douglas's young wife bravely came in from her sleeping apartments and took from Tzœlhnolle's father a dagger, which, however, she had soon to return to its owner. On the other hand, Tlœng, 'Kwah's nephew and presumptive heir, was pointing to Douglas's breast the Chief's own poniard, the same wherewith the latter had

---

1. These small pieces were mounted with a stout handle like a rocket.

fought the Naskhu'tins, and kept impatiently asking his uncle:

"Shall I strike? Shall I strike? Say the word and I stab him."

Which hearing, the women, screaming and crying, implored the Chief to have pity on the white man, promising all kinds of gifts if they spared his life. Nathadilhthœlh joined his advice to their entreaties and reminded his relative of the consideration with which he had so far been treated by the Company, and strongly counselled him not to allow any bloodshed. Then the two ladies, running upstairs, began to throw[1] in the midst of the crowd tobacco, handkerchiefs, pieces of attire, and other goods, which served for a time to divert the attention of the natives from the now fairly cowed Douglas. Then 'Kwah, who never had any real intention to kill the clerk, signified his acceptance of the gifts as a compensation for Tzœlhnolle's death, and bade his followers quietly return to their homes, as the "incident was closed."

The above is a careful digest of all the accounts of the affair by disinterested native and surviving Hudson's Bay Company parties, and the writer has no doubt as to its perfect correctness. Let us now return to Dr. Bryce's version of the same and scrutinize some of his statements.

In the first place, his misapprehension regarding the position of Stuart Lake is so much the more inexcusable, as a glance at any map of British Columbia would have shown him that that locality is not "just west of the summit of the Rocky Mountains." As a matter of fact, Fort St. James, on that body of water, lies almost two hundred miles west of the nearest peak within that range.

1. To throw to is, to a Carrier Indian, synonymous with to present, to give as a mark of deference; and the action of the ladies, by recalling the "potlatches" then in vogue, was well calculated to placate the invaders.

That Dr. Bryce is irretrievably mixed about the true location of his hero's residence is apparent from the fact that, two pages farther on, he speaks of the above incident as Douglas's adventure "in the Rocky Mountains," and again refers to his "stay in this part of the mountains."[1]

According to that writer, Douglas's motive in acting as he did was his wish to "enforce law." The reader knows by this time the real amount of legality there was in the execution of an untried individual, of whose identity he was not even sure. Indeed, so hasty and imprudent was his conduct in that connection that it eventually led to his recall from New Caledonia, where his life had become anything but secure. Hence, Dr. Bryce is hardly in order when he speaks of the "judgment having been deferred." As we already know, the Hudson's Bay Company in New Caledonia never held anything like a juridical trial.

As to the would-be stratagem resorted to by the Indians, none of the survivors or their immediate descendants ever heard of it. Such crookedness and premeditation are altogether repugnant to excited aborigines, even though they have to "deal with a doughty Douglas." We beg to assure the reverend gentleman that 'Kwah and his people were very little familiar with their intended victim's pedigree. To them he was but a poor young man in such straitened circumstances that he consented to attend to the most menial of occupations, fishing for a living, which they themselves left to their women.

But where the Winnipeg writer's remarks verge on the ludicrous is when he unhesitatingly declares that "the whole of the Nisqually tribe" rushed on to Douglas. We would like to know by what miracle of bilocation that tribe, whose habitat is in the State of Washington, over eight hundred miles to the south of Stuart Lake, should

1. p. 400.

145

J

have suddenly appeared at Fort St. James, even to oblige
'Kwah against the doughty Douglas. Evidently Bryce
might improve his geographical notions, or else he is very
careless in transcribing names.[1]

"This story has been harped in variations by almost as
many authors as have given us gunpowder plots." This is
from H. H. Bancroft,[2] who furnishes us himself with a
dramatized version of the incident, which he bases on
J. Tod, an excellent authority, to be sure, but one who was
at least eighty miles away at the time of its occurrence.
Moreover, we make bold to doubt whether that trader ever
went to the length of stating that one of the Fort George
murderers was killed by the Blackfeet. According to
Bancroft, Douglas, in search of the survivor, "found his eye
in close proximity to an arrow-point"; and yet he admits
that the Indian was hidden under "a pile of camp equi-
page," a rather uncomfortable position, we should say, to
bend his bow, the hard and powerful Carrier bow so much
dreaded by Mackenzie's men. Bancroft speaks of no
stratagem, but describes the fort gates as suddenly invaded
by two hundred savages with blackened faces, who finally
bind Douglas hand and foot and carry him away to the

---

1. His ethnographical notions concerning the aborigines he mentions are
hardly more satisfactory. He still speaks of the Indians north of the Crees as
the "Tinne," a misnomer to which the present writer has time and again
called attention in publications within the Doctor's reach. A page farther on
he states, that "to the Selish or Flatheads belong many of the tribes of the
Lower Fraser River, while the Shushwaps hold the country on the Columbia
and Okanagan Rivers" (p. 433). It is quite refreshing to learn that the
Shushwaps are distinct from the Selish. To be exact, Dr. Bryce should also
have stated that all, not many, of the tribes of the Lower Fraser (and many
more on Vancouver Island and the opposite mainland of the United States)
belong to the Selish group of aborigines. Again, we would like to know
what are that author's authorities for his statement that the Shushwaps'
habitat is "on the Columbia and Okanagan Rivers." (See Appendix C.)

2. "History of the North-West," Vol. II., p. 475.

mess room, where they lay him at full length upon the table. None of the Indians has heard of such an indignity as having been inflicted on the young clerk.

Even John McLean cannot be relied on when he relates that occurrence. He himself admits that its particulars were furnished him long after the event by Waccan, the interpreter; but at the time of the affray, J. B. Boucher, *dit* Waccan, was one hundred and forty miles away, on a "war expedition" to avenge the murder by the Babines of his half-brother,[1] Duncan Livingston. That half-breed, who had been from his youth a trusted servant of the Company, was then married to J. McDougall's daughter, and the fact that he was McLean's informant accounts for the heroic rôle that author attributes to [Waccan] the interpreter's wife, a rôle which was in reality played by Douglas's recently wedded spouse.[2]

After the humiliating experience above related, Mr. Douglas and his confederates of Fort St. James must have been in sad need of some restraining influence to keep them in the path of prudence and moderation while dealing with the Indians. This most providentially came to them in the shape of no less a personage than the Governor of the freshly reorganized Company, Mr. (afterwards Sir George) Simpson. That gentleman was himself but a young man so far as years go; but his official position and incumbent responsibilities, combined with his natural

1. McLean wrongly says "adopted brother."

2. Fearing for the legality of his marriage, Douglas was no sooner within reach of a clergyman than he sought to be re-married by a Rev. Mr. Beaver. At that early date the higher authorities of the Hudson's Bay Company had not as yet legislated on the subject; but in 1845 the Council held at Norway House on the 7th of June decreed (Resolution 85) that "in the absence of a clergyman, Chief Factors only solemnize marriages, and that no person be permitted to take a wife at any establishment without the sanction of the gentleman in charge of the district."

tact, made him a man of good counsel and worthy of his inferiors' deference.

Shortly after his accession to his high position, he decided upon a tour of inspection of the different posts retained after the amalgamation of the two companies, so as to be the better able to pass judgment on possible difficulties and proffer advice or take measures based on personal knowledge of the men and places. Starting on July 12th, 1828, from York Factory, on Hudson Bay, his party entered the Peace River region after the incredibly short time of a little over a month; yet he not only inspected most thoroughly all the forts lying along his route, but even had conferences with the natives and others to ascertain their needs and wishes and gratify them with an occasional bit of fatherly advice or even of discreet reprimand, as the case might be.

By the 17th of September, 1828, he was in sight of Lake Stuart. The Governor was a man of rare sense and penetration, who realized that to inferior minds externals and the paraphernalia of state are adjuncts conducive to an easier acquiescence in orders and direction.[1] Fort St. James was the emporium of New Caledonia, the capital of an immense district new to the Hudson's Bay Company. Therefore, it was resolved to impress its inhabitants, and especially the natives in its vicinity, with a sense of the importance of the new corporation through the honors paid its head.

1. At times he would even go further and resort to expedients which smacked somewhat of trickery, in order to enhance his prestige in the eyes of simple folk. Thus, in the course of his famous journey across the continent, he had a dog to the neck of which he had attached a diminutive music-box in such a way that, once started, its performance seemed to be due to the animal's throat. To this day Governor Simpson is remembered by the Carrier Indians as the "Great Chief whose dog sings," and none of them ever entertained the least doubt concerning the musical abilities of his dog.

As they neared the lake, which could be seen from a gentle elevation some distance back of the fort, they unfurled the British ensign, which was handed to the guide marching at the head of the procession. Then, preceded by the band, consisting of buglers and bagpipers, came the Governor on horseback, supported behind by Doctor Hamlyn and Chief Factor McDonald, also mounted ; twenty men packing burdens next formed the line ; then one horse loaded, and, lastly, Mr. McGillivray with his wife and family closed the rear.[1]

Arriving in view of the fort itself, the bugles sounded, a gun was fired, and the bagpipes struck up one of the favorite marches of the clans. Clerk Douglas, in the absence of his superior, now daily expected from Fort Alexandria, replied with cannon and musketry, after which he advanced in front of the fort to receive the distinguished visitor. After the mutual exchange of civilities, pipers and buglers entered the enclosure, and marching along the inside gallery contiguous to the palisade, paraded in full view of hundreds of wondering natives.

Two hours later a large canoe was sighted in the southwest, and amidst a renewal of military display, William Connolly returned to his post in company with a few employees. Next day the other canoes came up, bringing the outfits and the remainder of the fort's men, under the command of J. M. Yale.

In the face of all this pomp and apparent bravado, joined to the remarkable coincidence of the Chief Factor's return with his own party, the poor bewildered natives may well be excused for having supposed that the newcomers had no object in mind but to avenge the affront offered their Company in the person of Mr. Douglas.[2] The

1. "A Canoe Voyage from Hudson's Bay to Pacific," pp. 24-25.

2. The Governor's party consisted of at least thirty grown-up persons, and after Connolly's return the force disposable at the fort cannot have been less than sixty men.

invitation to a conference with the "Great Chief" was not calculated to dispel that impression. Yet it was accepted by the native population, and nobody had reason to regret his having yielded to the stranger's advances, since presents and friendly advice took the place of the violent scene the Indians had expected, and for which they had fully prepared themselves.

The chronicler of Simpson's doings and sayings during his journey—Archibald McDonald—says in his journal that "the chief that headed the party which entered the fort in the summer was pointed at with marked contempt, and it was only Mr. Douglas's intercession and forgiveness that saved him from further indignities," a not improper step on the part of the Governor and a generous conduct much to the honor of the young clerk, if truthfully recorded. We would, however, be more ready to give credence to either statement was not McDonald to add immediately after his mention of Mr. Simpson's superb contempt for the culprit, that "at the close of the harangue, the chief had a glass of rum, a little tobacco, and a shake of-the hand from the 'Great Chief'" [1]—a rather novel way of showing scorn, we should say. As to Mr. Douglas's magnanimous forgiveness, we shall see presently in what it consisted.

After the Governor's departure for the coast, the directing minds at Fort St. James seem to have been fretting more or less at the thought of the humiliàting part that gentleman and confederates had been forced to play in their encounter with 'Kwah and his people. Evidently they were bent on having the last word.

Even at that early date, and probably more then than ever, the recurrence of a New Year was the occasion of great gala at all the Hudson's Bay Company's posts in New

1. "Peace River," p. 28.

Caledonia. As the clock struck twelve at night, the servants would fire a volley with their muskets, and go in a body to pay their respects and offer their best wishes to the *bourgeois*, who would treat them to a good share of the cup that inebriates. In the forenoon it was the Indians' turn. Head chief and petty chiefs would lead their people to the fort, and, after a handshake with the presiding officer, the former would be presented with a whole suit of clothes and other commodities (in return wherefor they were expected to help the traders with their influence during the incoming year), while the others would receive minor gifts proportionate to the rank and dignity of the recipient. But the most appreciated of the favors conferred on that day was probably the share in the good Hudson's Bay Company's rum, which set everybody aglow, and eager for the dance which followed, when it did not occasion even more lively and less friendly scenes.

On New Year's Day, 1829, six months after the above-mentioned differences, the Company's authorities at Stuart Lake were extraordinarily generous in their distribution of spirits among the Indians, so much so that all the leading men in their midst got helplessly drunk, when, at a signal, all the women and such of the men as were not wanted were driven out of the fort, and the *engagés*, falling on the prostrate forms of the leaders, gave them such a drubbing as probably no Indian had ever received before. The head chief only was spared. It was felt that to touch 'Kwah would make matters altogether too disagreeable in the near future. His nephew Tlœng also managed somehow to crawl out of the lion's den.

The others were not a little surprised to find themselves bruised and swollen all over on regaining possession of their senses. Bad blood ensued, the natives became sullen, and it became evident that Douglas's life would be more secure on the banks of the Columbia than in the wilds of New Caledonia.

None of the authors who have mentioned the Douglas episode relate this finale. It is undoubtedly to this last incident that the mysterious remark refers that " there are other interesting circumstances connected with this affair," which the author found pencilled on the copy of McLean's book in the Parliamentary Library, at Victoria, British Columbia.

James Douglas managed to stay one year after the above recited occurrences. Then, " conformably to the orders of the Council,"[1] he bade farewell to Stuart Lake on the 30th of January, 1830,[2] leaving behind him his wife, with a sick infant daughter, who died on the 2nd of March of the same year. Two months later (5th May), Mrs. Douglas set out to join her husband, who in the course of five years was to rise to the coveted position of Chief Factor.

1. Fort St. James Journal.

2. All the authors have so far wrongly stated that he retired therefrom in 1828, and it may also be remarked that, although Alex. Begg seems to have been more or less acquainted with the Journal of Sir Geo. Simpson's voyage, to which he refers at the end of his " History of the North-West," he chronicles that event under the date 1822, instead of 1828 (*Ibid.*, Vol. II., p. 483).

CHAPTER X.

Connolly and Dease at Stuart Lake.

1829-32.

TO the outsider, one of the mysteries of the fur-trade is the voracious appetite of the Hudson's Bay Company for furs, such as manifested by its journals. The native hunters are no sooner back with their packs of pelts than, presto! they are hurried off to their hunting-grounds again. Should they wish to enjoy a little rest at home, the most opprobrious epithets— wretches, good-for-nothing scoundrels, lazy rascals, and the like—rain on their devoted heads from the pens of the chroniclers. Had there been a danger of the precious skins finding another destination than the warehouses of the Company, such eagerness would be intelligible ; but for years and years that corporation enjoyed the strictest monopoly within New Caledonia, and the uncontrollable avidity of its representatives there could have but one result : the utter extermination of the fur-bearing animals especially the beaver, towards which that region is now fast approaching. American aborigines are noted for their improvidence. Must we lay the same charge at the doors of the Hudson's Bay Company? A person not a fur-trader would be tempted to answer affirmatively.

Year in and year out, the Stuart Lake Journal is made up of the recital of the furs received from the natives. This is but natural. What to us seems extravagant is the desolation of the chroniclers when there remain hunters in their vicinity, and the loud exclamations of disappointment when a party's hunt has been a failure. Scorn and reproaches then seem the order of the day, just as jubilation and grateful encomiums attend the reception of the more successful trappers. Here is an example of the latter :

" 14th December, 1829.— . . . Chatlustas' little party brought in their hunts, which form collectively a very valuable and exceedingly respectable quantity of furs, consisting of eighty-two beaver skins, four otters, three marten, a cat [lynx], and a few [musk-] rats. The beaver is of the finest quality and very nicely dressed.

" The old man, who so far had been so lazy, having so highly distinguished himself by this display of energy, was in consequence treated with a becoming degree of civility and received a capot as a mark of Mr. Connolly's satisfaction. His son-in-law was gratified with a pair of cloth leggings, and his son with a breech-cloth. Then, to crown the whole, a quart of French rum was added for the general benefit, and with this they marched off in high glee."

This same avidity for furs at times prompted even little jealousies between the managers of the different posts, which at this late date we can afford to enjoy. At least one man has come down to us as a victim of that foible. His name was Alexander Fisher, and at the time of which we write he had just succeeded George McDougall in the charge of Alexandria. His neighbor in the south was Samuel Black, who was, some years later, to meet with a tragic death at the hands of his own Indians at Fort Kamloops.

Fisher was one of those men who seem weighed down with personal wrongs, real or imaginary, and who do not feel at ease unless they have somebody to fulminate against. Black, on the other hand, to judge from his private correspondence, must have been a good-natured man, who saw life through rose-colored glasses and had not a little sense of the ludicrous, as we infer from the following communication, which we are inclined to regard in the light of a satire on his correspondent's well-known foibles. He writes to Fisher on the 29th of October, 1832 :

" Lolo and three men leave this place to-day to make the usual round of the natives about the Canoe,[1] from thence across to North River, along Fraser River as far as the Canoe or thereabouts. Lolo has orders to trade all the salmon he can, and to send word to you to send for them for the use of your post.[2] He may trade about two thousand, *i.e.*, if the pass of fall salmon has been as abundant about Canoe as at Fountain, he may trade more ; but will send you some mark, besides the number of horses to be sent by you for the fish. Lolo may trade about the Canoe for the benefit of your post. . . .

" Lolo tells me of the many tricks wherewith you deceive the Indians, such as making holy water in wash handbasins, dressing up your cook to make him hold it, walking about the house with a whitewash brush in your hand with many mumblings and magical words, sprinkling the natives in said holy water, telling them that if they do not come to your place to dance and bring their furs with them this fall, they will be swallowed up like another Sodom into a fiery furnace or boiling caldron . . . thereby frightening the Indians from walking on God's earth and going about their usual occupations. However, as some of these poor devils may have resisted such an imposition on their understanding which you practise in order to get their furs, Lolo makes his usual tour among the natives belonging to this district,

1. Canoe Creek.

2. Two years before Fisher had himself asked for four thousand salmon from Black.

being instructed by no means or pretence whatever to interfere in any way or trade a single skin from any Indian that
has been accustomed to frequent your post. At the same
time he is to get information as to the truth of the reports
concerning your proceedings, and when he returns and
gives me the necessary proofs of so infamous tricks as afore-
said, I shall, for the remainder of the season, act accordingly
for the general interest of the Honorable Hudson's Bay
Company, not to get the Indians' furs for one year, but for
always, and in order to establish the respectability of the
Company . . . and make truth triumph against
jugglery, tricks and profanations of God's holy rites and
sacraments. . . ."

Fisher was prompt in his reply, of which we regret to
have but the first part before us. On the morrow of the
receipt of Black's letter he wrote from Alexandria :

" I have to acknowledge the receipt of your epistle of the
29th October on 6th November, per Lolo, your interpreter.
Under the mask or mantle of obliging me with salmon,
which you suppose is wanted for this post . . . you
direct your men and interpreter to continue to ruin the
trade of this district and run through the natives of this
establishment.

" In my letter of the 5th October I took the liberty to
request you to keep your men, women and children at your
own establishment or within its limits. A month thereafter,
day for day, your interpreter (Lolo) is again at the post or
fort of Alexandria, which amply bears me out in my statements that your threats of opposition have been put into
practice long ago and are still continued.

" There was no need of this salmon, as you knew well,
having sent a supply to me of 12 th. [12,000] prior to this
finesse of yours ; but I shall send for them, to save this
property from being lost to the Honorable Hudson's Bay

Company, Lolo having left them in the hands of the Indians. I regret to find myself situated as I am (your neighbor) ; for it is evident you wish to get me or yourself into trouble. I have with great caution avoided you. . . ."

Here Fisher's correspondence breaks off, and we feel we lose something by the disappearance of the sheet or sheets of paper containing his reply to Black's accusations of jugglery, etc., were it only the occasion of a good smile at the expense of the poor rapacious trader, who was in dead earnest, whatever may have been Black's real intentions or meaning.

Rapacious is a strong word, but Fisher's propensity for drawing unto himself by hook and crook undoubtedly warrants it. He was bent on appropriating the trade of others, though he was soon to complain again to headquarters at Stuart Lake of encroachments on his own territory, and though we shall see him vituperating a subordinate for appropriating one of his own men. Indeed, the Stuart Lake Journal for 1830 discreetly charges him with keeping by himself fifteen steel traps, instead of sending them up to headquarters, as directed by Mr. Connolly.

We have mentioned above George McDougall's departure from Alexandria. In 1827 he had accompanied the New Caledonia packet bound for the east through Tête Jaune Cache, then freshly discovered, which was to become famous in the annals of the Hudson's Bay Company west of the Rockies. From that time forth the Company was to send yearly two expeditions outside of the New Caledonia limits. One, composed of four or five canoes, which, with increasing prosperity and consequent wants, were soon to be discarded for as many boats, was despatched to Alexandria, there to meet the pack-trains, consisting of two hundred or two hundred and fifty horses from the Columbia, through Okanagan and Kamloops, loaded with the equipment of all the northern posts. The other party was sent east to Jasper House through Tête Jaune Cache, a route which in later years was abandoned for the Peace River Pass. The object of that expedition was to get a supply of leather, *i.e.*, dressed moose or cariboo skins, which, scarce in the west, Indians and *engagés* needed to make moccasins, bags, ropes, pieces of attire, etc.

The original Tête Jaune Cache, also called Leather Pass from the above mentioned circumstance, was at the first forks of the Fraser with the Rocky Mountains, at a place where an important branch comes from the north. A yellow-haired trapper (*tête jaune* being the French for yellow head) was responsible for its name, as that Indian, who was an Iroquois, used to cache or put up in a temporary store or shelter the furs he had procured in those mountain fastnesses. The scenery in the pass is "grand and striking beyond description. At the bottom of a narrow rocky gorge, whose sides were clothed with dark pines, or, higher still, with light green shrubs, the boiling, impetuous Fraser dashed along. On every side the snowy heads of mighty hills crowded round, whilst immediately behind us, a giant among giants and immeasurably supreme, rose Robson's Peak. This magnificent mountain is of conical form, glacier-clothed, and rugged."[1]

In the near vicinity of the pass roams a band of Shushwap Indians who, owing to the perfect seclusion of their quarters, were still, at a comparatively late date, destitute of most of the comforts of civilization. When Viscount Milton passed there in 1863 "they were clothed merely in a shirt and marmot robe, their legs and feet were naked, and their long black hair the only covering to their heads.

1. "The North-West Passage by Land," Viscount Milton and W. B. Cheadle, pp. 252-3.

Those Shushwaps of the Rocky Mountains inhabit the country in the neighborhood of Jasper's House, and so far as Tête Jaune Cache on the western slope."[1]

The route and distance of that pass, with which almost every Hudson's Bay Company employee within New Caledonia was for a long time so familiar, is best illustrated by a memorandum of Geo. McDougall's own trip, which lies before us :

"On the 18th of March, 1827," he writes, " I left Stuart Lake with a New Caledonia packet, to cross the Rocky Mountains by Tête Jaune Cache. From Stuart Lake I took five days to get to the Forks, or where Fort George now is. I remained there one day (say 23rd), writing and repairing sleds, etc. On the 24th we again started, proceeding up the Fraser River on the ice. The seventh day (March 30th), we got to Tête Jaune Cache, where we lost one day looking for Indians, to get provisions from them, but could not find them. On the 1st of April we left Tête Jaune Cache, but from having only temporary snowshoes, that could hardly support us on the snow, our guide, the Gauche, being so bad with . . . disease, could not keep up with us, which caused us frequently to lose our way, and owing to the quantity of snow, with the very soft weather we had when crossing the Portage, we only reached Jasper's House on the morning of the 18th of April, 1827."

Having taken a holiday hunting buffalo in the neighborhood of Fort Carlton, McDougall returned to Stuart Lake after the usual vicissitudes of a long journey. There he was sorry to find his brother James in a deplorable state of health, but felt some satisfaction in having brought him "his woman. She will be a good nurse for him," he

1. " The North-West Passage by Land," Viscount Milton and W. B. Cheadle, pp. 252-3.

wrote, after his return to Alexandria, where he was pleased to see that "hostilities had ceased between his own Carriers and the Chilcotins." But he had to remark that "sheer starvation had caused the death of many among our Alexandria Indians." [1]

This unfortunate state of affairs appears to have been chronic in that quarter, as we see from the following statements by Mr. Connolly, which add a little to our knowledge of the relations then existing between Black and Fisher.

"*Sunday*, 7th of November, 1830.— . . . I am sorry to learn that the fishery below has been so unproductive that the Indians had not been able to secure a sufficiency of provisions to meet their own wants, and that with much difficulty only 2,598 salmon have been obtained for the use of the men of the establishment. This quantity, added to the old stock, formed a total of 10,298 salmon ; but that number appears so insufficient to Mr. Fisher that he had sent to Kamloops for 4,000 more, which Mr. Black very kindly furnished him, although his own prospects of obtaining a stock adequate to the consummation of his post were by no means certain.

"In consequence of quarrels between the Indians who inhabit the banks of the Fraser River, called Atnahs [Shushwaps], and their neighbors farther down, the former entirely neglected their fisheries, and they are now all assembled at the rapid without possessing any means of subsisting. Such an assemblage of starved wretches so near the establishment gives us very just grounds of apprehension that they will fall upon our horses before the winter is over, but I hope that we will have the means of preventing them from carrying their depredations to any extent."

1. MS. letter, March 8th, 1828.

DOUBLY "CARRIERS."

Times were more cheerful at Stuart Lake. Would the reader like to learn how New Year's Day was spent there in 1830? It was kept not on the first but on the 14th of January, though the first of the month did not fall on Sunday. Might not the reason of that postponement have been that the whites at the fort were apprehensive of some kind of retaliation by the Indians on the anniversary of their own chastisement? What we know for certain is that the fort employees did not lose anything by having waited for their traditional holiday. Even the Journal man himself is naïvely proud of the good things that were spread at their mess. Let the reader rather judge for himself.

"14th of January, 1830.—This day was celebrated the return of the New Year, and nothing was heard but the sounds of mirth and jollity. Feasting, carousing, dancing and singing were the order of the day. The means of feasting were, all things considered, very ample, the men having received among them no less than fifteen dogs, thirty-four pounds of flour, one and a half quart of salt, and one pound of pepper. They were also gratified with the customary allowance of one pint of rum per man."

Ten days later other cares succeed, for the manager of the district, the carousals of New Year's Day. He becomes anxious about the fate of the new establishment at Chilcotin, which, on the 23rd of February, it is decided to abandon, a step which must have been countermanded at the last moment, as we see, some time after, the occupant of the place struggling against the ill-will of the natives.

Nearer home the Journal of the "capital" records the thousand and one little incidents whose aggregate forms what we call life. To-day it is Gagnon who is sent to burn some wood in order to make soap, which doing he allows the fire to spread, whereupon a general conflagration ensues in the woods behind the fort. On the morrow the blacksmith is shown us in the act of making an auger—not so bad for such a place. Next day, news of an alarming character is communicated by the Indians. The Mal-de-gorge—by which significant sobriquet is designated Nathadilhthœlh, the quondam youth who swam across Stuart River with a brother and a sister on his back—sends word that one of his people has fired at and seriously wounded one of several strange Indians who were skulking about their camp in the woods, an incident which causes the whole party to come home, to the great consternation of the authorities at the fort, who for some time endeavor vainly to coax the natives into returning to their hunting-grounds. Knowing that the deed will be avenged by the foreigners, probably now lurking in wait for their prey, nobody seems in a hurry to listen to the expostulations from the traders.

Then an event of a greater magnitude is recorded. It is the arrival, on the 12th of November, 1830, of Chief Factor Peter Warren Dease, who comes to succeed W. Connolly as manager of the whole district. But a few years before Dease was a Chief Trader, who conducted the material part of the Franklin Expedition from 1825 to 1827, and in the latter year he was in the far south in charge of the Flathead post. On the 13th of August, 1828, Gov. Simpson sent him, in the course of his famous journey overland, a Chief Factor's commission as a reward for his share in the above mentioned expedition.[1]

John McLean, who lived with him for a short time, says that he was one of the kindest and most considerate of men, a certificate of good character which is so much the

1. Dease had been made a Chief Trader in 1821. In his " Fur Hunters," Vol. II., p. 2, A. Ross mentions (under date 1823) an officer of that grade whom he calls *John* Warren Dease, though this can be no other than our new manager.

more precious, as the man who worded it was little accustomed to bestow such encomiums on H. B. C. people.

The change in the management of the district seems to have been so sudden and unexpected that we may not be much astray in supposing that Connolly's retirement was not altogether voluntary on his part. What may have been the reasons of his superiors in withdrawing, not to say dismissing, him from his post? It cannot be that they were dissatisfied with his management of the business interests confided to him, for never were these in so flourishing a condition. For this assertion we have the best of authorities, that of Governor Simpson himself. In a private letter addressed, in 1847, to one of Connolly's successors, the Governor writes that, in spite of the satisfactory state of affairs in New Caledonia, "there is still . . . much room for amendment to bring it up to the palmy days of Connolly, from which time it has been gradually declining."[1]

On the other hand, that gentleman never hints in his journal, which is quite detailed and full of notes of a personal nature, at any reason for being dissatisfied with his post until he suddenly chronicles the fact that Mr. Chief Factor Dease, who "has been appointed to New Caledonia," is to arrive on the morrow. We can suggest but one explanation. The part Connolly had taken in avenging, on New Year's Day, 1829, the affront offered his son-in-law, had come to the ears of the Governor and Council, who must have also learned of the restlessness it had caused among the natives. The time necessary to receive the intelligence of the true state of affairs and take the proper measures in consequence thereof had just

---

1. MS. letter from Norway House to D. Manson, July 1st. Simpson admits that " this decline in the returns is due chiefly to the gradual exhaustion of the country," a statement which fully bears us out in our initial remarks.

elapsed when Dease made his appearance at Fort St. James, unheralded by anybody but himself[1] only one day before his arrival.

That this is not a wild conjecture is shown by the fact that the resentment of the Stuart Lake Indians was known far and wide, and Francis Ermatinger, writing from Kamloops to J. McLeod at Norway House, the headquarters of the Company in America, had but lately said: "From New Caledonia we have had no communication through the winter, owing perhaps to the natives being still irreconciled to the death of the two murderers killed there in summer."[2]

Be this as it may, W. Connolly stayed a few months more at Fort St. James, apparently to familiarize his successor with the routine of his new position. In July, 1831, he was gone, never again to return. He seems to have been a most painstaking man, bent on succeeding by any means, fair or foul, in his search after pelts. He was certainly not sparing of intoxicants to the native trappers whenever luck had favored them.

Dease and Connolly probably went down together, the one to take up the outfit for the new fiscal year, and the other on his way to more civilized quarters. Thomas Dears, a senior clerk, had been left momentarily in charge of the district. In the account he sends his new superior of what had transpired at headquarters since his departure, Dears first mentions a great feast given by Chief 'Kwah, to witness which numerous Indians had gathered from all parts. For the sake of personal security he had kept all his men in the fort, and though he speaks of the whole affair as having passed off quietly, he is obliged to add, as a reminder of the danger of such gatherings:

1. Through a letter he wrote Connolly.
2. MS. letter, dated March 14th, 1829.

"On the Indians of Fond du Lac embarking . . . old Qua abruptly left his lodge with his bow and arrows. The Indians of Fond du Lac seeing him sally forth, they immediately put themselves on the defensive. At this moment a quarrel commenced in the fort between a Siccane and another Indian. They put a stop to the former quarrel, and by a little persuasion on our part, and as they did not seem very keen for battle, harmony was restored."[1]

Another particular which seems to have made more impression on the mind of Dease's lieutenant at Stuart Lake is the danger of a possible competition in the fur-trade from an unexpected quarter, as evidenced by the goods brought back by his Indians from a feast at the 'Upper Forks."

"It is reported by the Indians," he adds, "that they can get blankets at one beaver the point, shirts one, guns four, and so on. . . . From the assortment of articles, I think they must have seen Europeans frequently, that is to say, those of the Coast. Probably some vessel has remained some time among them. Anethlash, an Indian chief of the Coast, who was present at the Upper Forks' feast, told Yosecha's party that he intended paying them a visit with property for sale, and wished them to keep a few beavers on hand."

Then, to his evident chagrin, he has to remark that some of the Fraser Lake Indians have already gone there to trade. Reverting to happenings nearer home, he says that a party of six Babines had come to the portage between their lake and Lake Stuart to kill some of the Indians there. But he had been informed that, after stabbing a young man, they let themselves be appeased by the presents offered them, upon which happy termination Dears somewhat naïvely comments: "On hearing this

1. MS. letter, July, 1831.

it gave me satisfaction, for had they succeeded in their horrid intentions it would have prevented many from hunting."

A month later, August 16th, Dears speaks of an epidemic breaking out among 'Kwah's recent guests, and hints at further difficulties in other quarters.

"Mr. Roussain," he writes, "in his official letter to me (which I enclose for your perusal) says that Whoenke wishes to kill Wastiyaps. This I am of opinion that gentleman must have learnt from Whoenke's enemies, and from the information I have had and the general opinion here, I think he has not a few, and I presume it is only a report started by them to create a variance between the whites and him."[1]

That same month, from a very different quarter, came a bit of information which illustrates one of the minor difficulties against which the traders had to contend. The Sekanais of Finlay River had complained to William Todd, then stationed at Fort McLeod, that so far they had been supplied with an entirely inadequate quantity of ammunition, which at that time was given free ; but the fact soon became apparent that what had been sent them of that article the previous fall would have lasted throughout the winter had they not been so imprudent as to gamble it away with a party of Indians they met at the Rocky Mountain Portage. To them "they lost not only every load of powder, but likewise every other article of use with which they had been previously furnished, which was the cause of their suffering much in the course of the winter."[2]

1. Roussain was a Canadian then in charge of Fort Babine, who wrote, in a beautiful hand, excellent French, disfigured by unbecoming misspellings. In that connection we may state here that all the Hudson's Bay Company officers of that time were as much familiar with French as with English.

2. MS. letter from W. Todd to P. W. Dease, August 28th, 1831.

This same clerk, Thomas Dears, was, on Mr. Dease's return, entrusted with the charge of Fort Connolly, a change he does not seem to have relished overmuch, though he was more than pleased with the Sekanais who traded with him. But in such an isolated place in the far north, where he had six feet of snow at his very door, he thought a person was entitled to a remuneration commensurate with the inconveniences under which he labored. So, in a letter to Dease,[1] he remarked that if his salary was not increased to £100 he would leave the country in the autumn of 1833. His threat does not seem to have had the result anticipated, for this is about the last we hear of him in the mass of correspondence before us.

Another departure (this time probably a dismissal) was soon to leave a second place vacant at the opposite extremity of the district. The horses used in packing the outfits from the Columbia River to Alexandria were generally left to winter at the latter place, though some were at times sent to Fort Kamloops, where the cold was not so severe nor the snow so deep. Others passed the winter at Fraser Lake, and as early in the season as February (1832) several had already died of disease or of accident. In announcing this to his superior at Stuart Lake, their keeper, a certain D. McKenzie, tried to console him with the remark that "my philosophy teaches me to believe that there is a fate in these casualties, and all good Calvinists give belief to predestination."[2] One would hardly have expected to find a fur-trader talking theology in the wilds of New Caledonia. It seems, however, that his principles did not appear quite sound to his employers, who made haste to send him away to familiarize himself with other schools of thought.

1. February 5th, 1832.
2. MS. letter to P. W. Dease, February 20th, 1832.

Meanwhile, in the south Black's friend, Alexander Fisher, was constantly pondering over people's encroachments on his rights, and importuning Dease to such an extent with his recriminations that the latter assigned to him a band of Indians whose hunting-grounds were intermediate between Alexandria and Kamloops, a decision of which Fisher triumphantly notified Black by a letter dated September 14th, 1832.

A year later a clerk of many years' standing in the service came from the east, who was, after a brief stay in the country, to embody his impressions and give vent to his grievances in a book on the twenty-five years he had worked for the Hudson's Bay Company. John McLean is, among the Company's people, the only author who has ever written, from a personal knowledge, about New Caledonia.[1] As regards veracity, impartiality, keenness of mind in observing and sureness of judgment, John McLean is vastly inferior to Harmon, who, having no grudge against anybody, was not exposed to see his statements warped by the influence of personal feeling.

We will permit ourselves to quote but one instance of McLean's unreliability. Contrasting the Carriers' religious notions with those of the Ojibways, he says: " The Tekelly [he means the Carrier] says: ' The toad hears me!' "[2] for an oath ; while those Indians' sole formula in such cases was, in McLean's time, " The Being-on-high hears me." He asserts that they have no idea of a soul, no words to express the name of the Deity, of the spirit, or of the soul.[3] Yet from time immemorial they have called

---

1. We do not mention Chief Factor A. McDonald's " Peace River," which is merely the journal of Governor Simpson's voyage, nor Harmon's book, because its author was a North-West Company man. (See Appendix D.)

2. " Notes of a Twenty-five Years' Service in the Hudson's Bay Territory," Vol. II., p. 265.

3. *Ibid., ibid.*

the Deity *Yuttoere*, a spirit *ni*, and as for the idea of the soul, they have no less than three words to express it, according to the standpoint of the speaker, who may consider it as animating the body, as hovering about and thus presaging death, or as separated from the body in after life. Had McLean so many terms at his command to render a single idea?

McLean arrived at Stuart Lake in the fall of 1833. He soon had a reminder of the insecurity of life in the far west in the shape of trouble, which he says arose out of the drowning of seven or eight Indians on their way to Alexandria; but so involved is his account of the consequences of the accident that it is next to impossible to locate the disturbance which ensued. Both Stuart Lake and Fort Alexandria are mentioned, and after one has read our author, the impression left on the mind is that it occurred in neither of those places.

Of the returns which Dease took down to Fort Vancouver in the summer of 1834, McLean writes that they "might be valued at £11,000. The outfit, together with the servants' wages and incidental expenses, amounted to about £3,000, leaving the Company a clear profit of £8,000," which was probably correct enough, though the animus of the whole book seems to be more or less that of a philippic against the Hudson's Bay Company.

During Dease's absence the mantle of authority fell on his shoulders, and he improves his opportunity to decry the management of the post as regards the fare, which he declares, with every appearance of truth, was "scarcely fit for dogs."[1]

In the course of that summer (1834) a native, who had sometimes acted as interpreter, died after a few hours of agony, resulting from his having been caught in a bear-

1. "Notes of a Twenty-five Years' Service in the Hudson's Bay Territory," Vol. II., p. 250.

trap he had made, and which he was so imprudent as to test himself. His body was the first to be interred among the Carriers, and for that change of method in disposing of the dead we must credit the Company's people, who introduced it in pity to the unfortunate widows, who were exposed to the cruellest tortures at the burning of the body.

The year 1834 put an end to Peter Warren Dease's stay at Stuart Lake. Between 1837 and 1839 he was engaged, together with Thomas Simpson, a young relative of the governor, in the Arctic exploration, for which he was offered a knighthood, which he declined. Then, according to Malcolm McLeod,[1] the Imperial Government tendered him a pension of a hundred pounds sterling, and on his retirement from the Hudson's Bay Company he settled (in 1842) in the vicinity of Montreal.

As to William Connolly, who so abruptly left Stuart Lake in 1831, in spite of his successful labors on behalf of his employers, he was not destined to meet with so much good fortune. Yet the last echo of his after life which has come down to us has a somewhat joyous ring about it. "Mr. Connolly does not write me," we read in a letter from Chief Factor A. McDonald to John McLeod, "but I believe that, so far from his being in a dying state last spring, he was about taking to himself a better half . . . . at Tadousac."[2] He was still living in the course of 1848, since in a private letter from Sir George to the gentleman then in command of Fort St. James we read : "Connolly will scarcely believe that it is possible to collect so many furs in one season in his old and favorite district."[3] Finally he settled at Montreal, and at one time was even elected mayor of that city.

1. "Peace River," etc., "Notes," p. 76.
2. MS. letter, dated February 20th, 1833.
3. MS. letter, June 24th, 1848.

CHAPTER XI.

Peter Skene Ogden Takes Charge of the Country.

1834.

IN the course of 1834 arrived at Stuart Lake a man who for many years was to exercise a potent influence over the whole country. This was Peter Skene Ogden.[1]

The man who was to cut such a prominent figure in the annals of New Caledonia was a son of Chief Justice Isaac Ogden, of Montreal, and was descended from an old and honorable Scotch family. Though he was ever reticent about his age, one can safely assert that he was born in 1794. From the characteristics he evinced at a time when his natural abilities had won him an enviable place in the Hudson's Bay Company, it may be gathered that his youth was not passed without storms or, at least, incidents of a more or less innocent complexion.

At seventeen he entered the service of the North-West Company, where he, no doubt, expected to find the adventurous scenes in harmony with his own restless temperament. The Utah and Shoshone countries had the first-fruits of his labors as a fur-trader, and California received also

1. The Skenes belong to an old family, which owes its name to an incident which is said to have happened as far back as 1010. As Malcom II. was returning from the defeat of the Danes, he was saved from a ravenous wolf by a youth, who killed it with his dagger. Hence the name Skene, a modern derivation of the original *Sgian*, which means dagger. Some authors, and even Ogden's own clerks, spelt it Skeen.

occasional visits from him. As early as 1820 a manuscript
memoir by John McLeod speaks of him as of a man
already vested with some authority in the service of his
corporation. Four years later he was at Flathead Post,
in the Snake District, where he stayed until 1831. In
April of that year a party of experienced traders was
despatched to the North Pacific Coast, somewhere near the
mouth of the Naas River, to divert into the direction of
the Canadian concern a share of the fur-trade, which so
far had been mostly in the hands of the Russians. While
Captain Simpson was operating by water, Ogden had
charge of the land party. The expedition was a success
in so far as the reception it received was concerned ; but
owing to the high prices a keen competition forced
them to pay, they lost £1,600 on the 3,000 odd skins
they got.

In 1834 P. S. Ogden was sent to the capital of New
Caledonia, where he was to give the full measure of his
administrative abilities. At the same time a Chief Factorship put on his efforts the seal of his superiors' official
approval. He had been a Chief Trader since 1821.

P. S. Ogden was of middle stature, and has remained
famous among the Carriers for his great obesity. Indeed,
when he first appeared in their midst, the old men could
not help recalling Na'kwœl, who forms the subject of
our first chapter, and they maintained that the newcomer must be a reincarnation of their own patriarch.
Lively and yet dignified with his subordinates, imperious
though kind-hearted, he was generous while remaining a
vigilant guardian of his corporation's interests. On the
other hand, it may as well be confessed that he was subject,
like most men of his time and position, to those human
weaknesses to which all lack of social restraint exposed
him. Yet he was fairly faithful to a native woman he had

PETER SKENE OGDEN.

(From an oil painting.)

taken unto himself (and perhaps married) before he was promoted to his new dignity.

In private life, and especially with his friends, one of his chief characteristics was his inveterate penchant for tricks and good-natured malice. Even in his later years, when stationed on the Columbia, nothing would delight him so much as to befool those he cared for. Was a passing missionary, for instance, to warn him that he was in dead earnest and must absolutely leave by the next boat? Ogden would promise that his wishes would be complied with ; but in the meantime he would see to it that boat and crew were noiselessly off an hour or so before the appointed time. The poor Father had to put up as best he could with the old man's huge satisfaction at contemplating his guest's look of disappointment, and stay a fortnight longer under the Company's roof.

Sometimes, however, he found his peer among his intended victims. Witness a certain Father Chirouse, who is reported to have more than once outwitted him. Father Chirouse was a wily old soul, who was one day shopping with a little servant in Ogden's store while the manager was momentarily called away. The missionary coveted some rather expensive articles which the size of his purse did not allow him to purchase. Nothing daunted by the smallness of his means, he boldly ordered the boy to put up the goods into parcels, which he left in a conspicuous place.

After he had taken leave of his friend, his parcels were noticed on the counter by Ogden, who, recalling his tricky client :

" Just like you, Father Chirouse," he shouted ; "look at the parcels you forgot."

" I beg your pardon, Mr. Ogden, I took all my things away."

" I tell you you did not."

173

" Excuse me, but really—"

" No excuse; you are absent-minded, as usual. Take your parcels away."

" Really, I am sure they are not mine."

" They are, I tell you," insisted the imperious old man, who was bound to have the last word.

" Do you mean to say that—"

" I mean that I want you to take your things away."

" But—"

" Take them, I say, and if they are not yours—"

" They are not."

" Well, then, I give them to you."

This was all the wily missionary wanted. Without further ado he pocketed the goods he had not paid for, and the trickster was tricked.

Chief Factor Ogden was above all a fur-trader, and, though he must be credited with the honor of having practically introduced farming into the district, he felt very little sympathy for any other branch of business, and he had absolutely no patience with pursuits the object of which could not be counted in skins or pounds sterling. He had hardly been five years at his new post when, the interests of his charge having taken him on a visit to Vancouver, he thus summarized the news in a letter to John McLeod:

" Our profits will exceed ten thousand pounds. . . . Among the many good things their Honors from Fenchurch Street sent us last summer was a clergyman—and with him his wife—the Rev. Mr. Beaver, a very appropriate name for the fur-trade. . . . But this is not all. There are also five more gentlemen, as follows: two in quest of flowers, two killing all the birds in the Columbia, and one after rocks and stones. All these bucks come with letters from the President of the United States, and you know it would not be good policy not to treat them politely. They are a perfect nuisance."[1]

Another piece of news contained in the same epistle was that David Douglas had fallen into a bull pit and been gored to death. David Douglas was the botanist after whom the Douglas fir is now called. We have also, for the first time, the mention of a name which will occur frequently under our pen in the following chapters. "A young man," writes Ogden, "a young man, by name Maclean—his father was killed in Red River—is in the Snake country." This single line gives us a clue to the innate dispositions of the future New Caledonian. His father had died a violent death; he was himself to meet with a similar fate, and most of his children were to die on the gallows—a doomed family, indeed, and their end goes a long way to determine the nature of their acts.

But for the present we are concerned only with P. S. Ogden and his new field of action.

At the time when that gentleman assumed the command of New Caledonia, that country counted eight forts—St. James, on Lake Stuart; Babine, Fraser, and McLeod on the lakes of the same names; George and Alexandria on the Fraser, and Chilcotin in the valley of the Chilco River, to which was soon to be added Fort Thompson, as the embryo of what is now Kamloops was then called.

Fort McLeod, having no natural resources of its own, had to be entirely supplied with provisions, whereby we mean dried salmon, which was then, and remained until a very late date, the staple food of the Company's employees. In return therefor, the Sekanais trading at that post dressed not a few moose and cariboo skins, which they sold out to the man in charge of the fort, who in turn sent them to headquarters, Stuart Lake, though the main supply of

1. MS. letter, dated February 25th, 1837.

leather had to come from across the mountains. An idea of the hardships which attended the journeys to Forts Dunvegan or Jasper, where, as we have seen, the leather expeditions annually repaired, can be gathered from the fact that each member of the caravan was sometimes provided with eight pairs of mocassins, while the man in charge of the party received an additional supply of a score of the same to be used in case of an emergency.[1] All of these were intended for use during the trip.

Fort Alexandria was the northern terminus of the land route yearly followed by the Company's pack-trains, bringing from the south the equipments of the various New Caledonia posts. The task of the animals used for that important work was a most arduous one, and the letters of the managers of Alexandria are replete with references to the large number of horses which died on the way or at their winter-quarters, occurrences of which the authorities at Fort Vancouver, on the Columbia, professed at times to be unable to account for.

Fort Babine was famous for the quantity of salmon it yielded. From the point of view of a trader it was a place of but secondary importance, many of the Indians there taking their pelts to the Skeena River for barter with the native adventurers from the Coast. Another article which was derived from that post was a sort of putrid salmon grease, to smell which is nowadays sufficient to disgust any civilized nostril. Yet in those days it was relished by aborigines and Hudson's Bay Company servants alike. Owing to the usual abundance of salmon at Babine, the sleigh dogs of the Stuart Lake establishment were also generally sent to pass the summer there.

As to Fort St. James, it was, of course, the great emporium where converged every product of the country. Thence

1. MS. letter from J. Boucher to P. Fraser, August 29th, 1847.

these were distributed among the different posts by the officer in command of the district. This gentleman was shown every mark of respect ; his word was law throughout New Caledonia, and he was assisted by a corps of clerks and a large retinue of servants, who were kept for a double purpose ; they were intended as a body-guard and a sort of local militia in case of trouble with the natives, and at the same time they were expected to do all the menial work for which they had been hired—work of a cook, of a farm laborer, a boatman, a fisherman, a blacksmith, etc.

These, in case of a scarcity of provisions—a circumstance of rather frequent occurrence—were shifted from place to place, according to the economical conditions prevailing at the different posts. The danger of starvation was not unknown in New Caledonia, nor was it restricted to that district or to P. S. Ogden's time. As late as 1855 that gentleman's son, writing of a trip made in quest of leather to the Peace River forts, says : " The district was in a starving state, people being obliged to eat dogs and horses which died from bad treatment. It was with the greatest difficulty that I succeeded in getting back with my party, for when I reached Dunvegan there was not an ounce of provisions in the fort, and my men were obliged to go to bed supperless. Our sinews for the district were all eaten by the Dunvegan men previous to my reaching there."[1]

In the course of 1836 the following was the expenditure of provisions in the different posts under P. S. Ogden's jurisdiction : 67,510 salmon ; 11,941 of the smaller fish, plus 781 sturgeon and 346 trout ; 2,160 rabbits ; 153 ducks, 10 lynxes, 8 marmots, 3 porcupines, 1 swan, and . . . 14 dogs. Horseflesh, though not mentioned in 1836, was nevertheless recognized as an article of diet, and in the Company's book a column is reserved thereto. It

1. MS. letter to D. Manson, September 2nd, 1855.

was not until 1845 that the General Council forbade its use on the employees' tables.[1]

Fort Connolly, being situated within the territory of the Sekanais Indians, who live almost exclusively on venison, consumed in that same year 450 pounds of fresh meat, while the only other post which enjoyed a like luxury was Fort St. James, which is credited with an expenditure of thirty-two pounds of that article in one year among over thirty mouths.

With the exception of potatoes, of which a small quantity was grown near each post, especially at Fort Fraser, all food of a farinaceous nature, such as flour, rice, and beans, as well as bacon, tea, and sugar, was unknown to the servants of the Company then and for many years after Ogden's time, though the gentlemen (that is, the officers and clerks) were as well provided with these items as the extreme difficulties of the communications would allow. Even such luxuries as Madeira and port wines, together with an assortment of liquors, appeared at the mess of the latter.[2]

Dried salmon and cold water took the place of all this in the servants' quarters, and used to hardships as these generally were, more than once their stomachs proved rebellious against a regime of so primitive a character. This even led sometimes to serious consequences, as we see from a passage from a letter by D. E. Cameron, of Fort Babine : " Poor Couturier expired on the night of the 4th inst.," he writes. " He began to fall off and waste away ever since my return, from the effect, I firmly believe, which salmon has on some constitutions, as in the cases of J. B. Desmarais and Thibeault last year."[3]

1. Resolution 78.

2. In 1836 the allowance of spirits for the district was twenty-three gallons of Madeira, as many of port, and 12⅛ gallons of brandy.

3. To D. Manson, March 6th, 1845.

No wonder, then, if there was a general tendency to retire from the service after one's time had expired, and if some of the employees had not even the patience to wait so long, but deserted. If captured, they were as a rule mulcted in a fine of two pounds sterling (a sum which was then divided among those who had been instrumental in apprehending them), unless the local officers preferred to administer them a good flogging, as invariably happened in cases of larceny and other petty misdemeanors.

Such desertions were always reprehensible, and at times they greatly embarrassed those in charge of forts. "The scamp Martin, whom I had engaged to carry out this letter and the accounts, has gambled off all his clothing, and will not now come near the fort," writes McLean from Alexandria, "and I am obliged to postpone sending them till I can procure another courier."[1] Hence the harshness of the measures sometimes adopted, and the threats of even severer ones occasionally resorted to, as when it was reported through the district that a deserter, Jos. Jacques by name, was going to be sent, hands and feet in irons, to far-off Montreal, to serve as an example to the other servants.

In the course of 1836 thirty *engagés* went out of New Caledonia, as against twenty-six who came in. Most of these were French Canadians, half-breeds, or Iroquois. In every case they were duly hired by the signing of a legal paper in French, and then sent from Norway House to the district through Tête Jaune Cache, where they were met by a party of New Caledonians from Fort George.

The *engagés* were mostly single men, many of whom, once in the country, contracted unions, open or secret, with native women; but there were times when a man left a wife in the East and his prolonged absence too often had a demoralizing·effect, as when the wife of a native did not

1. To the same, January 4th, 1855.

hesitate to form a *liaison*, as Gov. Simpson delicately puts it, referring to an Iroquois who would not stay in the service unless his lawful wife was brought him from Canada.[1]

From all accounts there must have been, in P. S. Ogden's time, some thirty such men employed at Stuart Lake alone. To them, as to the Indians around and the subordinate officers in charge of the lesser posts, he was the embodiment of authority. He felt it himself, and acted accordingly. In contentious cases he was a judge and an arbiter, and his decisions were generally on the side of justice, even though the corporation he represented had to suffer thereby. Larance, one of his employees, had used a canoe without the permission of its native owner. " It would be as well," he writes immediately, "to make inquiries, so that the Indians may be paid for the same."[2]

Though at times rather brusque, he was on the whole considerate towards his subalterns, and feeling the weight of his responsibility, he more than once insisted on prudence when dealing with obstreperous aborigines. "The desertion of the men at the fort when in danger of being attacked," he wrote to Chief Traders Todd and Manson, "is a most convincing proof of the little reliance which is to be placed on them, and should be a warning to all that in our dealings with the natives great care and every precaution should be taken to avoid coming to acts of violence. From the latter we have nothing to gain ; on the contrary, everything to lose."[3]

He was impartial, and did not hesitate to lay the blame on his own men when they did not treat the Indians fairly, and he adds, in the course of the same circular : " It is

1. MS. letter from Red River settlement to D. Manson, June 15th, 1844.

2. MS. letter to J. McIntosh, October 20th, 1837.

3. October 22nd, 1845.

evident to me that to the dastardly conduct of Mr. McB. is to be attributed the violent conduct of the natives."

This same impartiality impels him to visit murder with terrible vengeance. The tragic end of his friend, Chief Factor Black, of Fort Thompson, who is not unknown to our readers,[1] fills him with horror, and he takes occasion of the event to recommend anew the greatest caution and prudence to his subordinate officers. " No particulars regarding this horrid murder have yet reached me," he writes immediately, " but still sufficient to call on me to warn you, gentlemen, how cautious and how guarded we ought to be on all occasions with Indians, and this most melancholy event, independently of long experience, teaches us never to place any trust or confidence in them. We are well aware that in this country our lives are constantly exposed, and in regulating our treatment of Indians neither too much severity nor leniency will answer ; but a medium between both is the most advisable."[2]

With this concern for his men's welfare and safety we might perhaps contrast the conduct of a contemporary with whom we are already well acquainted—we mean Chief Trader Alex. Fisher. That gentleman, who was then fifty-three years of age, was in command at Alexandria, and, though under Ogden's jurisdiction, exercised some kind of authority over Fort Chilcotin, which was then in the hands of a young half-breed called John McIntosh. Owing to the turbulent, and at times violent, disposition of the natives the latter had to trade with, his position was fraught with peril, a fact of which the older man, safe in his post among friendly aborigines, does not seem to have been fully aware, or, if he was, his conduct towards

1. Black fell at Kamloops, shot, in 1841, by the nephew of the Shushwap Chief whose death he thus sought, Indian fashion, to avenge.

2. Circular to the officers of the district.

McIntosh lays him open to the charge of unbecoming selfishness. In a very prolix communication, he wrote, under date of 11th June, 1837:

"Your letter of the 9th inst., in answer to mine of the 6th June by the Indian paid to carry an express to you purposely to obtain my man Chartier from you, I received yesterday evening, and I must confess that I do not find in that letter a single reason or the least necessity for detaining a man who is not attached to your own establishment and deprive me of his services when most wanted, much less to occasion you to break your word and not comply with my orders. . . . One moment's reflection would have told you that surely your story of the bull, the cow, the calf, the poisonous roots, the drowning of an Indian, the intention to murder a white man for the sake of revenge, etc., had nothing to do with the detention of my man. . . ."

Anybody, however so little acquainted with the psychic conformation of the native mind, would have been of a different opinion. In case of an accidental death among their kin, the first move of the Indians is to soothe their wounded feelings by seeking the death of others, especially of strangers. Hence McIntosh's position was certainly very precarious, and in that light it is hard to understand the following from Fisher:

"I should be very sorry that the Company should lose any of its servants for the sake of a pack of paltry small furs that you are not sure to get, and put such a valuable district in difficulties when there is not the least necessity to do so; for if the report is a true one, that the natives intend to kill Baptiste [Lapierre] when he returns to Tluzkuz, the reinforcement of my man Chartier is nothing to contend against a camp of Indians. . . ."

Then, to show the enormity of his correspondent's fault,

Fisher enters into an enumeration of the various jobs to do at Alexandria.

"Chartier could have worked at the buildings," he continues, "for in a short time hence there will be plenty of other things to attend to, weeding and hoeing potatoes, twenty bags of flour to grind, salmon fishing weirs to attend to, pickets of the fort to cut, hay to make, etc. . . . The idea of your breaking through the rules and regulations and not complying with my orders to you, exposing your men perhaps to be butchered by the natives without even asking my advice on the subject! . . . The whole is ill-becoming of you."

Despite this eloquent philippic, fear for his personal safety, and the instinctive tendency to self-preservation innate in every living being, seem to have been stronger in McIntosh than even the sense of that unquestioning obedience which was inculcated in every employee of the Company ; for we see him pleading against the compliance with orders, something quite unusual in the service.

" I would send you Chartier," he answers, "but really, my dear sir, I don't half like to remain here alone. Tapage is still unwell and not to be depended on ; he might get worse."[1]

But Fisher was unmoved, and replied at once in even less uncertain accents : " I request that my man be sent to me immediately on receipt of this letter, without any pretence for keeping him or for any consideration whatever."

Then he adds, somewhat curtly : " You seem to be an unfortunate man to transact business with.[2] What ! with Tapage you cannot take care of your fort for a couple of weeks or ten or twelve days, until the arrival of your people

1. Letter dated June 14th, 1837.

2. If the dear old man had only had a little experience of the sweets of life among the Chilcotins !

from Tluzkuz ! How did Baptiste Lapierre do, who kept that place for a whole season only with his wife and an Indian boy ? "

On behalf of poor McIntosh we would beg to answer that troubled times, such as usually follow a tragic death among the natives, are something quite different from the normal state of affairs when the latter, as a rule, are, unless maltreated, rather friendly to the whites. And then Lapierre, as his name indicates, was of French Canadian extraction, and people of that race have always had the knack of accommodating themselves to circumstances. Instead of showing that haughtiness towards inferiors which is only too common among representatives of the Anglo-Saxon race, they would rather stoop to conquer and thus make friends instead of enemies. Moreover, Lapierre had been thirty-four years in the Company's employ ; he was inured to danger, and could well afford to brave it.

Alex. Fisher, in spite of his professed objection to exposing the lives of the Company's servants for the sake of a paltry pack of furs, does not seem to have for a moment entertained these considerations, but ended his recriminations by saying :

" You certainly do not mean what you say, nor have you a regiment to keep up that place, nor can I dispense with the services of my man for that purpose ; so I send for him. And now I warn you that you must not, on any consideration, leave your post to come here or elsewhere until I find means to relieve you from your charge."[1]

Tluzkuz (Lhus'kœz) is the name of a small lake near the source of the Blackwater River, where the Hudson's Bay Company was then endeavoring to establish a post, which, however, did not become permanent until a few years afterwards, but was soon abandoned, probably

1. Alexandria, June 14th, 1837.

PACKING THROUGH THE MOUNTAINS.

because its returns did not warrant the expenditures it occasioned.[1]

That John McIntosh may have been justified in his fears for his personal safety in the midst of the naturally restive Chilcotins was shown by the fate he met later at the hands of the peaceful Sekanais. He was imprudent enough to boast that he would avenge, with his powerful "medicine" or magic, an insult he had received through the unwarranted familiarities of a lad with one of his wives, and it was but natural that the poor benighted Sekanais should have taken the scourge, which soon thereafter decimated their ranks, as the result of McIntosh's threat. At all events, his inconsiderate language cost him his life.

Such has always been the Indians' explanation of the unfortunate occurrence and of its causes, and the writer admits that he felt somewhat doubtful as to their veracity until he came on the following passage of a letter from Governor Simpson : "I notice what you say about the cause of the late John McIntosh's death, which, from all I can collect, arose in a great degree from his own want of sense in unnecessarily provoking the natives by threats of 'bad medicine,' and other injudicious conduct, for which he was long conspicuous." [2]

1. C. G. Nicolay, writing in 1846, counts Fort Lhus'kœz—which he calls Fluscuss and gravely locates "near the Russian territory"—as being still in existence at that time ("The Oregon Territory," p. 172). Ballantyne ("Hudson Bay," p. 56) spells the name Fluzcuz. The geographical notions of the former author are extremely hazy. Thus, while in one part of his little work (p. 98) he would have us believe that Fraser Lake is the source of the Fraser, in another (p. 172) he places "Forts St. James, McLeod, Conolly and Babine about the head-waters of Frazer's and Peace Rivers."

2. To D. Manson, July 1st, 1847.

CHAPTER XII.

The Country and Its Resources.

MEANWHILE, the ruler of New Caledonia was seeking ways and means of increasing the returns and diminishing the expenses of the various posts under his sway. The following entry in the journal he kept at Fort St. James tells us of the interest he took in every detail which tended to those ends:

"January 31st, 1840.—Cold. Mr. Anderson arrived from Fort George to-day. He did not come by Nantlais [Natleh or Fraser Lake], but by Nakasley [Na'kaztli or Stuart] River, a far shorter route, and one we shall in future follow—a great saving of time and provisions. Mr. Anderson brought the accounts from Alexandria as well as those from Fort George, and I am happy to remark that both have a considerable excess on their returns. I had scarcely penned my letters when Gagnon arrived from Alexandria with the Vancouver express. Mr. Todd has not accompanied it. All quiet on the Columbia."

In the course of 1841, the Thompson River District was added to New Caledonia. This necessitating a greater expenditure of provisions, we see Peter S. Ogden applying to the gentleman in charge of Fort Babine for at least thirty thousand salmon, the dearth of that fish having been exceptionally great during that year at his own place.

Lakes Babine and Connolly belong to the basin of the Skeena, while all the other posts, with the exception of that on McLeod Lake, whose waters are tributary to the Mackenzie, are situated within the valley of the Fraser. This was a most fortunate circumstance, for the salmon failing in one of the larger rivers and tributaries, its run was not necessarily small in the other. Owing to the great importance of that fish at that time in the eyes of the Company, and ever since, as the principal means of subsistence of the natives, a few words on the chief methods of procuring it will not be out of place.

In the first place, one should bear in mind that the salmon exclusively referred to in these pages is the so-called sockeye or red salmon (*Oncorrhincus nerka*). It is exceedingly gregarious in habits, and this peculiarity is taken occasion of by the natives to facilitate its capture.

Whenever this is practicable, as at Stuart, Babine, and Fraser Lakes, the Kamstkadals' method of salmon fishing is followed. This consists in staking across the whole width of the river and leaving for the fish only narrow passages—ending sometimes in long funnel-like baskets, sometimes in cylindrical traps of trellis-work—from which escape is impossible. By daytime the fish will generally keep clear of these traps, and congregate slightly below the weir, which prevents their progress upstream or into the lake; but at night they sometimes pack themselves in the box-shaped contrivances ready for their capture in such large numbers that it requires two strong men to lift these preparatory to their being emptied in their canoe.

But the Fraser and the Nechaco are much too deep and swift to allow of a weir being built across their raging waters. All the fisherman can do is erect a sort of lattice-work projecting a few feet only from the shore, and connect therewith, at the bottom of the water, a toboggan-like basket with an opening near its curved end. The fish passes through this into an uncovered conduit leading into a large latticed reservoir, where it is caught.

The apparatus becomes more intelligible by a glance at the accompanying figure, wherein we have a sectional view of the whole. The lines marked *a* and *b* show respectively the bottom and the surface of the water. "The upper part of the entrance basket *c* is flat, and serves at the same time as a bed for the canal *d*, which is formed by the addition of two long hurdles *e* on either side of the main or lower basket top. The salmon having entered at *c*, soon finds its way upstream blocked at *f*, where the basket is rather narrow; but as its instinct is decidedly against the wisdom of a backward course, so soon as it

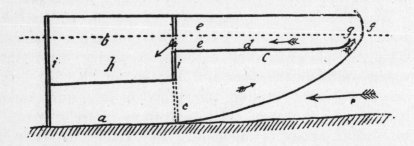

becomes aware of the free passage prepared at *g*, therein it runs and thence to the trap *h* laid out for its capture. *I* stands for one of the stakes which hold up the trap or reservoir, while they secure the whole structure against the action of the current."[1]

"To preserve their salmon, the Carriers and Chilcotins have recourse to the well-known method of drying. After the head has been cut off, they open and clean the fish, after which they expose it for a day or two to the rays of the sun. The spine and vertebræ are then extracted, together with the flesh adhering thereto, which is destined

1. "Notes on the Western Dénés," Trans. Can. Inst., Vol. IV., p. 89.

for the dogs' larder or used as bait when trapping. The fish is next gashed inside with a sharp knife as a precaution against putrefaction, and two wooden splinters having been driven through the flesh so as to keep its inside constantly open, it is dried beneath rough sheds by the action of the sun and air, aided by the fire and smoke underneath." [1]

Now that we are acquainted with Peter S. Ogden's personnel, its means of subsistence, and the way these are procured, we might as well peep discreetly into his account books and satisfy ourselves as to the amount of property there is in his different posts.

In 1836 he received, among other goods, the following articles from the Saskatchewan District: 500 large and 55 small dressed moose-skins, 3 large and 22 small dressed buffalo-skins, 25 moose parchment skins, and 30 pounds of sinews.

The dressed moose-skins were intended mostly for the manufacture of foot-gear, and their large number—considering that he had still 468 in stock and that he had also obtained 2 elk and 10 chevreau skins from Colville—is an irrefragable proof of the large native population then in his district. The sinews were, and continue to be, shredded into thread, with which leather is sewn, while the parchment skins were destined to serve as window panes and be made up into horse-bags and the like.

Among the articles in use at the different forts we notice the following, which would now be looked upon almost as curiosities: 1 blunderbuss; 7 hand grenades; 15 muskets and bayonets, four of which are described as worn out; 9 horse pistols, only four of which are in good order; 2 silk hat covers, 1 box wafers, 7 canoe awls, 1 drill bow, 1 bark canoe, 1 candle mould, 3 spears, and 2 carts.

1. " Notes on the Western Dénés," Trans. Can. Inst., Vol. IV., p. 29.

It is worthy of remark that Ogden's inventory, though still mentioning one bark canoe, also enumerates six wooden canoes. As we have already seen, but very few years before that gentleman's advent to the country the latter were quite unknown in New Caledonia, the only crafts then used by the Company being the canoes made of birch bark by its Iroquois *engagés*, while the natives themselves mostly adhered to the spruce-bark skiffs their fathers had used in pre-European times. So late as the autumn of 1848 we read in a letter from Thomas Charles, of Fort George, that "two men who deserted from Nant-lais cast up" there, and the significant fact is added that they travelled in a wooden canoe, which would seem to indicate that such embarkations were even then rare enough in that quarter to make it worth the while to mention their material.[1]

Among the articles for sale we find in the invoice of goods supplied New Caledonia from Vancouver for the outfit of 1836: Indian awls, used in making bark canoes or sewing leather; a great assortment of beads of all descriptions; three different kinds of belts; 412 blankets, which show that the "potlatch" was not unknown at that date; a large quantity of all sorts of *capots*, fine overcoats with cape and sometimes hood, a superior article; 7½ dozen cock feathers; a goodly number of "Indian guns," accompanied by a full supply of best gunflints; a few gross gunworms; a good many plain brass finger rings; 12 rolls Canadian twist and 1 bale carrot tobacco; 2 pounds vermilion; an assortment of quills and penknives; and, last but not least, five kegs of rum.

We have mentioned gunflints. At the time of which we write the guns in connection with which they were used were still a luxury which only a few of the New Caledonia

1. Letter to D. Manson, October 30th, 1848.

Indians could afford to buy. So late as the autumn of
1845 no other kind of fire-arm was known to them, as
we see Al. Anderson, of Fort Alexandria, forwarding to
Stuart Lake an assortment of one hundred and fifty gunflints. Nay, in 1851 (and much later) the Hudson's Bay
Company were still selling gunflints to the Indians.

INDIAN CROOKED KNIFE.

Since we have undertaken to review the resources of the
land during the first years of Ogden's reign, we should
not forget those items which are quoted as country-made
articles or country produce. The former comprise five
varieties of axes, two sorts of ice chisels (the implement
used by the Indians to break through the old or newly

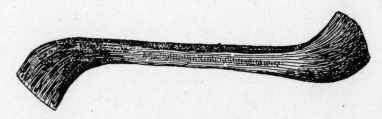

IRON SKIN SCRAPER.

formed ice, to cut the holes where they set their beaver
nets or go for their morning supply of water), some crooked
knives, the drawing-knives of the Western Dénés, a few
skin scrapers, a large number of beaver traps, and even
some door hinges.

The nature of these implements should not lead us to

form too high an opinion of the skilled labor then available in New Caledonia. The next chapter will enlighten us on the quality of some of those which were put in the hands of the Indians, even when they had been made at the very capital of the entire Western Department.

The country produce was reduced to a quantity of dressed skins and a few unimportant articles, mostly of leather, bags, mocassins, etc. Such resource as salmon was common, in varying degrees, to all the establishments, save that of McLeod Lake. As that fish is unknown through the basin of the Arctic Ocean, of which that lake is a distant tributary, the Indians trading there have to rely chiefly on the success of their hunts and the quantity of venison their chases may yield. This wanting, famine and starvation stare them in the face, unless they happen to be in the vicinity of a fort, when they can (or formerly could) generally count on the generosity of the officer in charge.

CHAPTER XIII.

Peter Skene Ogden Governs.

1834-44.

ON assuming the reins of the government of New Caledonia, Peter S. Ogden sent John McLean, the future author, to Fort George, a post which was then presided over by a Mr. Linton, to whom was assigned the charge of Fort Chilcotin, a very undesirable place. Yet the poor man was doomed to an even worse fate. In descending the Fraser on his way to Alexandria, in the fall of 1834, his canoe was upset by the drifting ice, and he was drowned with his whole party, consisting of his wife and three children, together with his interpreter, with his wife and child.

To that unenviable post John McIntosh was now sent, only to beg soon for an early withdrawal therefrom. However, he was induced to remain there for a while, and as one of the consequences he had with A. Fisher the little unpleasantness we have already chronicled. As years went on short lulls occurred in the Chilcotins' waywardness, which caused Ogden to write, in December, 1836, that the country was improving.

As could have been expected, this satisfactory state of affairs was not to last, and one year later Ogden was deploring, in a letter to A. Fisher, the chronic state of disaffection in that quarter. " The disaffected state of the natives towards our establishment at Chilcotin," he wrote, " has been, and continues to be, since my first coming to the district, a source of trouble and anxiety to myself and must be even to you. I have no authority vested in me to abandon a post in the district, and in my next communication to Governor Simpson I shall enter more fully in the subject."[1]

Another point, possibly of less importance, but to us even more instructive in view of the light it throws on the treatment of the Indians at that time, was touched upon by him in a letter to his immediate superior at Vancouver. " In regard to our axes of last year," he wrote to Chief Factor John McLoughlin, the head of the Pacific Department, " I beg leave to call your attention to the careless manner they are made, the edges being nearly half an inch thick and many of them not tempered, occasioning loud complaints by the natives all over the district."[2]

Little incidents, which are apparently of no importance whatever, will oftentimes serve to illustrate the straits consequent on isolation and the lack of communications with the civilized world. On the 27th of December the manager of the post, which was soon to be called Fort St. James, in honor of Sir James Douglas, was writing to Al. C. Anderson : " I forward you a pit saw file, and in doing so distress this place . . . I am much disappointed in seeing that you could not have assisted us with the loan of a couple of dogs, as it would have enabled us to have made but one trip to Bear's Lake. We, on all occasions, do all in our power to assist our neighbors."[3]

It is in that year (1836) that Fort Alexandria was removed from the east to the west side of the Fraser, and that, to attract the trade of the Babine Indians, Ogden

1. MS. letter, April 20th, 1837.
2. MS. letter, February 27th, 1837.
3. MS. letter, December 27th, 1836.

decided to move Fort Kilmars down to the northern end of Babine Lake. At that time the village near what is now called the Old Fort comprised one hundred and fifty inhabitants.

To A. C. Anderson is due the first detailed—we dare not say correct—statement of the native population within New Caledonia. Ever since the advent of the whites the number of the aborigines had been decreasing to such an extent that whole villages had been almost blotted out of existence. John McLean, while acknowledging the fact, asks in his book: "But what can be the cause of it? Here there has been no rum nor small-pox,"[1] by which statement the reader can gauge that author's reliability. Influenza and measles, added to the effects of strong drink and intercourse with unhealthy whites, were assuredly to blame for that state of affairs.

By Anderson's census, the native population stood as follows in 1839:

	Men.	Women.	Children.	Total.
Fort McLeod	49	40	113	202
Fort St. James	62	79	147	288
Fort Fraser	98	87	100	285
Fort George	75	50	62	187
Fort Alexandria	292	233	232	747
Fort Chilcotin	224	132	244	600
Fort Connolly	28	30	87	137
Fort Babine	69	47	65	181
Grand total				2,627

These figures call for a few remarks. In the first place, the present writer's long experience in enumerating natives, who are always more or less nomadic, has taught him that a good many omissions can hardly be avoided. The 747 inhabitants assigned to the establishment of Alexandria (comprising the native population of Quesnel and Black-

1. "Twenty-five Years' Service in the H. B. Territory," Vol. II., p. 296.

water) are to-day represented by less than 150 souls. That part of the district has always been the most exposed to the allurements of vice and liquor. As to the Babines, Anderson was evidently vastly in error, since we have seen that the population of one of the four villages on Babine Lake amounted to 150 souls. Nay, when the present writer first came in contact with them, they still numbered considerably over 300 souls, without counting those of Rocher Deboulé and Moricetown (not enumerated by Anderson), whose numbers, added to those of the Lake Babine, must have formed a total of upwards of 600 persons. Likewise, a census taken six years after that of Anderson, that is, when the population must have decreased, gave Fort George no less than 160 children, 30 widows and orphans, and 84 hunters, 20 of whom were single, and five had two wives—a detail which betrays the Company's lack of influence for good over the natives. These later figures would give us a total of 343 souls in 1845, as against Anderson's 187 for 1839.

Finally, Anderson's estimate for Stuart Lake falls also far short of the mark. Even at the present day the population inhabiting the shores of that lake, and whose territory is the equivalent of that of the 288 Indians he mentions, numbers no less than 346 souls. Nay more, as late as the year 1856, the authorities of the Hudson's Bay Company estimated at 12,000 the total native population of New Caledonia.[1]

And now, he who was undoubtedly the most conspicuous figure among all these aborigines, our old friend 'Kwah, was soon to be gathered to his fathers. So far back as 1836 we see him ailing more or less, and yet he would not relax from his usual duties, which seem to have been, in addition to hunting and trapping, the giving of

1. "Select Committee H. B. Co.," p. 367. See also footnote on p. 335 of the present work.

and assisting at native feasts, and being the husband of
four women. Indeed, one of his foibles was his remarkable uxoriousness, which in his days of sickness hardly
stood him in good stead, since, as the chronicler of the fort
quaintly remarks, the old man was sometimes in need of
medicine for "having indulged rather freely with the
ladys."[1]

The old Chief seems to have been an obliging neighbor
to the fort people. Besides his furs, he would bring them
whole beavers—meat and skin—and quarters of bear or
cariboo. During the fishing season Ogden and 'Kwah
must have made a sort of compact, which allowed the
former the use of the dusky chieftain's fishing traps
when he was absent. In return, the Company sometimes
gratified him with a turnip or an onion from its garden.
"Qua sent a whole beaver by a young man," we read in its
Journal; "at the same time he requested a turnip to
refresh himself after his trip down the river."[2]

Indeed, the Chief Factor and 'Kwah seem to have been,
in some respects, almost on the same footing in the establishment, and more than once the fort chronicler records
the visits he paid to the gentlemen. On the 16th of
November, 1837, he gave one of his feasts to the united
population of several villages, and, as usual, invited Ogden,
who for once chose to decline the honor, but sent, as a
substitute, a small quantity of flour, corn and sugar. The
wily trader seems to have that day forgotten the gift which
was the most appreciated by the banqueters, that without
which no feast was complete; but he was soon reminded
of it, a circumstance which prompted the remark, that "the
Indians are anxious to obtain rum; but they have fully
sufficient already, and I have refused them this. Promises

1. Journal, March 2nd, 1839.
2. *Ibid.*, September 14th, 1837.

are very fair now; but when the feast is over they will lose sight of all, and pass the remainder of the winter gambling. This was the case last year, and will consequently be the same again this time."[1]

Four days after this feast "Old Qua" is reported dangerously sick, an unwelcome piece of news to the fort people, since "this unfortunately prevents the Indians from starting" for their hunting-grounds. Three days later the Journal speaks of lamentations by day and night in anticipation of the Chief's demise, which is expected at any moment. The worst of it is that "not one will start" hunting. Indeed, the anxious traders plainly wish for his death, which "would cause a general move among them [the Indians], as a feast must be made,"[2] and furs gathered to pay for it. Two days later "Old Qua" is in a lingering state, hanging, as it were, between life and death. "I do most heartily wish," writes Ogden, "that some speedy change would take place; for, in the interim, all are idle around him, nor will one attempt to stir until a change takes place."

This change did take place, and it was for the better. The old Chief recovered enough to be able to attend again to his hunts as usual, though he was never strong again. His death occurred in the spring of 1840.

In the old representative of pre-European times, the defects proper to his race, and partly excused by his environment, were counterbalanced by some good qualities, inasmuch as, petulant and imperious as he was, he knew how to acknowledge a fault, could patiently bear the taunts of rancorous old souls, and was generous and faithful to his friends. He was buried quite close to the outlet of the lake, where his grave can be seen to this day. He left four wives to mourn his death, and of his children

1. Journal, November 18th, 1837.
2. *Ibid.*, November 27th, 1837.

'KWAH'S GRAVE.

With a grandson and great-grandson standing by.

sixteen (who grew up to man's estate) are now remembered. Considerably more than half the present population of the two villages near Fort St. James acknowledge him as their ancestor.

His third son—his first died in infancy—was to succeed him as head chief of Stuart Lake tribe, a man who proved to be energetic and deserved the name of "Prince," under which he was known to his death.

These appointments were made by the Hudson's Bay Company; for, as we have seen in our introduction, the primitive Carriers did not know of chiefs in our present sense of the word. The individuals thus honored were intended to be the spokesmen of the traders to the village folk, and help the Company in securing the departure of the hunters for their usual expeditions, and smooth over any difficulty that might arise between whites and reds. In return, they received certain annual gratuities, mostly in the line of wearing apparel.

As to their usefulness, P. S. Ogden had very pronounced opinions, and to a young clerk of a fort who wanted to create a second chief in his village, he remarked that one was more than enough, since in New Caledonia the institution of chiefs in our sense of the word is practically useless. Such men, he claims, give more trouble than help; they reign without governing.

This could certainly not be said of himself. True, he was not for ruling with a rod of iron, and he could be considerate for the lowliest of his men, though he visited misbehavior with sound corporal punishment. "Francois Boucher is on his return to Fort George," he wrote to one of his lieutenants, William Thew, then in charge of Fraser Lake. "He has received provisions for his journey, and will, I trust, not require any assistance. If he feels inclined to prolong his stay beyond the usual time it will be necessary that you give him a gentle hint about his taking his departure, as I find him rather dilatory in his movements."[1]

But in cases of attempted insubordination or carelessness in complying with orders, he could and would easily assert his authority. Thew, the very man he cautioned to show some consideration to a subordinate, has remained famous at Fraser Lake for his autocratic ways, his uncontrollable temper, and his cruelty to his men. This led to violent scenes, followed sometimes by desertion. We must say that in the beginning some of those who had to complain of him were unfortunately punished by Ogden, who was too prone to believe a gentleman against a plebeian. One of Thew's deserters was a Canadian, Letendre by name, whose escapade occasioned the following unpleasant correspondence.

Under date 20th October, 1840, P. S. Ogden addressed this question to Paul Fraser, the son of the discoverer, who was then a clerk in charge of a post :

" I have to request you to reply, per first opportunity, to the following charge brought against you by Mr. Thew : ' With regard to Letendre, I can only repeat what I have already stated to you, that upon my asking him the reasons that induced him to act in such a manner, he replied that had he not been, as it were, pushed or encouraged by Mr. Fraser to desert, he would not of his own accord have done so ; but from the frequent conversations that took place between him and Mr. Fraser and which the latter, according to Letendre's account, always contrived to carry on in a way that they should not be known to me, the latter made desertion appear so trifling, and the necessity of adopting it so pressing, as well as justifiable, that, as before mentioned, he was led unawares to follow a course which he himself afterwards

1. MS. letter, March 16th, 1840.

regretted and acknowledged as being improper. This is the sum total of his evidence as given by himself to me.'"

Paul Fraser had no difficulty in clearing himself in the eyes of his superior; but what is more interesting is the following statement written by Thew himself at the bottom of the page containing the copy of his accusation :

" Having by mere accident seen the above statement, wherein I am represented as being the individual from whom the charge originated, I consider it necessary here to deny the correctness of the above assertion. The facts are thus : Having come here in the fall on business, Mr. O., in the course of conversation, asked me the cause of Letendre having deserted, in reply to which I told him the reasons assigned by the latter when questioned by me, adding at the same time that I could not vouch for their correctness. Mr. O. subsequently wrote me to give him Letendre's statement in writing, which I accordingly did. I, however, never understood that such statement should be viewed in the light of a charge brought by me against Mr. Fraser, for I then observed that I placed no confidence in it. It is not to be supposed that I should have made use of it for any such purpose. I therefore cannot refrain from observing that it was exceedingly unfair in Mr. Ogden to make use of my name when he had no grounds or authority for doing so."

Before he had received any answer from Fraser, Ogden showed in a long communication to the same William Thew that he knew how to be jealous of the rights inherent to his position in New Caledonia. After having told him that instead of the five thousand salmon he had offered as his maximum quota towards the maintenance of the personnel of the whole district, he must furnish eight thousand, plus four hundred of a poorer quality for the dogs, the Chief Factor continues :

" I have now to convey to you my displeasure for your not sending the bull. The reason you assign, *viz.*, that Brunel was employed hanging up your salmon to dry, is a mere pretext, as Indians could have been procured, and granting that they could not, my orders must be obeyed, and no reasons that you may assign in the future will be considered satisfactory. I am here to direct, and you are bound to obey. If you again deviate from my instructions I shall be under the necessity of having recourse to such measures as would be the reverse of pleasant."[1]

Ogden had sent to Thew his interpreter, who was also his confidence man. The manager of Fraser Lake took umbrage at this step, which he construed as an attempt to obtain underhand information regarding his own doings and sayings, a surmise which prompts his superior to add : " I considered it necessary to send Waccan to Nantlais [Fraser Lake]. . . . Your surmises and opinions for my sending him have not made the slightest impression, and your remarks are uncalled for."

He then passes to the question of Letendre's charges against Fraser, and says : " In case this charge should prove to be founded on fact, it will be my duty . . . to submit the whole to the Governor and Council. Therefore I have to request that you forward the same statement to me under an official cover"; whereby we see how little foundation there is for Thew's assertion that he did not know that said statement was to be regarded in the light of a charge against a fellow-officer.

Under the weight of that blow (which was so much the more heavy as Ogden was little given to strike so hard in his official correspondence), all Thew could do to relieve his wounded feelings was to write at the end of that communication: " Part of the contents of the above is merely

1. Letter dated October 21st, 1840.

a vain show of authority." After which he no doubt felt better.

This did not prevent him from continuing to abuse his men, a proceeding which resulted, as usual, in complaints and desertions; but when he extended his ill-humor to the Indians who traded at his post the latter retaliated in kind, and more than once his life was in danger from them. Having once attacked an Indian of Stony Creek, he was assaulted by the fellow-tribesmen of his intended victim, and he would have been killed but for the intervention of the Chief of Fond du Lac, who stopped hostilities. It must be this affray, to this day well remembered by the Indians, which drew on him a letter from Peter S. Ogden, of which we give the chief passages :

" I regret to find so serious a misunderstanding between you, Dih, and others," he writes, " and as you call on me for my opinion on the same, I consider it my duty to comply. You also refer me to Mr. Lane for particulars. I see no necessity for applying to him, for I clearly see by your own showing that you acted most imprudently. I admit the provocation was great; but, coming from an Indian, there were other means than the rash and imprudent one you adopted to seek redress. You must bear in mind that if unfortunately in these quarrels blood was to be shed, the affairs of the district would be deranged to retaliate, and I am convinced that, had you given yourself time to reflect before you acted, your reflection would have led you to act in a far different manner, and could have at the same time made Dih as penitent and humble as by your account he is at present."[1]

Then he adduces his own personal experience to confirm the truth of his remark :

" Nearly a similar circumstance took place between my-

1. Letter, dated January 9th, 1841.

203

self and the late Old Qua, four years since," he says, "and without resorting to such measures the effect was equally satisfactory; for I lost no standing in the estimation of the Indians, and the old man from that day to his death never misconducted himself. It is not only our duty, but our interest also, so far as circumstances will admit, to avoid coming to extremes with the Indians. Look at our numbers compared to theirs; look at the many opportunities they may have of committing murder; look at their treacherous character [which, however, exists only in Ogden's mind]; look also at the weakness of our establishments in the summer[1] and the impossibility of obtaining assistance, and then judge for yourself if it is not more prudent to avoid quarrels than to engage in them."

After which he reminds Thew that, "without humbling yourself in the estimation of an Indian, . . . there is a certain tact in managing him, which, in course of time, experience and reflection will teach you."

In this, however, Peter S. Ogden was doomed to disappointment. Irascible Thew was incorrigible. On some trivial pretext he shortly after fell on one of the leading Indians of Fraser Lake, dubbed Saint Paul by the *engagés* of the fort, and gave him such a beating that, arming themselves with axes, the naturally peaceful villagers went in a body to the fort, a mile distant, broke open the gates, and rushed on the establishment, when the now fairly frightened autocrat came to a window, and, begging for his life, threw down gifts to the mob, promising at the same time to make Saint Paul a chief and compensate him for the illtreatment he had received, words which succeeded in calming the irritation of the natives and preventing further hostilities.

This unpleasantness, however, did not take place before

1. When most of the men are away on outfitting or leather expeditions.

some more desertions had reminded him of his altogether too disagreeable temper. " I remark that Baptiste Lapierre's desertion is fully confirmed," wrote Ogden, who was ever for punishing a wrong, however great might have been the provocation that had led to it, "and I trust that you have been most guarded in your instructions to Tastill in no way whatever to offer him the slightest inducement to return, as by so doing his punishment will not be half so great as if he had tasted the sweets and bitterness of an Indian life, and then you may rely on it that he will come supplicating to be taken back destitute of everything."[1]

Again Ogden was too sanguine. He did not realize the extent of the aversion engendered in the hearts of even the docile French Canadians by Thew's high-handedness. A month later the deserter was still at large. Lapierre, who seems to have been an excellent workman, was just then badly wanted for the brigade, while Mr. Tod was as anxious to obtain his services for the difficult post of Chilcotin. This leads the manager of the district to delude himself into the belief that he will soon prove to be a prodigal son, only too glad to be reinstated into the Company's paternal establishment.

" I am fully convinced in my own mind," he writes in April, 1841, "that Baptiste Lapierre is now heartily tired of an Indian life, and that it would require very little to induce him to return to his duty ; but the difficulty that appears to me to exist is what plan to adopt so as to make it apparent that we are independent of his services."

He then speculates as to the best mode of getting hold of him.

" Proceeding to the village and taking him prisoner is one plan ; but this, with the force we have, and the risk of coming to blows with the Indians . . . I feel reluctant

1. MS. letter, March 4th, 1841.

to adopt. It is, in fact, the last possible alternative. Sending an Indian and a man[1] with a promise of pardon, and, after his return, representing to him his age and the fact that this is his first fault, might answer ; but here again he may form an opinion that his services are of more consequence than they really are. Or, again, an invitation to the fort to settle some disputed Indian accounts for furs delivered during your absence, with a promise that no evil is intended, might answer even better, as it would do away with any favorable opinion he might entertain of himself."

None of these plans was to succeed. The best solution of the problem would have been the removal of Thew himself, a step which circumstances rendered probably impossible. Peter S. Ogden consoled himself with the thought that his suggestions had not had a fair trial.[2]

The reader should not think the above quotations too long, or the details they contain too minute, as we know of nothing better calculated to illustrate the workings of the mind and the consummate prudence and cunning of him who, for the time being, was the great magnate and first representative of authority within New Caledonia.

Before we pass to the review of happenings in other parts of Ogden's domain, we should perhaps say a word of Robert Campbell's expedition, in 1838, in the extreme north of British Columbia ; but though some authors make the northern frontiers of New Caledonia coincide with those of the Russian possessions, that territory was never considered to extend so far by those on the spot. True, Ogden was once advised from headquarters on the Columbia to extend his trading operations farther north ; but a trip he took to Fort Connolly convinced him of the moral impossibility of doing so.

1. *i.e.*, one of the employees.
2. April 17th, 1841.

If we mention the matter at all, it is because we remember that the population, in the midst of which Campbell established his ill-starred post, the Nahanais tribe, was of Déné extraction, and ethnographically one with the Carriers, the Babines, the Sekanais, and the Chilcotins. It may suffice for our purpose to remark that in 1838 R. Campbell, a young Hudson's Bay Company officer hailing from the east, having crossed the Rocky Mountains, started a post on a sheet of water called Dease Lake, four years earlier, by its discoverer, John M. McLeod.[1] Then, having passed over to the Stickeen River, he descended it to a point where he fell in with Coast Indians, the Tlingit, who took him prisoner with his companions. The whole party subsequently escaped to an Indian bridge, which they cut behind them to avoid pursuit by the natives. Some time later, a party of Nahanais having crossed over to Dease Lake, Campbell and his people succeeded in getting out of the country, when their fort was burnt by the natives.

Ogden had absolutely nothing to do with that expedition, and it may have been of interest to him only in so far as its field of action was the territory of the Nahanais, some of whom occasionally came to trade with his own people at Fort Connolly.

1. Who came from Fort Simpson, on the Mackenzie, by way of the Liard River, "with the view of controlling the western fur trade, which was then in dispute between the Russians and the Company" ("Through the Subarctic Forest," p. 55).

CHAPTER XIV.

Among the Babines.

BABINE LAKE is a long, very deep, and generally narrow body of water. Its length may be estimated at one hundred and five miles, while its greatest width hardly exceeds six. In places a sounding line will find as much as six hundred and eighty feet of water. Of an almost uniform breadth, save for a few indentations, as far as the end of its southern half, it then widens to the east, forming a multitude of islands, until it sends off two narrow branches right and left in a northerly direction, thus assuming the shape of an irregular crescent, with horns of a very unequal length.

It is at the base of these two projections, a little to the north of the fifty-fifth degree of latitude, that the Company first established its fort. But this was far from the salmon fishery, which was situated on the outlet of the lake, about thirty-five miles farther north ; and Babine Lake was then, with Fort St. James and Alexandria, the main source of salmon supplies for the various posts of the district. So far as 1836 we see Fort Kilmars, as the establishment on the northern lake was then called, contributing as many as twenty-thousand pieces towards the sustenance of the entire personnel.

Moreover, the Babines of that lake (especially those inhabiting its northern extremity) were in the habit of trading almost exclusively with the Tsimpsians of the Pacific Coast or their own congeners of what was then

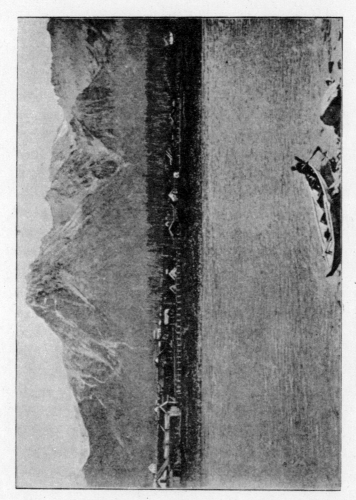

ROCHER DEBOULÉ AND THE SKEENA RIVER.

called the Fallen Rock—now Ackwilgate or Rocher Deboulé—at the junction of the Bulkley with the Skeena. The Coast Indians, more favored from a business standpoint than their brethren of the interior, used to trade, at reasonable terms, with the skippers of the vessels which patrolled the Coast, and, ascending the river in numerous flotillas, bartered for furs at a fair profit, but yet lower prices than those of the Company, the goods they had bought at home. Every year a regular fair, in which participated thousands of Indians, who could not always keep themselves orderly or peaceful, enlivened the forest at the foot of the beautiful mountain (Fallen Rock) which has given its name to the locality.

As a means of forcing back trade to its natural channel, as the Hudson's Bay Company would have it, it was resolved to remove Fort Kilmars, now badly in need of repairs, to the northern end of the lake, in the very midst of the disloyal Indians, and scarcely seven miles from the fishery. William McBean, an educated half-breed, born in 1790 on the east side of the Rocky Mountains, was then in charge of that post. Late in 1836 Mr. Ogden instructed him to make no further improvements on his buildings, but to prepare material for a new fort, to be erected at Hwo'tat, or the end of the lake.

Work progressed very slowly, as the natives, possibly less bloodthirsty than the Chilcotins, were even more noisy and restless. In a letter dated October 13th of that year, McBean gives us an insight into some of his troubles.

"When below[1] I was encamped close to Teeltzey's lodge, and about ten o'clock at night, when a number of Indians were assembled round my encampment, he stood at a distance, with a gun in his hand, and made a long speech, the substance of which was that he excused

1. *i.e.*, at the northern end of the lake.

himself for having stolen my canoe; would not own that he had ever said to an Indian he would shoot me, but that he heard I intended to shoot him, and, if true, I was welcome to do so.

"I insisted that my canoe should be paid five made-beavers, to which terms Tanewill [the Chief] agreed. Next morning I remained most of the day there, but Teeltzey was not inclined to make speeches, nor did he so much as show his face. They were many, but I think they were convinced now that with all their numbers they cannot intimidate me, nor must they think to make me run away from them when my duty calls me there."

At home he was not without his troubles. Early in 1837 he had sent two of his men on business to Stuart Lake, and finding that they were not back after an absence of twenty days, he began to fear for their safety. As he wrote to Mr. Ogden, he took occasion to mention one of those little incidents the aggregate of which forms what we call life.

"One of my bulls," he says, "very nearly killed him [Lefèvre, a servant], and should he recover at all, he may be a long time doing no work. Beside Lefèvre, the identical bull lamed and much injured an old Indian woman; in short, our lives were not safe with him, and being a most unmanageable brute, I shot him."[1]

Then, fearing the consequences of his act and a possible censure by his superior, he adds: "I am well aware that cattle have their value in this district, but you will own that men's lives are dearer. Had I not shot him, the Indians would." Which was quite likely.

In his next communication he hopes to be able soon to occupy his new fort, but that expectation was not to be realized. Work dragged on amidst numberless difficulties

1. To P. S. Ogden, February 20th, 1837.

from not too friendly Indians, so that, on the 27th of September, 1838, Peter S. Ogden ventured to inquire about the reasons for McBean's dilatoriness in occupying his new buildings. Had the half-breed told the whole truth, he would have confessed that the building material, though now ready, had not been so much as lifted from the ground. Indeed, it was not until over fifty years had elapsed that the new fort was erected with new timber.

McBean's ways, it may as well be remarked, were hardly of a winning nature. Though of a rather religious turn of mind—since, in 1843, we see him asking for a catechism, perhaps for his children[1] —he was so despotic with the men under him, so wily, and at times so dubiously honest with the natives, that he drew upon himself a most severe reprimand from Paul Fraser, who was not remarkable himself for his meekness, in the name of the manager of the district (momentarily absent).

A few months afterwards, October 16th, 1842, his charge was taken away from him, and while he was being sent to the solitude of Fort Connolly, William Morwick, a native of the Orkney Islands, who so far had been Ogden's cook at Stuart Lake, assumed the responsibility of directing the place, with the title of Postmaster, the limitations of his literary attainments not permitting him to aspire to the rank of clerk.

Whatever may be said of McBean's conduct at Babine, there is no doubt that he was a very shrewd man, who knew well how to behave among loud-mouthed natives such as were the Babines, even if he did not do so. The following directions, which he handed to his successor as he himself withdrew from his old post, fully prove it. He wrote :

1. He was even something of a religious fakir, making the Indians dance previous to addressing them on religious topics.

" In your dealings with the Indians be calm and patient, particularly with those of the end of the lake. Keep on good terms with the two chiefs Kishpin and Tanewill. As the majority of your Indians are in the habit of trading their furs with the Fallen Rock Indians, and as we are dependent on them for salmon every fall, it would be perhaps as well to keep them under in their demands, and so the less debts you advance the better. . . . You will have in mind that the Indians I have settled with are, on no account whatever, to have more debts until next fall, and then provided only they have paid what they have received."

Adverting to the insecurity of the place and the restlessness of the natives, he goes on to counsel prudence.

" When you shall have a number of Indians with you, it would be prudent to have your men employed about the fort, so as to be at your disposal at a moment's warning. Allow no Indian to sleep inside of the establishment."

Then the business man reasserts himself, and he ends his memorandum by renewing his wise caution against giving credit too easily, saying : " Be on your guard against some sweet-tongued fellows who, after my departure, will no doubt endeavor to get debt from you. Tah-han is one with many others."[1]

Unfortunately, poor Morwick was not long spared to follow these instructions. He may have proved somewhat rash himself, and, at all events, he had near him a man, Charles Toin, his interpreter, who, for the lack of that patience which is so necessary while dealing with the natives, was to precipitate matters and render his employer's probably good intentions of no avail. From the sworn deposition of an eye-witness, a Canadian named

1. Memorandum, October 16th, 1842.

Bonin, and the account of trustworthy Indians, here is what transpired at Fort Babine a month and a half after Morwick had taken charge of the post.

A Rocher Deboulé Babine named Lèkwè had killed a cariboo for the larder of the new officer, for which he wanted to be paid seven skins. Morwick, finding this sum too high, tried to induce the Indian to lower his price, in the course of which contention hot words were exchanged and a forcible encounter ensued.

This was on a Saturday. On the Indian retiring, Wm. Morwick is said to have loaded two muskets with powder and salt, and when on the morrow Lèkwè proceeded to take up again his recriminations, Toin applied to him several opprobrious names, after which, handing him one of the guns, he provoked him to a duel. The native, however, declined the proffered weapon, and taking hold of his knife, which was hanging from his neck,[1] he remarked that " he was not used to fighting with guns, but that if need be he could defend himself with his knife. Thereupon Toin retreated a pace or two and fired the contents of his gun upon Lèkwè, the wad . . . striking the left arm and lacerating it. . . . Then the Indian rushed on Toin and stabbed him twice in the arm with his knife, as the latter was endeavoring to escape from the room, whereupon he was taken hold of by Morwick and Bonin."[2]

Meanwhile the news was running like wild-fire through the native village that the officer had shot Lèkwè. Believing the latter to be dead, his son-in-law, whom the written deposition calls "Grand-Visage," instigated by a woman related to the supposed victim of the Hudson's Bay Company's manager, made for the fort, whose gate was now

1. The natives' wearing apparel formerly had no pockets.

2. Condensed from the deposition of Joseph Lefèvre *dit* Bonin, taken by A. C. Anderson, April 4th, 1843.

securely fastened, swearing he would wash out blood with blood.

At that time window panes were a luxury almost unknown in New Caledonia. Yet the sitting-room of the Babine establishment boasted the possession of two, each of which was framed in the parchment which otherwise closed the apertures in the walls. These being parallel to one another, a cross-light resulted, through which, even from the outside of the palisade, Grand-Visage could see Morwick walking to and fro, as the pickets were but loosely stuck side by side. Taking a steady aim through one of the interstices, he fired at him with mortal effect, Morwick falling shot in the head.

This happened on, or very near, the 15th of January, 1843. William Morwick was then only in his twenty-ninth year, and he had been in the Company's employ since 1832.

That same day Charles Toin succeeded in escaping, and, making all possible haste, came to announce the sad news to P. S. Ogden, who was just on the eve of taking his departure for a trip to Canada, as the East was then called. McBean, who had been summoned to Stuart Lake prior to going to his new field of action, was immediately charged, along with eleven other men, with the task of avenging the murder. Then, for the sake of formality, Ogden drew up the following document, which he addressed to McBean :

" In regard to the melancholy tidings received this morning of the murder of Postmaster William Morwick, and from the contradictory accounts we have received of this unfortunate event and the uncertainty if the two men left there are alive, or if the establishment be not destroyed, I deem it expedient, without loss of time, that you, with the party already named, proceed to investigate this affair

submitted it himself, assuring his co-tribesman that it was made in good faith. Upon this, after some hesitation, Grand-Visage emerged from his hiding-place, and accompanied by his daughter, who carried his musket, he proceeded to the fort, where all the Company's people were assembled.

As the Indian passed by one of the bastions standing in a corner of the palisade, two fatal shots brought him to the ground. William Morwick's death was avenged, and the Company was satisfied.

Not so, however, with the relatives of Lèkwè, the victim of Toin's aggressiveness, who now threatened to take up the gauntlet, and make the Company pay for its employees' high-handed proceeding. Apprised of their intentions, A. Anderson, the gentleman left in charge of the district by Peter S. Ogden, wisely wrote McBean that, should further hostilities ensue, or even be seriously contemplated, " it will be prudent to avert ill-will among the Atnahs by compromising the affair with the relatives of Lowquaw (the wounded man). In this we compromise none of our standing with the natives, seeing that we were the aggressors in this affair."[1]

Peace once restored, McBean went at last to take possession of his new establishment on Bear Lake, and one Duncan E. Cameron succeeded him at Babine.

From a passage in a letter from the manager at Fort St. James we gather how precarious was the position of the man in charge of that post. " From your experience now at the Babines," he wrote, " I presume I need not tell you, while surrounded as you are by so many Indians, to be strictly on your guard. Rest assured they are at all times most treacherous wretches, and you cannot take too many precautions."

1. Letter, dated March 4th, 1843.

This testimony to the innate depravity of the Western Dénés was penned by the old trader on Christmas Day, 1843. After a constant intercourse with that race, lasting over twenty years, and a ceaseless study of its character, the present writer begs leave to take exception thereto. Of course, the ministrations of religion, the acquaintance with the Gospel teachings and the fear of an after life, have had a powerful influence on that nation. Nevertheless, we can boldly affirm that most of the difficulties which ever arose between the white and red races can be traced to mutual misunderstandings, and a misconception of each other's characteristics. The natives did not understand their white brothers or their ways, any more than the latter could see the reason of so many, to them, uncalled-for outbursts and incomprehensible actions. Language is here the great barrier which separates races into so many antagonistic camps, each of which lives in perpetual suspicion of its neighbor's intentions.

Before continuing our chronicle, we may as well note *en passant* that, in the early part of 1844, McBean left the country. Officially speaking, this was on account of ill-health. We must remember, however, the isolation of his new post, where on one occasion he had to wait forty-three days for the return of his messengers, who, after having left Stuart Lake with a cargo of five hundred and eighty-four salmon, reached him with only two hundred and sixty-seven, the remainder having been eaten between two men and four dogs.[1] His request for a change of climate being

---

1. Letters to P. Fraser, February 13th and March 16th. If ill-health was McBean's real cause for retiring from the north, he must have subsequently found a wonderfully clever doctor or suitable climate, for he lived to a ripe old age, mostly in Oregon. On the 5th of September, 1847, he was in charge of Fort Walla-Walla, where he welcomed the first four Oblate missionaries who ever reached the Pacific Coast ("Historical Sketches of the Catholic Church in Oregon," p. 163).

granted, he left New Caledonia, nevermore to return.

D. Cameron, his successor in his former place, scarcely felt more at home in his post among the Babines. Haunted by the spectre of his murdered predecessor, he soon became morose, absent-minded, and tormented by ungovernable impulses which, in his moments of calm, led him to fear for the consequences of a possible rash act on his part. The following extracts from a private letter written after a year's stay in his new post speak for themselves:

"I have asked in my official letter to be relieved of my present charge on the 1st of January, which I beg you will take into your consideration, as my present feelings towards my *Red Brethren* are none of the most amicable. At times it is only by a violent and painful effort that I can keep my passions within the limits of prudence. I thought at one time that I had acquired a complete command of my worst passions; since the month of July it has been put to a severe trial. I fear that, should any of the Indians unfortunately attempt to be troublesome, this will lead to mischief."

He then proceeds to give the main cause of his difficulties:

"The Indians are none too well pleased because they cannot get goods on credit as usual, notwithstanding the little they have had to enable them to hunt so as to get them out of the way of mischief, merely for the sake of the consequences of any violence on my part—I apprehend none on the part of the natives. Well, with patience (I have much need of it), if I can only manage to curb my evil propensities for a few short months in order that I may get rid of the district, change of place and new scenes and intercourse with the civilized part of the western world may restore my lost equilibrium of reason—that is, if I ever possessed it."

He then asks for Charles Favel, a half-breed employee, to replace him pending the appointment of an abler man "to settle with these rascally Indians," and continues, not without a point of humor : " I am at intervals so completely lost that I fear I do not keep very correct accounts. I cannot trust my memory any more than a jealous husband would his wife."

He ends by an avowal too precious to be left unrecorded : " These wretches," meaning his Indians, "will impose when they can. Well, I cannot blame them ; they are apt scholars to learn roguery from the men " in the Company's service.[1]

In spite of his pessimism and his unsatisfactory mental condition, Cameron managed to live more than a year longer at Babine. On his withdrawal from that place he left the service altogether, and his post was momentarily abandoned. During that short stay troubles and anxieties continued to keep him in suspense and apprehension as to the future. On March 6th, 1845, he writes to Donald Manson, who had just succeeded P. S. Ogden in the command of Fort St. James :

" There is a great and serious commotion throughout the entire Indian population of this quarter, owing to that rascal Tanewill killing two Indians of this place, but belonging to a numerous sept of the Fallen Rock Indians. The latter are making every preparation for a campaign by withdrawing all their relatives and sending them to the Fallen Rock. I have dispatched a messenger . . . asking them if there were not ways and means of compromising the matter without any further effusion of blood. It would be better for all parties, for in killing Tanewill there will be no end of retaliation, and this will make matters worse."

1. To D. Manson, November 11th, 1844.

This last remark shows that he at least understood the Indian character. He adds, with a point of bitterness :

" I was interrupted by the arrival of my messenger, and truly I am well paid for my interference ! They say it's no business of mine, and they will act as they please, and making further allusions to the manner we punish murderers, they are determined to kill the Chief. From Indian accounts I have been in the necessity of keeping my men constantly under arms for the last three weeks."

Then, as usual, the trader asserts himself :

" This affair has put an end to hunting," he says, " and the salmon fishing will, I fear, in like manner suffer, as the natives do not go about. It will be impossible for me to attend to your request to transport salmon to the portage under the present excited feelings of the natives."

Always the same story. The Chief Tœnewill had lost a child, whose death being attributed to two brothers by the native conjurer, the old man had killed both, while the wife of one of them barely escaped destruction at the hands of the infuriated savage. The latter, knowing well that he who kills must be killed, had then appropriated as many of the logs destined to the erection of the new fort at the end of the lake as he needed, and having constructed therewith a regular blockhouse, was quietly awaiting the course of events.

Cameron's intervention, though prompted by the kindliest disposition, and based on the wisest foresight, was, however, premature. With the aborigine, the first effervescence must cool down before he can listen to reason. It is likely that that gentleman perceived his mistake and did not despair of mending matters, for some kind of a compromise was ultimately reached, as we learn from a later communication written by D. McLean, his successor in the command of Fort Kilmars or Babine. Under date of February 9th, 1846, he writes to his superior at Stuart Lake :

" There is at present a hollow peace between the Indians of this post and those of the Fallen Rock, but how long it may last it is hard to say. Tannewell has paid a good deal of property to the parents of the two Indians he killed. It is, however, reported that the Indians of the Fallen Rock have no good-will towards the whites, and threaten to give us some trouble. God help me! I am little able to contend against them with my force of three men should the rascals [most Indians were rascals to McLean] make their appearance with evil intentions."

Happily for McLean and others, an event of the greatest importance, the very first visit of a Catholic missionary to these far-off quarters, took place in the summer of the same year. We seem to feel the effect of the peaceful message brought by the first minister of the Gospel in the following extracts from letters by McLean :

" I am happy to say that all is quiet in this quarter, and the Indians, one and all, promise to exert themselves in the fur hunt."[1]   Again :

" The Prince [the head chief of the Stuart Lake sept] has given me no cause to be displeased with him.   Indeed, I am rather obliged to him for the manner in which he has spoken in favor of the whites to the tribes in this quarter."[2]

The Stuart Lake Chief had then seen two Catholic priests, and his advice to the Babines was one of the first-fruits of their teaching. The influence acquired from the start by the missionaries must indeed have operated some change in the restless dispositions of these Indians, when even a man of McLean's stamp was forced to write the

1. To Manson, November 3rd, 1847.
2. To the same, November (no date of day), 1847.

foregoing of Indians for whom but shortly before he could not find epithets opprobrious enough in his vocabulary, rich as it usually was in such terms. And these good fruits of the missionaries' preaching were not ephemeral. In October of the same year, after having noted the arrival of starving Indians from Stuart Lake, he states that "everything is quiet among the natives."[1] Exactly a month thereafter he writes: "I have no great reason to complain of the natives in my vicinity."

He then enters into a few details, which give us an insight into the resources of his post and the hardships which attended travelling on Babine Lake.

"I have now forwarded 30,000 salmon from this place," he goes on to say. "Lacroix, accompanied by an Indian, left on the 15th inst. in order to proceed to the Babines' Portage with 500 pkts. of salmon and eight of the Company's dogs with their harnesses; but owing to tempestuous weather and the splitting of their canoe, they could not reach their destination, and they returned here yesterday, after having left their salmon *en cache* at Tachette and losing six of the dogs."[2]

Leaving McLean to the minor troubles over which he had no control, we will now introduce to the reader those who wrought such a change for the better in the Indians he traded with, a change he duly chronicles, as we have seen, but without once referring to its cause.

1. October 22nd, 1847.
2. To Manson, November 22nd, 1847.

CHAPTER XV.

First Catholic Missions.

1842-46.

"WHILE many of the Company who spent their lives in the service of the Indians have given freely of their gold to the missionary cause, it is no doubt to the noble zeal and effective teaching of the Roman Catholic clergy, ever welcome at every post as brothers of the Cross in a common cause, that the Christian civilization of the North American Indian is mostly due." [1]

We might not be considered qualified to sing the praises of the Catholic missionaries throughout Canada. Our appreciation of their work among the natives, especially, might not appear disinterested. But nobody will venture to question the appositeness of the above statement who is told that it emanates from the pen of the late Malcolm McLeod, a gentleman whose very existence from the time of his birth practically belonged to the Hudson's Bay Company. He adds :

"I am a Protestant, as my father was, but we can bear no other testimony on this point. The priest and the trader have, in this case, gone hand in hand, and commerce has in truth, in this instance, been handmaid to religion."

As could have been expected, most of the financial aid granted missions by the Hudson's Bay Company went to co-religionists of the majority of its officers ; but the spiritual needs of its numerous servants, who were almost all

---

1. " Peace River," etc. Notes, p. 64.

CARRIER AND CARRIED.

Catholics, were by no means overlooked. The priest was ever welcomed at the different forts, and allowed to exercise his ministry among the people of his own faith.

However, for exactly twenty years after the coalition of the rival corporations, nothing was done to further the introduction of Christianity into New Caledonia. This should not be taken as meaning that the Indians never heard of a Supreme Being who rewards the just and punishes the wicked, through the French-Canadians and civilized Iroquois in the employ of the Company. Mr. Dease, during his short stay at Stuart Lake, had, with indifferent success, done his best to impart to those in his immediate vicinity at least a smattering of Christianity. Some years later a somewhat different route, apparently with the same goal in mind, was pursued by one of the clerks, William McBean, with whom the reader is now well acquainted. That gentleman has remained famous among the natives, who remember him as a sort of lay preacher whose hybrid religion betrayed his own Cree origin, since it consisted mostly of vague notions about the Deity and the primary precepts of the natural law, coupled with vain observances, the main burden of which was reduced to shouting and dancing.

About the same time (1834), but in the opposite part of the district, a movement affecting a larger area was agitating the southern Carriers. This can be traced to two natives of Oregon, who boasted a semblance of education received at Red River. According to J. McLean,[1] it spread with amazing rapidity all over the country, and its ceremonial was likewise restricted to singing and dancing.[2]

1. "Notes of a Twenty-five Years' Service in the H. B. T.," Vol. I., p. 263.

2. The writer has lately discovered, a little above Fort George, on the Nechaco River, one of the meeting-places of those early religionists, where could still be seen, beneath the overgrowth, remnants of the charred human

But more than those semi-pagan practices, the words and example of Mrs. Ogden, an excellent Catholic, effectively prepared the way for the missionaries. This should help Bancroft to solve the puzzle which arises in his mind at the sight of the treatment which the savages meted out to the first priest they saw, and whom, he remarks, they received " with open arms, as if informed by heaven of the benefits he should bestow ; and when he left they shed tears."[1]

It happened that some families of French Canadians had retired from the service of the Company and established themselves in the valley of the Willamette, Oregon. In conjunction with other free Canadians already settled in that quarter, they soon formed a population whose spiritual wants commenced, in the course of 1838, to be attended to by two secular priests,[2] the Revs. Norbert Blanchet and Modeste Demers.

For a long time the position of the courageous pioneers of the Gospel was very precarious, and their efforts among their own fellow-countrymen hardly as successful as they might have wished. " The conduct of the Canadians on the Columbia is far from edifying," wrote Mr. Demers, " and it contributes not a little to retard the conversion of the Indians, to whom they should be models."[3] What the

bones round which the natives would dance in a circle, to the sound of strangely-worded hymns, accompanied by invocations to the Trinity recalling the formula of the Sign of the Cross.

1. " History of the North-West," Vol. II., p. 537.

2. H. H. Bancroft, who, like too many of his kind, seems to be haunted by the bugbear of the Jesuit such as he exists only in the Protestant mind, explicitly states that they were Jesuits (" Hist. North-West," Vol. II., p. 536), and he accentuates his meaning by adding : " McLoughlin is quickly converted by Blanchet, and the Jesuits obtain the ear of the Governor." His mistake is on a par with that of an earlier writer who called the celebrated Father De Smet " Bishop of Oregon " (" The New El Dorado," p. 76).

3. " Rapport sur les Missions du diocèse de Quebec," Juillet 1845, p. 45.

bad example of the whites prevented them from doing at home they gradually thought of attempting abroad. In the course of their relations with the officers of the Company at Fort Vancouver, the two priests heard of the numerous Catholics living and dying without the ministrations of religion in the far north, and the thousands of unevangelized natives who had their habitat within what was then called the Siberia of America. With the double object of sounding the dispositions of the former, and of assuaging, if possible, their own extreme penury, they appealed for help to the head of the district.

Peter S. Ogden answered by asking for contributions from the well-to-do among his personnel, Catholic and Protestant. We have before us a circular in his handwriting, which we beg to reproduce, along with the response it received, as a feeble tribute of gratitude to the first benefactors of the Missions of New Caledonia. Under date November 15th, 1841, the Chief Factor wrote to the clerks under him :

" Messrs. Blanchett and Demers, the Catholic missionaries on the Columbia, requested me, prior to taking my departure from Vancouver last summer, to ask the inland servants of the district to contribute towards their mission, and I have to request that you will make application accordingly."

Then follow the names of the contributors, together with the amount promised or handed in.

	£	s.	d.
William McBean	3	0	0
Louis Gagnon	2	0	0
J.-Bte Boucher (*c*)	2	0	0
J.-Bte Boucher (*d*)	1	0	0
P. Gun	1	0	0
W. F. Lane	2	0	0
Pierre Letendre	2	0	0

	£	s.	d.
William Morwick	1	0	0
P. S. Ogden.......................	2	0	0
William Thew	1	10	0
Jos. Brunette	0	10	0
Jean Couturier....................	1	0	0
Paul Fraser	2	0	0
O. La Ferté	2	0	0
J. Tubault [Thibault?]..............	1	0	0
Pierre Roy........................	1	0	0

After these are found four names—John McIntosh, A. Bélanger, M. La Croix and C. Toin—all in Ogden's handwriting, but without any mention of any sum of money. As the copy of the circular preserved to this day was addressed to J. McIntosh, then in charge of Fort Babine, it is but natural to suppose that he sent in his subscription and those of his men without deeming it necessary to enter their amount on the communication just received.

The good missionaries on the shores of the Columbia must have been elated at the sight of such generosity on the part of strangers, some of whom did not even share their religious persuasion. So they set upon devising ways and means of repaying the kindness of their distant benefactors. This was, at the same time, an excellent pretext to try and extend the reign of the Gospel among the numerous Indians in the midst of whom the whites had thrown their lot.

The celebrated Father De Smet had just established his confrères at some distance from Willamette. In 1842 he went to see the Canadian missionaries at Vancouver, to consult them on the best means of extending their field of action. It was decided that the Rev. M. Demers would undertake to give that very year a mission to the inhabitants of far-away New Caledonia, while Father De Smet would return to St. Louis, and thence go to Europe to find new recruits to help in the good work.

Thus it was that Mr. Demers became the first apostle of the interior of what is now British Columbia,[1] the unimportant territories of Kootenay and Okanagan only having previously been visited by Father De Smet himself. To this day Demers' memory is held in grateful remembrance by the Shushwaps and the Dénés. Born at St. Nicolas, near Quebec, on 11th of October, 1808, he had studied for the priesthood at the Seminary of the latter city and been ordained on February 7th, 1836. The following year he was off for Red River, and thence, in company of the Rev. N. Blanchet, who was to become the first Archbishop of Oregon City, and of John Tod, an old Hudson's Bay Company officer fresh from a visit to the east, he proceeded to Colville and Vancouver. One of the first conquests of the new apostles was Governor McLoughlin himself, who thenceforth was to lead the life of a fervent Catholic, and by his example lighten not a little the task of the two priests among his subordinates on the Columbia. "He has ever been our protector," gratefully wrote Mr. Blanchet ; "he is the father of the orphans and of the afflicted."[2]

In furtherance of the plan of campaign agreed upon at Vancouver, Father Demers joined himself, at the beginning of July, 1842, to the caravan of the Hudson's Bay Company, which, under the personal supervision of Mr. P. S. Ogden, had come for the yearly outfit destined to New Caledonia. The two gentlemen seem to have enjoyed each other's company immensely. As to the missionary himself, he was loud in his praises of Ogden's "kind attentions and good offices, to which," he declares, "he was

1. And we might add of the Coast as well.
2. "Rapport," etc., p. 32.

exceedingly sensible, and which powerfully tempered for him the weariness and unpleasantness of such a long journey."[1]

The Rev. Mr. Demers was as fine a litterateur as he proved to be a devoted priest. He has left us a sketch of a day's travelling with the Company's brigade—as its pack-trains and flotillas were called—which is worth reproducing.

"Such caravans," he wrote, "are composed of large crowds of men and horses, the latter packing the baggage and merchandise destined to the different posts of the north. That assemblage of men, horses, and baggage unhappily renders progress slow and irksome. It is nine or ten in the morning before everything can be made ready for a start. One must seek out and gather the animals set loose and scattered in all directions the previous night. After long hours of waiting, the band is finally brought in, and the neighing of the horses, the yells of the *engagés*, the oaths forced on them by impatience, the contestations of the inferiors and the orders of the leaders result in a confused uproar not always flattering to scrupulous ears.

"At length, after having partaken on the grass of a meal of dried salmon, they load the horses, and at ten o'clock we are off. Progress is exceedingly slow, and full of more or less disagreeable incidents. We must face a fiery atmosphere, an enervating sun, a suffocating dust, with sometimes a hill to climb and a ravine to cross. The first days especially a person feels a general uneasiness, augmented by various inconveniences arising from the uncomfortable position he has to submit to while riding a horse already loaded with his chapel, his bedding, his household goods, and even his cooking implements. Fortunate is he if an untoward wind does not compel him to swallow

1. "Rapport," etc., "Lettre à Mgr. l'Evêque de Quebec," December 20th, 1842, p. 14.

waves of a thick dust which prevents him from seeing two
rods ahead.   A dull and monotonous sound of conversing
voices is constantly humming in your ears, which only the
crossing of a creek or a river can interrupt.   Then people
draw nearer one another, the horses hesitate, the drivers
shout and get angry; there are pushings, falls, and tumbl-
ings, with wrecks, which excite general merriment, and
furnish a theme for conversation and laughter during the
rest of the day.

"There is no halt until camping time, and the day's work
is over by three or four in the afternoon.   Then everything
is prepared for the night, the animals are unloaded and
sent out to feed, the outfit is set in order, small groups of
men insensibly form themselves in anticipation of the
forthcoming rest, the inevitable meal of dried salmon is
taken, and the sun has disappeared below the horizon."[1]

After five days' march, the entire party arrived at
Okanagan Forks, where Fr. Demers was well received
by the Indians who had been visited by Fr. De Smet the
previous spring.   There he baptized twenty-eight children
and went on with the pack-train until, at Kamloops (or Fort
Thompson, as the place was then called), he stood where no
minister of the Gospel had ever penetrated.   Useless to
say that he was received with open arms by crowds of
natives eager to contemplate at last that "black gown" of
whom they had heard so much.   But the requirements of
his company prevented him from staying there more than
two days, during which he christened a number of children.

On the 12th of August he was off again, and twelve
days afterwards he reached Fort Alexandria,[2] after having

1. "Rapport," etc., "Lettre à Mgr. l'Evêque de Quebec," December
20th, 1842, pp. 14-15.

2. By a strange confusion of names Demers says of Fort Alexandria that
"it owes its name to Sir Alexander Fraser, who discovered the river" on
which it stands (p. 17).   231

conferred the sacrament of baptism on eighty-five children whose parents he had found on his way up. The picture the young missionary gives of that then most important place is far from flattering.

" Its inhabitants," he writes, " know of no moral restraint. Among them the sacred laws of marriage are more loosely considered than in any other nation of North America. Promiscuity seems to enjoy an uncontested right ; suicide, murder, and a thousand other disorders follow, as natural consequences, this contempt for the laws of the family."

He goes even so far as to say that "it is not to be wondered at if they outdo even animals by the infamy of their conduct."

That there is nothing exaggerated in this sombre picture of the ante-missionary Carriers (to whom the whites had given all their vices without communicating any of their virtues), is attested by John McLean, who, little religious as he seems to have been, wrote four years later :

" The influence of the 'men of medicine,' who strenuously withstand a religion which exposes their delusive tricks and consequently deprives them of their gains— together with the dreadful depravity everywhere prevalent —renders the conversion of the Tekallies (Carriers) an object most difficult to accomplish."[1] And farther on he assures us that "the lewdness of the Carrier women cannot possibly be carried to a greater excess."[2] On the other hand, Harmon had already written that the men of that tribe quite often go without a vestige of clothing about them, a custom which does not denote too great a respect for modesty.

Such data are precious, as affording a basis wherewith

1. " Notes of a Twenty-five Years' Service in the Hudson's Bay Territory," Vol. I., p. 264.

2. *Ibid.*, p. 300.

we may now gauge correctly the extent of the transformation wrought in that race by the Catholic missionaries. The Alexandria tribe had practically succumbed before the onslaught of vice and intemperance ere the priest could definitely implant himself in its midst; but the Stuart Lake, Fraser Lake, Babine and other septs are to-day witnesses to what religion can do even with the most corrupt societies.

But we lose sight of our pioneer missionary. On August 24th he baptized twenty-eight children, and a week later thirty-eight, after which he proceeded to the capital of the country by boat, always with his friend P. S. Ogden and his entire party. At Fort George, where the brigade arrived on the 6th of September, he met but very few people, most of the Indians being away on their fall hunts. Only five of their children were admitted into the Church, and ten days afterwards the promised land was in sight, and he landed at Fort St. James.

As his stay there was to be unavoidably limited to three days, he employed every moment in preaching, instructing, and catechizing both whites and Indians, baptizing twelve children of the former and thirteen of the latter. To the adult natives he taught a few prayers and short hymns he had composed in the dialect of Alexandria, and to help in imparting religious instruction he made use of a sort of pictorial catechism or Bible history—due to the ingenuity of his confrère Mr. Blanchet,[1] in 1839—wherein the principal events and personages of the Sacred Scriptures and later chronicles were represented.

1. As will be seen farther on, Macfie ascribes the authorship of that little work to the Rev. Mr. Demers, while the writer's copy of the same bears the name of Mr. Blanchet as being that of its " inventor." That the latter was indeed the sole author of that " Catholic Ladder," as it was then called, is made clear by a passage of the " Historical Sketches of the Catholic Church in Oregon," pp. 84-85.

Commander R. C. Mayne, in his efforts to glorify at the expense of an earlier man a missionary whose work among the Coast tribes of the north became almost abortive as a consequence of his own contempt for religious discipline, chooses to sneer at the graphic aids Demers had recourse to, saying that "occasionally, too, might be seen in their lodges pictures purporting to represent the roads to heaven and to hell, in which there was no single suggestion of the danger of vice and crime, but a great deal of the peril of Protestantism."[1]   The reader will know the amount of truth there is in that estimate when he is told that the pictures of hell, of the deluge, of Cham the accursed, of the tower of Babel, of Sodom and Gomorrha, etc., figure prominently in that little catechism.   Does our critic suppose that such items were intended to exemplify the rewards due to the practice of virtue?   A work which is above all historical in scope could not well pass silently over the earliest heresiarchs or the introduction of Protestantism in the world.   Yet Blanchet's epitome of sacred history consecrates to both subjects but a very small part of its space.[2]

On the 18th of September Father Demers sang a high mass in the presence of all the fort employees, and on

1. "Four Years in British Columbia and Vancouver Island," by Commander R. C. Mayne, R.N., London, 1862, p. 306.

2. Matthew Macfie, in his work, "Vancouver Island and British Columbia" (London, 1865, p. 208), is much more impartial when he speaks of that little "catechism" in the following terms : "I was much interested in being shown by Bishop De Mers a rude symbolic Bible, devised by himself for the use of the Indian disciples of the Roman Catholic order.   It consists of a long slip of paper, on which the principal events narrated in Scripture, from the creation of the world to the founding of the Christian Church, are illustrated. The progressive development of the Church of Rome from that time to the present is also portrayed.   The advantage of the arrangement is that a large amount of general religious information is contained in a remarkably small compass."

the 27th of the same month he was back at Fort Alexandria, where he was to pass part of the winter under A. C. Anderson's roof.

Having caused a rude log church to be commenced under native auspices, our missionary set out again, this time for the valley of what is now called William's Lake, where he gave to the Shushwaps a mission of sixteen days' duration, which was blessed with the most consoling results. After christening thirty-two children, he returned (December 4th) to Alexandria, where he had the satisfaction of celebrating mass in the Indians' new church.

As an evidence of his desire to devote himself permanently to those distant missionary fields, we may note here that he made the acquisition, in the William's Lake valley, of a piece of land, on which a modest building was soon erected.

On the 3rd of January, 1843, we see him back among his beloved Shushwaps, who by that time had also put up a chapel, still without windows. A Siberian winter was then raging, and the apertures in the walls had to be hurriedly closed with pieces of rough parchment, which, to the discomfiture of flock and pastor, were eaten up by the dogs the very first night that they were used. The Indians were reduced to the necessity of setting snares for the capture of the delinquents.

Father Demers here records a little detail which graphically portrays the avidity of the people for his ministrations. " An extraordinarily large crowd used to encumber the chapel," he writes ; " so much so that one day I could not reach my place without passing over the shoulders of my neophytes, and I went from the doorway to the opposite end of the building without touching the ground."[1]

As usual, his time not taken up by other duties was

1. " Lettre à Mgr. l'Evêque de Quebec," p. 23.

employed in studying the Shushwap language and composing hymns and prayers for the use of his people. As a
result of his second campaign forty-one children received
the sacrament of baptism.

On the 21st of February, 1843, he bade farewell to his
host, Mr. Anderson, and, again in the company of his friend
P. S. Ogden, he made for Kamloops, where he arrived on
the 1st of March. At Okanagan Forks he finally parted
with that gentleman, and on April 13th he reached Fort
Vancouver, where he found his partner, Mr. Blanchet,
absorbed in prayer.

That same year, on December 1st, a bull from the
Sovereign Pontiff erected the Vicariate Apostolic of the
Columbia, with the Rev. N. Blanchet as its first titulary.
Important business calling the new bishop to Canada, Mr.
Demers was delegated to rule in his absence, while a Jesuit
Father Nobili, was assigned to the charge of the Catho-
lics of Vancouver. Since official cares hindered the former
from returning to his distant flock in the far north, it was
agreed that the latter should go to New Caledonia in his
stead.[1]

Therefore, in June, 1845, Father Nobili left for Stuart
Lake and way points; but his first visit, though precious in
the sight of the Indians as indicative of the fact that they
were not forsaken by their new pastors, could not accomplish much for the lack of time. He stayed five days at
Fort St. James, after which he had to leave by the boats
that went to Alexandria for a supply of wheat.

The following year he went back in the first weeks of

1. On the 30th of November, 1847, Mr. Demers was himself consecrated,
at St. Paul, bishop of the newly created diocese of Vancouver Island. From
1848 to 1852, he travelled through Eastern Canada and part of Europe in the
interest of his new field of action, assisted at the Council of the Vatican, which
he left in September, 1870; and had just time to return to Victoria, where he
died on July 21st, 1871, regretted by Protestants and Catholics alike.

BISHOP DEMERS.

(See p. 229.)

JOHN TOD.

(See p. 129.)

HON. JOHN WORK.

(See p. 275.)

JAMES A. GRAHAME.

(See p. 326.)

A. C. ANDERSON.

(See p. 195.)

autumn. As he intended to pass part of the winter at Stuart Lake, he soon repaired to Fort Babine, and he was the first minister of the Gospel ever seen in that quarter. D. McLean was then in charge of the Hudson's Bay Company's post on the lake of that name; he extended to him a cordial hospitality during the twelve days that he remained in his vicinity. The young priest then instructed the somewhat boisterous Indians dwelling near the fort and at the northern end of the lake, teaching them some prayers and a few hymns of a rather child-like character, which he composed in their own dialect. On the 25th of October, 1846, he baptized a large number of children and old people, to each of whom he gave brief certificates of admission into the Church, some of which are still treasured by the survivors. Finally, he presented the head men of the tribe with copies of an abridged edition of Blanchet's Pictorial Bible History, so that after his departure they might the better keep in mind and recall to their people the message that had been delivered unto them.

Father Nobili was of a very modest stature,[1] and seems to have been handicapped by a rather timid disposition, a circumstance which doubtless told against him in his dealings with the untutored savages of the northern wilderness. The observant eye of the natives could not but notice his extreme uneasiness on the waters of their large lakes, whereon he hardly ventured without being girdled with an appliance intended to keep him afloat in case of an accident.

This exaggerated diffidence undoubtedly detracted from his usefulness among Carriers and Babines, and when he returned to Stuart Lake he was a full month without being able to get the ear of his people, who happened to be busy

1. And he is, on that account, remembered by the Indians as the " Petit Père," or the " Little Father." 237

potlatching and feasting. But soon after the 1st of January, 1847, he made up for the lost time by a series of instructions, schooling, and catechizing, which did not end until the beginning of Lent, when he returned to the south by toboggan.

Thus ended the first missionary visits to the aborigines of New Caledonia. These were but skirmishes of the vanguard of God's army, and if the results did not prove of quite as permanent a nature as could well have been wished, this was due partly to the very limited time the missionaries could devote to their work, dependent as they were on the Hudson's Bay Company for their transportation, but especially because their efforts could not be followed up until most of their effects had disappeared with the lapse of time.

For fully twenty-one years no representative of any church was to continue the work of the two pioneers. In the meantime the devil was to ape their ministrations and thereby bear an indirect testimony to the worth of their efforts. Before we close this chapter we may as well record the fact that after Father Nobili's departure, numerous pseudo-priests, or would-be prophets, sprang up from all places, who, on the strength of dreams real or pretended, claimed supernatural powers, preached after a way, made people dance when they did not know how to make them pray, gave new names to their adherents, and otherwise counterfeited the work of the missionaries.

All villages of any importance, especially in the north of New Caledonia, boasted at a time the presence of some such self-appointed priest. The Babines were not to be outstripped in that race after notoriety. Their champion was a certain loud-mouthed man known as Uzakle, whose pretensions were the ultimate cause of a wonderful religious movement among the natives of the extreme north-west, both Tsimpsians and Dénés, a commotion which can rightfully be compared to the Messiah crazes of later days.

Among those whom Uzakle's preaching left incredulous was a middle-aged man named 'Kwes, a member of the band settled at Rocher Deboulé, none of whom had been privileged to see Fr. Nobili. He used to deride Uzakle's pretensions, and led a rather fast life. One evening he fell into a violent cataleptic fit, and when, aided (?) by the juggleries of the shaman or medicine-man, he recovered consciousness, he was dazed and speechless. When able to express himself, he declared in an incoherent way that " He who sits in the heavens " was punishing him for his incredulity and the irregularity of his past conduct.

The next night a new trance rendered him long power-less, and the services of the conjurer had again to be called into requisition. Similar attacks of catalepsy occurred on several subsequent nights, when it became customary for those near him to dance round his prostrate form, thus starting a movement which was to have far-reaching con-sequences. 'Kwes began to declare that he saw, floating in the air over the heads of every one, a bodiless head with wings[1] listening to the workings of each individual mind (*ni*), and he plainly intimated that his own mind (*pe-ni*) was penetrating into the inmost recesses of his credulous hearers' souls. Thenceforth, he said, he was to be called *Peni*, and under that name he soon became famous not only among his own congeners, but even among the Kitksons and Coast Tsimpsians.

Gradually he formulated a set of religious tenets, con-sisting of a mixture of Christianity with many beliefs and

1. Clearly a reminiscence of the Catholic doctrine concerning the Guardian Angels, though to this day his co-tribesmen resent the idea that he may have had any knowledge of the missionaries' teachings.

practices congenial to the native mind. He taught his followers to make the sign of the cross, composed songs with a strong religious bias destined to accompany heathenish dances, preached repentance and atonement for sin, introduced an organization whose object was to watch over order and morality, bestowed names on his adepts, in imitation, no doubt, of the christenings by the white priest he must have heard about, united native couples, and in every way played the part of a minister of religion. He went even further. As the number of his followers increased, he set upon prophesying, and declared that the future had no secrets for him. Strange to say, all the living witnesses, white as much as Déné and Tsimpsian, are unanimous in asserting that all his predictions have since been fulfilled to the letter. If we are to believe the modern survivors of his contemporaries, he went so far as to predict the introduction of the telegraph in the country, a feat which certainly defies any attempt at explanation.[1]

Another exploit, which might perhaps be laid to the credit of jugglery or of some kind of hypnotism, is attested by many eye-witnesses. In the course of his religious dances, he would introduce in his mouth the green, unmatured fruit of the amelanchier or service-berry bush, which, in the presence of all the spectators, would soon ripen to the extent of yielding a copious flow of dark juice.

But even the novelty of such feats will wear out. Fortunately Peni was a resourceful man. New trances, after several years, brought forth a renewal of interest in his mission, and the prophet accommodated himself to the circumstances by again changing his name into that of Sandrœsa. He died miserably at Babine, struck with apoplexy while playing the rôle of a common shaman.

1. See Appendix E.

CHAPTER XVI.

Manson's Tribulations.

1844-50.

B Y this time Peter Skene Ogden was at Fort Vancouver, where he had been appointed one of the Board of Management of the Western Division, to act in conjunction with the Chief Factors John McLoughlin and James Douglas. On the 15th of June, 1844, Donald Manson, who had crossed the Rocky Mountains with Connolly in the fall of 1825, was assigned to the command of New Caledonia.[1]

1. According to H. H. Bancroft, Dease succeeded Connolly only in 1831, while the latter gentleman was replaced in 1835 by Ogden, who remained in command of New Caledonia until some time after 1848 ("History of the North-West Coast of America," *passim*). Indeed, he positively asserts that "in 1848 . . . Chief Factor Ogden made his residence there," *i.e.*, at Fort St. James, on Lake Stuart, a statement which clearly implies that he then began to rule the district from that place. Our own assertion that Ogden's rule dates back from 1834 is based on mere circumstantial evidence, which, uncertain as it may be, we still prefer to Bancroft's unequivocal declarations. As to the two other dates, that author is evidently mistaken, as is usual with him whenever it is a question of New Caledonia history or geography. Connolly's own journal positively states that Dease was appointed and arrived in November, 1830, though it is known that he himself did not retire from the country before the following year; and as to Ogden having taken up his residence at Stuart Lake in 1848, that statement is ridiculously false. From June, 1844, all the correspondence, journals and other papers of Fort St. James go to prove that Manson was then in charge of the district.

The above had been written for some time when we ascertained by John McLean, who was on the spot when the changes he records took

With the exception of the second Ogden, Manson was the gentleman who reigned longest at Stuart Lake, having held the reins of power fully twelve years. At the time of his appointment he was merely a Chief Trader, and he was not destined to ascend higher in the Company's hierarchy. The new superintendent was a very different kind of a man from his immediate predecessor. As energetic and as zealous for the welfare of his employers' interests, his excitable temperament and his frequent recourse to "club law," as Sir George Simpson was wont to dub the kind of mitigated terrorism which obtained throughout the district during his management and that of his immediate successor, deprived his exertions of much of their legitimate results by alienating the hearts of his own men and of the natives.

Another circumstance which militated against his usefulness, especially when we consider that he came to the head of affairs after such Chief Factors as Connolly, Dease and Ogden, is that he never attained to the rank of those gentlemen, while he had under him no less than three officers, Paul Fraser, Alex. C. Anderson, and, later on, Donald McLean, who were Chief Traders like himself. Indeed, as we shall see, the first at least, who was an able man (though not without his failings) and a successful trader, seems to have harbored some secret leanings towards insubordination based on thoughts of inadequately recognized abilities. Manson could not help feeling the awkwardness of his position. It is but justice to state that, while doing his duty according to the dictates of his con-

place, that " on the 5th of May Mr. Dease took his departure from Fort Vancouver " (p. 250), and that "in the beginning of September Mr. Ogden arrived from Fort Vancouver " (p. 274), and as the date previously mentioned by that author, who strictly follows the chronological order in his account of events, is October, 1833, it is evident that Ogden's reign at Stuart Lake must have commenced in 1834.

FORT McLEOD.

science, he was officially courteous and even indulgent towards his subordinate, whom we might almost call his rival.

His official correspondence, at all events, shows him to have been considerate, and even at times patient, in his relations with the gentlemen in charge of posts—and a better writer, too, than P. S. Ogden, though by no means a faultless one—whatever he may have been in his moments of passion and in his occasional conduct relatively to his employees or servants.

His first care on assuming power was to avenge the death of John McIntosh, which, according to Sir George Simpson (who based his opinion on information due to Manson himself), "arose in a great degree from his [McIntosh's] want of sense in provoking the natives." The reader will soon become better acquainted with D. Mc-Lean's ideas and the special code of justice he kept ever ready for use in connection with the Indians on whose furs he was living. He it was whom Manson took up from Alexandria and appointed, first to the command of the leather party bound for Dunvegan, and then to the charge of Fort McLeod. At the same time, having ascertained that McIntosh's death was the act of only one Sekanais, the new ruler directed McLean to endeavor strenuously to impress on the minds of those he would meet the necessity of "destroying" the murderer. And as this end could not be attained without the co-operation of the whole tribe, he authorized his agent to offer a reward of two hundred skins to anyone who would deliver him up to the Company.[1]

But his thirst for justice—or vengeance—was not to be satisfied. The murderer of him who had boasted he would destroy his enemies with his "bad medicine," died himself

1. Letter, dated October 3rd, 1844.

shortly after his deed of the very disease whose appearance caused McIntosh's untimely end. That the unfortunate affair arose merely from the wish for redress on the part of a man who was thought to have been grievously wronged, Manson himself had to admit when he wrote to Sir George that "no insult or outrage whatever was offered to the family [of the deceased] or the fort, although the widow [he means *one* of the widows] remained there three days after searching for the body, which had fallen from the canoe" into the water of the lake.[1]

As an augmentation to Manson's cares, a new post, which was destined to be short-lived, was established at that time near one of the sources of the Blackwater River, on a small lake called Lhuz'kœz. This was intended for the benefit of both Carriers and Chilcotins, and its principal object was to prevent those Indians from disposing of their pelts in favor of the free-traders on the Coast. Anderson, the manager of Alexandria, spoke well of the prospects of the new fort, but Manson was not so sanguine. Although he admitted that it would undoubtedly pick up many skins which otherwise would find their way to the Coast, he feared it would injure the trade of Forts George and Fraser, which, in course of time, it actually did, thereby becoming the occasion of squabbles regarding the territorial rights of the officers in charge of the three places.

William Todd, a young man without experience, was first appointed to the new post (September, 1844), to be almost immediately replaced by a newcomer, Thomas Charles, who proved to be as careful and thrifty as the other was careless and negligent.

And now Manson's tribulations fairly commenced. These took the shape of desertions on the part of the servants and defections from the service on the part of officers at

1. Letter, dated February 2nd, 1845.

the very time when the latter were most needed. On his very first trip from the Columbia with the brigade, even before he had received the official intimation of his appointment to the command of the district, three of his men deserted, taking along with them what they thought necessary for a long voyage from the stock then in the boats. This untoward accident led Manson to call for energetic measures to repress an evil which, he said, was becoming of really too frequent occurrence. These, however, had not then to be resorted to by the authorities on the Columbia, as the culprits were shortly after apprehended by Anderson, of Alexandria, who sent them back to his superior.

A year later two of his crew absconded in the vicinity of the latter place, and when, after a harassing journey of thirteen days, the brigade reached Fort George, four more deserted ; so that Manson, who was, as usual, commanding the flotilla, had to hire Indians to help him man his five boats. These boats were in such plight from age and decay that they had to be calked two or three times a day, occasioning an expenditure of over three large kegs of gum.

At Fort George, having heard that two of his deserters were encamped a short distance below, he despatched his companion, Wm. Porteous, with two men, to take them back to their duties, and he had the consolation, after a time, to see his messengers return with the missing men, who for an excuse had only to say that they were altogether worn out and quite incapable of sustaining further the hardships of such a journey. Manson must have been warned to be kinder to his men, for in announcing these desertions to the Board of Management at Vancouver, he took particular pains to explain that "neither of them had any excuse for deserting, as they, as well as all the others, had been treated by [him] with the utmost kindness and indulgence."[1]

In view of these ever-recurring desertions, based mostly on the difficulty of ascending the Fraser with heavily loaded boats, he also recommended that a trail be cut from Alexandria to Stuart Lake, on which a train of one hundred and thirty horses would do in much less time the work of the annual brigades.

Such unfaithfulness on the part of the hired men could perhaps have passed unnoticed had it not been for the frequence of the escapades it led to, a frequence which called for some repressive measures when the truant employees reached the Columbia valley; but what must especially have grieved the new manager of the district was that one after the other the gentlemen or officers in charge of the different posts asked to be relieved of their duties.

First, we have W. Lane, of Fort Connolly, and Cameron, of Babine, who are anxious to leave as soon as possible. The latter even wants to start for Canada immediately after the 1st of January, 1845, a request which can evidently not be granted for the lack of a man to put in his place. At headquarters Manson describes his situation and asks for reinforcements; but, receiving no aid, he is constrained to momentarily close the important post of Babine (February 27th, 1845).

Then a third officer, Paul Fraser, applies for permission to go and join the brigade at Alexandria, preparatory to leaving the country, under the pretext that when he condescended to assume the charge of Fort McLeod he did so at Manson's own request and to oblige him. It seems that as Fraser was a commissioned officer, his appointment to any post or charge was within the province of the Governor, a circumstance of which he is duly informed by his imme-

1. Letter, dated September 25th, 1846.

diate superior in New Caledonia, who, after reminding him that he had himself nothing to do with that appointment, adds :

"I am sorry 'tis not in my power to grant your request for permission to meet the brigade at Alexandria next fall. . . . I trust you will consider well the step you are about taking, and, for your own interest as well as that of the concern, make up your mind to remain until some other gentleman can be procured from the Columbia to take your place."[1]

Fraser, in his quality of Chief Trader, had much to lose in disregarding this advice. He consented to stay a few years longer, and was recompensed therefor by being periodically put in command of the whole district during the manager's absences with the brigades from the end of April to some time in September of each year. He seemed to enjoy these interims, perhaps hoping that they might be changed into a permanent appointment, a conjecture which is warranted by the fact that when writing to his immediate superior he invariably addressed his communications to D. Manson "or the gentleman in charge of the brigade."

After Paul Fraser it was Maxwell's turn. It would seem, however, that a mere change of residence satisfied the latter, as we see him in the district a few years later.

The next to leave New Caledonia was very nearly its manager himself. In spite of his efforts to meet the views of the Board of Management, various causes conspired to deprive him of the fruits of his labors. In the first place, there was a notable decrease in the returns of the district. This did not meet with the approbation of the gentlemen at Vancouver. Then McLean, whom we have seen dispatched on a leather expedition, had returned too late in the fall, and,

1. MS. letter, February 9th, 1846.

being caught by the ice on the river, had been obliged to
cache his precious cargo, a proceeding which was deemed
dangerous to its safety. Again, when Manson asked for
a certain quantity of accoutrements for the horses of the
various pack-trains, his requisition had been thought extra-
vagantly large by P.S. Ogden, now a member of the Board,
who perhaps took this demand in the light of a reflection
on his own management of affairs while in New Caledonia,
an impression which was not removed by Manson when
that gentleman formally wrote that " when he took charge
of New Caledonia affairs he found everything of this
description worn out in tatters."[1]   Finally, in consequence
of the reckless conduct of young W. Todd, he could not
rely on his services to direct a fort, and therefore he declined
to comply with P. S. Ogden's instructions that his [Ogden's]
son Peter be sent out to Colville.

As a result of these adverse circumstances, Manson was
relieved of his charge and Chief Factor Lewis appointed in
his place (February 20th, 1846). Ill health on the part of
that gentleman had, however, forced him so far to remain
at Colville.

Manson took his disgrace manfully, and, without an
attempt at pleading with his superiors, he wrote them :

" On my departure from hence with the returns in April,
Mr. C. T. Fraser will be appointed to the charge until the
wishes of the Board of Management may be known. Myself I shall always hold in readiness to proceed wherever
my services may be found necessary."

The storm, however, abated, and, after oral explanations
at Vancouver, Manson was allowed to resume his post ; but
escaping Charybdis he encountered Scylla. Anxieties
greater even than those he had experienced by the defec-
tion of so many of his lieutenants, because of the unwar-

---

1. Letter to McLoughlin and Douglas, December 26th, 1846.

ranted conduct of a fifth, were in store for him on his return to Stuart Lake.

As early as the end of 1845, William Porteous, a character whose utter worthlessness was fully realized only after his removal from the district, asked to be relieved of the charge of Fort Connolly, where he had succeeded W. Lane. The isolation of the place was not evidently to his taste, and in wishing for a change he was in order. Where he was certainly wrong was in leaving it, as he did, of his own accord, a step the impropriety of which his superior endeavored to impress on his mind. It so happened that at that time Manson had absolutely nobody to put in his place, and he pleaded so forcibly with his subordinate that Porteous agreed to stay, on condition that he would give him another post if he returned from Vancouver, or that he would pledge himself to induce his successor to take a like measure in case he was to be permanently removed from his position in the district. On the strength of that promise, extorted when his superior was powerless, he returned to Fort Connolly.

But he was bound to hunt for pretexts to serve him as excuses to abandon his hated post. The Sekanais had resolved to attack his fort, he claimed, basing his apprehensions on information he had received from the Atnahs, information which Manson hardly believed deserving of credit when he very pointedly remarked that "should an attack be premeditated, the Atnahs themselves were the most likely to be the aggressors."[1]

Poor Manson had perhaps nobody but himself to blame for furnishing Porteous with such a flimsy excuse. It was only a few weeks since he had written him: "From Alexandria I am sorry to learn that Mr. C. T. Tod apprehended an attack on his fort [Kamloops] by the Okanagans and

1. Letter, March 24th, 1846.

Shushwaps combined, and led by Nicola, and in consequence has applied to Mr. Anderson for assistance, who
intended to start with six men immediately."[1]

Finally, on the 20th May, without permission or blowing
of trumpets, Porteous arrived at Stuart Lake, having again
abandoned his post. His excuse this time was that he
could find no means of subsistence at Fort Connolly, notwithstanding that he was well provided with nets and had
with him three men, two of whom were known to be expert
fishermen.

In view of this second escapade, Manson reconsidered
the promise he had been obliged to make to the fickle
employee, and told him that he must return to his post or go
out of the country under financial conditions not altogether
too agreeable to contemplate. The wretch chose the former
alternative. But he was no sooner back at Bear Lake than
he sent his superior a letter of recrimination, complaining
of the insufficiency of his salary, which he wanted to be
increased to £100 per annum. At the same time, he informed him that he was again coming out in the early spring.

Well might the care-worn manager write in disgust : " I
am at a loss what to do with the man, as by the time he
arrives here it will be too late to send him out with the
express, and I am of the opinion that it would be bad
policy to bring him out with the brigade. . . . I cannot help saying that this gentleman has given me a great
deal of annoyance and trouble since he was placed at Connolly's Lake, and has been most lavish and extravagant
with the property committed to his trust."[2]

To add still to his troubles, Manson had to let go, on
account of bad health, Maxwell, who had lately been
stationed at Fort George.

1. Letter, February 9th, 1846.

2. Letter to the Board of Management, February 25th, 1847.

For the lack of any other excuse, the inconstant Porteous now fell back on the extreme penury of his post, whereupon Manson wittily remarked: "That the fish in Connolly's Lake should have vanished so rapidly is most unaccountable to me as, during former years, fish were always taken during the winter months, and although perhaps in no large quantities, still this assisted in making the stock of salmon hold out longer."[1]

His correspondent had also asked for news of his dogs, and the answer was:

"I know of no animals of this description belonging to you at this place, and if the dogs you allude to are those which formerly belonged to Mr. Wm. Todd, I have to inform you that that gentleman before he left this place made over all his dogs, say seven, to the Company, and his account is now credited with that number."

But stubborn Porteous was bound to have his way. He again repaired to Stuart Lake, where Manson told him to stay with his *locum tenens*, P. Fraser, until the fall, when means would be devised to allow of his leaving the country. And lest he might forget these instructions, Manson notified him by writing to that effect, adding: "I consider it proper to inform you that any contravention to, or wilful neglect of, the orders you may receive from Mr. Fraser will subject you to the loss, not only of your four years' wages, but also the forfeiture of all you have in the Company's hands."[2]

Yet Manson had been out but two days with the brigade when Porteous, setting Mr. Fraser's authority at defiance, took an Indian and left for Alexandria, where his quondam superior took no notice of him, though he immediately wrote to Fraser, blaming that gentleman for

1. Letter, dated March 3rd, 1847.
2. Letter, April 18th, 1847.

having allowed him to go. To which his lieutenant pointedly replied, that his "keeping him by force would have, in his humble opinion, made matters worse, as in all probability he would have induced most, if not all, the men in his establishment to desert."[1]

Just then the truly despicable character of the man became apparent. Two Canadian eye-witnesses laid against him several accusations to the effect, mostly, that not only had he appropriated what pleased him of the Company's property, but that, when he left his post, he wilfully destroyed by fire all the doors, tables, chairs, and the floorings of his establishment.

This was the end in New Caledonia of a character who, fortunately for the Hudson's Bay Company, has remained without a peer in the annals of the district. Whatever may have been their failings, the great majority of its officers, even though of the secondary or non-commissioned class, have been men above reproach, so far as honesty and discipline are concerned, and almost all have displayed the greatest zeal in serving their employers' interests. On the other hand, it is safe to remark that, had not Manson been so short of men, Porteous' insubordination would not have lasted so long.

While that man was thus doing his own sweet will, his superior was not at the end of his troubles. Waccan, a typical Hudson's Bay man, was in his turn on strike for an augmentation of his wages. And here we may at once remark that he, at least, richly deserved such a recognition of his many services.

We must confess to a feeling akin to remorse for having tarried so long before doing justice to that unique character which, however, has sometimes already forced itself to our notice under its real name of Jean-Baptiste Boucher.

1. Letter, August 13th, 1847.

Waccan, the terrible Waccan, was the Company's gendarme and chief executioner in New Caledonia; he was the official avenger of the killed, the policeman who was dispatched to the villages in order to stir up the natives and send them hunting, or put a stop to the endless gambling parties, which prevented them from exerting themselves on behalf of the white traders. He was the general purveyor of Fort St. James; when famine stared its inmates in the face, he was deputed to various Indian camps, whence he never returned empty handed. He was the faithful steward; assigned to the guard of the salmon or fur convoys, he always saw to it that no harm came to the one and good care was taken of the other. Nay, more, he was the perpetual right arm of the successive managers, their *ex officio* lieutenant, who was repeatedly entrusted with the charge of the main fort during the absence of its official head. Chief Factors came and Chief Factors went, but Waccan stayed under all governments. Finally, he was by regular appointment the interpreter of the central post, and by birth nothing else than a poor French Cree half-breed.

His standing at the fort was neither that of an officer nor that of a servant. He had a house to himself, and enjoyed privileges denied the latter. Jean-Baptiste Boucher, or Waccan, as he was more generally known, was a relic of the heroic times of the district, having come to Stuart Lake with Simon Fraser in 1806, and he had remained in the country ever since.

He was the first white man—even half-breeds are whites to the natives—to take a Carrier girl to wife, which he did in January, 1811. But that union was not to last, as he soon after married Nancy, J. McDougall's daughter, by whom he subsequently had a host of children. Thenceforth he became indispensable to the traders who succeeded one another in the charge of New Caledonia, not only on account of his familiarity with the language of the aborigines, but especially owing to the wonderful ascendency he had acquired over the latter through his indomitable fearlessness and his boldness, which at times verged on rashness.

As early as 1827 we see him acting the part of the confidant and the trusted steward even over full-blooded whites. Almost every other page of the fort journal mentions his name, which in no instance that we can remember is coupled with words of blame or disapprobation. Under date April 3rd, 1827, we read:

" Waccan and Boisclair arrived last night from convoying the party from Connolly's Lake. They reached Tatla on the evening of the third day, which was excellent march, considering the weight of their loads. Waccan on his return collected ten cats [lynxes], forty-two martens, and one hundred and thirty hares from the Indians to be found along the Taché River."

And further, on the 5th of November of the same year:

" This morning Waccan, accompanied by five men, left this place in a large canoe for the Babine Portage ; they have, as load, leather intended for the Babine country. The object of sending Waccan is to prevent any waste of salmon whilst the people are carrying it across the portage, and at the same time to build a store at the west end of the same."

Had that one man been at the fort at the time of the Douglas episode, it is safe to say that things would probably have taken a quite different turn. His was, indeed, a name to conjure with among the natives ; but at that very time he was on Babine Lake, where, in the face of armed Indians friendly to his intended victim, he slew the murderer of his half-brother, Duncan Livingston, who on March of the preceding year had engaged himself to act in the capacity of interpreter at Babine.

Later on, in old Ogden's time, we see him play repeatedly the rôle of the policeman. "Waccan having threatened to clear out of the camp the young men who are too lazy to start themselves," we read in that gentleman's journal, "they took the hint and three started off this morning for Taché."[1] And again : " Waccan went to the Indian village and stopped the gambling."[2] A day later : "The Fond du Lac Indians took their departure; the alert of yesterday has had a good effect."

When it became a question of avenging Morwick's murder at Babine, Waccan's name suggested itself as a matter of course, and in his company the executioners of Ogden's justice felt safe.

And even now, when he was nearing his end, his services were called into requisition by Paul Fraser to effect the arrest of a man, Jos. Jacques, who had deserted his post in Mr. Manson's absence to join the relatives of his Indian wife in the vicinity of Fraser Lake, where he was said to be encamped. On the 18th of May, 1847, Paul Fraser wrote from Stuart Lake to Peter Ogden at Fraser Lake :

" I was pleased to learn that the abode of Jos. Jacques, the deserter, was so near Fraser Lake, and as you offered your services and requested those of Waccan with a man from this place to secure him, your wishes shall be complied with. It is indeed high time that some measures were adopted to put a stop to the scandalous practice of desertion now so prevalent in this district, and was Jacques taken from among the Indians and severely punished, it would, in my opinion, deter others from a similar conduct.[3]

1. Journal, January 5th, 1838.
2. *Ibid.*, February 21st, 1838.
3. Letter, dated May 18th, 1847.

Waccan, consulted on the subject, declared that the present was not the proper time to apprehend the villain, and that it would be preferable to wait until the Indians were gathered at Stella, at the opposite end of the lake, a suggestion which was immediately acted on. Then, on June 3rd, he left for Fraser Lake with a letter from the temporary manager of the district, in which Ogden was cautioned to be "much on his guard in case of treachery on the part of the natives, who, no doubt, will attempt to assist him to escape." But then, he added, "Boucher ('Waccan') is well acquainted with the Indians and their country, and you could not have a more competent person to assist you."[1]

Eight days later, Paul Fraser was agreeably surprised by the arrival of Waccan and Jacques, "who, having been cleverly outwitted, now professed the greatest repentance for his past conduct."

The last mention of the faithful old man we can find in the documents at our command is dated 27th of February, 1849, a circumstance which impugns the accuracy of a pencil note on the copy of John McLean's book now in the library of Parliament, Victoria, to the effect that Waccan died in the winter of 1847–48.[2] In a letter to A. C. Anderson, Manson, after having recited the killing of the instigator of a murder, the victim of which will form the subject of our next chapter, goes on to state that in the unsettled condition of the lower part of the country, in consequence of that high-handed measure, as well as to help towards the apprehension of the real culprit, he sends Waccan down to Alexandria.

1. Letter, June 2nd, 1847.

2. Said note is in the handwriting of an old Hudson's Bay Company officer, and it serves to prove that even such authorities are not always reliable.

"Waccan and six men leave here on the 1st of March prox. for Alexandria," he writes. "My principal reason for sending the old man is that he is known and respected by all the natives of the district, and therefore I am of opinion that his appearance there in the present state of affairs will have a very good effect."[1]

Waccan died in the spring of 1850 of the measles, an epidemic which devastated the whole district and made a host of victims. He left seventeen children.

Another object of anxiety for the manager of New Caledonia was the length and difficulties of the route his pack-train had to follow every year, and the great mortality among his horses which resulted therefrom. A. C. Anderson, his able lieutenant in the south, was so much the more prepared to share his uneasiness, as for many years the care of those animals had devolved on him. Moreover, the pretensions of the American Government made it apparent that Vancouver, the terminus of that route, would ultimately be found to be within American territory. Therefore, with the approbation of his superiors, that gentleman set out to explore the country between his place, Kamloops, and Fort Langley, on the Lower Fraser, with a view to finding a better route.

Starting on the 15th of May, 1846, he went by way of Cache Creek and Hat Creek, whence he passed through a gap in the hills until he reached the Upper Fountain, when he found it impossible to follow the Fraser. Then, striking westward by Lakes Seaton and Anderson, he made for the south by way of Lillooet, and nine days after his departure he fell upon the Fraser again; by five o'clock of the same day he was at Langley.

The country traversed had been mostly rugged and hardly fit for an important pack-train; but on his return

1. Manson to Anderson, February 27th, 1849.

he found somewhat better, by way of the Cascade range, through which, groping in the dark as it were, he had to retreat in order to try another defile, which allowed of his proceeding to Semilkameen and Lake Nicola.

He had accomplished his task thoroughly and, as Manson wrote to Sir Geo. Simpson, he " left nothing to desire in the shape of information. The return route is the shortest of the two explored. . . . Still a doubt as to its practicability remains."[1]

That doubt was well founded, as he discovered himself with his pack-train in 1848. Here is what he wrote to the Board of Management even before he had returned to Stuart Lake :

" When I last had the honor of addressing you from Langley, I gave you an account of our proceedings up to that date, and at the same time stated my fears as to the practicability of the new route. We have now tested its advantages and disadvantages thoroughly, and I have no hesitation in declaring it utterly impracticable for a large brigade such as ours. The rugged, rocky, mountainous and thickly wooded country which lies between Fraser River and the plains, say a distance of about forty-three miles, and which the brigade took ten days to pass, seven of which the horses were without food, is, in my opinion, sufficient in itself to condemn this route. These, however, are not the only impediments to the new road. The hosts of barbarians who are congregated on Fraser River at that season, and among whom we have recently passed under circumstances where neither courage, prudence nor precaution could avail to resist surprise or guard against treachery, is more than sufficient to deter us from again attempting that route."[2]

1. Letter, February 26th, 1847.
2. Kamloops, August 24th, 1848.

In a somewhat later communication he states that, on that road, in spite of every precaution, he lost no less than twenty-five pieces of merchandise and seventy horses. [1] He therefore dispatched one of his men, Peers, to minutely examine and report on Anderson's return route, and that gentleman had the good luck to find a pass free from most of the difficulties so far experienced.

But Manson seems to have been pursued by fate. Another kind of danger, arising this time not from nature, was in wait for his " brigade," as we shall see presently.

1. To Sir George Simpson, February 26th, 1849.

CHAPTER XVII

Alexis Bélanger and His Avenger.

AMONG the Company's servants in the early forties was a young man of pleasing appearance named Alexis Bélanger, who had quite a checkered career and was more than once a thorn in the side of his employers. As his life, his death and its consequences throw such a flood of light on the ways of the lonely traders in the wilds of what is now the northern interior of British Columbia at the time we have reached in our narrative, it is but proper that we should somewhat linger on the data we have been able to gather relative to his passage in the country and his tragic end.

The son of a French Canadian adventurer by a Cree woman, he never knew his father, and is said to have given way to boisterous rejoicing on the death of his mother, who had incurred his displeasure for having chastised him none too leniently in consequence of some misdeed of his. An orphan without friends, he entered the Hudson's Bay Company's service at the early age of thirteen (he had been born in 1816), and in due course of time he was sent to the headquarters of the New Caledonia District. He must have had good aptitudes for languages, since, in a relatively short time, he picked up the Carrier dialect sufficiently well to act as interpreter at Babine, where we first see him stationed with a salary of fifteen pounds a year.

Very friendly to the natives and rather bent on following

their ways, he was at times well beloved of his employers, though he was of a very inconstant disposition and of doubtful morality, as were most of his companions in the service. Married in 1837 to an Indian woman of Grand Rapid, he soon has a falling out with his local superior, whom he accuses of undue familiarities with his wife. This man, while admitting his guilt, retorts by writing to P. S. Ogden, then in command of the district : " Last fall . . . when you visited this post, I begged of you to give him a set down for his improper conduct. . . . Also, I attribute most of the blame to Bélanger's uncommon jealousy, who repeatedly questioned, quarrelled, and beat his wife on my account."[1]

The removal of his superior does not seem to have improved Bélanger's character, since a year later, early in December, 1838, he arrived at Stuart Lake, having been dismissed from Babine by John McIntosh, who had previously written flattering encomiums on his behaviour. That officer seems to have regretted his step, taken perhaps on the spur of the moment, for on June 13th, 1839, Mr. P. S. Ogden writes him in the following rather stiff terms :

" Your demand for Bélanger cannot be complied with. However injurious, as you represent, it may prove to your trade, it would be equally so in the eyes of your servants. Really, I can scarcely suppose how a gentleman of your long experience in the fur-trade should have formed such an erroneous opinion as to exalt such a worthless scamp. . . . Had you, when Bélanger just left you, or subsequently per Larance, sent me a correct statement of his misconduct, accompanied by a request that he should be sent back, he would now have been with you."

In spite of this rebuke, the necessity of an interpreter

1. Letter to P. S. Ogden, Babine, March 5th, 1837.

who was *persona grata* to such noisy Indians as the Babines have always proved to be, soon asserted itself more and more pressingly, and finally induced Mr. Ogden to reconsider his decision; but Bélanger's second stay with McIntosh was not any more satisfactory than the first. Instead of waiting to be dismissed, the fickle young man deserted his post, and on the 6th of January, 1842, the head of the Company in New Caledonia had to write again:

" In regard to Alex. Bélanger, I have to request you to allow him to remain with the Indians and take not the slightest notice of him, and when you send your after-trade here, you will devise ways and means of sending him here, as it is my intention that he should go out and finally rid the district of his worthless carcass."

In the spring of the same year Mr. Paul Fraser, temporarily in charge of Stuart Lake, repeats to McBean, of Fort Connolly, Ogden's order, with the special caution that "the man should on no account be allowed to enter into any of the Company's establishments, or to be in any way employed by any gentleman in the district."[1]

Unable to re-enter by the front gate, Bélanger tried the back door. Indeed, the above prohibitory words had not yet reached their destination when he caused himself to be temporarily hired by the man, Brasconnier, to whose care the message had been entrusted. The latter was returning to his post, Fort Connolly, with two dog-trains loaded with dried salmon, and, finding it more than he could do to drive both toboggans alone, he took upon himself to engage the services of Bélanger, who was lying idle with his wife's relatives at Grand Rapid, on Thaché River.

But, as if he could not get out of mischief, he and his compeer, no doubt to diversify their rather meagre menu,

1. Letter to McBean, March 2nd, 1842.

killed two of the dogs, which were McBean's private property, and regaled themselves on their meat. Arrived at Fort Connolly, Brasconnier told the most extravagant story as to how they had died on the way; but Bélanger ungenerously confessed to the whole truth, whereupon his benefactor received "a sound drubbing."[1]

Such apparently insignificant details are of use, since they reveal some of the difficulties the Hudson's Bay Company had to contend with. On the other hand, it is but just to remark that the poor fellows usually fared so poorly!

Despite the renewed warnings not to employ a "deserter who left the Company to abandon himself among the natives," as Bélanger was stigmatized at headquarters,[2] the latter must have been reinstated in his former position of interpreter, since Mr. A. C. Anderson, the acting superintendent of the district, having had an occasion to see him, says of the conference he had with him: "I have spoken to Alexis about his conduct, though I perceive in your letter you make no complaint against him, whence I infer that he has given satisfaction lately."[3]

He then commends the young half-breed to the care of his correspondent, who is requested to act fairly with him, inasmuch as his services are valuable.

In strict justice to all parties concerned, we may remark that the wrongs may not have been exclusively on one side. McBean himself, though apparently well educated, was but a half-breed, and the reputation he has left in the district is not of the best. While he was stationed at Fort Connolly he received the following rebuke, which must have been so much the more galling to him as it occurred in the course of an official letter:

1. McBean to P. Fraser, March 16th, 1842.
2. P. Fraser to McBean, April 1st, 1842.
3. Anderson to McBean, March 8th, 1843.

"If reports are to be credited, your dealings with those who have been placed under you are of so curt and tyrannical a nature as to cause one to blush to have them recited. I am really of the opinion that should the same come to the knowledge of the Governor and Council, or the gentleman superintending the Company's officers on the Columbia, the consequences would be most injurious to your reputation and future prospects in the Company."[1]

We must bear these words in mind while we read the following charges against Bélanger, preferred five years earlier by the same McBean, under whose orders he was at Fort Babine. These last we reproduce, not so much to accentuate the note of natural depravity, to which he had an undoubted right, as to give an authentic picture of the times and the country.

Under date of March 5th, 1837, McBean wrote to his superior at Fort St. James:

"I beg to call your attention to the following serious charges I have to make against my interpreter, Alexis Bélanger, who has been guilty of these faults since he visited Stuart Lake:—First, as to robbery. He robbed an Indian of his fur account, and, of course, the Company. On the 22nd ult. an Indian called Matitzey accused Bélanger of having robbed him of a lynx caught in one of his snares, and of eight salmon he had put *en cache* for marten baits. Larance says he was against taking it, but Bélanger would not listen to him. . . . The interpreter, finding that Larance would have nothing to do with the cooking of it, cut the animal as it was, meat and skin, of which they both ate. . . . Although I paid the Indian for his skin, meat and salmon, I had much to do to pacify him.

"Secondly, Bélanger is accused by Lefèvre [another

servant] of having stolen out of his trunk at the west end of the lake twenty-two balls and half a powder horn of powder belonging to the Company, which I had left in charge of Lefèvre, and with which they were to guard themselves against the natives, should they be ill-disposed, and also a piece of soap of Lefèvre's.

"Thirdly, disobedience to orders. . . . You told me, Sir, that Bélanger was engaged as interpreter and laborer. Upon this . . . I thought proper to order him below to assist the rest of the men with the new establishment.[1] I had to tell him three different times to be off that morning, and he would not start until he had eaten a good portion of putrid grease which a relative of his, an Indian, had given him ; and the day he left he encamped about five miles from here—the distance to the north end of the lake is just a day's march. The weather was delightful and favorable to travelling, but there he remained the rest of the day and the whole night, risking his property and gambling with the Indians."

McBean then proceeds to relate how, bidden by Lefèvre, who was in charge of the work, to help haul pickets for the palisade of the new fort, he flatly refused to obey, and immediately returned to McBean's own quarters.

Yet the indolent fellow must have subsequently profited by Anderson's kind words, for in the course of 1844 we see him at the head of a Hudson's Bay Company convoy, a circumstance which would seem to indicate that he had regained to a certain extent the confidence of his employers.

But the love of liberty and the Indian instinct in him were apparently too strong to conquer. When the Stuart Lake brigade was on the point of leaving for Alexandria,

1. He means the fort he was endeavoring to build at the northern end of Babine Lake.

in the spring of 1848, Bélanger was again a free man living in the vicinity of Fort St. James. The adventurous life of the boatman appealed to his taste for excitement, and he engaged himself to steer one of the outgoing five boats under the general supervision of D. Manson.

At that time there lived amongst the Indians of the Quesnel band a young man named Tlhelh, who, having lost his wife, had sworn to revenge her death on a white man. Such, at any rate, is the native account of the cause of the rash act that was to follow ; but it is to be presumed that there was another motive guiding Tlhelh in the choice of his victim. As early as the 3rd of March, 1843, A. C. Anderson, writing from Stuart Lake to W. McBean, notified him that he had just received a note from Mr. Lane, of Alexandria, stating that Natsilh and two other Indians were said to have gone off from Stella (Alexandria) in order to kill Bélanger, who was then stationed at the opposite extremity of the district. The fact that he was singled out for execution by very distant Indians can be construed, without rashness, as indicating that the miscreant had committed in that quarter another of his usual misdeeds.[1]

Be this as it may, the Stuart Lake brigade had been for a few days on its way back, and its boats had just been painfully poled up to the site of the Quesnel native village, when Nadetnœrh, Tlhelh's maternal uncle, scornfully addressing the young man, exclaimed :

" Here is the one who was to kill a white man. See how many of them have just passed ; how many did he shoot ?"

And seizing his nephew's gun, an old piece with a short barrel, he threw it away some distance in the direction of the river, shouting at the same time :

1. The Quesnel Indians then traded at Fort Alexandria, and were considered as belonging to that place.

"There goes that good-for-nothing gun!"

Tlhelh, mortified at thus being indirectly accused of cowardice, silently took up his arm, blackened his face with coal,[1] and ascending the cliff close by, came in full view of the brigade, which was already in the act of crossing the stream to avoid the angry billows caused by the meeting of the Quesnel River with the Fraser.

All the boats, the last of which was steered by Bélanger, had already left the left bank of the latter stream, when a detonation from a fire-arm took every boatman by surprise, a ball striking at the same time the water by the side of the last boat.

"My! they seem to be firing at us," exclaimed Bélanger, who continued to hold fast in the water the paddle he used as a rudder.

Presently he was seen to grow pale and, sinking slowly on the Indian next to him, he remarked that he thought he had been shot. Having reached the other side of the river, they put ashore, when a slight examination brought out the fact that a musket ball had traversed his breast. After attending to his wound, and bestowing on him what little care the circumstances permitted, Manson sent him back to Fort Alexandria, where he died eight days afterwards.[2]

Thus ended the brief but eventful career of "that rascal, that scoundrel, that good-for-nothing wretch," as his superiors never tired of calling him. Keeping these not any too friendly dispositions in mind, and considering that his untimely end does not seem to have been altogether unprovoked, one might suppose that his disappearance

1. The equivalent here of the war paint of the Plain Indians.

2. Tlhelh had then the whole crowd practically at his mercy, but never attempted to improve his opportunity, another proof that he had some reasons for the choice of his victim.

from the scene of the world should not have been too deeply felt. Yet a terrible vengeance was to be taken for his slaying, and even innocent blood was to be shed— with the approbation, we regret to say, of the higher authorities[1] of the Hudson's Bay Company—as the price of that "worthless carcass" of which Chief Factor Ogden had wished, some years before, to be rid.

The man to deal out that terrible retribution was readily found in the person of Donald McLean, who was then in charge of Alexandria. To judge from his spelling and his ideas concerning the natives, McLean was an American.[2] He had been born in the initial year of the nineteenth century, and had entered the service of the Hudson's Bay Company when in his twentieth year. A most high-handed man, he could hardly stand opposition, and had angry altercations even with his own superior, Donald Manson, who, as we have seen, was not himself of any too meek disposition.[3] Nevertheless, he seems to have been capable of repenting of a wrong when the offended party was of his own blood and race. As to the natives, he had for them the most perfect antipathy and treated them with the superb disdain of an American. In fact, his very contempt for that race and the rashness which resulted therefrom ultimately cost him his life. One of his favorite maxims while dealing with Indians accused of a grievous misdemeanor was: Hang first, and then call a jury to find them guilty or not guilty!

Such was the man whom, in the month of January, 1849, we find with Montrose McGillivray at the head of fifteen armed men sent by D. Manson in search of Tlhelh, who had, naturally enough, taken to the woods.

1. Whom we must charitably suppose to have been misinformed.

2. We must remark, however, that some think he was born in Scotland.

3. See MS. letter of McLean himself to D. Manson, dated February 8th, 1854.

Arrived at the Quesnel village, they noticed that, though this was deserted, three huts on the opposite (or right) side of the river seemed to be inhabited. Repairing thither, they entered one, where they found Tlhelh's uncle with his step-daughter and babe.

"Where is Tlel?" cried out McLean through his interpreter, Jean-Marie Boucher, as he rushed in.

"Tlhelh is not here," answered Nadetnœrh.

"Well, where is he? Tell me quick," insisted McLean.

"How can I know his whereabouts?" replied the old man; "all I know is that he is not here."

"Then you shall be Tlel for to-day," declared the white man, who, firing with two pistols he held concealed about him, missed the mark, but finally shot the Indian dead with his musket.

Hearing the report of firearms, his son-in-law, who was just then busy in the next house cutting with a hatchet the leg bones of a deer he had killed the previous day, ran to his assistance, but was himself repeatedly shot till he fell lifeless on the snow. Which seeing, his young wife, a half-breed, with a child in her arms, sought a place of refuge in the cabin, when a man from outside (whom the writer has known for many years) sent her, perhaps by mistake, the contents of his musket, large deer shot, which crushed out the head of the babe and finally lodged itself in the mother's shoulder.

Not content with this exploit, the avenging party turned its attention to the third hut, where dwelt a very determined old man, who, bolting his door, defied them to come in, assuring them of the death of the first who dared force an entrance. Unable to accomplish otherwise their ends, they tried the roof of the hut, and McLean had already cut a hole therein, when, peering in, he was astounded to find himself at the end of the barrel of a gun, and had barely time to drop out of sight when it exploded.

This ended for a time the search after Tlhelh, the real murderer, who, despite the three deaths just chronicled— the woman survived—was still at large.

For this unwarranted slaying of three perfect strangers, of whose identity he was not even sure, and two of whom were most certainly innocent, McLean received the following encomium, which his employer, Donald Manson, did not scruple to send to Sir George Simpson and his Council :

" I have every cause to be well satisfied with the conduct of both Mr. McLean and Mr. McGillivray, as well as the men employed in this important duty, for the readiness with which they undertook the task and the promptitude displayed in executing all there was in their power to accomplish at that time. Messrs. McLean and McGillivray while under my command have always given me entire satisfaction, and in this last important duty I feel much indebted for the handsome manner in which they have executed my orders, so far as it was in their power."[1]

From which it seems clear that employed and employer were equally sanguinary, and that they were animated more by the thirst for vengeance than by the wish to obtain justice for the wrong done their corporation.

1. MS. letter, February 26th, 1849. In view of the above communication the reader will easily understand the reasons which prompted the cautious qualifications noticeable in the following statement by Sir George Simpson before the Select Committee appointed in 1857 to consider the state of the British possessions in North America: "I scarcely know a case, there may have been perhaps a few cases, in which our servants have retaliated " for murders at the hands of the natives (" Report from Select Committee on the H. B. Co.," p. 61). He declares that " the Indians are usually punished by the tribe to which they belong " (*Ibid.*), an assertion which could certainly not be construed as applying to New Caledonia.

That there is nothing exaggerated in our account of the affair, the most minute detail of which is vouched for by eye-witnesses, can be inferred from the character of the leader such as illustrated by the following passage of an official letter to the ruler of the district :

" The murderer of the deceased Bélanger is alive," he writes under date of March, 1850. " This I have discovered beyond a doubt, having sent J. M. Bouché and Turcot to the spot where he had caught his stock of salmon for the winter. A party of fifteen Taotins[1] are in search of him, having volunteered their services and expressed their determination to kill him. Many of the Nascotins[2] are, doubtless, friendly towards the scoundrel, who was at their village when the brigade passed, and while here. This I discovered by threatening death to those who should conceal him. And most assuredly if my will was only concerned, the black, ungrateful, bloodthirsty, treacherous, and cowardly scoundrels [he means those on the trade with whom he lived] should have prompt justice for it ; hang first, and then call a jury to find them guilty or not guilty."

Such summary executions must have had their critics at the time, for he continues thus : " I wish the glib-tongued speakers and ready-penned writers against the Company were placed for a few years in the unchristianized Indian country. They would, I suspect, change their sentiments. I know my own. and shall not be easily induced to change them."

That the Lhthau'tenne or Alexandria Indians did *volunteer* to kill their fellow Carrier is more than can be believed by one who knows their feelings towards their own congeners. Tradition, on the contrary, has it that the man

1. He means Lhthau'tenne, or people of the Lhthakhoh (Fraser River).

2. More correctly, Nazkhoh'tenne, the people of the Nazkhoh (Blackwater River).

who made an informer by threatening death was no sooner back at his post than, unable on account of professional duties to absent himself for any considerable length of time, he did not rest quiet until, by dint of cajoleries first, and then of threats, he engaged for the pursuit of the missing man another of his uncles, Neztel, with three other Indians.

Handing the former a gun, he promised him one hundred skins[1] if he brought in the scalp of his own nephew, at the same time threatening dire vengeance if he returned without it.

" Look at this gun," he is reported to have said in his usual haughty tone ; "its contents will find your heart if I see you come back empty-handed."

The distracted old man started with his three companions on his melancholy mission. After many fruitless attempts at finding his tracks, they finally came upon Tlhelh's retreat. He was crouching with his mother, in a nook of the Cottonwood River, under the shelter of a few fallen trees covered up with brush.

At the sight of the approaching party, the outlaw sprang out and tried twice to fire at the intruders, but his musket would not go off, which seeing, he seized his bow and arrows, and was on the point of using them when Neztel, who carried his gun sideways on his left arm and was slyly getting it ready for use, exclaimed :

" Stop, my nephew ; 'tis I, your uncle."

Upon which Tlhelh somewhat relented, and the old man, turning slightly around, discharged his gun at him with mortal effect. Tlhelh fell into the water, and being dragged

---

1. About $60.00. The natives say that he promised only sixty skins for the deed, in which case he must have kept the balance for himself. At any rate, he was authorized to offer one hundred skins as a reward for the slaying of Tlhelh.

out by Neztel's companions, his scalp was cut off; when, suddenly seized by remorse at his unnatural act, the old man, in a moment of passing dementia, attempted the lives of his own companions, and failing to succeed, offered himself as a target for their guns. When finally he had been calmed down, the entire party united in rendering the last honors to Tlhelh's remains, which were cremated on the spot.

The natives still recount, with unhidden glee, how, on his return to Alexandria, Neztel whipped McLean's face with the scalp of his nephew.

Such were the ideas of justice prevalent in those days throughout New Caledonia. To punish a misdeed by untutored savages, white men, who should have known better, turned themselves savages and paid back tooth (or rather teeth) for tooth, the innocent sometimes sharing the fate of the guilty. Arrest and trial as a consequence of a fault were something utterly unknown among the lords of the lonely North.

Such summary executions were, no doubt, considered measures dictated by the requirements of self-defence; but people will probably be found who would wish that at least a semblance of legal proceedings had been resorted to, had it been only to show the natives that such punishments were demanded by the exigencies of society instead of proceeding from a thirst for blood and revenge. As it is, the result on the native mind was disastrous; that system simply confirmed the Indians in the propriety of their hereditary feuds and the rightfulness of their unending reprisals.[1]

1. From a judicial standpoint, Manson's conduct in this instance was quite unwarranted, since he offered a reward for the *head* of the Indian who had *wounded* Bélanger, whose death he did not learn until some time after (see letter to Ferd. Mackenzie, then at Alexandria, October 16th, 1848).

Moreover, in the present case, one feature of the utmost barbarity was especially indefensible; we mean the scalping of a close relative, a custom utterly repugnant to the feelings of the Western Dénés, who never practised it even in connection with their enemies. To the shame of our own race be it said that, on this occasion, it was forced on unwilling Indians by a white man who had ever ready for use against them the epithets of scoundrels and barbarians.[1] We are well aware that Ross Cox, on the faith of his informant, Jos. McGillivray, relates[2] cases of scalping by the Carriers of Alexandria, which he says took place as early as 1827. But the latter have always declared that the gruesome practice was adventitious among them, and the fact that their exceedingly rich language does not so much as possess a word expressive of that act bears them out in their contention.

[1]. To add to the coloring of the picture which we endeavor to draw of the times and of the people to whom we have introduced the reader, we may be allowed here a remark which will bear us out in our contention that, instead of trying to elevate the inferior race, the representatives of the Hudson's Bay Company rather stooped to the level of the natives. In a previous monograph (" The Western Dénés," Proc. Can. Inst.), we have stated that, at the end of one of those treacherous massacres which the aborigines called victory, the guilty party—we mean the victor—would improvise a dance to the tune of a song, the main burden of which would be the last words of his victim. And so it came to pass that Donald Manson, the superintendent of an immense district, a man whose duty it was to use the influence of his position in the interest of civilization, did not scruple to celebrate, Indian fashion, the " victory " of his subordinates. Assembling his men and some of the natives in the large hall of his fort, he would make them dance, and ask them as did McLean : " *Tlelh tatqa ?* " (Where is Tlelh?) To which the dancers would reply : " *Tlelh hulœrh* " (Tlelh is not here), and then whirl about amidst the plaudits of the crowd.

[2]. "Adventures on the Columbia River," p. 321, New York, 1832. His graphic account of the bloody differences between the Lower Carriers and the Chilcotins should be read in connection with the entry of Connolly's Journal, reproduced on p. 124 of the present work. It fully corroborates our own surmise as to the date of said extract and consequently of the establishment of Fort Chilcotin.

CHAPTER XVIII.

"Club Law" in New Caledonia

1850–1856.

THE year 1850 opened with the following personnel distributed throughout New Caledonia:

Fort St. James (Stuart Lake), Chief Trader Donald Manson, assisted by a few clerks.

Fort McLeod............Clerk Donald McLean.
Fort Fraser.............. " Ferdinand McKenzie.
Fort George............. " Peter Ogden.
Alexandria.............. " H. N. Peers.
Babine.................. " Thomas Charles.
Fort Connolly...........Postmaster William Todd.
" " .... " M. McGillivray.
Thompson's River........Chief Trader John Tod.
" " ....Clerk George Simpson.

By this list it will be seen that the two posts of Chilcotin and Lhuz'kœz had already been abandoned.

At the same time our old friends P. S. Ogden and James Douglas formed, with Chief Factor John Work, what was styled the Board of Management of the Columbia Department, and the first-named gentleman was, besides, at the head of Fort Vancouver, while Douglas commanded at Fort Victoria, which he had himself called into existence in 1843 on the south end of Vancouver Island. Another ex-clerk of Stuart Lake, James M. Yale, now a Chief Trader, had charge of Fort Langley, on the Lower Fraser, which was that year converted into a depôt for the north, where all requisitions had thenceforth to be sent.

The personnel detailed in the above list was evidently inadequate to the needs of the district. Ever since Connolly had left Stuart Lake, the numbers of the "gentlemen" had been decreasing, until it had become hardly possible to conduct properly the affairs of the country. Good returns could not reasonably be expected from several posts, owing to the inexperience or the carelessness of the men in charge. Against this Manson had recriminated, but to no purpose; men could not be spared for New Caledonia, the Siberia of the Western Department, where ruled a man who might have been a whit meeker. Thus, for instance, both Wm. Todd and M. McGillivray were but postmasters whose inefficiency was well known. Indeed, the manager had several times vowed never to trust Todd with a post again; but, with his lack of men, what could he do? He warned the authorities on the Columbia that he would not be responsible for the consequences, and gave the young man an appointment. Again, F. McKenzie had been taken *in flagrante delicto* of negligence while in charge of Alexandria, and he had been relieved of that post only to be entrusted with another. Peers and Charles were promising clerks, but their years were few in number and their experience limited. D. McLean and P. Ogden were the only reliable men at Manson's command, to whom we might add John Tod, were it not that the ties which bound his post to New Caledonia were becoming lighter and lighter.

As to Paul Fraser, he was under a cloud, and on the official list we quoted from he is designated as one of the three disposable men. Charges of intemperance, which, by request, his immediate superior at Stuart Lake had had to investigate, only to find them not unfounded, added to a state of failing health which required medical aid, had caused him to sever his connection with the northern district. In 1850 he was appointed to the command of a party of twenty-four men composing the Saskatchewan brigade from York to Edmonton, and some time after we see him in charge of Fort Kamloops.

In that same year, 1850, Manson himself very nearly left the district under the plea of ill health. He had been granted a leave of absence, and Mr. Yale had been appointed to his place. Added to the reason he gave for his application therefor, it would seem as if there had been a secret motive—that of disappointment at being left so long in the rank of Chief Trader. His old friend James Douglas seems to have understood his true feelings when he wrote him:

"I sincerely hope the state of your health will not render it necessary for you to take advantage of the leave of absence granted by the Council. It will, in my opinion, be fatal, for a time at least, to your prospects of promotion in the service. I most earnestly advise you not to leave New Caledonia until you receive your expected step."[1]

Yielding to that friendly warning, D. Manson did not avail himself of the favor granted him. Governor Colville thanked him for staying at Fort St. James, and re-appointed him to the command of the whole district, but with the significant proviso that it was "understood that the Board of Management have the power of altering these appointments, so as to meet the exigencies of the business."[2]

Poor Manson, in spite of the sacrifice he had made in staying in his northern wilderness, was not destined to go up that step wherewith Douglas had baited him into keeping his post. Yet he was an able man, and untiring in his

1. Fort Victoria, November 27th, 1850.
2. York Factory, July 10th, 1851.

endeavors to promote his employers' interests; but his methods with his subordinates militated against his promotion in the service.

We have said that Paul Fraser had been appointed to the command of an important brigade in the east. These expeditions were at all times and everywhere attended with hardships and even danger; but it is safe to say that nowhere did they entail labor and difficulties as in New Caledonia. Hard on beasts, they were far from pleasant for man. The authorities tried route after route without ever obtaining satisfactory results. Now that Fort Langley was the depôt for the north, they set upon carrying their goods by way of Fort Hope Mountains, at the foot of which they erected a fort in the winter of 1848–49. But in 1850 the trail they had cut there was still so rough that J. Douglas directed the superintendent of New Caledonia to send men in advance of the brigade in order to render it passable to the horses.

In spite of these precautions horses continued to die by the dozen, and complaints became so frequent and so pointed that the authorities in the south got tired of the subject.

"You refer to the subject of the transport horses, a certainly endless theme," wrote a gentleman from Fort Victoria,[1] "and one which I did not expect to hear renewed after the great trouble and expense we have had in providing the large supply of horses, no less than 63, sent into New Caledonia last year. . . . The loss of horses in the interior for the last few years has been a subject of remark throughout the country, and there is a very general impression that the New Caledonia horses are both overloaded and neglected on the journey."

In cases of illness or accidents such expeditions were

1. Probably J. Douglas (signature wanting), April 12th, 1854.

hardly more pleasant for men. Witness that Iroquois, Michel Kanawokon, who was killed by the Indians Manson had hired to take him to Fort Hope, as he was so sick that he could not walk. The vagabonds, getting tired of carrying him, shot him through the head.

Another and more unexpected kind of danger arising from such expeditions had already caused an even more deplorable catastrophe. We have seen Chief Trader P. Fraser in charge of Fort Kamloops. Paul Fraser was a man who, conscious of his own abilities, would brook no opposition or even mere neglect in the execution of orders. His correspondence with the heads of the various posts in the North is a witness to the truth of this assertion.

"You will, on receipt of this," he once wrote P. Ogden in the absence of their common chief, "give me a reply in writing to the following : 'Why did you not forward Tappage with the Indians . . . as requested in my instructions to you of the 13th July?' By the arrival of the Indians from your quarters, I was informed that the Indians employed by the incoming brigade had reached you some time back, and instead of sending them hither, as you were in duty bound to do, you detained them to work at your hay. The consequence is that the boat has been detained and my orders disobeyed."[1]

If he was so curt with his brother officers, we may well imagine what must have been his temper while dealing with the servants. At that time clubbing and flogging were the devices resorted to in order to enforce obedience or punish a wrong. Now, it happened that for some offence, the nature of which is not remembered, he gave (at Kamloops) to one of his men, a French Canadian named Falardeau, such a brutal beating that the poor fellow died of it. As Baptiste, an Iroquois, was planing

1. Letter, August 13th, 1846.

and bending the planks intended for the luckless man's coffin, Fraser happened to pass by.

"What are you doing with these boards?" he asked of the Iroquois. "Rough, unplaned boards are good enough for that rascal."

The Iroquois, surprised at such a remark under the circumstances, stared a moment at his master; then, with the brutal frankness proper to his race:

"Hehm! when you die you may not have even rough boards to be buried in," observed the laborer.

Two months later Paul Fraser was on Manson's Mountain, seated in a large tent by the side of Manson, who accompanied his brigade, and the men were variously employed in preparing the camp when a crash was heard, and a big tree, which a Canadian was felling, came down on the tent, instantly killing Paul Fraser, who was reading his correspondence. So it was that he who had grudged a decent coffin to the victim of his own brutality had to be returned to Mother Earth without any kind of coffin.[1]

Paul Fraser was a son of Simon, the discoverer and founder of New Caledonia. He had been born in 1799 at Glengarry, Ontario, and was in the service of the Hudson's Bay Company since 1828.

His was by no means a solitary instance of cruelty to employees. Nay, he was considered one of the most patient among the officers. Such were the straits to which the traders in the far north were sometimes reduced for the lack of means of subsistence, that punishment by means of long detention could not be thought of. The club and the whip were resorted to in all cases of misconduct, unless it was thought that the fist of the officer well applied on the nose of the servant would suffice. Tied up,

1. This must have happened late in the spring of 1852.

sometimes to a ladder, the delinquent received the number of lashes merited by his conduct.

In these executions there was at least a semblance of formality, and the culprit could be persuaded that he received nothing but what was demanded by the requirements of justice. What was utterly reprehensible was the excessive violence, the uncalled for cruelty of the officers caused by fits of passion, when the men were mercilessly beaten with clubs or pounded upon until they were left senseless. Things came to such a pass that Sir George Simpson had to censure publicly such practices in an official communication addressed to Mr. Manson.

"I am sorry to state," wrote the Governor-in-Chief, "that the service in New Caledonia is very unpopular among the people in consequence of reports spread of the rough treatment experienced at the hands of the Company's officers. There is at present here a retired winterer from your district, one François Lacourse, who states that he was very severely beaten by Mr. Ogden, who knocked him down, kicked him, and injured him so seriously that the man has since then been subject to epileptic fits. He states that on another occasion you aimed a blow at him with an axe, but fortunately missed him and only cut open his coat, which he exhibited here; and he further adds that you afterwards presented him with a suit of clothes as reparation for the injuries.

"These are the *ex parte* statements of Lacourse and they may be in part false; but taken in connection with other cases of late years, they afford ample evidence of the existence of a system of 'club law' which must not be allowed to prevail. We duly appreciate the necessity of maintaining discipline and enforcing obedience; but that end is not to be attained by the display of violent passion and the infliction of severe and arbitrary punishment in hot blood. When a servant is refractory or disobeys orders he should be allowed a full hearing, his case examined fairly and deliberately, and, if guilty, either taken out to the depôt, put on short rations or under arrest—in fact, almost any punishment rather than knocking about or flogging.

" I have to beg you will make the foregoing remarks known to Mr. P. Ogden, Mr. McLean, and other officers in the district, and I trust we may hear of no more of these disagreeable affairs."[1]

And in a post-scriptum Sir George, who, like most of the governing minds, was fairness itself, added :

" Reverting to the case of Lacourse, we learn that he was mulcted of a year's wages for attempting to desert and misconduct. We beg you will distinctly understand that neither you nor any other individual officer in the service has the power to inflict fines on the Company's servants. If a case arise in which you think such punishment is deserved, your duty is to report the case specially to the Board of Management. As regards Lacourse, we have directed that the wages of which you deprived him be placed to his credit."

Such as are naturally inclined to pity the poor and the lowly may here find some consolation in the thought that, after all, the humble Canadian workman may have been indirectly instrumental in preventing high-handed Manson from getting his much-coveted Chief Factorship, which would have doubled his income without increasing his labors.

The Governor of the Company was so intent on being understood that in a private letter, written a day later, he again takes up the same subject, saying :

" You must really put a check on the 'club-law' that

1. Norway House, June 18th, 1853.

prevails in your district. It makes the service so unpopular that it is difficult to induce men to join it. . . . We hear that McLean and Ogden use their fists very freely, and I think you should caution them on the subject."

No wonder, then, if the peaceful Canadians did not enjoy the company of such pugilistic gentlemen. From Fraser Lake, John D. Manson, himself not a model of meekness, was writing to his father at Fort St. James :

" I spoke to Lebrun about his removal to Stuart Lake (Fort St. James). He seems to take it very much to heart, and said that surely you would never think of taking him back to a place where he gave thirty pounds to get away from. He also said that he so much regretted that sum of money that he swore an oath he would never return to remain at the same place. His answer was a flat refusal."[1]

Thirty pounds sterling was more than the yearly wages of the best paid laborers. Had the manager of New Caledonia again arbitrarily kept from a man his entire salary ?

We have just seen McLean and Ogden blamed by the Governor for using their fists too freely. Manson might have taken this as a gentle hint at his own methods, for in that respect he was perhaps the most guilty of all the officers in his district—with the exception, however, of McLean, who had no peer when it was a question of ungentlemanly conduct. Indeed, so freely had Manson used his fists and feet less than two years previously[2] that he had grievously compromised the safety, not only of himself, but of his whole establishment. He was in his rights at the origin of the encounter which occasioned the trouble ; but with a little tact and forbearance none of the disagreeable results he had afterwards to deplore would have ensued.

1. January 14th, 1856.
2. About November, 1851.

As we have seen, 'Kwah's successor as head chief of the Stuart Lake Indians was a third son, whom the French Canadian and other employees had dubbed " the Prince." That man was independent and rather haughty in his ways, and perhaps slightly aggressive in his dealings with the white traders. Tall and powerfully built, his strong will commanded the respect and obedience of all his subordinates. In a word, for a Carrier Indian, he was an ideal chief.

He had now two wives, one of whom, the eldest, he would generally leave in the village when he was called away for a short time. The younger, a half-breed, was his inseparable companion. Ill reports came to his ears concerning the conduct of his first wife, reports which implicated the reputation of Jean-Marie Boucher, serving then as an occasional interpreter. As the Prince was one day reproaching in the public hall of the fort the half-breed for his want of propriety, Manson came in, who, on ascertaining the cause of the altercation, ordered the Chief out.

The latter, however, instead of meekly submitting, made for the manager with his fist. Manson, of course, paid him back, which so enraged the Indian that, seizing a large yard-stick, he was on the point of using it against his adversary, when of a sudden it was snatched away from behind in such a way as to inflict a severe wound on his own temple, which caused him to fall unconscious at Manson's feet. The unexpected cause of the accident was no other than John D. Manson, who, bending on the now prostrate form of the Chief, helped his father to give him such a pounding that he had finally to be carried away senseless.

As soon as the Prince came to, he sent couriers to the neighboring villages with messages asking the men to come and help him annihilate the whites, and for three days Indians were seen pouring in from all quarters.

"JEM" BOUCHER.

By this time Manson and his people were at their wit's end. It was already some years since the manager himself, ever confident in his own resources, had dismantled the fort and taken down its palisade and bastions, and now hordes of savages were to assail him! Peter Ogden, a congenial character, was just on his way from McLeod's Lake with James Boucher, the eldest son of the terrible Waccan, who had inherited some of the latter's influence over the natives. A courier was immediately dispatched to hasten their arrival.

Meantime the buildings were put as much as possible in a position to sustain a siege, should this become necessary; the windows were blinded, arms and ammunition were distributed and such precautions taken as might help the whites in their critical situation. Fortunately for the traders, other counsellors than the Prince were at work among the now numerous bands of natives. His own elder brother, who was secretly dissatisfied with the secondary rank he occupied in the tribe, together with a most influential "nobleman" baptized in his infancy by one of the missionaries, were indefatigable in their endeavors to remind the people of the instructions of the "black-gown" and keep down the rage of the wounded Chief.

After much parleying and repeated gifts of tobacco by the whites, through the intermediary of J. Boucher, the Prince's stubbornness was finally vanquished, and, secretly flattered by Manson's supplicating attitude, he consented to go, at the head of the long file of his followers (who kept discharging their guns as they went, to warn the traders of what they might have done), and receive the valuable presents publicly bestowed upon him as a compensation for the injuries he had received.

But from that day forth there never was any great

friendship between him and the representatives of the Hudson's Bay Company. The Chief treasured up his sense of wounded dignity to such an extent that in the following years he frequently made himself really disagreeable to them. Once he went so far as to construct to himself a sort of native fort on the banks of the Stuart River, intending thence to shoot Manson as he left with his brigade.

Unable to harm him to any perceptible extent, the traders secretly vented their animosity against him by calling him names in their journal, of which here are a few entries :

"The Prince is out of temper to-day, and does not want us to hunt along the river."[1] "The Prince of Darkness dispatched his imps to seek for prey,"[2] which, being interpreted, means: The Chief sent in his followers for a supply of provisions. "Prince on hand. Gave in about seventeen martens ; grumbled as usual and made himself disagreeable."[3] "The Prince of Darkness was as disagreeable as ever, with tremendous demand for debt."[4]

This covert enmity between the Chief and the Hudson's Bay Company's representatives at Fort St. James could not be of any advantage to the latter, inasmuch as the Indians were bound to side with the former, and the thoughtless among them would not scruple to injure their interests by any means in their power. "Some blackguard has stabbed the young cow very severely," writes the chronicler under date 25th June, 1862. "I complained to the

1. Journal, March 29th, 1865. The country adjoining Stuart River was the Chief's hereditary domain, on which, by native law, he had exclusive control.

2. *Ibid.*, February 6th, 1866.

3. *Ibid.*, April 7th, 1865.

4. *Ibid.*, September 26th, 1866.

Prince, who tried to discover the delinquent without success." Two days later, a new cause of complaint is recorded. "The Indians have again severely wounded another of our animals with an arrow. If they go on at this rate there will be soon an end to all amicable feeling between the whites and the aborigines."

While these minor happenings were taking place at the capital of New Caledonia, measures pregnant with the most important consequences had been inaugurated at the future capital of British Columbia, whereby the Queen's Government in London had first taken cognizance of Fort Victoria, on Vancouver Island, where presided James Douglas, the quondam fisherman of Stuart Lake. On the 13th of January, 1849, the British Government had ceded that island to the Hudson's Bay Company on condition that within five years they establish thereon a colony of British subjects. A first governor, Richard Blanshard, had been appointed, who had resigned in 1851, when J. Douglas succeeded him as the Queen's representative on the Pacific, and became the head of a government which, though composed almost entirely of old Hudson's Bay Company men (John Tod, Roderick Finlayson and James Cooper), was to represent other interests than those of the fur-trade. In the meantime, Douglas kept his place at the head of the trading concern known as Fort Victoria and as a member of the Board of Management of the Columbia division or Western Department.

These details, while not directly affecting affairs in distant New Caledonia, were necessary for the perfect understanding of the present narrative.

From the little settlement which Douglas was laboriously forming round his fort, he watched with interest the passing of events in the Old World, and especially the various phases of the Crimean war, which then engrossed the attention of both hemispheres. Its most salient features he would communicate to Manson, whose combativeness he knew and whose delight for such information he well guessed.

" We have items of English news up to the 15th August," he once wrote to that gentleman. " Sebastopol was still obstinately maintained by the Russian army. . . . Having sent all my papers the other day to Fort Simpson, I have none at present to send you. The next file, however, will be reserved for your service."[1]

Pugilistic McLean came to the rescue, sending him from Fort Thompson (where he had succeeded Paul Fraser) a few newspapers containing the latest available intelligence concerning the war. At the same time he proceeded to give him news of a very different character—news that was to herald a new era for the fur-trade and the country generally. He wrote under date of October 29th, 1855 :

" Gold is abundant at Colville, and I suspect that many, if not all, of our men will be off in that direction before long. Mr. McDonald gives favorable accounts as to the richness of the mines, and says that people from all quarters and of all sorts were gathering to the diggings, Messrs. McKinley and Anderson among the number."

A month sooner Douglas himself had sounded the same note of alarm :

" I hope and trust," he said in a letter to Manson, " that the gold fever so prevalent here will not penetrate as far as New Caledonia, at least until next year, when you may expect trouble in abundance."[2]

Yet we venture to think that this was better news to Manson than the tales of sickness and misery that were communicated to him from Fort Connolly and Alexandria

1. October 2nd, 1855.
2. September 10th, 1855.

and the extreme penury, verging on starvation, brought in his own vicinity by the failure of the salmon run. From the former place he was told that many Sekanais had died, while all that the survivors near the fort could do was to crawl about. There also the superstitious mind of the natives having full play, the Nahanais had shot one of their own medicine-men, to whose machinations they attributed their misfortunes.[1]

At Alexandria, where Peter Ogden had lately assumed command, the new manager complained of the dilapidated state of his fort, declaring that he had not even parchment skins wherewith to close his windows. Ogden mentioned also the utter lack of provisions in his establishment and the starving condition of the surrounding Indians, which led him to fear for the safety of the Company's horses in his keeping.[2]

At home Manson had to feed his numerous personnel on rabbits and turnips, a diet which, in the absence of all farinaceous foods, is hardly adequate to the needs of a working man. Then, reverting to the glittering reports from the south, embodying the prospects of a possible fortune, he decided to write to that Board of Management which persisted in denying him the Chief Factorship, to which he thought himself so well entitled. He asked the gentlemen composing it for a leave of absence for the outfit of 1857, reminding them that for the last nineteen years he had held with credit a Chief Trader's commission. At the same time he warned them that, should his request be overlooked, he would find himself in the necessity of leaving the service.

His request was refused, a step which, after his own ulti-

1. Wm. Todd to D. Manson, January 5th, 1856.
2. To D. Manson, October 11th, 1855.

matum, was tantamount to a dismissal ; and in the course of 1857 he left New Caledonia never to return. After various vicissitudes, he established himself on a farm in the Willamette country, which was ultimately destroyed by an inundation.

Peter Ogden, the half-breed son of Peter Skene, succeeded him in the command of the district.

CHAPTER XIX.

Golden Cariboo.

1856–62.

IT is somewhat remarkable that the precious metal which was to have such a lasting influence on the red man's destinies within what is now British Columbia, was first discovered by representatives of his race. The Indians, who so far had been little else than the wards of the Hudson's Bay Company, were themselves to sound the death-knell of that powerful corporation's supremacy in their midst, and unconsciously, but not less certainly, proclaim the approach of a new era, when a contest would be established between their own forces and those of the incoming civilization which would leave them vanquished, demoralized, and verging on their ruin, both moral and material.

H. H. Bancroft constitutes himself the echo of a rumor according to which Chief Trader McLean procured at Kamloops gold dust from the natives of the Thompson River as early as 1852.[1] If this statement be founded on fact, the discovery must have been of very little importance, since we have seen the same man singing, at least three years later, the praises of mines within the American territory, without saying a word of any in his own vicinity. But it is certain that in 1856 or 1857 gold was found in rocky crevices on the banks of the Thompson River. McLean,

---

1. " History of British Columbia," p. 348.

having examined the grounds, sent to Victoria for iron spoons to dig out the nuggets. These were furnished, and he was instructed to give as much encouragement as possible to the Indians willing to devote their time and energies to that purpose.

But lest the Hudson's Bay Company's employees should be tempted to abandon their posts for the more exciting and generally more lucrative occupation of mining, and to prevent the untimely breaking up of the little settlement he was planting near Fort Victoria, Governor J. Douglas issued a proclamation declaring that all the gold *in situ* belonged to the Crown and forbidding all persons to " dig or disturb the soil in search of gold until authorized in that behalf by Her Majesty's colonial government."[1] That authorization was granted on payment of ten shillings a month, and even then the right to exercise that privilege was subject to such vexatious conditions that Douglas's act was ultimately declared *ultra vires*.

In the meantime these stipulations served to momentarily restrict mining to the native population ; but the gold thus obtained, to be of any use to its finders, had to be disposed of to the agents of the Hudson's Bay Company, the only parties who could turn it into account, and these, again, had to make it over to the mints, the nearest of which was then in San Francisco. The first lot of the precious metal to leave the limits of what is now British Columbia found its way into that city, where it was taken in February, 1858, by the Company's steamer *Otter*.

On its becoming noised about in the western metropolis that new and promising diggings had been found in what was still the nameless North, a party of some thirty prospectors left in the following March to investigate and report on the nature of the grounds. Leaving Victoria

2. " History of British Columbia," p. 353.

for the Fraser, they ascended that river up to within a short distance of Fort Yale, where they discovered Hill's Bar, which yielded gold in such quantities that a first band of four hundred and fifty of their friends took passage on the steamer *Commodore*, and left for the new Eldorado on the 20th of April. The ranks of the adventurers were soon swollen by thousands of newcomers, who, having first to land at Victoria, surrounded Douglas's erstwhile peaceful quarters by a lively city of tents. At this sight, the wily Governor increased the tax on miners to $5 per head.

In connection with the original little party of thirty or thereabouts, an adventure is related which well illustrates the sordid eagerness of unprincipled whites for lucre at any price, and their utter disregard of the welfare of others.

"One day, while the party were working away with their rockers on the bar, a boat belonging to Captain Taylor arrived with a load of whiskey, which he was selling to the Indians for $5 worth of gold dust per bottle. Many of them became drunk, and the white men on the bar, fearing for their lives, offered to purchase all the whiskey he had aboard for his own price. He declined the offer; so the miners, taking the law into their own hands, marched down to the boat one morning with their guns at full cock, and while a few of them stood guard over the captain, the others broke in the heads of the casks and emptied the whiskey into the Fraser River, giving Captain Taylor an hour to get out of sight, which he lost no time in doing."[1]

This praiseworthy action, prompted less by a consideration for principles than by the craving for personal safety (the Indians at the place were ten to one white man), did not suit some of the natives, who, having tasted the for-

1. "The Year Book of British Columbia," by R. E. Gosnell, 1897, pp. 89-90.

bidden fruit, regretted the departure of its dispenser, and were inclined to convert their displeasure into overt acts of hostility. The providential arrival of Douglas, however, saved whites and Indians from any bloodshed, and it is gratifying to see that the Governor's remembrance of the adventure at Stuart Lake stood him in good stead in his dealings with the Lower Fraser Salish.

A California expressman, "Billy" Ballou, having volunteered to serve the miners in his professional capacity, the latter entrusted him with samples of their gold, which, at that time, they obtained at the rate of $100 to $150 a day, a step which resulted in a further increase of their numbers.

Among the gold-seekers was a young man, Peter Dunlevy, who, unlike most prospectors and miners, was to cast his lot with the new country and become one of its pioneer settlers. When he came to the northern mines, in 1858, Indians in the vicinity of Fort Yale had massacred a number of whites, among whom was a woman. Nothing daunted by the prophets, who were predicting him all kinds of terrible eventualities as the unavoidable result of his rashness, young Dunlevy went up into the very heart of the disaffected territory without meeting with any molestation at the hands of the natives. There is nothing like being fair and honest, and as he was wont to say many years after, "the whites never had any trouble with the Indians until the latter got whiskey."

After having worked on a bar some three miles above Yale, Dunlevy went up the Fraser until he reached the mouth of the Chilcotin River.

He had been toiling there for some time with shovel and pick, when one day he was accosted by a stalwart Indian who, after having looked attentively at the yellow dust left in the young man's pan, remarked that if the latter would meet him after sixteen days at a certain spot, which he carefully indicated in a rough map improvised on the sand, he would show him a place where the same material was abundant. True to his word, the native, who proved to be the son of the Kamloops Chief, introduced Dunlevy to what was to become famous as the Horsefly mines.

In 1859 many of the miners, pressed by their ever increasing numbers and the limitations of the original goldfields, went up even farther, until they reached the mouth of the Quesnel River, which they ascended, there to find a number of rich bars. On one of them, Snyder's Bar, as much as $1,000 worth of gold was taken by three men in one day. On the north and south forks of the same stream good paying bars also were discovered.

The influx of white population caused by these discoveries prompted the foundation in that same year, 1859, of New Westminster. This immediately became the capital of a new colony, which, absorbing New Caledonia as far north as the Skeena River, on the one side, and the Finlay on the other, took in Forts Yale, Hope and Langley, with the adjoining territories to the forty-ninth parallel, under the name of British Columbia. The original Columbia of the Hudson's Bay Company had been found to flow in its lower course within American territory, and the name of the new colony suggested the fiction of an equivalent for the lost region.

We have referred to Ballou's venture. His was indeed the pioneer express within the new colony, in the sense that he offered to convey letters and parcels to destination with a certain amount of regularity. As to carrying the same for a scheduled pecuniary consideration, the Hudson's Bay Company had anticipated the American by fourteen years. As early as June 7th, 1845, the Norway House Council had decreed that postage on letters from strangers was thenceforth to be charged west of the Rockies. Letters to or from the Columbia, not exceeding half an ounce, were to be taken to destination for a consideration of one dollar, and twenty-five cents was to be paid for every succeeding half ounce.[1] Bearing in mind the times and the difficulties attending travelling, these terms were at least as reasonable as those of the new government of British Columbia, which charged the same sum on a letter from New Westminster to Antler Creek, a much shorter distance, and at a time when the increase in the white population rendered communication much easier and less dangerous.

In 1860 Keithley Creek was discovered by George Weaver and his companions, and various other creeks were soon added to the number of the streams which yielded a bountiful supply of the yellow metal. The Quesnel River itself gave, in the summer of 1860, employment to some six hundred miners, who earned from ten to twenty-five dollars per day, and several nuggets were picked up in that region weighing from six to eight ounces apiece. Ferguson's Bar then yielded as much as sixty dollars a day per man.

New discoveries followed one another in quick succession, until the Cariboo mountains, which so far had known hardly any other sound than the hoot of the owl, with the occasional stamp of the deer and the shrill notes of the Carrier's love-song, were now alive with the thump of the miner's pick and the rattle of his rocker. Harvey Creek, Goose Creek, Antler Creek, and other streams which were soon to become famous for their auriferous deposits, successively claimed the attention of gold-seekers, until those discoveries culminated in the finding, in 1861, of Williams Creek, the richest gold-field in the world, which was

1. Resolution No. 105.

struck by a man known as "Dutch Bill." Among the many claims taken up on that creek several yielded from $20,000 to $60,000 a year, and one man named Cameron did not leave the country before he had amassed $150,000 in gold dust.[1]

The miners generally went in small parties of two or three, bound together by the ties of partnership, while such as were possessed of capital would constitute themselves into regular companies employing men who worked for wages. One of these concerns once realized 180 pounds of gold as the result of one day's work,[2] while, later on, another, the Ericson Company, took out 1,400 ounces of the precious metal in six days,[3] and 1,926 ounces the following week. This last amount was equivalent to at least thirty thousand dollars.

Yet many of the miners were hardly better off for their luck than mere Hudson's Bay Company laborers, since, in their folly, they spent their money almost as quickly as they made it. The story is well known of the man who, having made some thirty or forty thousand dollars in the mountains of Cariboo, wasted the whole sum in champagne, wherewith he treated all persons present, as well as the neighbors and passers-by, and crowned his exploit by smashing with twenty-dollar gold pieces a costly mirror hanging in the bar-room.

Others, who deserved a better fate and were instrumental through their discoveries in making large fortunes, died poorer than the very latest arrivals at the diggings to which they gave their names. Witness the discoverer of Williams Creek, the German William Dietz, who shortly

1. H. B. Hobson, in the Year Book of British Columbia, p. 89.

2. "Travel and Adventure in the Territory of Alaska," by Fred. Whymper, London, 1868, p. 15.

3. *Ibid.*, p. 16.

after his good luck in Cariboo was living in Victoria broken down and dependent on charity. One of his companions, a Scotchman named Rose, met with an even less enviable fate, having died of starvation in the woods after attempting to record his sufferings on his tin cup, on which he scratched a few broken words.

In the meantime others were making thousands and thousands of dollars with their shovels and picks. Thus, a certain Cunningham realized, on an average, nearly $2,000 a day during the whole season, and Diller's claim produced the enormous amount of one hundred and two pounds of gold, or almost $20,000, in one day.[1]

These and other fabulously rich finds being noised about gave such an impetus to the mining industry that crowds flocked from all parts to the new diggings. Things came to such a pass that, to keep his men at their posts, Jas. Douglas had to increase their wages by £10 a year.

The first explorers had been practically all Americans, hailing mostly from San Francisco. The Canadians and other Britishers were slower in availing themselves of the treasures hidden throughout the Cariboo valleys ; but once they did move in the direction of the gold-fields, which were theirs by virtue of political arrangements, neither the difficulties of the route they had to follow, nor its extreme length and tediousness, could induce them to turn their backs on the promised land. While thousands of them went to the new diggings by way of Panama, others there were who preferred to run directly across the continent through the great Canadian North-West plains and Rocky Mountains. Several such parties left Quebec and Ontario in the very first days of May, 1862, and passing through the American cities of Detroit, Milwaukee

1. " The North-West Passage by Land," by Viscount Milton and W. B. Cheadle, p. 362.

and St. Paul, reached the Red River settlement one after the other or in combined companies composed originally of two or three smaller parties.

For the sake of safety through the hordes of Plain Indians, they all assembled in the vicinity of Fort Garry, deciding to proceed thence in a body under the leadership of a Mr. Thomas McMicking. Mrs. Margaret McNaughton, the widow of one of the young men of the party, which now consisted of some one hundred and fifty persons, has found in the vicissitudes of their journey overland the material of a well-written little book,[1] from which we learn that after several adventures, such as the desertion of their original guide—an accompaniment almost *obbligato* to all long expeditions throughout the wilds of British North America—they came in view of the Rocky Mountains on the 13th of August, soon after which they entered the great Tête Jaune or Leather Pass, with which our readers are already well acquainted.

As they were getting short of provisions, and their animals fared even worse in the mountain fastnesses, where no feed could be found, twenty of the party, in order to save, if possible, the remaining oxen, decided to try a route overland indicated to them by some Shushwap Indians, which was to lead them to the headquarters of the Thompson River, while the remainder, with the captain of the entire expedition, entrusted their lives to the treacherous waters of the Fraser.

After various adventures and many a perilous passage, in the course of which were drowned four of those who had preferred the swift and less cumbersome canoe to the large unwieldy, but safer, rafts chosen by the others, they finally reached the Quesnel River on September 11th, 1862, when

1. "Overland to Cariboo," Toronto, 1896.

they disbanded, some proceeding to the goal of their journey, the Cariboo mines, while others scattered throughout the country, adopting a variety of pursuits, some taking even to farming. The smaller party also lost two men on the Thompson, and dispersed on striking Kamloops. On the morrow of their arrival at that place, the Irish wife of a German named Schubert, who had accompanied them from Fort Garry, gave birth to the first white child born in that locality.

An independent band, led by Dr. Symington, which arrived at Tête Jaune Cache eleven days after the main party, suffered great privations on its way to the "Golden West," but was helped along by the Shushwaps of the mountains and the Carriers of Fort George, and, making for the south, ultimately reached Victoria.

On foot or by raft, such of the McMicking party as hailed from Queenston had covered very nearly, if not quite, one thousand nine hundred miles.

A fourth and somewhat later party met with such a tragical fate that its bitter experiences seem to have deterred others from following in its wake. It consisted of only five Canadians, namely, three brothers called Rennie, and two men known respectively as Helstone and Wright, who similarly repaired to Tête Jaune Cache, where they bought two canoes for their trip down the Fraser. With a view to greater security while shooting the rapids, they lashed these together, with the result—which would have been easily foreseen by less inexperienced boatmen—that their craft, becoming unmanageable in the midst of the raging waters of the torrent, was swamped, with the loss of most of their property. None but two of the Rennie brothers could swim ashore, while the other three men reached a rock in the middle of the stream, where they remained for two days and two nights without a morsel of food and suffering severely from the cold of the opening winter.[1]

When they were at length hauled over by means of a rope thrown to them from the shore, they were so frost-bitten and exhausted that they could proceed no farther ; which seeing, the two Rennies, who had already spent two days in working out their release from their narrow prison, provided them with a quantity of firewood, and, having parted in their favor with almost all that remained of their scanty provisions, they set out on foot to seek assistance at Fort George, which was not very far distant. But so little inured were these men to the hardships incident to the wilds of New Caledonia[2] that it took them twenty-eight days to cover a distance which they had expected to traverse in six, and which an Indian could easily make in three.

Natives were then despatched from Fort George to lend assistance to the unfortunates left behind, who were expected to have slowly followed the two Rennie brothers, after recuperating a little from their terrible experience on the lonely rock in the Fraser. But the Indians soon returned, alleging the depth of the snow as an excuse for the failure of their journey.

"Other Indians, however, discovered the party some time afterwards. Helstone and Wright were still alive, but, maddened by hunger, had killed Rennie. When they were found they had eaten all but his legs, which they held in their hands at the time. They were covered with blood, being engaged in tearing the raw flesh from

1. "Red River," by J. J. Hargrave, p. 234.

2. Hardships which were still enhanced by the lack of any trail, the daily thickening of the snow on the ground, and the necessity they were at to look to the woods for their means of subsistence at a time when they had lost the proper weapons to procure the same.

the bones with their teeth. The Indians attempted to light a fire for them, when the two cannibals drew their revolvers, and looked so wild and savage that the Indians fled and left them to their fate, not daring to return.

"The following spring a party of miners, on their way to Peace River, were guided by Indians to the place where these men were seen by them. The bones of two were found piled in a heap; one skull had been split open by an axe, and many of the other bones showed the marks of teeth. The third was missing, but was afterwards discovered a few hundred yards from the camp. The skull had been cloven by an axe, and the clothes stripped from the body, which was little decomposed.

"The interpretation of these signs could hardly be mistaken. The last survivor had killed his fellow-murderer and eaten him, as shown by the gnawed bones so carefully piled in a heap. He had, in turn, probably been murdered by Indians, for the principal part of the dead men's property was found in their possession."[1]

1. "The North-West Passage by Land," by Viscount Milton and W. B. Cheadle, pp. 237, 238. The joint authors we quote from are probably right in their last conjecture. In the estimation of the primitive Dénés there were in the world two classes of individuals unworthy of life, cannibals and madmen. Though members of their family in the east were sometimes impelled by hunger to eat even their own relatives, perpetrators of such revolting deeds were never safe afterwards, especially as it was then current among those tribes that cannibalism engendered a dangerous appetite for human flesh.

CHAPTER XX.

Improvements and Trials.

1862-64.

TURNING to less gruesome scenes, we may remark that it would be neither just nor fair to other pioneers to suppose that the overland strangers were the only wayfarers whom the thirst for gold led into the inhospitable wilds of New Caledonia. That very year (1862), two months before the McMicking expedition put in an appearance at Quesnel, " Jem Boucher cast up [at Fort St. James] from Alexandria, along with a party of five miners, *en route* to Peace River."[1] This was on the 10th of July, 1862. Exactly a month thereafter another band of prospectors, bound for the same destination, was camping close to Fort St. James. In the spring of the following year (1863), about seventy gold-seekers arrived at Stuart Lake in small detachments, among whom were two large boat-loads of miners, who, on June 2nd, came up all the way from Victoria, bound for the Finlay or Peace River. This last party had been not less than three months and a half on its way up to the capital of New Caledonia.

Surely such indomitable energy and admirable perseverance deserved some recognition in the shape of help

1. Fort St. James Journal.

towards greater travelling facilities. The right man to procure these was then in the right place. Ever since he had become governor of Vancouver Island, James Douglas had shown himself to be a great promoter of roads. He went even so far as to cherish the hope of connecting British Columbia with Eastern Canada by means of a waggon road, crossing the Rockies in the vicinity of Kootenay. This project failing, through no fault of his, he turned his attention towards the " Golden North."

At first it was customary for the miners to outfit at Victoria, and then make for Lake Douglas by steamer, whence they proceeded along the Pemberton Portage and the other lakes, on which steamers also plied, up to Lillooet. They were then forty-seven miles from Clinton. A waggon road had just been constructed (1861) between the two places by Gustavus Blin Wright, the great road-builder of the interior, a man of great energy and daring plans, with whose further ventures we shall soon become acquainted. It was then decided to connect the terminus of this highway, Clinton, with Fort Yale, along the forbidding defiles of the Fraser, and push through the green timber up to the great interior as far as the Cariboo mines.

A mule trail had already been cut from Yale to Boston Bar, a distance of twenty-five miles. This was converted, in the course of 1862-63, into a regular waggon road, which was built in three sections by as many parties. From Boston Bar to Clinton, as many as five different contractors had the work in hand ; and it is a wonder that, with so many minds at work, the result should have been such a uniformly perfect piece of engineering that even to-day

1. Mostly along the wall-like slopes of the meandering gorges, at the bottom of which the furious Fraser hurries its turbid waters to the bosom of the Pacific Ocean.

the traveller who lazily glides along the banks of the Fraser in the comfortable cars of the Canadian Pacific Railway cannot help admiring the audacity and skill displayed in its construction.

Gustavus B. Wright pushed the work through the green timber and the alkali belts up to Alexandria,

THE
CARIBOO
WAGGON ROAD.

which he reached in 1863, and the forty miles intervening between that place and Quesnel Mouth were also completed that same year. But it took two years to finish the road up to Barkerville, in the heart of the diggings.

By this time a considerable settlement had sprung up at the confluence of the Quesnel with the Fraser, and Barkerville—named after W. Barker, a lucky miner—was beginning to assume the airs of a town, with hotels where a not too clean blanket spread on the floor of a loft did duty as a bedroom ; where meals were served for a consideration of $2.50, though they consisted generally of nothing else than bacon and beans, unless one chose to add to the bill two dollars for three eggs and sixteen for a bottle of champagne. As late as 1864, potatoes sold there at ninety dollars a hundred.

Nay, more, even journalism, that now indispensable adjunct of civilization, was not slow in penetrating within the wilds of New Caledonia. In 1865 the "Cariboo Sentinel," a small four-page weekly, began to appear at Barkerville, and was sold at the moderate price of one dollar a copy. As the editor, a Mr. Wallace, was at the same time his own compositor, pressman, advertising agent, publisher and collector, there can be no doubt that his was a paying undertaking.

The same conditions which were the occasion of such expensive living in the valleys of the Cariboo produced a diametrically opposite effect in the vast territory to the north thereof, which for many years to come was to remain beyond the control of the new powers established at New Westminster ; for even in New Caledonia proper—we mean that part of the country peopled exclusively by aborigines—economical conditions were beginning to undergo a change, due to the introduction in that district of flour and rice, bacon and beans, tea and sugar for the Indian trade, and to a limited extent for the use of the Hudson's Bay Company employees as well. So far, only the clerks and higher officers had known these luxuries at their mess.

To Peter Ogden, the manager of the district at Fort St. James, who had now been promoted to a Chief Tradership, this happy innovation was due. His co-operators in New Caledonia, in 1864, were : At Stuart Lake, his own son, Peter Skene, with Messrs. Webster and Tebbitt ; at Fort Connolly, William Todd ; at Fort George, Thomas Charles, and at Fort McLeod, Ferdinand McKenzie, the three last gentlemen being the only relics of Manson's personnel. At Fraser Lake ruled J. Moberly, who was not to remain long faithful to his employers, while at Babine reigned Gavin Hamilton, and William Manson, a son of the former superintendent, presided at Alexandria.

It would seem as if the direction of affairs had been deemed open to criticism or calling for inspection at headquarters, for in the spring of that year Chief Factor Finlayson arrived at Fraser Lake in company with Chief Trader Ogden, reaching the capital of New Caledonia on the 3rd of June, 1863. After a three days' stay there, he took passage on one of the two boats of Davis, a man in the employ of P. Dunlevy, of whom more remains to be said, as far as Fort George, where, on the completion of the business which had occasioned his trip to the north, he took a canoe for Alexandria.

By the side of the boon conferred on the country by its opening to the commodities of civilization came a terrible curse, which, at the end of 1862, afflicted the southern part of New Caledonia, and almost converted it into an immense graveyard. Smallpox, brought up from the Coast, played havoc among the Chilcotins, decimating them until almost those parties only who were away in the mountains were left to represent the tribe. Coming north, the plague next attacked, in November, 1862, the Southern Carriers stationed in the valley of the Blackwater, who, flying through the woods crazed with fever and fright, communicated the contagion to the inhabitants of Peters Lake, where only eight persons survived. Then it extended its ravages from Hehn Lake, at the source of Mud River, to St. Mary's and Morice Lakes, where the immense majority of the natives succumbed. Two small villages still remain on St. Mary's Lake; but the scourge wiped away those which existed on the other sheets of water.

At first corpses were hurriedly buried in the fireplaces, where the ground was free of snow and frost. Then the survivors contented themselves with throwing down trees on them; but soon the dead had to be left where they fell, and the natives still relate in their picturesque language that grouse used to do their wooing on the frozen breasts of human corpses.

Fortunately, the very violence of the disease, added to the inclemency of the weather, prevented its spreading farther north, as very soon any camp attacked thereby became powerless and incapable of exertion, even of an attempt at flight. Fraser Lake remained untouched by the plague, and at Stuart Lake the only echo of the calamity was this mention in the fort's Journal : " Late this evening Mr. Moberly arrived from Fraser's Lake. He reports all well in that direction, but apprehends that the natives there will suffer privations, and that many of them are dying of the smallpox, thus putting those here in an alarming state and all applying for a second vaccination."[1]

In the face of the new order of things, so suddenly thrust on the Hudson's Bay Company, one may be tempted to ask what was its attitude. Writers there are who declare that it was one of latent, but none the less certain, hostility. Mining and trapping are contradictory terms, they claim ; those pursuits are mutually exclusive and radically

1. Journal, December 10th, 1862.

inimical to each other. Therefore the traders were bound to resent the influx of the gold-seekers.

This may have been the case in some parts of the country, but the Journal of Fort St. James at any rate does not warrant us in crediting the representatives of the Company in the north with such intolerant views. The governing minds of the south were, indeed, apprehensive in the beginning for the steadiness of their own men in presence of the inducements held out by mining, and they may also have been secretly adverse to contemplating placidly the threatened destruction of their supremacy in the country ; but their agents at the capital of New Caledonia at least had no words derogatory to the character of the strangers or condemnatory of their intrusion. They seemed rather to bestow a discreet smile of condescension and half-concealed pity on such as passed their post on their way to the ill-starred Peace River mines.

They could even afford to hold out to them a helping hand in their misfortunes, and at times even clerks served them in the capacity of guides through the woods. " The miners started off this morning with nine pack-horses and Mr. Hamilton as conductor "[1] is one of the entries in the Journal of that time ; and a week later : " Four unfortunate miners arrived this morning from the McLeod's Lake road. They went as far as Salmon River, and in crossing the river in a raft they lost all their mining tools and provisions."[2] At times the chroniclers seem even more hopeful than the miners themselves. " Perrault arrived with all Léon's property on account of bad news from the mines," we read under date of July 26th, 1863. " However, the mines may turn out quite the reverse yet, as many are still prospecting down Finlay's branch. Those returned are broken miners,

1. Journal, May 28th, 1863.
2. *Ibid.*, June 6th, 1863.

many of whom never mined, but gambled for a livelihood."

The one thing which the Company would not tolerate,
and was ever ready to resent, was the intrusion of free
traders within its preserves, and for this few of those who
have studied human nature will be prepared to blame it.
Unfortunately, the influx of miners was so closely connected
with the origin of free trade that at length the one must
have come to be looked upon with suspicion as the immediate cause of the other. The mining wave came and went,
leaving behind the fur-trader, who, perhaps little successful
in his pursuit of gold, tried his hands at amassing furs.

Sometimes just the reverse happened. The successful
miner, having acquired a certain competency, invested it in
a stock of such articles as are mostly in demand in the
Indian trade, and bartered out the same for furs. Thus did
P. Dunlevy, whom we left at Horsefly, and who started in
that line as early as 1861. The Shushwap Indians were
his first customers, and for six years Beaver Lake, to the
south-east of Soda Creek, was his headquarters.

Though he succeeded fairly well, his competition was, on
account of distance, hardly as much felt, or at least his presence as objectionable, as that of two retired miners, Peter
Toy and Ezra Evans, accompanied at first by a third
partner, who established a store at the village of Pinche,
barely thirteen miles from Fort St. James. As a matter of
course, from that day forth all the energies of the Hudson's
Bay Company's people were concentrated towards one single
object—to drive the audacious intruders out of the country.
To that effect a clerk, G. Hamilton, with two laborers left
on October 15th to erect an outpost, or guard-house, as they
called it, to counterbalance the action of the opposition
traders. The site of the new post was admirably well
chosen. The hunting-grounds of all the Pinche Indians

lying to the east of Lake Stuart, they had to pass the Company's guard-house, situated on Rey Lake, five miles to the east of Pinche, when their furs could easily be intercepted.

So far, good and well. But here our sympathy with the old Company must cease. Instead of confining themselves to strictly honorable means of competition, its agents did not scruple to stoop to measures which are every way reprehensible. Their journals are very reticent about such methods ; but there is yet at Stuart Lake an abundance of eye-witnesses, and even one of the guilty parties, through whom their conduct can easily be ascertained.

We read in the Fort St. James Journal, under date December 16th, 1865 : " Jem Boucher with Desmarais off to Pinche with liquor for Mr. Hamilton and Peter Toy." Three days later the return is announced of the party, accompanied by G. Hamilton and Jas. Bird, a kind of postmaster set over the guard-house on Rey Lake. Two more days elapse, when it is remarked that " Grosse-Tête," one of 'Kwah's sons, " is at the fort in a good state of mind." And on the morrow we see that Hamilton and Bird, who had returned to Pinche, arrived from that place with " all the Pinche Indians in their train."

This is innocent enough. But what were the real facts ? A keg of liquor had been taken to Pinche expressly for the Indian trade. This, on reaching its destination, was, by the addition of water, converted into two kegs and immediately sold out to the Indians. Anybody, man or woman, would bring a marten and receive in return a bottle of the exhilarating beverage. The original supply soon failing, Bird was dispatched for another keg, which went off as quickly as the first. All the furs available being now in Hamilton's possession, he returned to the fort with

J. Boucher and Bird, followed by all the Indians, who were endeavoring to proceed to a feast, to which they had been invited by their tribesmen near the outlet of the lake. But such was their state of intoxication that they could make but six miles during the whole day. As they were camped for the night, another keg of liquor was brought them from Fort St. James and immediately traded out. So that when they did get to the fort, men, women and children were, like Grosse-Tête, " in a good state of mind," though hardly able to stand or walk.

As to Peter Toy himself, if we are to credit the natives, he never resorted to so dishonorable means (perhaps because he never was in a position to do so), and of course, after a time he had to give up the contest.[1] One of his original partners, a certain W. Cust, took it up himself at Fort George, and managed to eke out a living there for a few years.

But perhaps the most galling to the Hudson's Bay Company of all such ventures was when their own men profited by the knowledge acquired in the service of the real gains realized in the fur trade to sever their connection with the great corporation and set up themselves opposition stores. This J. Moberly did, and others have done after him, only to find out the error of their ways. Even at this late date, we can well imagine the smile of satisfaction which illuminated the countenance of the scribe as he wrote on the 16th of June, 1865 : " Mr. Moberly arrived from Fraser's Lake, who has given all his furs to the Hudson's Bay Company, and leaves the country with a debt of about two thousand dollars—$2,000."

1. That trader is the same of whom Gen. Butler speaks as being a Cornish miner (" The Wild North Land," p. 288 ; " Far Out," p. 64, *et seq.*).

CHAPTER XXI.

From Chilcotin to Omineca.

1864–1871.

SO inviting were the gold-fields of Cariboo that it was thought one could not make them too accessible. Some were for following Mackenzie's route and cutting a trail from Bentinck Arm to the Upper Fraser, and a party of Royal Engineers was even sent to examine and report on it. A more numerous faction agreed with Mr. Alfred Waddington, who, almost since the inception of the mining operations, had protested that the advantages of a public highway through Bute Inlet were incomparably superior. This route, he claimed, would render that journey 175 miles shorter than by the Fraser River valley. His intention was to establish regular steam communications between Victoria and the head of that inlet, and thence build a waggon road up the Humalhkhoh River, through the Chilcotin territory, whose exceptional resources in agricultural and grazing land would thus be opened to the settler.[1] So sanguine was he of success that, even after the Fraser River route had

1. If we are to credit Fred. Whymper, A. Waddington was the first to publicly advocate the expediency of a transcontinental railway to unite British Columbia with the eastern provinces. That gentleman duly explained his scheme before the Royal Geographical Society, and his proposition received some amount of attention in the public press of Canada, though it was generally branded as premature.

been adopted, he organized a private company and, early in 1864, sent a force of sixteen men to battle against the innumerable difficulties presented by the Coast range of mountains and force their way through the forbidding gorges, where rocks thousands of feet high towering over roaring torrents, by the side of glittering glaciers and perpetual snows, seemed a constant menace to the lives of the road-makers.

Yet, great as the difficulties presented by nature undoubtedly were, those arising from the restlessness of the inhabitants of those wilds were even more formidable, as the strangers learned at their own expense. We have had more than once to refer to the turbulent character of the Chilcotin Indians. So late as 1864, their appearance and costume did not betray much contact with representatives of European civilization, and in the absence of all missionary influence their inner self had undoubtedly remained even more refractory to humane ideas. A traveller thus describes a small band of them he met at Bute Inlet:

"They had rings through their noses, were much painted, and wore the inevitable blanket of the Coast. For the rest, there was nothing very characteristic in their costume, some having a shirt without breeches, some breeches without a shirt. Two of them were picturesque with their wolf-skin robes, hair turned inwards, and the other side adorned with fringes of tails derived from marten or squirrel."[1]

On the 29th of April, 1864, two of these savages, hungry and tired out after a vain ramble through the mountains, asked for something to eat of a Jim Smith, who had been left in charge of some provisions and was keeping the

---

1. "Travel and Adventure in the Territory of Alaska," by Fred. Whymper, London, 1868, p. 19.

ferry on the Humalhkhoh. Their request having met with a haughty refusal, aggravated by insulting epithets, the younger man, enraged at such a reception at a time when he was so needy, shot his insulter, and, hastening with his companion to a camp of Indians, told them of the words and fate of the ferryman, and the whole band transported themselves to the night quarters of the road-makers. Then, very early in the morning of the 30th, they fell on the sleeping workmen, on whom they dropped their tents, and, by firing at them and running knives or launching axes into their bodies, killed fourteen of them. " One of the survivors, Petersen, a Dane, . . . hearing the shots, jumped out of his blankets and was immediately struck at by an Indian with an axe ; he stepped aside just to see it fall heavily on the ground, and a few seconds after this was shot in the arm. Faint, and bleeding copiously, he plunged into the river by, and its swift waters carried him down half a mile over the stones and snags, bruising him much. He managed to reach the bank, and was soon after rejoined by Mosley, a man who had escaped almost unhurt. . . . The third man, Buckley, an Irishman, who afterwards joined them, had been stabbed repeatedly by the Chilcotins, and fell, faint from the loss of blood, remaining unconscious for hours, and they left him, imagining he was dead."[1]

These men, after various adventures, eventually reached the Coast, when they repaired to Nanaimo and Victoria, where they told the melancholy news of the fate of their companions:

Three weeks after the Humalhkhoh massacre some men under a Mr. McDonald, hailing from Bentinck Arm, with a pack-train of forty-two loaded animals, met with a similar

[1]. " Travel and Adventure in the Territory of Alaska," by Fred. Whymper, London, 1868, p. 19.

fate, only one of them escaping unhurt, though some of them died game, as, for instance, the leader, whose horse having been shot under him, mounted another, which was also shot down, when he took to the bush and, standing behind a tree, kept the Indians at bay, firing at them with his revolver until he fell bathed in his blood.

The total number of the Chilcotins' victims was eighteen, including the squaw of McDougall, one of the party, who had, but too late, apprised the whites of the fate that was in store for them.

" The Indian is to-day very little understood," wrote an author almost forty years ago. We may add, in our own name, that he has remained so to most readers. It stands to reason that the Chilcotins, who, in spite of their undoubted restlessness, had not once attempted the lives of the traders at Alexandria, and even at the fort built in their very midst, whose " garrison " was always ridiculously weak, must have had some motive in going to such extremities. The rebuke administered by the ferryman was but the spark which lighted the fire of discontent which for some time had been smouldering in their breasts. That plunder was not their aim is evident from the fact that, eight years after the massacre, the tools and belongings of their victims were found in the identical spots where they had been left. The murderers' reasons were made apparent through private information which found its way into the startled communities at Victoria and New Westminster, only to be indignantly repudiated by A. Waddington in a letter to the *British Colonist.*[1] That gentleman did not deny that the trifling of the whites with the Chilcotin women was one of the main causes of the disaster, though he gallantly exculpated his own men

1. June 13th, 1864. Dr. Grant in his " Ocean to Ocean," admits (p. 326) that " provocation had been given them."

from any such guilt. Then, publicly defying contradiction, he asked:

"Is it true or not that, the year before last, Lieut. Palmer or his sergeant, on their way through to Alexandria, broke through some well-known Indian usage, and that Lieut. Palmer knocked down the son of the second chief of the tribe, who resented it, and that Lieut. Palmer then threatened to shoot him, on which the young man returned with fifty armed Indians, bared his breast, and dared him to do so? The Indians were too powerful, and Lieut. Palmer desisted; but surely that affront has never been forgiven."

He then states that, about the same time, the whites brought the smallpox to Bella-Coola, whence it spread to Nakuntlun, then the principal settlement of the Chilcotins, killing one-third of the whole tribe.[1] "I myself saw the graves of perhaps five hundred Indians," declares the writer, who adds that, shortly after, two white men, Angus McLeod and a certain Taylor, went and stealthily gathered the blankets of the dead which had been thrown away in the bush, and were therefore infested with smallpox, which they sold out again to the Indians without revealing their origin, thus causing a second visitation of the plague, which carried off the second third of the native population, whereupon he pointedly exclaims: "Is it to be supposed that such diabolical deeds did not arouse the hatred of the Indians?"

But the harm was done, and the question now was to prevent a repetition of its consequences by meting out adequate retribution to the murderers. A reward of two hundred and fifty dollars was offered for the apprehension of any of them; but it was evident that without concerted action under the auspices of the colonial

---

1. This is the first visitation of the plague mentioned in our last chapter.

government itself no satisfactory result could reasonably be expected. Therefore military expeditions were fitted out in different places.

On June 13th volunteers from New Westminster arrived at Victoria, where they were joined by a goodly contingent raised in the latter place. Governor Seymour, who had just succeeded Douglas, freshly knighted (1863), put himself at the head of that force, and left two days later by the *Sutlej* for Bentinck Arm, where he took as allies some thirty or forty of the Bella-Coola Indians. Meanwhile forty miners from Cariboo had formed themselves into a posse under the leadership of Judge Cox, an eccentric character, and, soon joined by still another party headed by our old acquaintance, D. McLean, whom the perspective of Indian slaughter had brought from his retreat on the Bonaparte, had already transported themselves in the midst of the hostile district before Seymour's forces came up.

Cox's party, now numbering sixty-five men, had just camped at a place which seemed to have been occupied but lately by the Chilcotins. In the morning of July 17th, McLean, who pooh-poohed all warnings of danger and declared to whites and Indians that "when the Chilcotins would see him they would bend down their heads and he would kill them with a club," went on reconnoitring in company of a single Indian, Jack, of Alexandria. After having crossed a prairie where they were the observed of several pairs of unfriendly eyes, they climbed a rocky hill, the top of which they were just nearing when Jack thought that he heard a gun snap.

"Pshaw!" contemptuously exclaimed McLean, in answer to the Indian's remark, "they would not shoot us. They are too much afraid of me."

He had scarcely finished the sentence when he fell dead,

shot by Anukatlh, a Chilcotin, who was never apprehended,[1] so that the death of him who had ill-treated and
slain so many natives remained unavenged.

On the very evening of the day when he was executed—
for his slayer afterwards declared that he had killed him
as a punishment for his harshness to the Indians, but had
spared Jack because he was guilty of no crime—Seymour's
volunteers effected their junction with Cox's party, and
the combined force now numbered some two hundred men.

For about a month the search after the murderers was
carried on without result. Little by little, however, the
Chilcotins came to trade with Cox's men, and near the
middle of August it became noised about that some of
the suspected murderers had come to the camp of Alexis,
one of the native chiefs. Cox immediately dispatched one
of his most trusty Indians to induce them to surrender,
pledging his word of honor that, as they had acted under
provocation and in ignorance of the white men's laws, their
lives would be spared, and if they would promise henceforth to behave well they might even receive presents.

The pursuit of the murderers in the inaccessible retreats,
where they had taken refuge, independently of the great
cost it entailed,[2] was becoming more and more hopeless on
account of the difficulty of victualling the pursuers, and
there was hardly any prospect of capturing " anything but
mosquitoes," as a paper of the time put it. Hence the
expediency of asking the guilty parties to surrender.

Somewhat skeptical as to the worth of the stranger's
words, the Chilcotins, eight in number, sent, on the 15th of
August, " one of their slaves to Mr. Cox's camp to ascertain the terms of surrender. Cox packed the slave with a
sack of flour and other articles, and sent a message to the

1. He died scarcely three years ago.
2. The expedition cost the country £16,000.

effect that they desired to make friends with them, and invited them into the camp. About noon of the same day Tellot [the principal man wanted], with his party, accompanied by their families, came into camp and found to their surprise that they were surrounded by armed men, who informed them that they were prisoners, and ordered them to lay down their arms. All, with the exception of Tellot, complied, but he grasped his musket by the muzzle and smashed it into atoms against a tree, and drawing his knife dashed it on the ground, and coolly folding his arms across his breast, invited them to shoot him, remarking with scorn depicted on his countenance, that "'King George' men were great liars."[1]

The eight Chilcotins were immediately taken to Quesnel, where they underwent a regular trial. Two of them being retained by the Crown as witnesses, five were found guilty of murder, and hanged in the presence of a great concourse of Indians convoked (and some of them paid) for the circumstance, while the eighth was sentenced to imprisonment for life, but escaped on his way down.

Most of the murderers were never caught, and Waddington's road, which in preparatory surveys and actual work had already cost $60,000, had to be abandoned.

The Carriers were more fortunate or behaved better in their first serious encounter with the whites. Since twenty years or more it had been felt that quicker communications between the Old and the New Worlds than those afforded by the mail packets were very much wanted. An American of great initiative, Cyrus Field, had repeatedly attempted to supply that want through his then novel plan of a trans-Atlantic cable ; but nature and fate had so far

1. *The British Colonist*, September, 1864, after the New Westminster *Columbian*. It would seem that Cox was in good faith when he made his promises to the Chilcotins, but that these were disregarded by the Colonial Government.

baffled his efforts. Deeming his undertaking doomed to failure, the Americans had resolved to unite the two hemispheres by means of a telegraph line traversing the mainland of British Columbia and the Russian possessions— now Alaska—whence the wire would be laid down Behring Straits across to north-eastern Asia.

To that effect some financiers formed a company called the Western Union Telegraph Company, which had the line through British Columbia surveyed in 1865, while the actual building work thereon commenced only in the spring of the following year, under the direction of Mr. Edward Conway. Colonel Bulkley was one of the directing minds of the company, and his name was given to the important river which flows into the Skeena some one hundred and sixty miles from its mouth.

In September, 1866, the building party had reached a point forty miles north of the Kispiooks River, when news was received to the effect that Cyrus Field had at length been successful in laying his cable across the Atlantic Ocean. This, however, did not entirely stop the proceedings. It was felt that after a time the wire might refuse to work, as had happened on a previous occasion. Exploring went on during the winter months until the brook now called Telegraph Creek was reached, when it became evident that the enterprising American's success was destined to be permanent.

The efforts of the Western Union Telegraph Company were thus rendered abortive. The undertaking was not, however, to remain entirely without results. We have already seen that as early as 1862-63 the mining wave, whose centre was the mountains of Cariboo, had surged about until it had reached the region immediately to the east of Fort St. James, which was already beginning to be called Omineca, after one of the tributaries of the Finlay, the Omœn River.[1] While prospecting for the telegraph line, some of the men had heard of the isolated mines back of Stuart Lake, which were as yet undeveloped, and, upon the breaking up of the party, they turned their attention to the search after the precious metal. Among them was a French Canadian named Vital Laforce, who soon struck rich pay on a creek which is now called after him.

The success of the new miners could not long be kept secret. Indeed, the very mystery with which some of them tried to surround their operations added zest to the ardor with which the Cariboo miners and others endeavored to investigate for themselves. In a short time, the Stuart and Skeena Rivers were dotted with boats and canoes full of prospectors. Henceforth, in the Fort St. James' Journal, which at that time is extremely dull and laconic, we hear of nothing but the arrival or departure of such gentlemen as Dancing Bill, Black Jack, Dutch Harry, Red Alick and French Franck.

The Stuart Lake route led them to Fort St. James, whence they originally went to Lake Tatla by way of Thache and Middle Rivers. From Tatla Lake they plunged into the endless groups of mountains at the base of which flowed the creeks Vital, Manson, and Germansen, which rolled their noisy waters over the yellow dust. The miners hailing from the Skeena had to cross the Babine mountains onto the lake of the same name, as far as a bay some thirty miles south of the fort, whence G. B. Wright had built a waggon road, over which was carted the freight which Pat. Hickey and others brought in large boats.

This was in 1869-70. The following year the Omineca

---

1. Omœne-khah, in Sekanais—*khah* stands for river. Bancroft sagely remarks, after an Hudson's Bay Company man, that it is called "after a species of whortleberry growing there and forming a staple article of food of the Indians!" Omœne-khah is a Sekanais word which means "lake-like or sluggish river."

mines saw their best days, though the country never fully justified the expectations entertained by the miners accustomed to the fabulous yields of Williams and other creeks. It is estimated that $400,000 was obtained during that year by about 1,200 people. So great, indeed, were the anticipations of some people, prominent among whom was G. B. Wright, that, despite the formidable difficulties opposed to navigation in the shape of bars and rapids in the rivers, a steamer—well named *Enterprise*—was built and, after incredible hardships, brought up to Fort St. James, in front of which she arrived on Sunday, 6th August, 1871. She was designed to ply between that place and Tatla Landing, but once she had gone north she never returned to Stuart Lake, as a direct trail to the diggings had just been cut, which was immediately adopted by the miners. Mr. Edgar Dewdney was the gentleman whom the gold-seekers had to thank for the trail leading from Stuart Lake to Omineca. He cut it in 1871, and in the same year Captain William Moore rendered a similar service to the same class of men by improving an old Indian trail from Hazelton, on the Skeena, to Babine.

CHAPTER XXII.

Some of the Later Pioneers.

IN the midst of this influx of strangers, so near its doors, what became of the Hudson's Bay Company? The old corporation fared tolerably well, though its wards, the Indians, were getting sadly demoralized in more ways than one. Slowly, but surely, the young town of Quesnel was assuming the airs of a rival to the post of Fort St. James, whose commercial supremacy was seriously threatened. The Company had not, it is true, been slow in founding an establishment at the new place; yet Peter Ogden did not relish the idea of seeing his Indians go and trade at the southern post, especially when the guilty parties were such influential men as the very Chief of the village nearest to him, whose principal function, he thought, should have been to keep his people loyal to the local representatives of the Company. Some entries of his journal betray that secret jealousy, as, for instance, the following: "Prince (the Chief) made an appearance, seeming no better for his trip to the promised paradise of Quesnelle."[1]

Meanwhile, things were fairly lively in his own vicinity. A saloon, that unavoidable token of that which some call civilization, had been erected, wherein the fort chronicle says that "grand entertainments"—and something else—were given. To offset the usual effects of the kind of goods

1. July 10th, 1867.

plentifully supplied in said institution, two gentlemen, Peter O'Reilly and W. H. Fitzgerald, were acting as the representatives of the Colonial Government. In a new country, among aborigines whose language they did not understand and whites who only too often imagined that they were above every law because they had crossed the limits of civilization, their path was full of thorns, and mistakes were to be expected, especially in cases where Indians were concerned.

In the latter part of November, 1871, one of the lesser chiefs of Babine Lake had bought a sack of flour of a Mr. Nelson, with a view to publicly distribute its contents to his fellow-villagers. When the whole crowd had assembled in his lodge, it was found that the sack contained nothing else than ashes. Indignant at the mean trick played on them, the Indians sent two of those who knew a few words of English to recover the flour, which had been paid for. As the trader would not accede to their demand, they helped themselves to the article they considered theirs, after which they had their promised "potlatch."

A few days later, Judge O'Reilly happened to pass by. The white man laid a complaint before him, and, as no interpreter could be found, Chœnnih, the Indian who had taken the sack of flour, was condemned to six months' hard labor and sent to Victoria.

Accompanied by three armed white men, two of whom preceded him in the narrow trail, Chœnnih sullenly went on, wondering at the kind of justice the white chief was dispensing, when, having managed to disengage his hands from the irons that bound them, he sent the two first guards rolling down a precipitous hill, where the third man soon rejoined them. A few minutes after, he was out of sight, a free man again.

A regular mail service was also established, in connection wherewith R. Sylvester and a certain Brick won golden opinions for their efficiency as public servants. The end of that same year, 1871, saw also the first Canadian Pacific Railway survey through the district, under the direction of Mr. Charles Horetzky.

Peter Ogden, the ruler of New Caledonia, did not live to see the glory of those days. He died on the 9th of October, 1870, after having held the reins of power since 1856, with the exception of the outfit of 1868-69, when James A. Grahame replaced him, as the wisdom of his administration seemed open to question.

At the time of Ogden's demise there were in the district three commissioned officers, namely, Messrs. H. Moffat, Wm. Manson, and Thomas Charles. All believed that Mr. Moffat was a superior man, well fitted to take charge of the district. The authorities of Fort Garry thought otherwise, and Mr. Gavin Hamilton, heretofore a simple clerk, was at once promoted to a Factorship and entrusted with the direction of affairs; whereupon the above-mentioned gentlemen sent in their resignation.

G. Hamilton had the advantage of being very well connected. His grandmother was a near relative of Lord Macaulay, the historian, and by his maternal side he was a nephew of Dr. J. Rae, the explorer, while one of his cousins was Sir Robert Hamilton, at one time Governor of Tasmania. He was born on January 1st, 1835, at Stromness, in the Orkney Islands, and having signed a five years' apprenticeship to the Hudson's Bay Company, he sailed for America on the 17th of August, 1852, and landed at Victoria in January of the following year.

His first station was Fort Langley, where he served under J. M. Yale, "a fine specimen of a trader, though a very diminutive man," as Hamilton wrote many years after. From the start Hamilton knew how to win the hearts of the natives with whom he came into contact, and even the worst among them took kindly to him. Yet he resigned in August, 1857, but was persuaded by Chief Trader Ogden to stay in the service and accompany him up to Stuart Lake.

To show the wonderful fearlessness of the man, we may mention that in 1855 he saved from a burning store-house seventy or one hundred barrels of gunpowder, with the assistance of men whom he rallied after the first shock of fright and buoyed up until the end of the terrible ordeal. For this feat he received a premium of £100, and his men were also proportionately rewarded.

G. Hamilton, who had married Peter Ogden's daughter, seems to have always taken kindly to the Indians, and this goes a long way to explain his success among them. He was also possessed of some knowledge of medicine, and soon became renowned for his surgical skill, a circumstance which added not a little to his popularity among his dusky wards.

He was moreover constantly friendly to the miners, whose goods and working implements he would store without caring for the construction his superiors in Victoria would put on his action. It is only natural to suppose, however, that his kindness did not extend to his opponents, the free traders.

One of these, P. Dunlevy, we have already seen tempting fortune among the Shushwaps who resorted to Beaver Lake to barter their furs for the white man's goods. Ambitious to extend his operations and augment his gains, he dispatched, in 1870, a boat loaded with sundry articles for the Indian trade up the Fraser, Nechaco and Stuart Rivers. Three years later, yearning for even greater laurels, he inaugurated his annual trips through the Peace River district, passing through the McLeod Lake region, which had never known the sweets of commercial competition. To further his ends, he established a post at Giscome Portage, a section of land named after a man he had for some time in his employ as cook. Outposts farther down towards the Peace were similarly established until, despite the proverbial loyalty of the Sekanais Indians to the Hudson's Bay Company, he accumulated quite a competency, some of which, however, he subsequently lost through no fault of his.

For some years he had sent as his agent through the wilds of the north a man whose nickname of " Twelve-foot Davis " was due to his having "jumped," or irregularly acquired, a plot of land 12 feet wide which ultimately yielded its owner $1,000 per foot. Davis's luck, however, does not seem to have rendered him either rich or honest, since, after having been several years in Dunlevy's employ, he went north with a load worth $20,000, crossed therewith the Rocky Mountains, sold out the goods to the Indians, and never returned to deliver the furs he had received as their equivalent.

A little incident is still related by Peter Dunlevy which illustrates both the straits sometimes forced on people whose abilities fitted them for posts far above the estate of. a miner, and the rapacity of certain Indians who seemed determined to make the most they could of the new circumstances thrown upon them.

After the first rush to the Omineca gold-fields, he was going up to Manson Creek in company with E. Dewdney,[1] who then filled some official position in connection with the colonial administration of the district. While Dunlevy attended to the horses, Dewdney had to do the cooking. Unfortunately, the latter was absentminded enough to leave, more than once, the matches of the little party so near the fire that finally, when they

1. Afterwards Lieut.-Governor of British Columbia.

arrived at Tsinkœt or Head Lake, none of that humble, but none the less important, article was left. In this predicament it was decided that Dunlevy was to go on until he could find some Indians and get from them a new supply of that commodity.

Arrived at the bridge erected on Stony Creek by the telegraph building party, he was met by an Indian who, throwing up his hands in a forbidding way, bade him pay for the use of the bridge.

" But it does not belong to you, and you did not build it," argued Dunlevy.

" No ; but I keep it in repairs," answered the native.

" How much do you want ? "

" Half a dollar."

To save himself trouble and ingratiate himself with the dusky native, from whom he expected to get the much needed matches, the white man paid his toll. Then he asked for the object of his mission, remarking at the same time that he was but the fore-runner of a great man, a big *taye*, who must be well treated and was shortly to make his appearance.

As they were parleying, Dewdney came on, but was immediately stopped by the Indian, who required the customary payment for the right to pass over the bridge.

" How much do you want?" queried the mystified official.

" One dollar," answered Mr. Indian.

Turning to his companion, Dewdney asked :

" How much did you pay yourself? "

" Fifty cents."

Then to the Indian :

" How is it," he said, " that you ask of me double of what that man paid ? "

" Oh ! your companion is a " cultus "[1] man, while I know that you are a chief," answered the native.

1. *i.e.*, common, plebeian.   329

Thus it was that Dunlevy's intentionally good offices turned to the detriment of him on behalf of whom they had been preferred. Dewdney mildly avenged himself on his companion by representing him as a great doctor, which little trick caused Dunlevy to be daily besieged by crowds of natives, whom he generally cured with no more dangerous prescriptions than copious draughts of Hamburg tea.

Even more successful than Peter Dunlevy was another pioneer whom the gold fever likewise brought up to Cariboo, namely, James Reid, the amiable gentleman who lately represented the interests of that district in the Dominion Senate. Plucky and dauntless from the start, he ascended, by dint of sheer perseverance and the exercise of sound judgment, all the rounds of the social ladder, until he occupied the very top of it in the country of his adoption.

Born in August, 1839, in Hull, Province of Quebec, he came, when barely twenty-three, to Victoria, where he arrived on the 20th of April, 1862, with P. Hickey, another pioneer who left his mark in the annals of the district. In the fall of the same year we find him at Quesnel, then composed of a single cabin. Thence he proceeded to the gold-fields of Barkerville and vicinity, where for some time he found fortune rather spare of her smiles. Living was then exceedingly costly, and fabulous prices had to be paid for the most essential commodities of civilized life. The late senator long remembered having eagerly seized a damaged sack of flour, for which he paid the modest sum of $62.50 and went away exulting over the good bargain he had struck.

Such onerous conditions are not conducive to contentment, nor will they lead to a prolonged stay, unless they are accompanied by a corresponding luck in one's search after the precious metal. No wonder, then, if shortly after we see young Reid working in the humble capacity of assistant on a farm in the Lillooet district.

A little incident, unimportant enough in itself, exemplifies the daring of the young man and his stubbornness against adversity, at the same time as it gives us a clue to the reason of his ultimate success. Out of a job owing to the return on the farm of the man he had momentarily replaced, he was asked to help in driving from the 150-Mile House, on the waggon road, a band of cattle destined for the miners. Reid was without a horse, and did not even possess a whip. Nevertheless he boldly stationed himself in the very midst of the animals, some of which were bound to be more or less vicious and therefore dangerous to a man on foot and armed with only a stick. Yet he did not leave his post until he reached Barkerville. So unmindful of danger was he that he thought he had accomplished the most ordinary task, and it was not until some years after, when he was nearly gored to death by an unruly ox, that he realized the reasons for the encomiums he had received at the end of his memorable drive.

Mining remained, however, his favorite pursuit. For fully seven years he followed it without tangible results until 1868, when, feeling unwell and broken down, he was offered and accepted the agency at Barkerville of the Barnard Stage Company. The savings he was thus enabled to accumulate permitted him to invest some money in a claim which, in 1869, commenced to yield very satisfactory returns. Other ventures followed which proved equally successful. Among these we must mention the establishment of a store, to which he was led by a merchant offering him at a loss certain deteriorated articles which the latter could not sell. This line of business was entered into in 1873, and by means of judicious investments and additions to his stock Mr. Reid easily came to possess the most complete store in Quesnel.

In spite of his now assured prosperity he remained the same unassuming gentleman people had but a few years before seen pursuing the most arduous paths. When, therefore, a vacancy occurred in the Dominion Parliament, caused by the death of the previous member for Cariboo, Reid easily conquered the suffrages of his fellow-miners and others in the north, and was elected in 1881. At the next general elections, the acclamation of his constituents told of his success as a Member, and finally, in October, 1888, his political future was assured by his being raised to the rank of a Senator.

When he died on the 3rd of May, 1904, regretted alike by political foes and friends, he was possessed of a snug fortune, which he had amassed without ever catering to the appetite for strong drink generally so prevalent in a new country, where the gentler sex is hardly represented, and where too many see in the saloon the most unfailing stepping-stone to prosperity. In his case, as in that of many others, *labor improbus omnia vincit*, it is owing to sheer labor and the display of untiring energy that his undertakings have been crowned with success.

Returning to Stuart Lake, we may chronicle the arrival, in 1876, of a young man belonging to an old Hudson's Bay Company family, Alexander Campbell Murray, who was to become the superintendent of New Caledonia at a time when the glory of that district would be mostly a thing of the past. A. C. Murray was born in 1859 and is to-day in charge of Fort St. James, where he follows, within a more limited territory, the traditions of enterprise and honest activity of his predecessors.

HON. SENATOR JAMES REID.

CHAPTER XXIII.

Laudetur Jesus Christus !

1861-1880.

WHILE earthly goods were thus eagerly sought after, the more important interests of the soul were not overlooked. Ever since 1861 Anglican clergymen visited their Cariboo co-religionists every summer until the fall of 1869, when a church was built by the same at Barkerville and consecrated under the vocable of St. Saviour. Its first incumbent was the Rev. Mr. Reynard, who was appointed by Bishop Hills. The former gentleman attended at the same time to the spiritual wants of the inhabitants of Quesnel belonging to his denomination. To judge from the parish registers, the first years of that mission were not without success. But the efforts of the gentlemen in charge of it were always restricted to the white population, and to this day there has never been a Protestant Indian within the limits of New Caledonia.

As to the Catholic missions in the district, we have already seen that they date back from 1842, but were interrupted in 1847. With the exception of the accidental visit of Brother Antoine, a sort of lay reader, who passed some time at Stuart Lake in the early sixties, nothing could be done for the northern missionary fields until 1861, when the mainland part of the province, or that part which was then exclusively called British Columbia (by contradistinc-

333

tion to Vancouver Island, which formed a separate colony),
having been entrusted to the care of the Oblates of Mary
Immaculate,[1] the Rev. Charles Grandidier was sent to visit
the Cariboo miners, as well as the Indians of the different
villages he would find on his way up.

This was no light task, as most of the journey had to be
made on foot and in the midst of all kinds of privations.
Leaving Fort Hope on the 3rd of July, 1861, he went up
by way of Douglas and Lillooet, where he had some difficulty in obtaining the ear of the natives, who, though first
ministered to by a representative of his own Church, had
just been prejudiced against it by a Protestant minister.
From Quesnel he went to Antler Creek, William's Creek,
etc., meeting with some recognition among the French and
Irish miners toiling there, though his missionary services
hardly obtained as satisfactory results as he had expected.
Even at Alexandria his ministrations did not seem much
in demand, but for a quite different cause. The natives,
having heard that his visit was to be of short duration,
treated him with studied coolness, thinking thus to force
him into fixing his residence in their midst. There he
realized the terrible ravages of fire-water and profligacy
among the aborigines.

Three years later, the Rev. Father L. Fouquet followed
in his footsteps, though with less difficulty, as he had the
advantage, as far as Quesnel, of the newly-built waggon
road. He had been instructed to spy out the land, with a
view to establish a permanent mission in the north, and
he reported favorably on Quesnel; but the valley of the San
Jose, or William's Lake, was ultimately chosen as the most
propitious spot for that purpose. Father Fouquet's minis-

1. O.M.I.; founded in 1816, at Aix, France, by C. J. E. de Mazenod,
afterwards Bishop of Marseilles. As is his wont in such cases, Bancroft
converts them all into Jesuits ("History of British Columbia," p. 718).

trations, though not meeting with all the encouragement they deserved, seem to have been more acceptable to the Catholic population of Cariboo.

His journey was especially remarkable for having been the occasion of the first visit of a minister of the gospel to the land of the Chilcotins.[1] Unhappily, he could see nothing but their land, and after four days' travelling he had to return to Alexandria without having met one of the natives. Yet, that tribe must have heard of his advances as, when those of its members who were responsible for the Waddington massacre had been condemned to death, they unanimously begged for his services previous to being executed ; but the letter containing their request—which had been entrusted to a Protestant clergyman—reached him too late for him to act accordingly.

The glory of being the first missionary to that tribe was reserved for the Rev. J. M. McGuckin, a young priest who was also entrusted with the task of establishing St. Joseph's Mission, near William's Lake. Thence he would go and stay for a number of months at Richfield, among the Cariboo mountains, where the Catholics had erected a church, with adjoining apartments for the priest.

In the meantime, the Indians of northern New Caledonia were clamoring for the visit of a Catholic missionary.

1. In his Journal, written eleven years after the occurrences it relates, Father J. Nobili, whom we have seen walking in the footsteps of Rev. M. Demers, says : "The 24th October [1845], I visited the village of the Chilcotins. The mission lasted twelve days," etc. ("Western Missions and Missionaries," p. 514). The substitution of Chilcotins for Babines is a remarkable slip of the pen, which, however, can hardly mislead the careful reader, as both the dates mentioned and the statistics produced by the missionary make it evident that he had no intention to claim any practical acquaintance with the Chilcotin tribe. He estimates at 1,190 the number of the Indians who resorted to Fort Babine, and, exclusive of the Chilcotins, whom he does not enumerate, he puts down at 4,138 the native population of New Caledonia in 1845, quite a difference from Anderson's total of 2,627, which comprised 600 Chilcotins.

Left to themselves for twenty years, they had not, in spite of the numberless irregularities which, as a matter of course, had cropped up amongst them, forgotten their pioneer priests, Fathers Demers and Nobili, nor had they altogether forsaken the practices and duties of a religious life. Therefore, when, in 1867, one of their chiefs happened to meet Rev. Fr. McGuckin at Quesnel, he could not refrain from asking him to go and visit his people in the north. That request having been communicated to the proper authorities at New Westminster, the answer was that not only a priest, but the Bishop himself, would go and see them.

That Bishop was the Rt. Rev. L. J. D'Herbomez, the first dignitary appointed to the new Vicariate of British Columbia—comprising the mainland part of the province of the same name—created by Pius IX. in 1863. Born in 1822 at Brillon, in the diocese of Cambrai, France, he had entered the Order of the Oblates, and been sent in 1849 to the Oregon missions. After a six months' voyage by way of Cape Horn, Father D'Herbomez arrived at Fort Vancouver in 1850, and after having occupied several responsible posts, he was finally consecrated Bishop of Miletopolis at Victoria, on October 7th, 1864.

Pursuant to his promise, the prelate left New Westminster on April 18th, 1868, taking as a companion Father Lejacq, the gentleman who was destined to found the second mission within New Caledonia. After a laborious ride on horseback from Fort Yale to the new residence of William's Lake, the Bishop stationed there his companion, taking with him Rev. Fr. McGuckin, the gentleman who had already won golden opinions among the Cariboo miners.

The two missioners left Quesnel on the 12th of May, and after the usual incidents of a spring journey through

Rev. J. M. Mc Guckin C.M.I.
Rector of
Church of our Lady of the Holy Rosary.

the wilds of the north—crossing on rafts of swollen streams, loss of horses, mosquitoes, etc.—they reached the native village near Stony Creek, where they gave their first retreat. There the Bishop inaugurated that part of the Oblates' missionary system which has since yielded so satisfactory results. Instead of adding to the innate cupidity of the natives by allowing them to see an occasion of pecuniary gains in the visit of a priest, Bishop D'Herbomez declared to those who questioned him about the price he was prepared to pay for the loan of the canoe he needed to go to Stuart Lake that, after he had travelled five hundred miles exclusively in the interest of their souls, he would be ashamed to acknowledge them as his children if they wanted to be paid for a service which, after all, was to benefit, not himself, but their own co-tribesmen.

From Fraser Lake the party returned by way of Lake Dontenwill, and after eight long days' journeying down the Nechaco and up the Stuart River, they reached Fort St. James on the Monday after Pentecost. The Bishop and his companion were hospitably received by Peter Ogden; but to show the Indians that no other consideration than their own good had prompted their voyage, they elected to establish their headquarters in the close vicinity of the native village.

At Stuart Lake, as well as in every locality visited by the Bishop, it was made clear to the Indians that thenceforth, in order to merit the uninterrupted ministrations, and possibly the permanent residence, of a priest in their midst, they would have to make serious efforts to live up to the rules laid down for their guidance. In consequence, polygamy was solemnly abolished never again to appear, gambling and conjuring were severely proscribed, and the use of intoxicants renounced by every adult kneeling to the Bishop. In consideration of these pledges each village received a flag whereon were engraved, round the symbol of our redemption, the significant words "Religion, Temperance, Civilization," than which no others could better express the aim of the missionaries. To ensure the fulfilment of those promises, a chief with a captain or sub-chief and a few watchmen were appointed in each locality.

On the 8th of June, 1868, the missionary party embarked for Babine, where they found an enormous crowd just ready for the celebration of one of their "potlatches." After instructing for three days Indians who thought of nothing but their delayed feast, the Bishop, who desired to be in a position to judge for himself, allowed them to go on with their festivities, after which he cautioned them against the features of the same he found to be the most incompatible with a Christian life.[1]

On his way back the Bishop repeated at Fort George the religious exercises he had given at the other places, after which he went with his companion to the principal diggings of Cariboo, where he stayed ten days. This sufficed to give him a most advantageous idea of the miners and, in general, of all the settlers he met. At Richfield he blessed a church and a bell, and the local paper did not tire of singing the praises of the Catholic clergy so long as he was in the midst of the Cariboo mountains. At Alexandria the party met a goodly assemblage of Carrier and Chilcotin Indians, who profited not a little by their preaching.

The following year, 1869, it was Father Lejacq's turn. It is impossible to follow him throughout all the vicissitudes of such a long journey. Almost everywhere he was pleased

---

1. Those feasts have since been completely abolished all over the district, as experience has shown that anything recalling to the mind of the natives the old observances of a heathenish life was only too calculated to take them back to the disorders they had renounced at the time of their admission into the Church.

with the reception he met with and the respectful attention with which his instructions were listened to. At Stuart Lake especially everybody craved the favor of being baptized ; and when it became known that only old or feeble persons would be admitted to the sacrament of baptism, all began to complain of some incurable disease or to ridiculously exaggerate their age.

The dispositions of the Babines were not so edifying. Measles had but lately played havoc among them, and Tsimpsian traders had seized that opportunity to indispose them against the priest, who, they averred, carried sickness and death wherever he went.

But a little incident which had taken place shortly after the Bishop's passage in the country yielded Father Lejacq a text for a good philippic against that and many other false notions only too current within that tribe. A child having fallen grievously sick, a conjuror or shaman had declared that he could easily cure him, but had been rebuked for daring to set at naught the "great priest's" formal prohibition of all such deviltries, whereupon he had laughed away the parents' scruples, who had finally delivered up their little one for the exercise thereon of his black art. In the midst of his dancing, rattling, and howling he had suddenly fallen with his face to the ground as if in a trance.[1] People had thought this a part of his

1. According to the original notions of the Western Dénés, disease was caused by evil spirits which entered the body, generally as a punishment for some fault against the natural law, an infringement of the immemorial ordinances concerning tabooed food, the proper preparation for hunting and trapping and various concomitant observances, and the restrictions governing the relations of the sexes—sequestration or isolation of the women monthly and after child-birth, and the many precautions against their legally impure state. Still more often those evil spirits were believed to obey the ill-will of such persons as the sorcerers, who enjoyed the greatest influence over them. Other sorcerers or shamans were then called into requisition in order to undo what the former had done, that is, to exorcise the spirit out of the patient.

"ceremonies"; but when, after waiting a long time, they had ventured to wake him up, they had felt the cold of death on his brow.

Father Lejacq was the first priest to visit the Fallen Rock or Ackwilgate, where he witnessed one of the great fairs annually held there. The large gatherings of alien tribes consequent on those occasions were always dangerous, and inimical to peace and order. He soon had a proof of this. His guest asked him one day whether everybody was not bound to pay his debts.

"Certainly," answered the missionary.

Whereupon the Indian, going to an Atna—a native of Tsimpsian parentage—forcibly took away from him all the goods he had brought to barter for furs, remarking:

"You owe me so many blankets; therefore, on the advice of the priest, I take this as payment of the same."

Furious at hearing this, the Atna swore he would kill the white man, and for some time it looked as if Father Lejacq's days were indeed numbered. Yet he managed to stay four weeks among those Indians, many of whom came in only after a time from their distant hunting grounds.

One morning two Atna young men, whose faces were painted, while their hair was knotted in a tuft on top of their heads and adorned with eagle feathers, rushed, gun in hand, into the lodge of the great chief Telusa, which was then the missioner's headquarters. After the moments

To that effect, amidst a tremendous tumult of drumming and singing by his attendants, the conjuror, dressed up in the spoils of his personal totem, rattle in hand and dancing to the time of the song, worked himself up to such a degree of frenzy that he was supposed to have become possessed of his own particular spirit or genius, the image of which he directed towards the prostrate form of the patient. Then, falling suddenly on his victim, he sucked out of his or her naked body a diminutive reptile, a nail or other impurity, which he represented as the materialized form of the cause of the complaint!

of silence prescribed by native etiquette, they addressed his host in these terms:

"We have come as representatives of our nation on the Naas River to ascertain your dispositions. Our warriors, to the number of three hundred, are camped a day's journey from here. They tell you: Will you trade with us? We have goods. Would you prefer to fight? We have guns."

Kularhnet, in the absence of the head chief, answered that as the man of God was his guest nobody could think of war. Shortly after, the whole crowd was in, trading and singing, dancing and potlatching. The missionary vainly attempted to address the strangers on religious topics—the Atnas are of those who have ears that they may not hear.

Father McGuckin, who had for some time been stationed at Richfield, was to be the messenger of the good tidings in 1870. Circumstances led him even to visit the Sekanais of Fort McLeod, who received him with open arms and gave him the greatest consolations. Their congeners of Bear Lake were granted the same favor, and the devoted priest, though sick and tired out, crossed over the snow-capped mountains which lie between the Skeena and Fort Connolly, living on marmot and dried salmon, in order to give them an opportunity to learn of their Redeemer and of their duties to both Creator and creature.[1]

Father Lejacq succeeded him in 1871, and it soon became evident that the good dispositions of the natives were of a permanent character, as in the absence of the priest they tried hard to live up to his teachings. They faithfully kept

1. Notwithstanding Bishop N. Blanchet's contention that Mr. Demers, in the course of his apostolic excursions throughout New Caledonia, went as far as Bear Lake ("Rapport sur les Missions du Diocèse de Quebec," Juillet, 1847, p. 22), that place had never been visited by a missionary before Fr. McGuckin's voyage in 1870.

up the organization for the repression of vice established among them, observed the Lord's Day and the Friday abstinence, and hardly ever failed to say their morning and evening prayers in common. Even the Journal of the traders at the fort is a witness to the fidelity of the natives to the chief observances of the Church of their adoption. Here are two of its entries :

" *Good Friday*, April 15th, 1870.—A collection of Indians from all quarters to hold out mass (?!) till Easter Sunday. Singing and praying is now quite the order of the day in the church."

" *Easter Day*.—Holy ceremonies kept by the men and Indians."

Such perseverance deserved recognition. Therefore it was resolved that, despite the scantiness of the Bishop's resources in personnel and pecuniary means, a mission would be established at Stuart Lake. In consequence, early in the spring of 1873, the Rev. Fathers Lejacq and Blanchet went up to Fort St. James, and while the former evangelized the neighboring tribes, the latter, helped by the Indians of the lake, erected the modest buildings and the church which to-day form the Mission of our Lady of Good Hope, on Lake Stuart.

We will forbear praising either Father Lejacq or his work in New Caledonia, but must be allowed a quotation or two from an author who speaks *de visu*, and who, in his quality of Protestant clergyman, cannot be accused of undue tendency to lyrism in a case like this. Of the missioner himself Rev. D. Gordon writes, in his volume on " Mountain and Prairie " :

" On our way we met Père Lejacques, the missionary of this district, whose charge embraces the whole territory between the forks of the Skeena and Fort McLeod, east and west, and between Fort Connolly and Fort St. George (*sic*),

STUART LAKE MISSION.

(From a photo taken shortly after 1873.)

north and south. After leaving the valley of the Skeena and of the Nasse, all the Christian Indians of the interior throughout this northern district are Roman Catholic. The mission is under the direction of the Oblate Fathers, and the missionaries, if all like the devoted Père Lejacques, are ' in journeyings often and in labors abundant.' "[1]

Concerning the most distant portion of his flock, Mr. Gordon says that " among our packers was the Achwilgate prince, as we called him. . . . It was gratifying to notice that they had prayers each evening, one of their own number leading their service."[2]

The Sekanais, in his opinion, " appear to be throughout this district quiet, trustworthy and industrious."[3] As to the mission itself, he remarks that " about a mile above the fort there is an Indian village possessing a pretty little church, and houses which have an air of neatness and cleanliness not always found among the Indians."[4]

The year 1880 put an end to Father Lejacq's residence in the north. That some of his successors and their charge have not degenerated too much from the high standard he had set up in the wilds of New Caledonia will be shown by the following passage from a book by another eye-witness, Henry Somers Somerset :

" Father X. is the Catholic missionary, and we had made his acquaintance almost as soon as we arrived, and thus came in contact with one of the most remarkable men in North-West America.

" Père X. was, of course, a Frenchman, but his English was irreproachable. It is something of a surprise to find a *savant* and a man of learning working amongst the Indians

1. " Mountain and Prairie," p. 123.
2. *Ibid.*, p. 90.
3. *Ibid.*, p. 134.
4. *Ibid.*, p. 7.

in a lonely northern mission.   But, judging by his congregation, it was evident that his talents were not thrown away.   The Carrier Indians are immeasurably superior to their relations, the Beavers.   They build log houses, and many speak English, and read books and a monthly review in the native tongue, printed in the syllabary which their priest has invented for them.   This is one of the many extraordinary achievements of this prince of missionaries who not only is his own editor, compositor and printer, but has invented a most ingenious syllabary, which is easily learnt ; so that Indians, who have no idea what writing is, have been known to learn to read and write this language with perfect correctness after two or three days' instruction.   Of course, their manner of life is not that of the civilized man, for their employment remains unchanged, and they still hunt and fish like other Indians ; but they have been given many of the advantages of civilization, and none of its evils."[1]

1. " The Land of the Muskeg," pp. 226-228, London, Heinemann.

APPENDICES.

APPENDIX A.

List of the Superintendents of New Caledonia from its Origin to this Day.

Simon Fraser..........1805-09
John Stuart............1809-24
William Connolly 1824-30
Peter Warren Dease....1830-34
Peter Skene Ogden.....1834-44
Donald Manson........1844-56
Peter Ogden 1°........1856-68
J. A. Grahame.........1868-69

Peter Ogden 2°........1869-70
Gavin Hamilton........1870-79
J. M. L. Alexander 1879-86
Roderick Macfarlane ...1886-89
W. E. Traill 1889-93
Alexander C. Murray 1°.1893-97
W. E. Camsell.........1897-98
A. C. McNab........1898-1901

A. C. Murray 2° ....1901—

S. Fraser retired before the coalition of the North-West and Hudson's Bay Companies.

J. Stuart was made a Chief Factor in 1821, the year of the coalition.

W. Connolly was made a Chief Trader in 1821 and a Chief Factor in 1825.

P. W. Dease was made a Chief Trader in 1821 and a Chief Factor in 1828.

P. S. Ogden was made a Chief Trader in 1821 and a Chief Factor in 1834.

D. Manson was made a Chief Trader in 1837 and was never promoted higher.

P. Ogden was made a Chief Trader in 1854 and died with that rank.

J. A. Grahame was made a Chief Trader in 1854, a Chief Factor in 1861, Sub-Commissioner in 1872 and Commissioner in 1874.

G. Hamilton was promoted from a Clerkship to a Factorship in 1872.

J. M. L. Alexander was made a Junior Chief Trader in 1875 and a Factor in 1879.

R. Macfarlane was made a Chief Trader in 1868, a Factor in 1872 and a Chief Factor in 1875.

W. E. Traill was made a Junior Chief Trader in 1879 and a Chief Trader in 1883.

None of his successors attained a commission.

We owe these last details to an old and well informed Hudson's Bay Company officer.

APPENDIX B.

Captain G. Dixon, wondering at the degree of perfection in the art of carving attained by the aborigines of the North Pacific Coast whom he visited in 1787, remarks that "this art s far from being in its infancy; a fondness for carving and sculpture was discovered among this people by Captain Cook; iron implements were then also in use, " before any contact with the whites. And he adds that " it must doubtless be a considerable time ago" that iron was introduced on that coast ("A Voyage to the North-West Coast of America," pp. 243-44). When, in 1741, Behring first reached the mainland of America, he found among the inhabitants of the Fox or Eastern Aleutian Islands "long iron knives, apparently their own manufacture" ("Ten Months among the Tents of the Tuski," p. 9). It is open to question whether iron was then really indigenous to that quarter; it is much more likely that the supply of it was derived from the Russian merchants of Eastern Siberia. As early as 1648 a trading expedition consisting of seven vessels, four of which seem to have been lost and perhaps drifted to the coast of America, reached the Gulf of Anadyr, opposite the mouth of the Yukon. Now, as the natives of the coast of Eastern Siberia had from time immemorial intercourse with America, directly by way of Behring Strait, or through the Aleutian aborigines, "who seem to migrate from island to island, and many to the mainland of America" ("Ten Months among the Tents of the Tuski," pp. 9-10), it becomes evident that there is nothing extraordinary in the fact that in 1730 an iron axe should have found its way to the basin of Lake Stuart, some 200 miles from the North Pacific Coast.

The American aborigines are proverbially nomadic, and, but a few years ago, the present writer had a good instance of the possibility of barter between natives from the remotest points in the circumstance that, on Wrangell Island, in Alaska, he found a couple of Indians from the distant Mackenzie side by side with a survivor of the Chinook nation, whose seat was on the banks of the Lower Columbia, perhaps 2,000 miles from the original home of the two Dénés.

APPENDIX C.

Unsatisfactory as the Rev. Dr. Bryce's treatment of New Caledonia affairs undoubtedly is, his handling of matters Catholic or French is even worse. Personal preferences and religious bias should never be allowed to influence a serious historian's assertions. One may inadvertently fall into errors of fact or even of judgment; but nobody should attempt to write history who is prejudiced against any of the parties he would have to speak of. Now, when the necessities of his narrative lead him to treat of the stand Riel and the Red River half-breeds took against the high-handed and blundering representatives of Eastern Canada, whose acts were afterwards publicly disavowed by their own superiors at Ottawa, that author's equanimity is so shaken that he sees among the French Catholic element nothing but rebels, plotters and conspirators—"foreign priests with Jesuitical cunning," p. 461; "fledgling Fenian priests, [priestly] princes of plotters," p. 466; "violent and dastardly [priests]," p. 467; "ecclesiastics . . . who had no love for Britain, no love for Canada, no love for any country, no love for society, no love for peace," p. 460—in a word, missionaries who, though admired by others for having consecrated their lives to the welfare of Indians and half-breeds, are to our author on a par with anarchists and outlaws.

He seems so blinded by prejudice that he sees priests where there are no priests and Jesuits where there are no Jesuits. O'Donoghue did, indeed, study with a view to taking orders, but he was never promoted to the priesthood. As to poor Father Lestanc, he never was anything but an Oblate missionary, though Bryce seriously writes that he "has generally been credited with belonging to the Jesuit Order" p. 466. Then, again, what does he mean by a "Fenian priest"? The Fenians, belonging to a secret society, fall under the ban of the Church. Does our Doctor suppose for a moment that what is forbidden to the laity is allowed to the clergy? Just the reverse is true in some cases. A Fenian priest is as rare a bird as a white crow. It is a matter of regret that the fear of rendering himself ridiculous did not stay his pen before it was too late.

Then, again, according to that writer, these hated ecclesiastics formed "a greedy and foreign cabal planning to seize the country," p. 461. But just one page before he had stated that they "had no love for any country." Why, then, should they have been so eager to seize a country they detested?

This part of Dr. Bryce's book bristles with contradictory and illogical assertions, most of which the lack of space prevents us from noticing. To one point only shall we venture to draw the reader's attention. At the risk of startling writers of Dr. Bryce's school, we dare say that, in our humble opinion, there never was anything like a Red River Rebellion. A rebel is "one who opposes the lawful government to which he owes allegiance." Now, against whom did Riel and the majority of the Red River settlers rise in 1869? Not against Great Britain, since our author has himself to admit that they at least pretended to remain loyal to that country. With the exception of O'Donoghue and a mere handful of politicians, they would not change their allegiance, and all those "foreign priests" of whom Bryce speaks so disparagingly were strongly in favor of retaining the British connection, in the same way as the French Canadian clergy of 1776 saved Canada from the revolted American colonies by their staunch loyalty to the British flag. Then against whom did Riel and his people rise? Against Eastern Canada, as everybody knows. But did they owe allegiance to Canada? Not in the least. Bryce himself admits (p. 464) that when McDougall, the man sent by the eastern provinces to represent them on the banks of the Red River, issued his famous proclamation authorizing a recourse to arms against Riel and his friends, the transfer of the country to the newly formed Dominion had not as yet been accomplished. Therefore it is plain as daylight that Riel and his people in their first uprising were not rebels, and that consequently there never was anything like a Red River Rebellion.

The settlers of the Red River valley were then in about the same position as the Newfoundland colonists of to-day. Let Dr. Bryce suppose for an instant that he is one of the latter. People come to his country sent by Quebec, who form "an irritating, selfish and aggressive expedition, taking possession of the land before it has been transferred . . . and assuming the air of conquerors" ("History of the Hudson's Bay Company," p. 459) "giving harsh treatment" to the native settlers, surveying the land and cutting roads exactly as they please in spite of the protests of the islanders, who feel themselves threatened with being dispossessed of their farms. Suppose that those loud-mouthed French Canadians declare that whether Mr. Bryce and his fellow pioneers like it or not, their country is going to be annexed to a newly formed political body, that the English language is to be proscribed in favor of the French, which will be forced on them, and that their children will soon have to attend Catholic schools, though their conscience is strongly against them. How will the good Doctor feel? Probably the same as the original settlers of Manitoba did when they were similarly treated by the Ontario people who represented the newly fledged Ottawa Government. That their apprehensions were not groundless later events have only too fully demonstrated.

As to the Rev. Dr. Bryce's aspersions on Fathers Lestanc and Ritchot and the Roman Catholic clergy in general, they are unworthy of a man of his calling. We are prepared for the amount of truthfulness there is in his charges when he makes of the one a Jesuit who never was a Jesuit and of the other a Frenchman though he was born and raised in Canada. Conscious of our own familiarity with that phase of Canadian history, we simply oppose our word to his and declare that all those gentlemen were ever loyal to the British connection and acted most honorably during the whole crisis. Any fair-minded person who wants to be enlightened on the events of 1869-70 has only to read the late Archbishop Taché's admirable " Page of the History of the Schools in Manitoba," a most moderate and well documented brochure printed at Dr. Bryce's very door. We wonder how it is that a writer who, in his list of references, gives several times the title of the same book bearing on his subject should have so persistently ignored that most important pamphlet. He should not be afraid to refer to the original and official sources of information it contains.

APPENDIX D.

Exception has been taken to this statement by a party well informed on North-West American matters, on the ground that a little book called " Traits of American Indian Life and Character, by a Fur Trader," must swell by at least one the number of H. B. Co. authors who wrote from personal experience about New Caledonia. But, after months of patient study and unceasing enquiries, we can only repeat what we remarked after a hasty examination of the volume, viz.: that the strength of our assertion remains unimpaired, because, though evidently inspired to a great extent by a New Caledonian, who could have been none other than P. S. Ogden, the book was certainly not written by that gentleman.

It was recognized that Ogden's rich fund of information on the native tribes with which he had associated should not be allowed to perish with him, and, as early as 1845, J. Dunn wrote in his "Oregon Territory" (p.196) : " I should very much like to see issued from the press the 'Memoirs of the eccentric Peter Skein Ogden.'" Now, intrinsic evidence is not wanting which betrays an undeniable connection between Ogden and the scenes which the author is supposed to relate from personal experience. The former's antecedents prior to his advent into New Caledonia entirely tally, as to dates and places, with the life the latter admits to have led before he went there. We have referred to the great friendship existing between Ogden and S. Black, of Kamloops. But the author of the book expressly states, under circumstances which unmistakably point to Ogden as being the speaker, if not the writer : " Black " (for which name the B—— of the book evidently stands, as is shown by the tragic death of the person referred to) "was one of my oldest and worthiest friends." P. S. Ogden first saw Stuart Lake in 1834, the very same year when the first departure from the traditional custom of burning the dead took place among the Carriers, a custom which, as was to be expected, disappeared only by degrees. Now, in 1835, the author is exceedingly curious to witness the cremation of a corpse at Stuart Lake, an experience which he plainly intimates was then new to him. Moreover, all the information in the book bearing on happenings in New Caledonia after 1834 is as reliable as that on events taking place in the same country prior to that date is inaccurate. Needless to insist on this point.

And yet we claim that P. S. Ogden was not the author of that book. In the first place, that gentleman, though well educated, was naturally averse to literary work. His letters, of which we have read hundreds, are made up of stereotyped formulas and wearisome verbal repetitions. Nobody who turns from their stilted and often incorrect style to the elegant English of the "Traits of American Indian Life" will dream for a moment that the same hand could have penned both. Turning to the subject matter of the little volume itself, the reasons for rejecting the hypothesis of Ogden's authorship grow even more cogent. Anybody acquainted with that gentleman's practical good sense and his honesty of purpose will refuse to believe that he could have unnecessarily consented to stultify himself by ridiculous contradictions, mendacious assertions, and attempts at claiming for himself honors which every New Caledonian then knew perfectly well belonged to another. Yet this is what we find in the book under discussion. Though published only in 1853, that volume, or rather its framework, was prepared in 1838, since the would-be author says (p. 57) : " Six years ago, being the spring of 1832, I was stationed . . . . at the newly formed settlement of Fort Simpson, at the mouth of the Nass River." P. S. Ogden did indeed go there in 1831 ; but note now the contradictions of the scribe. "Ten or twelve years ago," he writes, meaning therefore 1826 or 1828, "I was stationed at Fort Killmaurs, in the Babine country" (p. 71). We turn to p. 22 of the book and read : " In the year 1823 I was appointed to the command of an expedition destined to operate southward of the Columbia. During the six succeeding years I was employed in the perilous and disagreeable duty involved in this adventure." Was that pretended author at the same time "in the Babine country" and "southward of the Columbia"? Nor is this all. He is mistaken by three or five years as to the date of the foundation of Fort Kilmars, and claims to have made a journey to a place now called Moricetown, where Ogden most certainly never was, while the trader who first visited it just as undoubtedly never wrote a book. On the way to that village he locates a native hamlet at the outlet of Babine Lake, which is fully 15 miles therefrom ; he follows for a time a river which does not exist, etc. But here is the climax. He writes (p. 72) : "It had been my lot to superintend the cutting of the first stick of Fort Killmaurs." As that post was established in 1822, it follows that when he was "strolling on the banks of Stuart's Lake . . . in the autumn of 1835," it must have been 13 years since he had first resided among the Babines, a tribe of Indians who not only practised cremation, but had even taught that custom to the natives of Stuart Lake. And yet, on that autumn day of 1835, our author is irresistibly impelled by his "curiosity excited before now by the accounts [he] had *heard* of the barbarities exercised on these occasions, more especially towards the women" (p. 129), to try, at great personal risk, to witness the burning of a body then in course of process a short distance from the lake !

This must suffice to show that the book in question was evidently the work of an outsider, who patched up several accounts of a country he had never seen, prominent among which were probably P. S. Ogden's notes or verbal information, incorrectly recorded after one of those journeys to Canada which the exigencies of his charge annually forced on him. Who was the obliging scribe? The firm which published the volume now simply answers : "The MS. of the book 'Traits of American Indian Life and Character' was received by us from the Hudson's Bay Company on account of Duncan Finlayson, and was edited by Mr. Rich" (Letter dated 12th Dec., 1904). D. Finlayson was brother-in-law to Lady Simpson, and the inference deducible from the above statement that he was indeed the party who compiled the little work under consideration is strengthened by the fact that the "author" of the same dedicated it to that lady "as a small tribute of affectionate regard." But D. Finlayson never was in New Caledonia, and therefore could not have written "from a personal knowledge."

A work whose existence would militate to a greater extent against our original assertion is A. C. Anderson's Prize Essay (See Appendix F). But then its scope is restricted to modern British Columbia, and it has hardly anything to do with New Caledonia matters.

APPENDIX E.

Since the lines referring to these apparently incredible circumstances were first printed, we came across an anecdote in an old book which we feel so much the more inclined to reproduce by way of apology for having recorded facts which will task the credulity of more than one reader, as the principal witness of the occurrences mentioned in that volume is one of our old acquaintances, W. Lane. On p. 388 of his "Ten Months among the Tents of the Tuski" Lieut. W. H. Hooper, who was with one of the parties sent in search of the ill-fated explorer, Sir John Franklin, writes :

"During the time that Mr. Lane was stationed in New Caledonia he received a visit from an aged Indian of the Carrier tribe who had been with Sir Alexander Mackenzie in one of his trips of discovery to the sea coast and had the reputation of being a great medicine-man. As he had not paid a visit to the fort for several years, his appearance excited some surprise, and he was asked why he came. He replied that he had come to look at the fort and its inmates for the last time. 'Did you ever,' said the old man, 'hear thunder in the winter time ?' Mr. Lane replied in the negative. ' Then,' rejoined the Indian, ' when in two moons' time you hear a clap of thunder, send to my lodge and you will find me dead.'

" Within fifteen days of the appointed time Mr. Lane did indeed hear a solitary burst of thunder ; the nephew of the old Indian, who was the fort interpreter, started off directly to his uncle's lodge, and on arrival found that he had just expired. The realization of this prophecy did not in the least surprise the rest of the Indians, who had expressed their entire conviction of its fulfilment."

Hooper had that story from Mr. Lane himself.

APPENDIX F.

Authorities Quoted or Consulted.

(N.B.—The following works bear more or less on some of the subjects treated in this History. A few other books on British Columbia refer only to the southern part of the Province or to the Pacific Coast.)

Anderson (A. C.).—"Dominion at the West." Victoria, 1872.

Anonymous.—"Biographical Dictionary of Well-Known British Columbians." Vancouver, 1890.

"Guide to the Province of British Columbia." Victoria, 1877.

"Historical Sketches of the Catholic Church in Oregon." Portland, 1878.

"Papers Relative to the Affairs of British Columbia." London, 1859-62.

The British Colonist (a daily newspaper). Victoria, 1864.

"Rapport sur les Missions du Diocèse de Quebec." 1845-47.

"Traits of American Indian Life and Character." London, 1853.

Ballantyne (R. M.).—"Hudson Bay." London, 1896.

"Handbook to the New Gold Fields." London, 1858.

Bancroft (H. H.).—"History of British Columbia." San Francisco, 1890.

"History of the North-West Coast of America." 2 vols. San Francisco, 1884.

Barrett-Lennard (Capt. C. E.).—"Travels in British Columbia." London, 1862.

Begg (Alexander).—"History of British Columbia from its Earliest Discovery to the Present Time." Toronto, 1894.

(A namesake).—"History of the North-West," 3 vols. Toronto, 1894.

Bryce (Rev. Dr. George).—"The Remarkable History of the Hudson's Bay Company." Toronto, 1900.

"Holiday Rambles." Winnipeg, 1888.

Butler (Gen. Sir W.).—"The Wild North Land." New York, 1903.

"Far Out : Rovings Retold." London, 1880.

Cogswell (O. H.).—"History of British Columbia." Victoria, 1894.

Cornwallis (Kinahan).—"The New El Dorado." London, 1858.

Cox (Ross).—"Columbia River." London, 1832.

Dawson (Dr. G. M.).—"Report on an Exploration made in 1887 in the Yukon District and Adjacent Northern Portion of British Columbia." London, 1898.

D'Herbomez (Bishop L. J.).—Letter in "Missions des Oblats de Marie Immaculée." Paris, 1870.

Dixon (Capt. G.).—"A Voyage Round the World." London, 1789.

Downie (W.).—"Hunting for Gold." San Francisco, 1893.

Dugas (Rev. G.).—"L'Ouest Canadien." Montréal, 1896.
" Le Mouvement des Métis à la Rivière-Rouge." Montreal, 1905.

Dunn (John).—"The Oregon Territory." Philadelphia, 1845.

Fitzgerald (J. E.).—"Hudson's Bay Company and Vancouver's Island." London, 1849.

Fleming (Sandford).—"England and Canada." Montreal, 1884.

Franchère (G.).—"Narrative of a Voyage to the North-West Coast of America." New York, 1854.

Franklin (Capt. John).—"Journey to the Shores of the Polar Sea." 4 vols. London, 1829.

Gordon (Rev. D. M.).—"Mountain and Prairie." London, 1880.

Gosnell (R. E.).—"The Year Book of British Columbia." Victoria, 1897.

Grant (Rev. Dr. G. M.).—"Ocean to Ocean." London, 1877.

Greenhow (R.).—"The History of Oregon and California." London, 1844.

Hargrave (J. J.).—"Red River." Montreal, 1871.

Harmon (D. W.).—"A Journal of Voyages and Travels through the Continent of North America" (original and New York 1903 editions).
"A Concise Account of the Principal Animals which are found in the North-Western Part of North America" (do).
"An Account of the Indians living West of the Rocky Mountains" (do).

Hazlitt (W. Carew).—"British Columbia and Vancouver Island." London, 1858.
" Great Gold Fields of Cariboo." London, 1862.

Hooper (Lieut. W. H.).—"Ten Months Among the Tents of the Tuski." London, 1853.

Horetzky (Chas.).—"Canada on the Pacific." Montreal, 1874.

Hudson's Bay Company.—"Report from Select Committee." London, 1857.

Johnson (R. Byron).—"Very Far West Indeed." London, 1872.

Laut (A. C.).—"Pathfinders of the West." Toronto, 1904.

Lejacq (Rev. J. M.).—Letters in "Missions des Oblats de Marie Immaculée." Paris, 1874.

Macdonald (D. G. F.).—"British Columbia and Vancouver Island." London, 1862.

Macfie (M.).—"Vancouver Island and British Columbia." London, 1865.

Mackenzie (Sir Alexander).—"Journal of a Voyage through the North-West Continent of America." (Original London edition and Toronto reprint.)

Martin (R. M.).—"The Hudson's Bay Territories and Vancouver's Island." London, 1849.

Masson (L. R.).—"Les Bourgeois de la Compagnie du Nord-Ouest." 2 vols. Quebec, 1889.

Mayne (R. C.).—"Four Years in British Columbia and Vancouver Island." London, 1862.

McCain (Charles W.).—"History of the S.S. *Beaver*." Vancouver, 1894.

McDonald (Archibald).—"Peace River: A Canoe Voyage from Hudson Bay to the Pacific." Ottawa, 1872.

McGuckin (Rev. James).—Letter in "Missions des Oblats de Marie Immaculée." Paris, 1873.

McLean (John).—"Notes of a Twenty-Five Years' Service in the Hudson's Bay Territory." 2 vols. London, 1849.

McNaughton (M.).—"Overland to Cariboo." Toronto, 1896.

Milton (Viscount) and Cheadle (W. B.).—"The North-West Passage by Land." London, 1865.

Montreal (Bishop of).—Journal. London, 1849.

Morice (Rev. A. G.).—"Au Pays de l'Ours Noir." Paris, 1897.
  "Notes Archæological, Industrial and Sociological on the Western Dénés." Toronto, 1894.
  "Déné Sociology." Ottawa, 1892.
  "The Western Dénés; their Manners and Customs." Toronto, 1890.

Nicolay (Rev. C. G.).—"The Oregon Territory." London, 1846.

Paquet (E. T.).—-"Fragments de l'Histoire de la Paroisse de Saint-Nicolas." Lévis, 1894.

Pemberton (J. D.).—"Facts and Figures Relating to Vancouver Island and British Columbia." London, 1860.

Petitot (Rev. E.).—"Traditions Indiennes du Canada Nord-Ouest." Alençon, 1887.

Pike (Warburton).—"The Barren Ground of Northern Canada." London, 1892.
"Through the Sub-Arctic Forest." London, 1896.

Rattray (Dr. Alexander).—"Vancouver Island and British Columbia." 2 vols. London, 1862.

Rawlings (Thomas).—"The Confederation of the British North American Provinces." London, 1865.

Robinson (H. M.).—"The Great Fur Land." London, n.d.

Ross (A.).—"Adventures of the First Settlers on the Oregon or Columbia River." London, 1849.
"The Fur Hunters of the Far West." 2 vols. London, 1855.
"The Red River Settlement." London, 1856.

Simpson (Sir Geo.).—"Narrative of a Journey Round the World." London, 1847.

Simpson (T.).—"Narrative of the Discoveries on the North Coast of America." London, 1843.

Smet (Rev. P. J. De).—"Western Missions and Missionaries." New York, n. d.

Somerset (H. S.).—"The Land of the Muskeg." London, 1895.

Taché (Archbishop A.).—"A Page of the History of the Schools in Manitoba." Winnipeg, 1893.
"Esquisse sur le Nord-Ouest." Montreal, 1901.
"The North-West Difficulty." London, 1874.

Taché (J. C.).—"Forestiers et Voyageurs." Montreal, 1884.

Turner-Turner (J.).—"Three Years' Hunting and Trapping in America and in the Great North-West." London, 1888.

Twiss (Travers).—"The Oregon Question." London, 1846.

Wade (M. S.).—"The Land of Heart's Desire." Kamloops, 1905.

Whymper (F.).—"Travel and Adventure in the Territory of Alaska." London, 1868.

Willson (Beckles).—"The Great Company." 2 vols. Toronto, 1900.

INDEX.

Ackwilgates, 7.

Ackwilgate village, 209.

A'ke'tœs, 11 ; killed, 12.

Aleutians, 346.

Alexandria, Fort, its site reached by Mackenzie, 44 ; established, 122 ; terminus of the land route, 176 ; occupations of the servants, 183 ; moved to opposite side, 194 ; its inhabitants immoral, 232 ; dilapidated, 289.

Anarhem, village of, 16.

Anderson, A. C., mistaken as to the terminus of S. Fraser's voyage, 81 ; blamed, 194 ; takes census of the natives, 195 ; counsels moderation, 217 ; seeks a new route, 257 ; on Bélanger, 263.

Anecdotes, principal : Na'kwœl and the lame man, 10 ; Khadintel and Khalhpan, 15, 19 ; 'Kwah and Arrow-Heart, 29 ; 'Kwah and Harmon, 89 ; 'Kwah and Douglas, 140, et seq.; Father Chirouse and P. S. Ogden, 173 ; D. McLean and Tlhelh, 269 : Paul Fraser and the Iroquois, 280 ; D. McLean and the Chilcotins, 318 ; P. Dunlevy and E. Dewdney, 328 ; Father Lejacq and the Atna, 340.

Anglican clergymen, 333.

Animals in New Caledonia, 2, 4.

Anreon, 127.

Armor, at Lillooet, 17 ; on the Pacific, 35.

Arrow-Heart, 28 ; killed, 29.

Articles in use, queer, 189 ; of home manufacture, 191.

Askettihs, 79.

Astor, John Jacob, 94.

Atéte, 11 ; killed, 12.

Atnahs, 51 ; and Fraser, 74 ; great smokers, 74 ; in trouble, 160 ; cause trouble, 340 ; trade with Babines, 343.

Authorities, list of, 353.

Axe, first iron, 9 ; lost and found, 10; greatly prized, 28; first brought by the whites, 55 ; home made, 194.

Babine, Fort, founded, 125 ; a great place for salmon, 176 ; its site, 208 ; its removal decided on, 209 ; insecure, 212, 217 ; abandoned, 220 ; not founded by P. S. Ogden, 351. See Kilmars.

Babine Indians, their habitat and characteristics, 4 ; origin of their name, 6 ; their own origin, 7 ; first mentioned in literature, 87 ; gamble and dispute, 97 ; bent on massacre, 165, 166 ; enumerated, 196 ; trade with Coast Indians, 208 ; their doings, 212, et seq.; said to be treacherous, 217 ; displeased, 219 ; restless, 220 ; take the law in their own hands, 325; their number in 1845, 335 ; their new religion appreciated, 335.

Babine Lake, 2, 3 ; first sighted by Europeans, 92 ; its appearance, 208 ; yields plenty of salmon, 223.

Bad River, 39.

Bagpipes, 149.

Ballou, W., 294.

Bancroft, H. H., inaccurate as to the character of the country, 2 ; unfair, 53 ; mistaken, 56 ; unjust to Fraser, 59 ; unnecessarily punctilious, 59 ; too bickering, 60 ; mistaken as to the topography of fort on Stuart Lake, 64 ; inaccurate as to distances, 68 ; ungenerous, 78 ; on Fraser, 82 ; wrong as to date of the erection of Fort Chilcotin, 124, and Fort Babine, 125 ; gives a fanciful account of the Douglas episode, 146 ; mistaken relatively to the status of first missionaries, 226 ; inaccurate concerning dates, 241 ; wrong regarding the etymology of a name, 322, and as to the O.M.I., 334.

Barkerville, 306, 331.

Barret-Lennard, Capt. C. E., mistaken, 64.

Baskets, salmon, 40, 187.

Bear Lake, 3 ; first mentioned in literature, 56 ; its position, 134.

Bears, brown, 4; grizzly, 60.
Beaver, abundant, 38.
Beaver Creek, 21, 131.
Beaver Indians, 30; they oppress the Sekanais, 31; encroach on their territory, 36.
Beaver, Rev. Mr., 147, 174.
Begg, A., on the limits of New Caledonia, 1; wrong with regard to the establishment of the first new Caledonia post, 65; concerning the identity of the river discovered by S. Fraser, 71; as to the founding of posts by Douglas, 133; and as to the date of Gov. Simpson's voyage to New Caledonia, 152.
Bélanger, Alexis, 215; his origin, 260; dismissed from Babine, 261; reinstated, 262; deserts his post, 262; a free man, 266; his life in danger, 266; shot, 267; his death avenged, 269, *et seq.*
Bella-Coola, 317.
Bentinck Inlet, 49, 313.
Berries, 2, 67, 88.
Bible History, 233.
Bird, James, 311.
Black, S., and Fisher, 154; is murdered, 181.
Blackwater Indians. See Naskhutins.
Blackwater River, 3; reached by Mackenzie, 48; fort established, 244.
Blais, at Stuart Lake, 68; at Fraser Lake, 70.
Blanchet, Rev. George, 342.
Blanchet, Rev. Norbert, 130, 226; composes a pictorial catechism, 233; elected Bishop, 236; wrong as to the terminus of Fr. Demers' missions, 341.
Blanshard, R., Governor, 287.
Boucher, J. B. See Waccan.
Boucher, Jem., helps Manson, 285; and liquor, 311.
Boucher, J. M., 284.
Bows and arrows, 27, 39; penetrating power, 47.
Brasconnier, 262, 263.
Bridge, Indian, cut down, 207.
Brigades, described, 230.
British Columbia, organized, 295.
British Columbians, first, 55.
Brown, W., 125.

Bryce, Dr. Geo., wrong as to topography, 64; one of his statements contested, 72; inaccurate in his phraseology, 100; relates the Douglas episode, 140; mistaken as to facts, geography and ethnology, 144, *et seq.*; unfair concerning Red River matters, 347, *et seq.*
Buckley, 315.
Buffalo, 38, 159.
Bugles, 149.
Bulkley, Col., 321.
Bulkley River, 3, 321.
Bull, unmanageable, 210.
Burial among the Carriers, first, 170.
Burning of the dead, 6; of a chief, 69; of a woman, 87; of a man with two wives, 91; in the woods, 96; and P. S. Ogden, 351.
Bute Inlet, 313.
Butler, Gen., 312.

Cable, Atlantic, 321.
Cameron, D. E., on dried salmon, 178; at Babine, 217; uneasy, 219; tries mediation, 220; and fails, 221.
Campbell, R., 206.
Canadian colony in Oregon, 226.
Canadian courts, 99.
Canadian miners, 298; drowned, 299.
Canadians, French, liked by the natives, 184; conduct not edifying, 226.
Cannibalism, acts of, 301.
Cannibals, not secure among the Dénés, 302.
Cannon at the H. B. Co. forts, 113, 143, 149.
Canoes, large birch-bark, 37; sprucebark, 61; wooden, 190; wrecked, 39, 80, 193, 223; stolen, 210.
Cariboo, deer, 4, 10, 213.
Cariboo mines, 296, *et seq.*
"Cariboo Sentinel," 306.
Carrier Indians, their habitat and characteristics, 4; reason of their name, 6; originally more nomadic, 21; first seen by Mackenzie, 40; they spurn his overtures, 41; first intercourse with the whites, 43; their wearing apparel, 60; they receive Fraser at Stuart Lake, 61; described by Fraser, 62; violent, 95; jealous, 96; first union of one

Carrier Indians (*Continued*)—
of their women with a white man,
253; well behaved, 320; their
pagan practices abolished, 338;
superior Indians, 344. See also
Alexandria, etc.
Carrier Lake, 54.
Catholic clergy, saves Canada to England, 348; loyal, 349. See Missions, Missionaries.
Census, 195; inaccurate, 196; partial,
by Father Nobili, 335.
Chalh'tas, 11; killed, 13.
Charles, T., on deserters, 190; thrifty,
244.
Chartier, wanted by Fisher, 182.
Cheadle, W. B. See Milton.
Chichanit, 11.
Chiefs, formerly unknown, 5; ap-
pointed by the N. W. Co., 55, 88;
by the H. B. Co., 199.
Chilcotin Indians, 4; make war on
the Carriers, 15; first mentioned in
literature, 76; unfriendly to the
whites, 194; visited by smallpox,
307; massacre the whites on the
Humalhkhoh, 315; on Bentinck
Arm, 315, 316; five hanged, 320.
Chilcotin, Fort, erected, 122; de-
pends from Alexandria, 181.
Chilcotin River, 2, 3.
Children shamefully treated, 16, 18.
Chinlac, 14; destroyed, 19; passed by
Fraser, 60; made a rendezvous, 68.
Chippewayan, Fort, 35, 49.
Chirouse, Father, 173.
Chœnnih, 325.
Chronology, pre-European, 19.
Clerks, of the H. B. Co., 105.
Clubbing, 279, 280; condemned, 281.
Cogswell, O. H., mistaken, 54.
Columbia River, 71; terminus of
brigades, 122, 158, 167.
"Commodore," steamer, 293.
Connolly, Fort, by whom established,
133; when established, 133, *et seq.*;
its diet, 178.
Connolly, W., 126; appointed Chief
Factor, 129; communicates with
J. Douglas, 133; meets Sir George
Simpson, 149; rewards successful
hunter, 154; retires from the dis-
trict, 164; his after life, 170.
Conway, Edward, 321.

Cook, Captain, 64.
Courts, Canadian, 99.
Cox. Judge, 318; makes promises to
Chilcotin murderers, 319; his pledge
ignored, 320.
Cox, Ross, renders wrongly a tribal
name, 74; on scalping, 274.
Credit, 112; forbidden, 219.
Cremation of the dead, 6. See Burning.
Crimean War, 287, 288.
Cunningham, miner, 298.
Cust, W., 312.

Dances, 15, 226.
Davis, "Twelve-Foot," 328.
Dawson Lake, 2.
Dead, disposal of the, 6. See Burial,
Burning.
Dears, T., on liquor, 116; on Stuart
Lake happenings, 165; on his
salary, 167.
Dease Lake, a short lived post, 207.
Dease, P. W., 162; retires, 170;
instructs the natives, 225.
Demers, Rev. M., 130, 226; undertakes
the New Caledonia missions, 227;
his early years, 229; starts for the
North, 229; describes a caravan,
230; baptizes children, 231, *et seq.*;
mistaken as to origin of a name,
231; he works at Stuart Lake, 233;
back at Alexandria and William's
Lake, 235; returns to Kamloops,
236; made a bishop, 236.
Dénés, Western, their habitat, 4, 5;
social organization, 5; customs, 6;
means of subsistence, 7; moral
characteristics, 7; origin, 7; not
"Tinne," 146; troublesome in cases
of accidents, 182; not treacherous,
218; degraded, 232; did not practise scalping, 274; and cannibalism,
302; nomadic, 346. See also
Babines, Carriers, Chilcotins, Nahanais, Naskhutins, Sekanais.
Desertions, 179; at Fraser Lake, 190;
in Thew's time, 200, 205; from
the brigade, 245; from Fraser Lake
again, 255; of Bélanger, 262.
Desmarais, J. B., 178.
Dewdney, E., 323, and Dunlevy, 328.
D'Herbomez, Bishop, 336; visits
New Caledonia, 337.
Dietz, W., 297.

Diller's claim, 298.

Dixon, Captain George, on iron implements, 346.

Douglas, David, 175.

Douglas, James, born, 128 ; his salary, 129 ; head fisherman at Stuart Lake, 131 ; sometimes in low social positions, 132 ; collects fish and furs, 133 visits Alexandria, 133 ; marries, 138 ; his greatness, 139 ; his life in danger, 140, 141 ; fires at Tzœlhnolle, 142 ; is apprehended by 'Kwah, 143 ; married before a clergyman, 147 ; receives the Governor, 149 ; retires from Stuart Lake, 152 ; founds Victoria, 275 ; becomes Governor of Vancouver Island, 287 ; his correspondence, 288 ; imposes onerous burdens on the miners, 292 ; goes to the mines, 294 ; increases the wages of the H. B. Co. employees, 298 ; a promoter of roads, 304.

Douglas, Lady, 138 ; intercedes for her husband, 143.

Drunkenness, first case of, 87.

Dunlevy, P., 294 ; reaches Horsefly River, 295 ; becomes fur-trader, 310 ; goes north, 327, *et seq.*

Dunn, J., quoted from, 350.

Dunvegan, Fort, 99, 176.

Elk in New Caledonia, 38.

Engagés, 104, 151, 179. See Servants.

"Enterprise," steamer, 323.

Ermatinger, F., 164.

Errors. See Mistakes.

European wares in early times, at Stuart Lake, 9 ; among the Naskhutins, 44-48 ; on the Findlay, 56, *et seq.*; at Fond du Lac, 69 ; on the Lower Fraser, 79 ; at an early date on N.W. Coast of America, 346.

Evans, Ezra, 310.

Expeditions, stores and leather, 157 ; leather, 176 ; of R. Campbell, 206, 207 ; military, 318.

Expenditure, 177.

Express, 294 ; rates, 296 ; to the north, 325.

Factors, Chief, 98, 107, 108 ; inspecting, 108 ; in charge of important posts, 110, 177.

Factors, 109.

Fair, large annual, 209, 340.

Falardeau, ill-treated, 279.

Fallen Rock, 8, 209 ; first visited by a missionary, 340.

Fare, poor, 169, 289 ; costly at the mines, 306 ; gets better in the north, 306.

Faries, Hugh, arrives in New Caledonia, 70 ; first man in charge of Fort George, 72.

Farming introduced, 174.

Fauna, 4.

Favel, Charles, 220.

Feasts, 6. See Potlatch.

Field, Cyrus, 320 ; successful, 321.

Finlay, James, 52.

Finlay River, 3, 36.

Finlayson, Duncan, author, 352.

Finlayson, Rod., 287 ; visits Stuart Lake, 307.

Fir, Douglas, 2.

Firearms, 30, 31.

Fisher, Al., 154 ; corresponds with S. Black, 156 ; rapacious, 157 ; annoying, 168 ; in command of Alexandria, 181 ; reproves McIntosh, 182 ; intransigeant, 183.

Fisheries, 131 ; unproductive, 131, 132 : salmon, 187.

Fitzgerald, W. H., 325.

Flints, gun, 190.

Flogging, 279, 280 ; condemned, 281.

Flour, first traded to the natives, 111, 306 ; ground at Alexandria, 183 ; given as a bait, 319 ; costly, 330.

Fond du Lac, 69, 165, 203, 255.

Forts, H. B. Co., 113 ; of the aborigines, 216.

Fouquet, Rev. L., 334 ; wanted by the Chilcotin murderers, 335.

Fraser, Fort, built, 69 ; burnt, 87.

Fraser Lake, 3 ; discovered, 68 ; and vicinity described, 69.

Fraser, Paul, on liquor, 116 ; accused by Thew, 200 ; an able man, 242 ; kept against his will, 247 ; momentarily in charge of the district, 248 ; on desertion, 255 ; reprimands McBean, 264 ; under a cloud, 276 ; autocratic, 279 ; killed, 280.

Fraser River, reached by Mackenzie, 40; mistaken for the Columbia, 71; explored by Fraser, 73; differentiated from the Columbia, 79.

Fraser, Simon, born, 53; establishes Rocky Mountain Portage House, 54; prepares for his voyage west, 56; starts on his trip, 58; reaches Stuart Lake, 61; quoted from, 62; caters to the whims of the natives, 69; passes his first winter at Stuart Lake, 70; starts to explore the Fraser, 73; describes that river, 74; meets with frightful experiences, 75, *et seq.*; reaches the salt water, 79; confronted by new dangers, 80; promoted, 81; dies, 82.

French Lake, 3, 69.

Frobisher, Jos., 33.

Furs, received at Alexandria, 123; collected by James Douglas, 132; avidity for, 153; good hunts recompensed, 154; procured by means of tricks, 155.

Gambling, 28, 265, 310.

George, Fort, established, 71; native population, 196; reached by Demers, 233.

Giscome Portage, 59, 328.

Gold, first discovered, 288; on the Thompson, 291; first exported, 292; fabulous sums realized, 296, 297, 298.

Gordon Lake, 69.

Gordon, Rev. D., quoted from, 342.

Gosnell, R. E., misled by Bancroft, 123.

Grahame, J. A., 326.

Grandidier, Father, 334.

Grand Rapid, 66.

" Grand Visage," kills Morwick, 214; builds to himself a fort, 216; is decoyed and killed, 217.

Grant, Cuthbert, 99, 100.

Grant, Dr. G. M., on the Chilcotin massacre, 316.

Greenhow, R., mistaken as to the climate of New Caledonia, 2; regarding the dates of the discovery of the Fraser and of the establishment of the first N. C. fort, 49.

Groseillers, M. C., 102.

Grosse-Tête, 311.

Guns, introduced, 30; in early use, 37; fired off to impress the natives, 48; in New Caledonia before the whites, 57; displayed by Fraser's men, 62; and himself, 74; on the Lower Fraser, 79; flint, to a late date, 191.

Half-breeds, on the war-path in Red River, 99; often promoted in the H. B. Co., 106.

Hamilton, Gavin, 307; opposes free traders, 310; and liquor, 311; succeeds P. Ogden, 326; a favorite with the natives, 327.

Hargrave, J. J., quoted, 301.

Harmon, D. W., quoted from, 30, 38, 92; goes to New Caledonia, 85; his journal, 86; chastises 'Kwah, 89; goes to Babine, 92; then to Fraser Lake, 92, 94; returns east, 97; a religious man, 99.

Hazelton, 9.

Hazlitt, W. C., and his book, 7.

Hehn Lake, 69.

Hickey, P., 322, 330.

Hill's Bar discovered, 293.

Hooper, Lieut. W. H., on iron implements, 346; on the prophetic power of the shamans, 352.

Hope, Fort, established, 278.

Horetzky, Ch., mistake of, with regard to the altitude of Lake Stuart, 64; drecting survey C.P.R., 326.

Horsefly mines, 295.

Horses, first mentioned, 73; over a precipice, 76; loss of, 167; wintering at Alexandria, 176; eaten, 177; lost while convoying, 259, 278.

Hotels, primitive, 306.

Houses of the Carriers, 40.

Hudson's Bay Company, 33; slow, 52; its origin, 102; an efficient corporation, 103; its personnel, 104; officers, 106; its moral influence on the wrong side, 115; countenances vendettas, 115; redeeming traits, 119; governed by Sir Geo. Simpson, 121; abuses the Stuart Lake Indians, 151; loses, 172; appoints chiefs, 199; favors the missions, 224; practises vendettas, 270; not intolerant, 309; except with free traders, 310; keeping its own in spite of the miners, 324.

Humalhkhoh River, 313, 315.

Incantations, 6, 10, 339, 340.
Indians, see Carriers, Dénés, etc.; injure H. B. Co.'s property, 286, 287; massacre the whites, 294; described by traveller, 314.
Influenza, 195.
Interpreters, 38, 104.
Inventory of the district, 189.
Iron goods, see European wares; long known on the N. W. Coast of America, 346.
Iroquois, 95; trapper, 158; *engagés*, 179, 190; killed, 279.

Jacques, Joseph, deserts, 255; captured, 256.
Jasper House, 98; reached, 159; destitute of provisions, 177.
Journal, Stuart Lake, on murders, 95; on occupations of James Douglas, 130; part of it lost, 133; on Fort Connolly, 134; on murder of woman and child, 136; on salmon, 160; on a new route, 186; on smallpox, 308; on the mines, 309; the queer names it records, 322.

Kamloops, visited by Father Demers, 231; threatened by the natives, 249.
Kanawokon, 279.
Keithley Creek, 296.
Kescel, 27.
Khadintel, 14; dances, 15; avenges Chinlac massacre, 16, *et seq.*; remarries, 19.
Khalhpan, 15, 16; bewails his fate, 18; is laughed at, 19.
Kilmars, Fort. See Babine, Fort.
Kitksons, 7.
Knives, ancient, 13. See European wares.
Kularhnet, Chief, 341.
'Kun'qus, 16; falls in battle, 18.
'Kwah, 23; prepares for war, 24; kills Tsohtaih, 25; reception of his followers, 27; gambles, 28; kills Arrow-Heart, 29; appointed chief, 88; chastised by Harmon, 89; hunts, 134; invades Fort St. James, 143; meets the Governor, 150; gives a feast, 164; threatens strangers, 165; becomes sick, 196; a good neighbor, 197; dies, 198; pacified by P. S. Ogden, 204.
'Kwes, Indian prophet, 239.

Labrets, 6.
Lacourse, Francois, ill-treated, 281.
Ladder, primitive, 76.
Laforce, Vital, 322.
Lakes, 2, 3.
La Malice, 55; causes trouble, 58; sick and unruly, 60; sent off, 67; fails to bring the goods, 70.
Lane, W., 246; tells the story of a shaman, 352.
Langley, Fort, a southern depot, 276; in charge of J. M. Yale, 326.
Languages, native, 41; different, 42; recorded, 51.
Lapierre, Baptiste, deserts, 205; his capture discussed, 206.
Larance, in bad company, 264.
La Roque, 85; in Oregon, 94.
Leather Pass, 158.
Lebrun, abhors Stuart Lake, 283.
Lefèvre, injured, 210.
Lejacq, Father J. M., 336; at Rocher Déboulé, 340; revisits the district, 342; founds Stuart Lake Mission, 342; appreciated by a Protestant, 343.
Lèkwè, fired at, 213.
Lestanc, Father, not a Jesuit, 347.
Letendre, deserts, 200.
Lewes, T., on New Caledonia profits, 112; appointed to Stuart Lake, 248.
Lewis and Clarke, 71.
Lhus'kœz, Fort, 182, 184; founded, 244.
Linton, drowned, 193.
Liquor among the Indians, 31, 36, 37; first tasted by N.C. aborigines, 90; the H. B. Co. continues to supply it, 116; restrictions by the same, 117; wilfully abused of, 151; as a premium on good hunts, 154; refused by P. S. Ogden, 197; on the Fraser, 293; on Lake Stuart, 311.
Livingston, D., 147; his death avenged, 254.
Log church erected, 235.
Lolo, interpreter, 155.
Loring, Lake, 3.
Lynx, 60, 254, 264.

Macaulay, Lord, 326.
Macdonald, D. G. F., on the Western Dénés, 5.
Macfie, M., mistaken, 65; on Demers' Bible History, 234.

Mackay, Alexander, 37 ; meets with a stirring experience, 45.

Mackenzie, A., 34 ; starts for the West, 35 ; meets first party of Sekanais, 38, 39 ; quoted from, 40, 45 ; his first intercourse with the Carriers, 40, *et seq* ; reaches the sea, 49 ; secedes from the North-West Company, 50 ; his " Voyages," 50, and philological shortcomings, 51.

Mail, first, 92, 295 ; rates, 296 ; regular service established, 325. See Express.

Mal-de-Gorge, 22. See Nathadilhthœlh.

Manson, Donald, favors liquor for the Indians, 118 ; succeeds P. S. Ogden, 241 ; his character, 242 ; his difficulties, 244, *et seq.* ; to P. Fraser, 247 ; is relieved of his charge, 248 ; on a troublesome officer, 250 ; remonstrates with him, 251 ; on Anderson's route, 258 ; praises McLean, 270 ; celebrates the success of a vendetta affair, 274 ; handicapped by an inadequate personnel, 276 ; reappointed to the district, 277 ; reproved, 281 ; assails the Prince, 284 ; resigns conditionally, 289.

Manson, J. D., 283 ; assails the Prince, 284.

Manson, William, 307.

Marriage, orders about, 147.

Massacre, Chinlac, 15, *et seq.* ; Stuart River, 22 ; of Naskhu'tins, 25 ; of Sekanais, 31 ; of Beavers, 32 ; Seven Oaks, 99 ; Humalhkhoh, 315 ; Bentinck Arm, 316 ; their causes, 316, 317.

Masson, Sen. L. R., wrong as to the topography of Fort St. James, 64 ; another of his statements contested, 72 ; mistaken concerning the identity of native tribes, 74.

Maxwell, 247 ; retires from the country, 250.

Mayne, Commander R. C., on Demers' Bible History, 234.

McAulay, Lake, 3.

McBean, W. B., 129 ; born, 209 ; has a difference with a Babine, 209 ; despotic, 211 ; sent to Fort Connolly, 211 ; instructs his succes-

sors, 212 ; retires to Oregon, 218 ; as a lay preacher, 225 ; is reprimanded, 264 ; complains of Bélanger, 264, 265.

McCain, C. W., mistaken, 49, 105.

McDonald, killed, 316.

McDonald, Archibald, arrives at Stuart Lake, 149 ; his statement regarding 'Kwah discredited, 150 ; on W. Connolly, 170.

McDonnell, Capt. Allan, 82.

McDonnell, J., 129, 136.

McDougall, George, 94 ; at Alexandria, 124 ; goes to Tête Jaune Cache, 157 ; his account of his trip, 159.

McDougall, Hon. Wm., 348.

McDougall, James, 53 ; returns to McLeod Lake, 55 ; his first winter at McLeod Lake, 70 ; at Stuart Lake, 90 ; goes to Babine, 92 ; clerk at Stuart Lake, 129 ; sick, 159.

McGillivray, Archibald, 58.

McGillivray, Montrose, 268, 270.

McGuckin, Father J. M., 335 ; visits the Sekanais, 341.

McIntosh, John, at Fort Chilcotin, 181 ; killed, 185 ; for cause, 243.

McKay, J. W., on the Chief Factors, 110.

McKenzie, Ch., complains, 106.

McKenzie, D., and his Calvinistic ideas, 167.

McKenzie, Ferdinand, 276, 307.

McLean, Donald, on his Chief Tradership, 109 ; first spoken of, 175 ; on desertions, 179 ; reports improved conditions at Babine, 221, 222 ; his characteristics, 268 ; kills Nadetnœrh and others, 269 ; is praised, 270 ; on the Indians, 271 ; he forces a native to scalp, 272 ; succeeds P. Fraser, 288 ; retired on the Bonaparte, 318 ; is killed, 319.

McLean, John, relates the Douglas episode, 140, 141 ; inaccurate, 147 ; mistaken as to the native language, 168 ; at Stuart Lake, 169 ; goes to Fort George, 193 ; on the morals of the Carriers, 232.

McLeod, Angus, 317.

McLeod, Fort, established, 54 ; headquarters of the district, 84 ; its resources, 175.

McLeod, John M., quoted, 93.

McLeod, John, written to, 93, 170.

McLeod Lake, 2 ; discovered, 53.

McLeod, Malcolm, on the elk, 38 ; unjust to S. Fraser, 79 ; as to Harmon's status, 98.

McLoughlin, John, 128 ; converted, 226, 229 ; charitable, 229.

McMicking, Thomas, 299.

McNaughton, Mrs., 299.

McTavish, S., 33, 50, 51, 52.

McTavish, John George, 94.

Measles, 195, 257.

Medicine-men, 6 ; their way of exercising their art, 10, 339, 340 ; pretended, 137 ; come to grief, 339 ; wonderful prediction of one fulfilled, 352.

Milton, Viscount, quoted from, 158, 159 ; on rich claims, 298 ; on a case of cannibalism, 302.

Miners, first regular party of, 292 ; take the law into their own hands, 293 ; extravagant with their money, 297 ; at Fort St. James, 303 ; their original route to the north, 304. See Prospectors.

Mines, See Cariboo, Omineca.

Mining, discouraged by J. Douglas, 292 ; in Cariboo, 296, *et seq.*

Mission founded, at William's Lake, 335 ; at Stuart Lake, 342.

Missionaries, good work of, 222, 224 ; well received, 226 ; appreciated by non-Catholics, 342, 343.

Missions, Catholic, 224, *et seq.* ; 333 *et seq.* ; Anglican, 333.

Mistakes, of Bancroft, 2 ; of Greenhow, 2 ; of Macdonald, 5 ; of McLeod, 38 ; of Mackenzie as to language, 42 ; of McCain and Rattray, 49 ; of Greenhow regarding two different points, 49 ; of Mackenzie, in his vocabularies, 51 ; of a biographical dictionary, 52 ; of historians concerning Fraser's age, 53 ; of Nicolay relative to a date, 54 ; of Bancroft as to Bear Lake, 56 ; of Barret-Lennard concerning the origin of a name, 64 ; of Bancroft, Bryce and Masson as to geography, 64 ; of Horetzky with regard to the altitude of Lake Stuart, 64 ; of Macfie and of Begg, 65 ; of Bancroft anent distances, 68 ; of Rattray on three different points, 68 ; of Begg concerning the identity of the Fraser, 71 ; of McLeod, 79 ; of Anderson with regard to the terminus of S. Fraser's voyage, 81 ; of McCain relative to the status of a Chief Trader, 105 ; of Bancroft as to the date of the erection of Fort Chilcotin, 124, and Fort Kilmars, 125 ; of a dictionary concerning J. Douglas, 131 ; of Bryce as to the Douglas episode, geography and ethnology, 144, *et seq.* ; of Bancroft relative to the Douglas episode, 146 ; of authors as to the date of J. Douglas's departure, 152 ; of Begg with regard to the date of Gov. Simpson's voyage to New Caledonia, 152 ; of Al. Ross, 162 ; of John McLean regarding the religious ideas of the Carriers, 168 ; of Nicolay relative to the geography of New Caledonia, 185 ; of Bancroft as to the status of the first missionaries, 226 ; of Cornwallis concerning Fr. De Smet, 226 ; of Father Demers anent a name, 231 ; of Bancroft as to dates, 241 ; as to the date of Waccan's death, 256 ; of Bancroft relative to the etymology of a name, 322 ; of Father Nobili concerning the Chilcotins, 335 ; of Dr. Bryce concerning Red River matters, 347, *et seq.* ; of Bishop Blanchet with regard to the terminus of Father Demers' missions, 341 ; of an anonymous author relative to New Caledonia matters, 349. *et seq.*

Moberly, J., 307 ; arrives at Stuart Lake, 308 ; is bought out, 312.

Monopoly, 153.

Montreal, 33, 50, 120, 170, 179.

Moore, Capt. Wm., 323.

Moose, 38.

Morice Lake, 2 ; and smallpox, 308.

Moricetown, 8 ; population of, 196 ; first visited, 351.

Morwick, W., appointed to Fort Babine, 211 ; has a difference with an Indian, 213 ; is killed, 214.

Mosley, 315.

Murders, 95; of Iroquois, 97; of Chilcotins and Carriers, 124; of a woman and child, 135; of women, 136; of employees at Fort George, 137; of two Indians, 220; of Bélanger, 267; of innocent persons by D. McLean, 269; of Tlhelh by his uncle, 272; of white men by the Chilcotins, 315, 316.
Murray, A. C., 332.
Mutiny among Mackenzie's crew, 46.

Naas River post, 172.
Nadetnœrh, incites to murder, 266; is killed, 269.
Nagailer Indians, 51.
Nahanais Indians, 5; visited by R. Campbell, 207; shoot a medicine-man, 289.
Na'kwœl, 9; is put down, 11; aging, 13; dies, 14.
Naskhu'tins, 21; go to war, 22; massacred, 25; their chief village visited by Mackenzie, 48; friendly towards a murderer, 271.
Nathadilhthœlh, saves his sister, 22; intercedes for J. Douglas, 144; his camp attacked, 162.
Nation Lake, 3.
Nation River, 3; passed by Fraser, 59.
Nechaco River, 3; unnoticed by Mackenzie, 51.
Nelson, trader, 325.
Nets, ancient fish, 13, 131.
New Caledonia, 1; physical aspect, 2; flora, 2; lakes, 2, 3; rivers, 3; origin of the name, 64; its status in connection with the H.B. Co., 103; everything in tatters, 248.
Newspaper in Cariboo, 306.
New Westminster, its site passed by Fraser, 81; founded, 295.
New Year's Day, 37; drinking, 87, 90; festivities described, 150, 151; feasting, 161.
Neztel, 272; kills his nephew, 272.
Nicolay, Rev. C. G., inaccurate regarding a date, 54, and geography, 185.
Nobili, Father, 236; shy, 237; on the native population, 335.
Noblemen, native, 5; killed, 22.
North-West Fur Trading Company, 33; coalesces with the H. B. Co., 101.

Norway House, American headquarters for the H. B. Co., 121, 179.

Oblates, founded, 334; their missionary system, 336.
O'Donoghue, 347.
Officers of the H. B. Co., 107; generally conscientious, 252.
Ogden, Peter, blamed by Paul Fraser, 279; at Alexandria, 289; succeeds Manson, 290; dies, 326.
Ogden, Peter Skene, his parentage, 171; goes to Naas River and to Stuart Lake, 172; his characteristics, 172, 173; with missionaries, 173; on the Indians, 180; on the murder of S. Black, 181; inclined to kindness, 200; reproves Thew, 202; on tact with the natives, 204; gives instructions regarding the avenging of Morwick's death, 214, 215; on the Dénés, 217; favors the missions, 227; on Bélanger, 261; the inspirer, not the author, of an anonymous book, 350, 351.
Okanagan Forks, 231, 236.
Omineca mines, 322, *et seq.*
Omineca River, 3; etymology of the name, 322.
O'Reilly, P., 325.
Origin of the Dénés, 7.
"Otter," steamer, 292.

Pacific Fur Co., 94.
Pack River, 3; ascended by Fraser, 54.
Palmer, Lieut., high-handed, 317.
Pambrun, P. C., at Fort Kilmars, 125; his history, 129, 130; at Stuart Lake, 129.
Parchment for window panes, 130, 214, 289.
Parsnip River, 3; its source reached by Mackenzie, 39; ascended by Finlay, 52, and by Fraser, 54.
Peace River, 52; mines, 309.
Peni, 239; works wonders, 240.
Personnel in New Caledonia, under S. Fraser, 70; under Connolly, 129; under P. S. Ogden, 175; under Manson, 275; under P. Ogden, 307.
Petersen, 315.
"Pesta," an armor, 17.

Peters Lake, 3, 69.

Pike, Warburton, quoted, 207.

Pinche Indians debauched, 311, 312.

Pinche River, 66.

Pine, black, 2.

Poll, Deed, of the united Companies, 101 ; new, 108.

Polygamy, 115 ; at Fort George, 196.

Pond, P., 33.

Population, native, on Lake Stuart, 65 ; on Babine Lake, 92 ; around Alexandria, 123 ; of the whole district, 195 ; decreasing, 195 ; in the north, 335.

Porteous, William, 245 ; dissatisfied with Fort Connolly, 249 ; escapes to Stuart Lake, 250 ; departs from the country, 251.

Postmasters, 105, 211.

Potatoes, grown at Fort Fraser, 178 ; costly at the mines, 306.

Potlatch, 6 ; countenanced by the H. B. Co.'s people, 115 ; given by 'Kwah, 164, 197.

Pouce-coupé, 137.

Priests, see Missionaries ; counterfeit, 238 ; cannot be Fenians, 347.

Prince, the, at Babine, 222 ; assailed by Manson, 284 ; threatens Fort St. James, 285 ; makes himself disagreeable, 286 ; trades at Quesnel, 324.

Produce, country, 192.

Profits of the H. B. Co., 111, 112 ; according to McLean, 169 ; in P. S. Ogden's time, 174.

Prophets, false, 238, 240 ; true, 352.

Prospectors, gold, go overland to Cariboo, 298, *et seq.*; eat one another, 301.

Provisions, costly, 306, 330.

Quesnel, J. M., arrives in New Caledonia, 70 ; accompanies Frazer, 73.

Quesnel River, 3 ; as a mining field, 295, 296.

Quesnel, village, 269 ; flourishing, 306 ; as a trading post, 317.

Radisson, P. E., 102.

Rae, Dr. J., explorer, 326.

Railway, transcontinental, 313.

Rattray, Dr. A., 49, 68.

Red River troubles, earlier, 99, 107 ; later, 347, 348.

Reid, Sen. Jas., 330 ; his strenuous life, 331 ; his final success, 332.

Religion of the natives, 5, 225 ; in later times, 238.

Religious excitements, 225, 239.

Rennie brothers, their awful experiences, 300, *et seq.*

Rey Lake, 2.

Reynard, Rev. Mr., 333.

Riel Rising not a rebellion, 348.

Rising of the natives, against J. Douglas, 140, *et seq.*; against Thew, 203, 204 ; against Manson, 285 ; of Riel against Canada, 348.

Rites, propitiatory, 27.

Rivalries between trading Companies, 52, 102 ; between local traders, 154.

Rivers, 2.

Road, waggon, 304, 305, 313, 322.

Rocher Déboulé, 209, 239.

Rocky Mountain Portage, 54.

Rose, miner, 298.

Ross, Alexander, mistaken, 162.

Ross, Charles, 125 ; at Fort Connolly, 134.

Ross, John, killed, 34.

Roussain, Mr., 166.

Route, convoy, 70 ; a new one sought, 71 ; another adopted, 122 ; still another proposed, 246 ; a different one sought, 257, which is found unsatisfactory, 258 ; another still, 278 ; to the Cariboo mines, 304, 313 ; to Omineca, 322.

Russians early equip a trading expedition, 346 ; furnish iron to the natives of America, 346.

Salmon, abundant at Stuart Lake, 68 ; staple food of the natives, 95 ; sent by S. Black, 155 ; its bad effects on some constitutions, 178 ; the way to catch it, 187 ; from Babine Lake, 223.

Saloon at Stuart Lake, 324.

Samalh'ti, 19.

Scalping, 115 ; ordered by an H. B. Co. officer, 272 ; Tlhelh scalped, 273 ; repugnant to the Western Dénés, 274.

Schubert, 300.

Sekanais Indians, 4 ; their original habitat, 29 ; oppressed by the Beavers, 30, *et seq.*; they retaliate, 32 ;

Sekanais Indians (*Continued*)—
  great gamblers, 166 ; first visited by the missionary, 333 ; good Christians, 342.
Selkirk, Lord, 99.
Semple, Gov., killed, 99, 100.
Servants of the H. B. Co., 104 ; re-engaged with difficulty, 112 ; desert, 179 ; their morals, 179.
Seven Oaks, skirmish, 99.
Seymour, Gov., 318.
Shamans, 6. See Medicine-men.
Shares of the H. B. Co., 107.
Shushwaps, 43 ; found among Carriers, 44 ; vocabulary of their language, 51.
Simpson River, or Skeena, 136.
Simpson, Sir Geo., 80 ; winters at Lake Athbaasca, 120 ; an able man, 148 ; visits Stuart Lake, 149 ; on McIntosh's murder, 185 ; reproves Manson, 281, 282.
Simpson, Thomas, 170.
Skeena Valley, 57 ; long unvisited by whites, 58.
Skenes, the, 171.
Skins received, 189.
Smallpox, 307 ; at Bella-Coola, 317.
Smet, Father De, 226, 228.
Smith, Jim, ferryman, 314.
Snyder's Bar, 295.
Soap, eaten, 62 ; made at Stuart Lake, 161.
Soda Creek, 74.
Somerset, H. S., quoted from, 343.
Sorcery, 28.
Soullier, Lake, 2.
Spaniards, 35.
Spirits, first introduced at Fraser Lake, 87 ; allowed the officers, 178. See Liquor.
Squirrel, causes emigration, 8.
Starvation, at Fort St. James, 67, 88 ; in the Red River colony, 129 ; in the woods, 135 ; on the Peace River, 177.
Steamer at Stuart Lake, 323.
Stickeen River, descended by R. Campbell, 207.
St. James, Fort, its site first visited, 55 ; founded, 63 ; personnel, 94 ; the great northern emporium, 176 ; reached by Father Demers, 233.
St. James' Journal, Fort, on murders, 95. See Journal.

St. Louis, 229.
St. Mary's Lake, 3, 69 ; visited by smallpox, 308.
Stony Creek, 69.
Strathcona, Lord, 128.
Stuart, John, 58 ; passes his first winter in New Caledonia, 70 ; rides by the Fraser, 76 ; succeeds Fraser, 84 ; his connection with the District, 85 ; characteristics, 93 ; goes in search of a new route, 94 ; buys out the Pacific Fur Co., 94 ; on the resources and the aborigines of New Caledonia, 95 ; retires from the district, 126 ; unhappy in his domestic life, 127 ; dies, 128.
Stuart Lake, 2 ; discovered, 62 ; described, 63, 64 ; its altitude, 64 ; its population, 196.
Stuart River, 3.
Sturgeon, 3.
Subscriptions, for mission work, 227, 228.
Sunday work, 119.
Superintendents of New Caledonia, 345.
"Sutlej," steamship, 318.
Syllabary invented for the Indians, 344.
Symington, Dr., 300.

Taché, Archbishop A., 349.
Tanewill, Chief, 210, 212.
Tatla Lake, 2.
Tax on miners, 293.
Taya, Chief, 14.
Taylor propagates smallpox, 317.
Taylor, Capt., and whiskey, 293.
Telegraph line, predicted, 240 ; built, 321.
Tête Jaune Cache, 157 ; the route of the newcomers, 179 ; reached by overland party of miners, 299.
Thachek village, 16, 19 ; populous, 28, 69,
Thaché River, 66.
Thalhthan village, 5.
Thew, W., 199 ; accuses Paul Fraser, 200 ; takes exception to P. S. Ogden's statements, 201 ; is reproved, 202 ; causes discontent, 203.
Thompson, David, explorer, 93.
Thompson River District, 186.
Titles in the H. B. Co., 107 ; sought after, 109.

Tlhelh, 266 ; shoots Bélanger, 267 ; is killed by his uncle, 272.

Tlœng, threatens Douglas, 143 ; escapes from Fort St. James, 151.

Tluzkuz. See Lhus'kœz.

Tobacco, 36 ; wondered at, 62 ; among the Shushwaps, 74.

Tod, John, 129, 276 ; a member of Douglas's first Government, 287.

Todd, William, on liquor for the Indians, 116 ; appointed to a new post, 244.

Tœneza, 5. See Noblemen.

Tœyen, 55 ; goes to meet Fraser, 61 ; deposed, 88.

Toin, Charles, causes trouble, 212 ; escapes to Stuart Lake, 214.

"Tonquin" ship, captured, 37.

Toy, Peter, 310.

Trade, articles of, 55, 111 ; native produce, 130 ; in P. S. Ogden's time, 190.

Traders, free, 309 ; disliked, 310. See Toy, P.

Traders, Chief, 98, 107, 108 ; Junior Chief, 109 ; two of them simultaneously in New Caledonia, 242.

Trading, 57 ; with the sea coast Indians, 63 ; how it was done at the forts, 111 ; profitable, 112 ; prosperous at Babine, 125 ; on the Skeena, 165 ; and bartering, 175 ; for liquor, 311.

Trains, dog, 133, 194.

Traps, salmon, 187, 188 ; bear, 169.

Tremblé Lake, 2.

Trials, judicial, unknown in New Caledonia, 118, 145, 273.

Tsalekulhyé, 20 ; killed, 22.

Tsechah, 9. See Fallen Rock.

Tsimpsians, traders, 57, 88 ; serious competitors, 165 ; with the Babines, 176, 209.

Tsinkœt Lake, 24.

T'sœlkwet, 25, 26.

Tsohtaih, 25 ; his body gives the alarm, 26.

Turner Lake, 3.

Tzœlhnolle, James Douglas's victim, 142.

Utzi-lla-e'ka, 27.

Uzakle, Indian prophet, 238. See Peni.

Vancouver, Fort, 103, 194, 227.

Vancouver Island, ceded to the Hudson's Bay Company, 287.

Vendettas, countenanced by the H. B. Co., 118 ; at Babine, 221. See Wars.

Vicariate Apostolic of the Columbia, erected, 236.

Victoria becomes the capital of Vancouver Island, 287.

Vowell Lake, 3.

Voyageurs with Mackenzie, 38.

Waccan, 58 ; accompanies Fraser, 73 ; on the war-path, 147 ; goes to avenge Morwick's murder, 215 ; his status in the Company, 253 ; gets married, 253 ; his services, 254 ; as a policeman, 255 ; captures a deserter, 256 ; is sent to Alexandria, 256 ; dies, 257.

Waddington, Alfred, and his road, 313 ; on the causes of the Chilcotin massacre, 316.

Waggon road, to Canada, 304. See Road.

Wallace, editor, 306.

Walla Walla, Fort, 130, 133, 218.

War, 15, *et seq.*; 22, 23, *et seq.* ; Crimean, 287, 288.

Weaver, Geo., 296.

Western Union Telegraph Co., 321.

Wheat, raised at Alexandria, 122 ; ground by hand, 183.

Whitefish, 66.

Whymper, Fred., quoted, 313-315.

Wig, ceremonial, 18.

William, Fort, 53, 128.

Williams Creek, 296.

Williams Lake Mission established, 335.

Window panes, parchment, 130, 214 ; eaten by dogs, 235.

Woman purchased, 58.

Work, John, 275.

Wright, G. B., roadmaker, 304, 322.

X. Y. Company, 50, 51, 53.

Yale, Fort, its site reached by S. Fraser, 79 ; its Indians massacre the whites, 294.

Yale, J. M., at Stuart Lake, 129 ; suspended, 138 ; meets the Governor, 149 ; a good trader, 326.

Yœntœlh, 17.

Yokogh, 131.